LAN SURVIVAL

A Guerrilla Guide to NetWare®

LIMITED WARRANTY AND DISCLAIMER OF LIABILITY

ACADEMIC PRESS, INC. ("AP") AND ANYONE ELSE WHO HAS BEEN INVOLVED IN THE CREATION OR PRODUCTION OF THE ACCOMPANYING CODE ("THE PRODUCT") CANNOT AND DO NOT WARRANT THE PERFORMANCE OR RESULTS THAT MAY BE OBTAINED BY USING THE PRODUCT. THE PRODUCT IS SOLD "AS IS" WITHOUT WARRANTY OF ANY KIND (EXCEPT AS HEREAFTER DESCRIBED), EITHER EXPRESSED OR IMPLIED, INCLUDING, BUT NOT LIMITED TO, ANY WARRANTY OF PERFORMANCE OR ANY IMPLIED WARRANTY OF MERCHANTABILITY OR FITNESS FOR ANY PARTICULAR PURPOSE. AP WARRANTS ONLY THAT THE MAGNETIC DISKETTE(S) ON WHICH THE CODE IS RECORDED IS FREE FROM DEFECTS IN MATERIAL AND FAULTY WORKMANSHIP UNDER THE NORMAL USE AND SERVICE FOR A PERIOD OF NINETY (90) DAYS FROM THE DATE THE PRODUCT IS DELIVERED. THE PURCHASER'S SOLE AND EXCLUSIVE REMEDY IN THE EVENT OF A DEFECT IS EXPRESSLY LIMITED TO EITHER REPLACEMENT OF THE DISKETTE(S) OR REFUND OF THE PURCHASE PRICE, AT AP'S SOLE DISCRETION.

IN NO EVENT, WHETHER AS A RESULT OF BREACH OF CONTRACT, WARRANTY OR TORT (INCLUDING NEGLIGENCE), WILL AP OR ANYONE WHO HAS BEEN INVOLVED IN THE CREATION OR PRODUCTION OF THE PRODUCT BE LIABLE TO PURCHASER FOR ANY DAMAGES, INCLUDING ANY LOST PROFITS, LOST SAVINGS OR OTHER INCIDENTAL OR CONSEQUENTIAL DAMAGES ARISING OUT OF THE USE OR INABILITY TO USE THE PRODUCT OR ANY MODIFICATIONS THEREOF, OR DUE TO THE CONTENTS OF THE CODE, EVEN IF AP HAS BEEN ADVISED OF THE POSSIBILITY OF SUCH DAMAGES, OR FOR ANY CLAIM BY ANY OTHER PARTY.

Any request for replacement of a defective diskette must be postage prepaid and must be accompanied by the original defective diskette, your mailing address and telephone number, and proof of date of purchase and purchase price. Send such requests, stating the nature of the problem, to Academic Press Customer Service, 6277 Sea Harbor Drive, Orlando, FL 32887, 1-800-321-5068. APP shall have no obligation to refund the purchase price or to replace a diskette based on claims of defects in the nature or operation of the Product.

Some states do not allow limitation on how long an implied warranty lasts, nor exclusions or limitations of incidental or consequential damage, so the above limitations and exclusions may not apply to you. This Warranty gives you specific legal rights, and you may also have other rights which vary from jurisdiction to jurisdiction.

THE RE-EXPORT OF UNITED STATES ORIGIN SOFTWARE IS SUBJECT TO THE UNITED STATES LAWS UNDER THE EXPORT ADMINISTRATION ACT OF 1969 AS AMENDED. ANY FURTHER SALE OF THE PRODUCT SHALL BE IN COMPLIANCE WITH THE UNITED STATES DEPARTMENT OF COMMERCE ADMINISTRATION REGULATIONS. COMPLIANCE WITH SUCH REGULATIONS IS YOUR RESPONSIBILITY AND NOT THE RESPONSIBILITY OF AP PROFESSIONAL.

LAN Survival

A Guerrilla Guide to NetWare®

DENI CONNOR
MARK ANDERSON

Foreword by John McCann

AP PROFESSIONAL
Boston San Diego New York
London Sydney Tokyo Toronto

This book is printed on acid-free paper. ♾

AP PROFESSIONAL
955 Massachusetts Avenue, Cambridge, MA 02139

An Imprint of ACADEMIC PRESS, INC.
A Division of HARCOURT BRACE & COMPANY

United Kingdom Edition published by
ACADEMIC PRESS LIMITED
24–28 Oval Road, London NW1 7DX

Library of Congress Cataloging-in-Publication Data

Connor, Deni
LAN survival : a guerrilla guide to NetWare / [Deni Connor, Mark Anderson] ; foreword by John McCann.
p. cm.
ISBN 0-12-194480-8
1. NetWare (Computer file) 2. Local area networks (Computer networks) I. Anderson, Mark, 1956- . II. Title.
TK5105.7.C675 1994
004.6'8--dc20 94-13938
CIP

Printed in the United States of America
94 95 96 97 98 IP 9 8 7 6 5 4 3 2 1

Contents

II All the Beasts in the Jungle

III Toning Your Survival Instincts

Appendices

FOREWORD

With the ever-increasing presence of networks in our computing life, it is important to understand and accept them for what they are. Computer networks or LANs are a tool to help accomplish a need, more than likely a business need. As with any tool, understanding how and when to use it will help you control it. Computer networks or LANs are not a simple tool; they can be incredibly complex since they are comprised of hundreds or thousands of individual components.

Overall, a computer network or LAN is a tool, but with its complexity, understanding all the interrelationships can be a formidable task. This is where *LAN Survival: A Guerrilla Guide to NetWare* comes in, namely to help conquer understanding the basic and complex components of a computer network or LAN. In addition to this base understanding, knowledge of how the components interrelate is presented in concept and practice.

For those new to or involved with networks or LANs, LAN Survival provides an overall view of how to put a network together and keep it running. This alone is a pressing need for most people involved with computer networks. With this book in hand you will garnish greater knowledge of how a network "works" and how to use this most important business tool.

John McCann
NetWare Sophist
May 1994

Acknowledgments

Our hearty thanks to all the people who helped us with this book: to Margaret Dornbusch and Ed Tittel, for their editing talents and tireless reviews; to Terry Ahnstedt, who wrote the LAN Compass under duress and without complaint; to our bosses, Kathy Murphy, publisher of *NetWare Solutions* magazine, and Jim Weakley of Thomas-Conrad Corp., for putting up with our strange work schedules; to Tony Lopez, Shane Weaver and Jennifer Hinnenkamp of Two Dudes and a Chick Design, who supplied the network illustrations for the book; to Susan Price of Susan Price and Associates for producing the manuscript; and to Carole McClendon and Belinda Catalonia of Waterside for their gentle pressure and support of this project. We also want to thank our families and friends for their unconditional support when we were grouchy, thoughtless, or simply complaining too much about how much we had to do. Finally, thanks to Naomi for fueling us with chocolate chip granola cookies and to Kevin, B.J. and Phylis, for being there when we needed them the most.

ABOUT THE AUTHORS

DENI CONNOR

Deni Connor is the editor of *NetWare Solutions* magazine and a former technical editor for *LAN Times* magazine. She was media relations manager for Thomas-Conrad Corp. Connor writes a newsletter for Motorola on the PowerPC microprocessor, and has written product reviews and articles for *Datamation, PC Today, Reseller Management, Windows User, InfoWorld, Computer Shopper, PC Novice,* and *ComputerWorld.* She is the coauthor of IDG's *NetWare for Dummies.*

MARK ANDERSON

Mark Anderson is a product test engineer at Thomas-Conrad Corp. and the technical editor of *NetWare Solutions* magazine in Austin, Texas. He has written for *NetWare Solutions* magazine and *LAN Times.* Mark is an Enterprise Certified NetWare Engineer and a Microsoft Certified Systems Engineer. He wrote several chapters of *Unleashing Novell DOS 7* for Sams Publishing Company.

PREFACE

INTRODUCTION

Two adages describe the different approaches people take to administer a local-area network (called a LAN for the rest of this book):

1. Simon says.
2. There's nothing common about common sense.

Either people act without thinking and perform tasks because someone tells them to, or they consider the problem, devise a possible solution, and then act. As you become familiar with NetWare, Novell's client–server network operating system, you'll meet both types of people. You'll see people who panic and say, "I don't care why it works this way—I just want to know how to fix it," and you'll find people who sit back and calmly say, "OK, tell me the symptoms." You can guess which approach we think is better.

The person who acts without forethought will have to ask for directions the next time, and the next, and the next. He won't remember which path took him to his destination and will forget all the shortcuts he was supposed to have learned. The person who ponders the situation before acting will be in better shape to conquer the beasts and barriers the networking jungle throws at him or her. Managing a network with the second approach—call it the "common sense" approach—works better than responding with sheer panic or trying to remember the steps in a list you forgot as soon as you read it.

This book will supply you with a little of both approaches to network administration. We'll talk heavily about the logic of networking and why things work the way they do. We will tell you the hows and whys of network decision-making. This book will show you where common sense will help you not only sharpen your focus, but also eliminate threatening situations. Throughout this book we'll follow these discussions with quick lists and decision charts you can use as you pick your way around the LAN. We'll talk about NetWare in general and not about a particular version. The NetWare manuals exhaustively cover NetWare installation and its commands and utilities; we refer you to them for more specific information. We'll talk about the principles of networking the NetWare way. We won't talk about a particular version except where it is absolutely necessary. If we think it's necessary to talk about important information that is version-specific, such as NetWare's Directory Services, we'll tell you so. Each chapter is planned to help you organize your trek in as efficient a manner as possible.

We'll spend a lot of time helping you plan your journey and document your tracks. We think that preparing for your voyage, and then acting, is the approach to network administration that will allow you to solve network problems best, often with a modicum of effort. With proper planning, you can prevent much of the Tinker-Toy–like looks of many networks. We also think that the "Simon says" approach to network management is for use only after you know how to manage your network with the logic-based approach. With this book, you'll be able to survive your traverse across the network jungle, approach obstacles with caution, find the next watering hole with some surety, and never worry that you are headed in the wrong direction. We won't tell you that finding your own way and negotiating obstacles will be as easy as having someone plot your course for you, but we will tell you that when you're the master of your plan, the jungle is yours also.

Whether you're administering a local-area network (LAN), a group of standalone PCs, or a group of your colleagues, some of the same approaches and rules apply. These are the most important rules for surviving NetWare LAN administration:

- Take a deep breath. Count to 10, or 20 if necessary.
- Plan your approach, and don't panic.
- Rely on the tools you have to help you solve the problem.
- Implement your plan.
- Learn from what you do wrong.
- Revise your plan as necessary.

Having the common sense to sit back and clear your registers before you react, to think things through before you start a project, and then to act, will keep panic at a minimum. Pangs of panic that do surface will be kept to a reasonable level. Then, by relying on the tools you have at hand, such as trade publications, documentation, or books like this, you can make problem resolution easier. Once you've learned the routine, you'll be able to change it when you need to. You'll likely make some mistakes that you'll be responsible for fixing, and you'll have some successes that you can't explain. LAN administration is a continuous learning process—even for the best of us.

Who Should Read This Book

If you're like many network administrators, you inherited your LAN or it inherited you. You aren't trained to be a NetWare administrator, much less an expert troubleshooter, but then again, you probably don't blanch when you're put in front of a PC. You take things in stride and learn to do them better each time. That's the reason we hope someone chose you to be the network administrator—you can adapt peaceably to any habitat.

Specially trained network administrators are becoming more commonplace as the market for NetWare grows. You'll meet them as you network within the LAN community. They are the people you should emulate, if you are lucky enough to be able to work with them. Most often, however, you're not. The network is your responsibility and yours alone. Training classes and user groups can help. Books can supply information too. No approach will provide the complete solution to networking management, although some come close.

This book is for those curious individuals who want to explore networking so they can become master pathfinders and not succumb to the "tenderfoot" rank all too many people earn. *LAN Survival* will give you the fundamentals for building a strong networking foundation, one you can modify as you need to or leave alone once everything works just fine.

What You Will Learn

You'll learn how to survive administering a NetWare LAN via a logic-oriented approach. This approach is an extension of caring for standalone PCs. Many of the same principles apply. We teach you how to apply these principles to keep your LAN up and running.

Throughout this book, you'll see decision charts that will help you decide what you logically should do next. We supply quick lists (we call them Flash Lists) that will help you with the process of eliminating problem areas, pointers to the LAN Compass program in the back of the book, and tips you'll want to remember as you learn about NetWare.

How This Book Is Organized

LAN Survival is organized in chapters that build upon principles you have learned in the preceding chapters. In addition, the book is divided into the following three sections:

I. This LAN Is Your LAN (A New Continent)
II. All the Beasts in the Jungle (Networking Nuts and Bolts)
III. Toning Your Survival Instincts (Troubleshooting)

Each section is further divided into individual chapters.

This LAN is Your LAN discusses the hows and whys of networking. It tells you how to choose file servers and workstations and how to select the other networking devices you'll use on the LAN. In addition, we'll talk about the applications you put on the LAN, how to plan where applications are put, and the features that make for a NetWare-aware application. Last of all, this section will tell you how to protect your investment by backing up data and implementing NetWare security, and will discuss the records and important documentation you should keep.

All the Beasts in the Jungle details the nuts and bolts of networking. It discusses the common LAN access methods, the topologies they use, and the implementation and management of each.

Toning Your Survival Instincts will sharpen your instincts and give you tips, plans, and methods for LAN troubleshooting. The section ends with some of the more common problems you'll see and suggests answers for them.

You'll also want to refer to the individual appendices, which cover the Open Data-Link Interface Specification, the glossary of terms, and the list of common NetWare commands; a list of sources for networking equipment and information has also been provided.

Surviving in the LAN environment doesn't need to be a task fraught with formidable barriers, inaccessible pathways, and more unfriendly, hungry animals than you can shake a stick at. LAN administration can, at times, be fun, albeit never stress-free. With that said, let's cut through the undergrowth and explore the jungle of networking.

part

This LAN Is Your LAN

I

You've inherited responsibility for the LAN. Now you wonder exactly what does this LAN consist of and why should you care? You may need to decide how to implement each of the components of the LAN, or you may need to start from scratch and purchase and gather the components yourself.

A LAN, in the sense of this book, consists of a file server that processes user requests, PC workstations users can work from, media which joins the workstations together, and a network operating system that allows them to communicate. Simple, you say. It is—once you've learned to negotiate the hows and whys of networking.

The following chapters will help you do just that. They'll tell you how to select and install workstations, what you need to have for a file server, where to position network printers and how to manage them, and how to organize the file server's disk space so that users can make use of it efficiently and quickly. We'll discuss keeping your network secure, keeping your data safe, and managing the applications you will need to put on the network. Negotiating the network jungle is nothing more than learning to follow the right paths, look for the right signs, and learn from the dead ends you run into. The basics of networking will get you started on the right foot.

chapter 1

LANs: Foe or Friend?

You've inherited a LAN—the problem is, you don't quite know what it is. You've heard that it's called a *local-area network* (LAN, for short) and that it's supposed to let PCs talk to each other, but you're skeptical. What you see when you are led into your office as the official LAN administrator is one of two things. It's either a PC with cables coming out of the back of it that looks much like any other PC you've seen, or it's a simple red box sitting next to a PC and a bunch of cable that doesn't look like anything much at all.

What Is This Thing Called A Network?

This is an easy question if you look at the question in an easy way. People tend to complicate matters and answers when it's not necessary. A network, simply put, is a forum, a method, or a means that lets more than one item communicate with another.

Remember the two tin cans joined by string you used when you were a child to talk to your buddy across a field, or the Walkie Talkies you got for Christmas that didn't work very well, but once in a while you could get your message across. Now that you're grown up, you use one of the largest networks in existence—the telephone system—and perhaps you employ another form of networking—glad-handing with people when you're trying to find a job. All these forms of communication are networks—they allow two or more devices or people to talk to each other and share data or experiences.

Collections of connected PCs grouped in close proximity to each other are called *local-area networks* (LANs). They occupy a defined area that is local. Close proximity is a loosely used term—here it means that the PCs are roughly within the same building. In its finished form, a LAN is a collection of computers connected by a medium (the cabling) that allows the communication and sharing of information among the computers. Easy.

A LAN, then, is limited by the area it takes up, typically a building or a group of buildings in close proximity of each other. When PCs proliferate and the network grows past the boundaries of the LAN, or when more than one physical network is present and they are joined together by devices that transfer traffic from one network to another, the entity becomes an *internetwork*. (See Figure 1-1.)

When LANs grow to include forms of communication other than traditional media, such as public data or private leased lines, they become *wide-area networks* (WANs). If these networks span great distances such

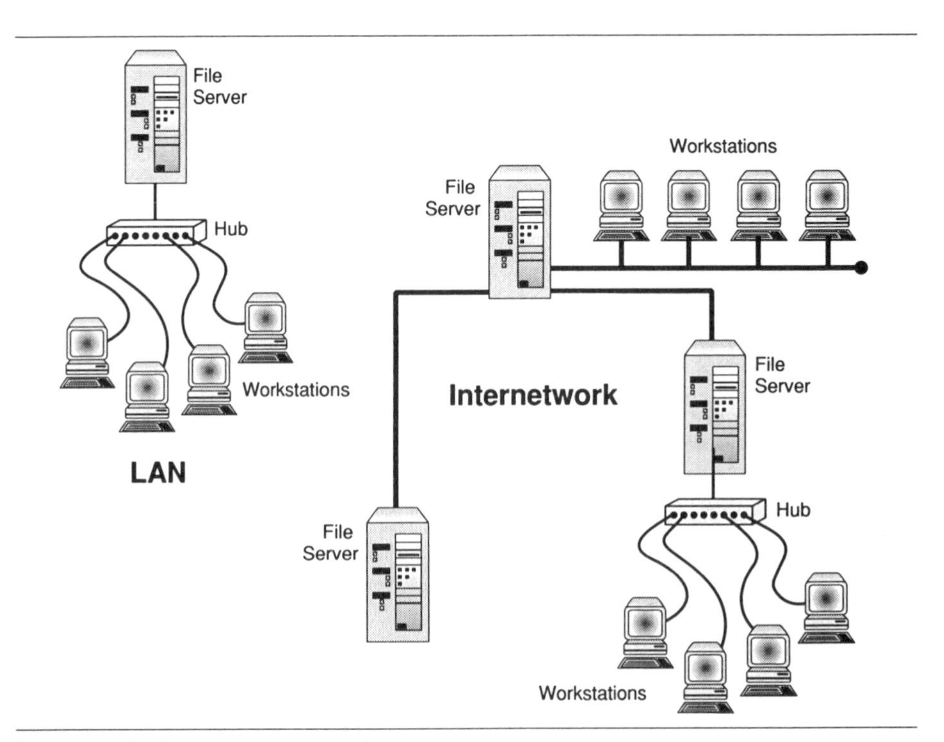

Figure 1-1. *LANs and internetworks.*

as from San Francisco to Omaha to Dallas, they are most definitely WANs. If they span an area like metropolitan Chicago, many people call them *metropolitan-area networks* (MANs). (See Figure 1-2.) HANs are becoming more common, too—it's our acronym for a home-area network. Mine has two nodes. Mark's has three. Whatever you call them and whatever their geographic boundaries, they allow communication and information sharing between PCs.

The terminology blurs for networks once in a while. Say, for example, you have two networks, one in one building connected to another

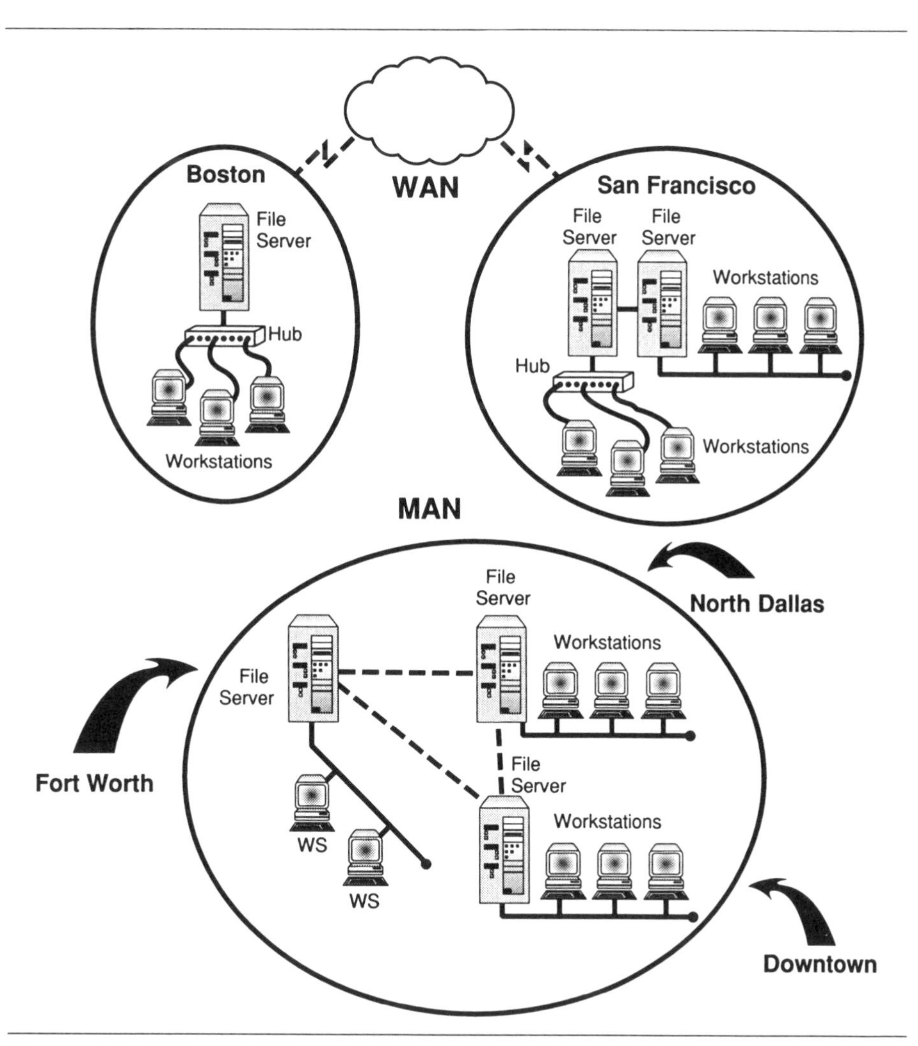

Figure 1-2. *WANs and MANs.*

in a building next door. Does this mean that you have a WAN or only an internetwork? Probably, in this case, because the buildings are next to each other and not part of a larger campus, city-wide, or geographically dispersed network, you have only an internetwork. When distances separate the separately connected networks, and some form of communication takes place between them over a medium other than a wire you own, you have a WAN.

LANs, internetworks, WANs, MANs, and even HANs are built not only to let PCs talk to each other but to let people share common resources and information. That may be an expensive printer or access to a large database, as we'll see later.

First, though, let's dispense with a question that might be in your mind.

Why Me?

At this point you're probably wondering what you've gotten yourself into, and why you volunteered to manage this LAN or internetwork just because you know more about PCs than anyone else in the office. You'll soon find out. Administering a LAN involves little more than common sense. You just need to learn what's common and what's not. Networking is not a jungle of twisting, twining vines and pitfalls waiting for a victim. If you know the right paths, you'll be able to "keep the LAN up" as they say in the business, and be a success at doing so. It's that easy, or is it?

With that said, we hope you're at least intrigued. LANs aren't the strange creatures many make them out to be, and your curiosity about what makes the LAN tick plays a big part in administering it. To tweak your curiosity, let's start with some basic explanations. We'll expand from there.

Who Put You in Charge?

Someone, your boss's boss or someone higher up the chain of command, "bought the LAN." At least that's what he or she thinks. It's your job to put it together. This person may have gotten a package deal that includes all of the equipment and software that makes up the LAN, or he or she thinks that buying the network operating system

(NetWare, in this case) was the important decision. The rest of the pieces may be left up to you. In any case, you'll probably find that one of the pieces of hardware or software that's supposed to let one PC talk to another is missing, and it's your job to find out and fix it.

You were the likely candidate because of your affinity for PCs. You've fixed the office copier, you know how to use the fax machine, and whenever anything needs to get done in the office and it involves some mechanical device, you're the one who takes charge and gets things working. In this case, you'll learn a lot about getting things working and keeping them that way—it's now your job. Get used to it.

Why Network? Why Not?

Let's start first with an explanation of why someone decided that your company should network. You'll undoubtedly need to explain it to someone else whose life at the office is altered by it. This may be your successor when you successfully move on to somewhere else, or it may be one of the users you'll become responsible for.

A LAN lets PCs communicate with each other to save people the time and the expense of running around like cats with their tails on fire. Via the LAN, you can exchange messages with other workers. You can communicate lunch plans or gossip about the boss. Most importantly, you can get things done faster because you only have to work with resources someone else manages. You can share a spreadsheet with another co-worker and get the job done faster.

On the LAN, you'll share a common storage space with your co-workers, and you'll get your own private locker for storing your private files. You won't have to fight with Bob anymore, who is always hogging the printer trying to get a manual printed when all you have to do is print out the schedule for the next trade show. You'll simply make the printing request, and the rest will be done automatically. And you'll do all this communally, so that neither you nor your co-workers know that it is happening.

Many people consider networking only because it allows them to share an expensive printer. (See Figure 1-3 on the next page.) Tying PCs together with cable and installing an operating system and a network operating system seem to be a lot of trouble just to share a printer when you could simply get a device that would let you switch the printer connection from Bob's PC to yours. When your network of co-workers grows beyond just a few of you, you can imagine the problems it will cause.

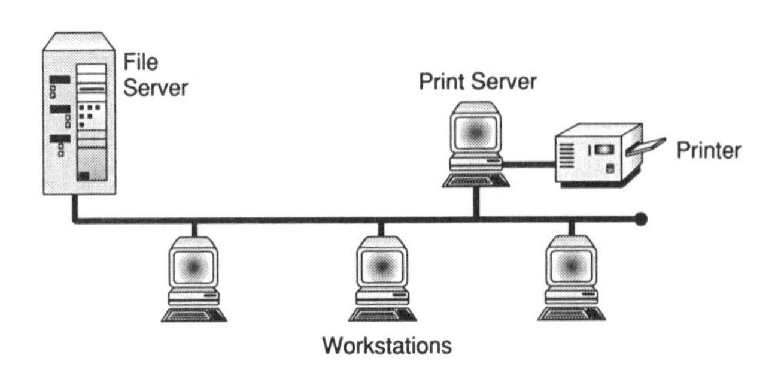

Figure 1-3. *Printing as a shared resource.*

Besides a shared printer, you'll want to be able to share other resources too, such as access to massive amounts of storage. Your standalone PC may be limited by the amount of hard disk space it has, and you keep wanting more. Your boss is resistant because she can't imagine why you, of all people, have to have more than 300 megabytes (MB) of memory. You do graphics work you say—case closed. On the network, data is stored in a common area amounting to gigabytes (GB) of information that is accessible by all users. Suddenly your graphics files consume only a small part of this common storage.

On the network, you also can create private areas called *user directories* where you can store your latest football pick list or the budget report you've been working on for accounting. Each of these areas will be protected, too. No one will be able to walk up to your PC and steal your thoughts if you carefully observe the rules of networking. Figure 1-4 on the next page shows both public and private network areas.

Those are the obvious benefits of networking—printer sharing and access to massive amounts of storage. But there are other, more subtle, benefits when you look beyond the surface of networking.

People Tend to Work in Groups

At the office, people tend to work in groups or teams. Decisions are made by the group, and each person has his or her part of a project to get done. The people in the group want to be able to communicate with each other, and the LAN is a logical way to do it. Via the LAN, users

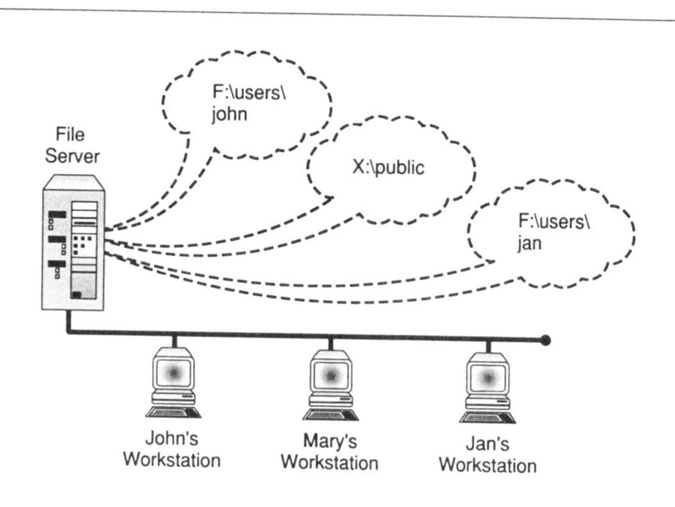

Figure 1-4. *Public and private areas.*

can send messages to their fellow co-workers via electronic mail, schedule appointments, brainstorm electronically, or make decisions via scheduling and groupware packages.

Most of us have worked with PCs for so long now that offices don't have typewriters. Carbon paper is a thing of the past. With a LAN, you simply replicate your message to the four or five other people you work with, and let the LAN do the rest, communicating the data to everyone so that everyone's in touch.

To Access Other Computers' Data

Networks traditionally allow an individual user's workstation (PC) to access information from a common source, in this case, a file server. This server, equipped with oodles of storage, processes the request for data and provides the warehouse facilities for the data. Money is saved by adding additional storage only to this file server, and not to each workstation on the network.

Other networks, called peer-to-peer networks, may exist where you actually can share the data on your own workstation or retrieve data from someone else's, but these networks tend to be more limited in their capabilities. We'll talk about file-server–based networks here.

To Share Expensive Peripherals

Devices such as high-speed modems, printers, and plotters are expensive, especially if you need to equip each PC with one of each. LANs let you share these devices, which operate off the file server or another workstation, saving money in the bargain and resources that may not be used by every user all the time.

To Have Safe and Secure Data

Fewer people back up the data on their computers than those who do not back up. With a network, data that can be shared automatically can also be backed up automatically. Backup is a tedious affair. Relying on your own means to back up your data when you're tired and ready to go home for the day is no way to run a LAN. You can install a tape backup unit on each PC on the network and make users back up the information before they leave, or you can simply ignore the fact that only the most diligent will back up the files they change.

A simpler approach is to install a tape backup unit on the file server or on a workstation attached to the file server that can back up the shared information on the server or on each workstation. You'll need to buy fewer tape drives this way, and the money you save can be spent on a higher-capacity backup drive and faster, more reliable, tape backup software.

To Increase Productivity

Increasing productivity goes hand in hand with working in groups. Very few people work alone, not relying on someone else to get their jobs done. Imagine typing a report that needs to go to 15 people. To distribute it, you need to get it to the mail room and someone needs to deliver it, or if your office is like some we know, you'll have to deliver it yourself. If you doubt that sending information over the LAN saves time because, after all, your office is pretty small, take down the LAN sometime and see what the users say.

To Be Able to Upgrade with Minimal Impact

Because LANs allow the sharing of resources such as applications and data, they allow a network administrator to upgrade easily everyone's software when a new revision comes out. Because in the type of LAN you'll be managing most information is stored on the file server, you'll save the time and expense of upgrading each user's workstation when a new copy of Lotus 1-2-3 comes out.

To Allow PCs of All Types to Talk to Each Other

One of the least obvious reasons for networking is also one of the most important. In many large offices, the art department uses Macintoshes, the scientists use UNIX-based machines, and everyone else uses PCs. Each machine is a different entity. You have groups of entities. With the LAN, you can camouflage these differences, as Figure 1-5 shows. Macintosh users can send mail to PC users, and PC users can forward the mail to those on the UNIX part of the LAN.

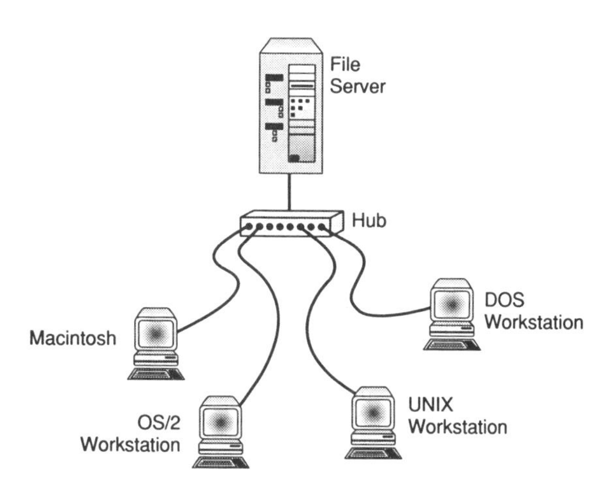

Figure 1-5. *LANs promote heterogeneous environments.*

To Make Everything Equal

Right in line with letting all types of users access the shared data on the file server, with a LAN you also provide equal protection for all users. Very few offices have the latest workstations (486 or more recently Intel's Pentium-based machines). You are likely to find 286s mixed with 386s, mixed with 486s. Each has applications it needs to use, which are stored on the file server. The file server can be a very powerful device, such as an Intel 486 66-megahertz–based machine, and can provide rapid access to PCs and machines of all types.

LANs also allow you to standardize applications you use. Consider the company that has 250 employees, all with PCs. With a LAN, you can upgrade everyone to the latest software and supply it from the file server. The versions of applications are consistent. They don't vary between Jim in accounting and Sherri in the travel department unless you want them to. Each user can share and share alike. As the network administrator, you control it all. That's how important this job is. Your actions can make or break the LAN.

chapter

2

Network Basics

Types of LANs

There are three predominant, traditional network types: the host–terminal network, the peer-to-peer network, and the client–server-based network. If you've been around computers much at all, you've probably worked on at least one of these networks and may not have known it. Each of these networks has similarities to the others, but each is also different. Each allows communication between devices and allows users to share resources.

Host–Terminal

Traditional mainframe and minicomputer environments operate with a central intelligent "host" machine that serves the need of terminals. Terminals, at which users work, are attached via media to the host computer. These terminals are "dumb," by nature, and incapable of processing information on their own—the host performs all actions for them and simply relays screens of information to the terminal so the user can see what's going on. Terminals don't have a central processing unit (CPU). When a terminal needs information, it logs onto the central computer, a mainframe in this case, and is served by the mainframe. All its operations rely on the mainframe for execution.

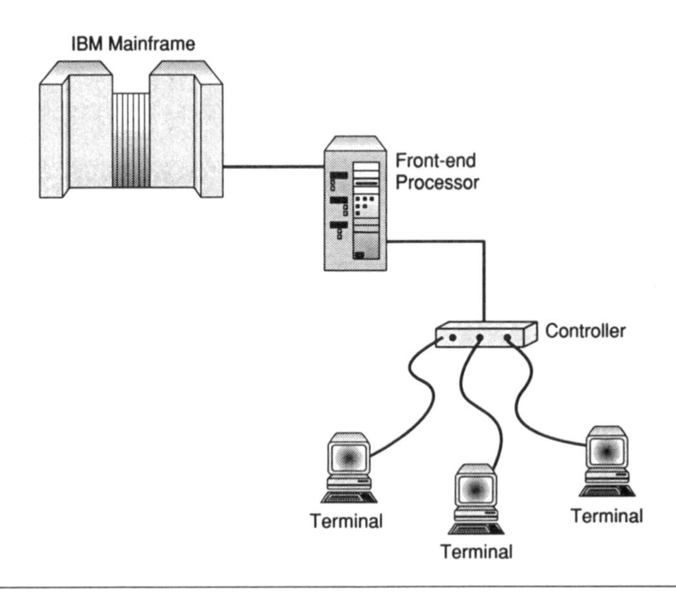

Figure 2-1. *A traditional host-terminal network.*

Terminals operate in a timesharing mode, where each terminal shares the mainframe's processing time with the other terminals on the network. Host–terminal networks are hierarchical in nature—all the processing is centralized at the mainframe host. It is not distributed among the host and the terminals. The mainframe contains all the storage and other peripheral devices, such as printers, the terminals need. (See Figure 2-1.)

Peer-to-Peer

Another form of networking is peer-to-peer networking, in which all machines are equal to each other—they each share information and provide information to other PCs on the network. In addition to sharing peripheral devices such as printers, each workstation may also share disk drives with the other computers on the network. These drives contain the applications and data users rely on to do their work.

In a peer-to-peer network, no one machine is the host, and all PCs on the network are intelligent, which allows them to process information on their own if the network is down.

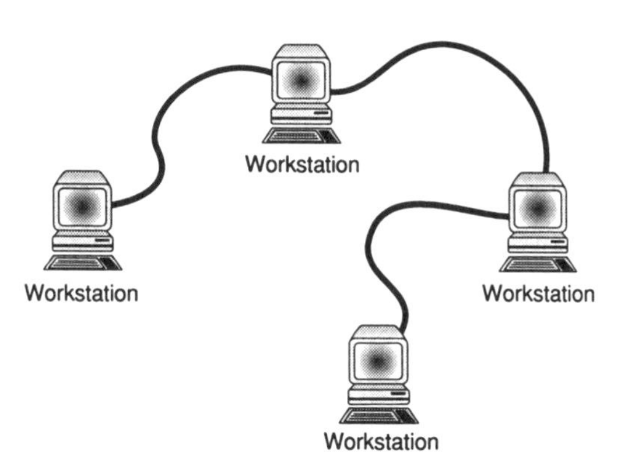

Figure 2-2. *A peer-to-peer network implementation.*

Peer-to-peer networks operate more slowly than client–server-based networks because each PC shares its processing time between its own jobs and the jobs of others. PCs can be designated as servers (they answer requests for information) or as clients (they request information), or as both clients and servers. (See Figure 2-2.)

The most common NetWare implementations of peer-to-peer networking are NetWare Lite and Personal NetWare. These networks should be considered by any user with a small number of network users (between 2 and 20) and light network traffic.

Other peer-to-peer network implementations from vendors are Artisoft's LANtastic, the most popular of the peer-to-peer networks, and Microsoft's Windows for Workgroups. Both of these peer-to-peer networks interoperate with Novell's NetWare.

Client–Server

NetWare v2.x, v3.x, and 4.0 are called *client–server implementations.* These network operating systems consist of intelligent PCs called *client workstations* that request information of, and are served by, dedicated PCs called *servers.* These workstations can operate by themselves if the network is not there and can process information independently of the file server if the application the workstation is using dictates it. (See Figure 2-3 on the next page.)

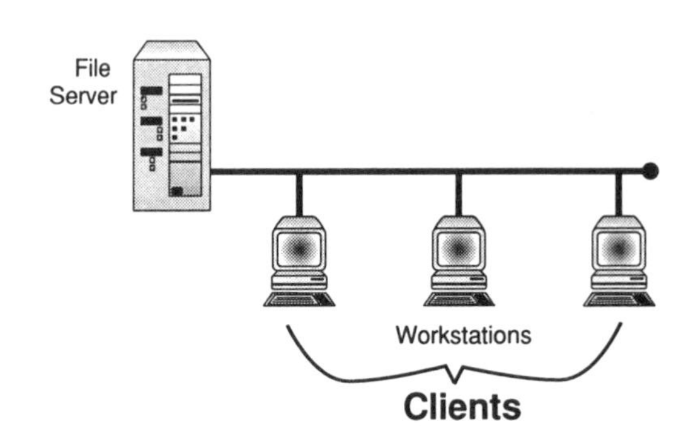

Figure 2-3. *A client-server network.*

Other network operating systems that use the client–server model are Banyan's VINES and IBM's LAN Server.

What Comprises a LAN?

Networks are comprised of several major components. These components interact with and rely on each other to provide network communications. The components are

- the server
- the workstations
- the operating system
- the network operating system
- the media

Server

The server, the central component of the distributed network, is responsible for processing and answering requests for services from the other devices on the LAN. In a distributed network, the server normally acts as the repository for common information and applications that all workstations use and process.

The most common type of server is the file server, which provides file access to individual workstations on the network. Other types of servers provide printing services and are called *print servers*, database services (database servers), and access to fax capabilities (fax servers). Each of these specialized servers works in cooperation with the file server to receive the files and data it is supposed to service for the workstations.

In NetWare v3.x and 4.x, the program that provides the file server capabilities is called *SERVER.EXE*. This executable file is started from the DOS command line. In previous versions, the program is called *NET$OS.EXE*. In these earlier versions, you boot the machine directly to the network server program.

The NetWare file server also contains two programs, AUTOEXEC.NCF and STARTUP.NCF, which correspond roughly to the AUTOEXEC.BAT and CONFIG.SYS files in DOS. The AUTOEXEC.NCF file contains the commands that bring up the file server. STARTUP.NCF contains the commands that load the disk driver information the server needs to boot.

A NetWare file server can be a 286-, 386-, or 486-based machine, depending on the NetWare version. Versions 3.x and 4.x require a 386 or higher machine.

Workstations

Each client on the network is called a *workstation*. These workstations request information from the server. To communicate with the server, each workstation loads a shell (in v2.x and v3.x) or a requester (4.0), which determines if the request is for a DOS file or application or for a network file or application. Depending on the nature of the request, the shell routes the request to the appropriate component. (See Figure 2-4 on the next page.)

Each workstation contains an adapter called a *network interface card* (NIC for short), which controls its interaction with the network. Each adapter has a software-based driver, which tells it how to operate.

Workstations may consist of DOS-, UNIX-, OS/2- or Macintosh-based machines. The Windows environment is also supported.

Media

Workstations are joined to the file server and other devices via media or cabling, which takes the raw data that needs to be transmitted and carries it to its destination. Media types range from relatively inexpen-

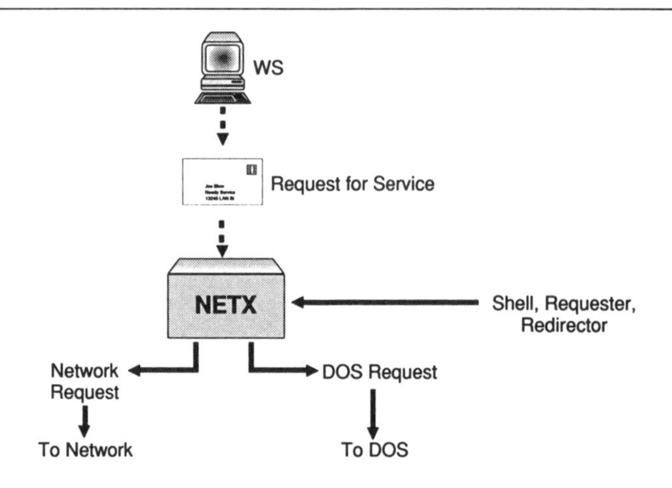

Figure 2-4. *How the NetWare shell works.*

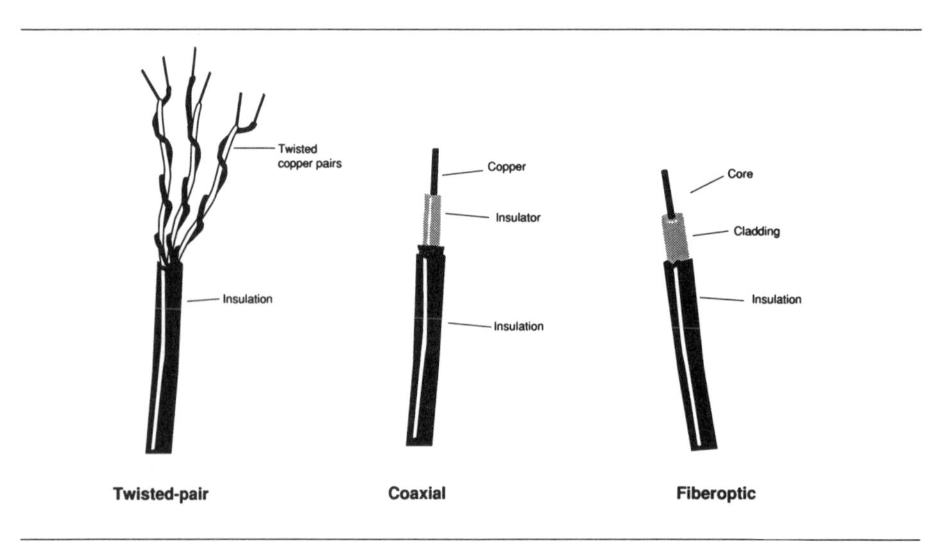

Figure 2-5. *Different media types.*

sive unshielded twisted-pair to coaxial cable to fiber-optic cable. Wireless forms of communication also exist which rely on the airwaves to communicate information. (See Figure 2-5.)

The medium determines the rate that data is transferred across the network and, many times, the manner in which workstations access the LAN.

Operating System

The network operating system NetWare is built on a native operating system. Originally a system that operated on CP/M-based and then DOS-based machines, NetWare now works on a variety of platforms —UNIX, Sun's Network File System (NFS), and the Macintosh Operating System. In NetWare 4.0, requests are sent to DOS, which handles requests for DOS files and information, and defers network requests to NetWare.

Network Operating System

The network operating system, in this case, NetWare, is responsible for the operations of the network as a whole. It provides file and directory access, system security, and resource sharing. The network operating system works in concert with the operating system to service the needs of its users.

Other Related Networking Concepts

In addition, there are other components of the network that determine how workstations and file servers communicate across the media to each other. Like any telephone conversations, rules exist that govern how information exchange takes place. These rules are called *protocols*. Working in concert with protocols are *network access methods*, which define how information (data) is placed on the media. Two types of media access are common in local-area networking: token-passing, in which an entity called a token governs how the workstations will communicate; and Carrier Sense Multiple Access with Collision Detection (CSMA/CD), which specifies a method in which workstations listen to the media for activity before communicating.

Topology

Each media access method defines how the network is laid out—its topology. In networking, several topologies and combinations of topologies exist. They are the bus topology, the star topology, and the ring topology. A variant of the ring topology is used by the Fiber

Distributed Data Interface (FDDI). You can consider that the topology gives you a map of your network.

Bus Topology

In a bus topology, all devices are attached linearly to a central cable or backbone called a bus. Workstations are daisy-chained from one to another. To expand the network, you break it into segments, each interconnected to a bus. The ARCNET and Ethernet access methods use bus topologies most often. Data traffic on the bus is heard by all workstations but accepted only by the workstation to which it is addressed. (See Figure 2-6.)

Ring Topology

The ring topology is similar to a bus topology except that the bus is joined at both ends into a physical ring. Data exchanged between workstations traverses this ring from one node to the next, finally reaching its destination. Token-ring, as its name implies, is a media access method that uses a ring topology. (See Figure 2-7 on the next page.)

Star Topology

In a star topology, each workstation radiates from a central device called a concentrator or hub. Signals pass from the sending workstation through the hub and then on to their destination. ARCNET and

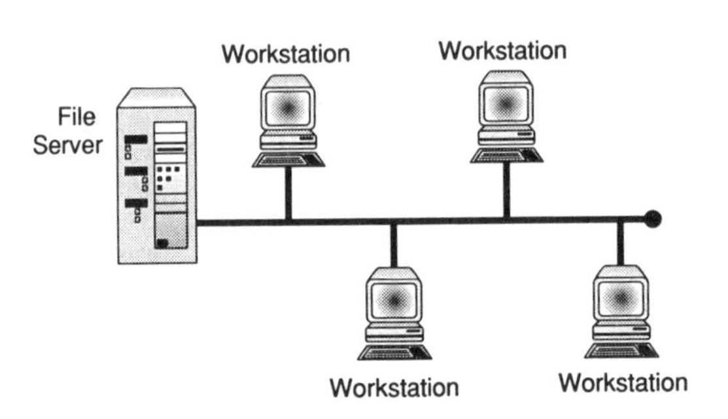

Figure 2-6. *A bus topology.*

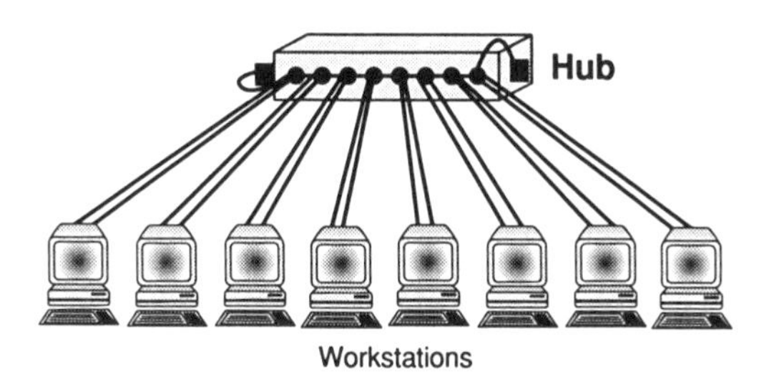

Figure 2-7. *A typical ring topology.*

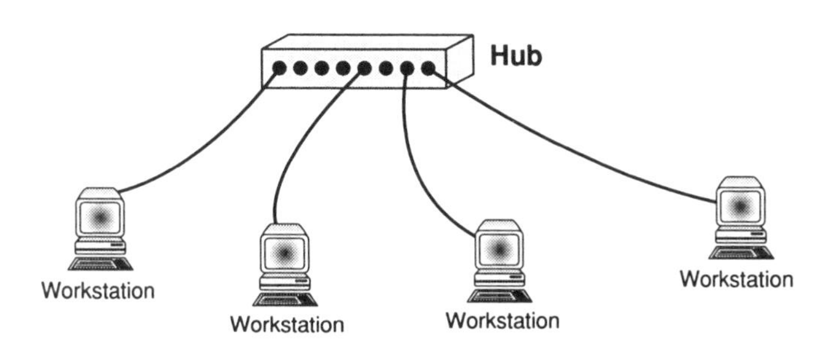

Figure 2-8. *A star-topology network.*

unshielded twisted-pair Ethernet (10BASE-T) use star topologies. (See Figure 2-8.)

Protocols

The manner in which workstations communicate with each other is governed by protocols or rules. In NetWare, the two major protocols are the Internetwork Packet Exchange (IPX) and the Sequenced Packet Exchange (SPX). We'll talk more about them in Chapter 12: Protocols, Access Methods, and Media.

VERSIONS OF NETWARE

Since its introduction in the early 1980s, NetWare has undergone a series of transitions. It has changed from operating on a Motorola 68000-based machine that used the CP/M operating system to operating on DOS Intel-based, UNIX, or Macintosh machines. Over the years, NetWare has increased the number of users it supports and made changes in the network security, which controls who can get into the LAN and who can't. As a result of enhancements to the original network operating system, Novell has introduced a number of versions that support several different hardware and operating system platforms. Some versions of NetWare for the DOS platform are virtually defunct these days. Others still have many users working on them. The currently sold versions of NetWare that operate on DOS machines are v3.12, 4.0, and SFT III NetWare.

NetWare v2.x (Including v2.15c and v2.2)

NetWare v2.x, which includes both version 2.15c and v2.2, was introduced in 1986. NetWare v2.x operates on 286- and 386-based machines and has the ability to use the file server in either a dedicated or nondedicated mode. NetWare v2.x supports from 5 to 100 users and allows up to four individual networks to run from a single file server. This version of NetWare introduced the capability to incorporate Macintosh computers into the network and allows servers to be linked together to form an internetwork.

NetWare v2.x allows disk mirroring and duplexing, use of Novell disk coprocessor boards (DCBs, a disk controller that can manage disk requests independent of the file server), and supports value-added processes (VAPs), which are specialized applications that run on the network file server and are integrated into the network operating system when the server is booted.

This version of NetWare lets up to 1,000 files be opened at one time and supports disk drives larger than 255MB of RAM. It supports a maximum of 16MB on the file server and a total of 2GB of disk storage. Up to 255MB of space can be assigned to each volume and partition, and up to 32 volumes and physical drives are allowed per server. (See Table 2-1 on the next page.)

Features	NetWare v2.2	NetWare v3.12	NetWare 4.x
Number of users	5–100	5–250	5–1,000
Maximum file server RAM	12MB	256MB	4GB*
Maximum disk storage	2GB	32TB	32TB
Maximum volume size	255MB	32TB	32TB
Maximum partition size	255MB	No limit	No limit
Maximum # of open files	1,000	100,000	100,000
# of volumes per server	32	64	64
# of drives per server	32	4,096	4,096
NLM/VAP support	VAP	NLM (Ring 0)	NLM (Ring 3)
Client support	DOS, Macintosh, OS/2	DOS, Macintosh, OS/2, NFS	DOS, Macintosh, OS/2, NFS
TCP/IP support	No	Yes	Yes
# of adapters per file server	4	64	64

* Current technological limit

Table 2-1. *A comparison of NetWare versions.*

NetWare v3.11

Novell introduced NetWare v3.x in 1990. It supports from 5 to 250 concurrent users and operates on 386 or higher file servers. NetWare v3.x, or 386 as some users call it, supports up to 100,000 open files, each up to 4GB in size. It supports drives larger than 255MB and volumes up to 32 terabytes (TB) in size. The NetWare v3.x file server can use 2.5MB to 4GB of RAM and can support up to 64 LAN adapters per server. Up to 32 drives can be combined to form one volume, each up to 32TB in size, with a maximum limit of 64 volumes per server supported.

NetWare v3.x supports up to 4,096 disk drives and offers support for native Macintosh, OS/2, and Sun Network File System (NFS) clients. In addition, NetWare v3.x has provisions for TCP/IP and the encapsulation of NetWare data in TCP/IP frames.

In NetWare v3.x, passwords are encrypted instead of being sent in clear-text across the network. This improves network security. NetWare v3.x also uses NetWare Loadable Modules (NLMs), an extension of the VAP concept, which allow server-based applications to be dynamically loaded when they are needed and unloaded when no longer needed. NetWare v3.x also allocates file server RAM dynamically.

Four types of NLMs exist: disk drivers, LAN drivers, applications, and name spaces. Disk driver NLMs, which have the .DSK extension, provide the intelligence a disk drive needs to interact with the file server. LAN drivers (.LAN) perform a similar function for LAN adapters. Applications and utilities that vendors write as NLMs have the .NLM extension. Namespace NLMs allow Macintosh, UNIX, or NFS client operation.

SFT Level III NetWare

System Fault Tolerance Level III (SFT Level III) has the same features as NetWare v3.x, with two exceptions. It presently does not support Macintoshes or NFS machines.

NetWare 4.x

NetWare 4.x, Novell's latest operating system, is a true 32-bit network operating system that Novell has designed for large network installations. NetWare 4.0 supports up to 1,000 users and allows NLMs to operate in Ring 3, which provides protection to the network operating system. In NetWare v3.x, NLMs run in Ring 0, the same space the network uses. As a result, if an NLM misbehaved or did not operate correctly, it could corrupt the operating system. With 4.0, vendors and users can test NLMs in Ring 3, a protected area, before moving them to Ring 0, where they will run faster.

NetWare 4.x also introduces some dramatic features. It offers file compression and data migration. In file compression, data may be compressed on the network to afford more disk space, and uncompressed when the network operating system needs to use it. Data migration allows less-often-used data to be stored to an off-line storage device, to free the file server drive. In addition, NetWare 4.x allows the administrator to suballocate files to less than 4-kilobyte (KB) blocks. In previous versions, data, even if it was not 4KB long, was stored in 4KB blocks, thus wasting disk drive space that could be used for other storage. The biggest feature of NetWare 4.0 is its support for Network Directory Services (NDS), which allows users to look at the internetwork as a single entity and find resources in a yellow-pages–like fashion. (See Table 2-1 on the previous page.)

Personal NetWare

Personal NetWare, Novell's peer-to-peer network and a successor to NetWare Lite, supports from 2 to 50 users.

Choosing Which Version You'll Use

The version of NetWare you use will be determined by the number of users you have, the type of equipment you must support, and the features you want. The majority of systems being installed today are v3.12. 4.x is still new and users are currently still trying it out. Novell expects that 4.x will appeal to users that have enterprise and other wide-area needs, and that the rest of its users will be satisfied with v3.12, as well as NetWare Lite and Personal NetWare.

chapter

3

Care and Feeding of the Network

The Importance of Documentation

One of the most important lessons you'll learn is to document what you do whenever you use the LAN. Recording everything about the LAN—its components, the amount of memory the file server and each workstation uses, the characteristics of each workstation, and every operation you perform—is a tedious, but necessary, affair. LAN documentation is like having insurance when disaster occurs. You hope you'll never need it, but when you do, you'll be able to rebuild from scratch after a disaster happens. Software packages are available that help you document your LAN, but for a small LAN (one of 20 nodes or less), or for one that requires minimum maintenance, these packages can be expensive.

Most of the time, you'll be better off to keep a notebook about the LAN—call it your LAN Log—that records everything you'll ever want to know. In this record, you'll want to keep a myriad of facts. You'll want to record every action you take against the LAN. You'll want to take a physical inventory of the LAN and record it here, list the logical structure of the network by directory and volume, note how users and applications are organized within this directory structure, and keep lists that help you maintain the LAN and then recover from disaster if one happens. This log will give you an audit trail of your actions and let you retrace your steps, if necessary. From this log, you'll learn how your LAN behaves and you'll be able to make up a baseline of normal performance and activity.

Documenting your actions and the characteristics of the network is a tiresome but important task. It can mean the difference between floundering around in the bushes and cutting a clear, concise path through the jungle. After each step you take, write down a description of it. Stanley Livingston is remembered only because his diaries were found. Let your LAN Log chronicle your LAN adventures.

Tip

Keep a log of all your actions on the network. Document when you make changes to the hardware or software configuration of the devices on your LAN.

Physical Workstation Inventory

For each workstation on the LAN, you'll want to keep information that will let you reconstruct the workstation's configuration if a machine fails and a new one needs to be installed. Include on this list the vendor you purchased the equipment from, its warranty length, and the device's serial number. Follow that information with repair estimates, maintenance contract, and the documentation you receive with the machine. Create a file for each workstation. Place this information in it.

On the machine, place a permanent number you can use to track the machine even if it moves from one place to another. Duplicate this number in the file you keep. In addition, record the adapters that are in the machine and their interrupts and base memory address settings. Also record the type of video adapter the machine contains, the amount of RAM it has, and the hard disk space. Since so much information is necessary to keep on top of network maintenance, we've designed a form you can use to record this information. (See Figure 3-1 on the next page.)

Logical Workstation Configuration

The workstation's logical configuration is as important as the amount of RAM and the size of the hard disk. In your files, you'll want to keep

Device # ________________ Location ______________________________

Node ID ______________________________

Person assigned to ________ Machine type ____________________ (286, 386, 486)

Vendor ____

Processor speed ____________________________

Bindery name assigned to ____________________

Amount of RAM ____________________________

Manufacturer of BIOS ________________________

Hard disk capacity ________ Hard disk type ____________________________

Disk controller ______________________________

Diskette drives ❑ 3.5″ ❑ 5.25″ CD-ROM ❑ Yes ❑ No

LAN adapter vendor ______________ Model # ______________ Bus type ______

Interrupt set at ____________________ Base memory _________ DMA _________

Media type ____

Speed (if token-ring) ❑ 4Mbps ❑ 16Mbps

Other devices ____________________________ Manufacturer ________________

Other devices ____________________________ Manufacturer ________________

Other devices ____________________________ Manufacturer ________________

Figure 3-1. *Workstation inventory.*

copies of the AUTOEXEC.BAT file, the CONFIG.SYS file, and the SHELL.CFG or NET.CFG file. Place these listings or copies of them on a diskette and place them in the file for that workstation. Include information on the applications the user has on the workstation or that he or she uses. Include the configuration files for any applications that reside on the workstation. If trouble occurs, you'll want this baseline to recreate the workstation's state before the trouble began.

Tip
Update workstation worksheets as you make or observe changes.

Flash List
A Quick List of Things to Record

1. The AUTOEXEC.BAT file
2. The CONFIG.SYS file
3. The NET.CFG file
4. The SHELL.CFG file
5. The WIN.INI and SYSTEM.INI file for Windows workstations
6. All the applications a user runs
7. If a menuing system exists, what its name is and how it works
8. A copy of the user's login script
9. The security profile for the user
10. Any configuration files applications use

File Server Configuration

Once you've finished recording the information on each workstation on your network, you can start to inventory the file server. While much of the information is the same, information about the logical characteristics of the disk are important, as is more detailed information on the groups of users on the file server and the applications they use. Figure 3-2 on the next page shows a sample form you can use.

Tip
Lock your LAN Log in a fire-proof safe and store it someplace it won't get lost. Even though the file server is the heart of the networking jungle, consider your LAN Log to be your passport.

Logical File Server Configuration

Most important, after adding the hardware configuration, is to know what the logical contents of the file server are. This inventory includes all applications operating on the file server and their directory loca-

Device # ________________ Location ______________________________

Node ID ______________________________

Network # ____________________________

Person assigned to ________ Machine type ____________________ (286, 386, 486)

Vendor ____

Processor speed ________________________

Supervisor-equivalents ____________________

Amount of RAM ________________________

Manufacturer of BIOS ____________________

Disk controller manufacturer ____________________________________

Hard disk space __________ Hard disk type ______________________________

Diskette drives ❑ 3.5″ ❑ 5.25″ CD-ROM ❑ Yes ❑ No

LAN adapter vendor ______________ Model # ______________ Bus type ______

Interrupt set at ____________________ Base memory _________ DMA _________

Media type ____

Speed (if token-ring) ❑ 4Mbps ❑ 16Mbps

LAN adapter vendor ______________ Model # ______________ Bus type ______

Interrupt set at ____________________ Base memory _________ DMA _________

Media type ____

Speed (if token-ring) ❑ 4 Mbps ❑ 16 Mbps

LAN adapter vendor ______________ Model # ______________ Bus type ______

Interrupt set at ____________________ Base memory _________ DMA _________

Media type ____

Speed (if token-ring) ❑ 4 Mbps ❑ 16 Mbps

Other devices ____________________________ Manufacturer ________________

Other devices ____________________________ Manufacturer ________________

Other devices ____________________________ Manufacturer ________________

Figure 3-2. *File server hardware configuration.*

tions, how the directories on the server are organized, and files, drivers, and NLMs that are loaded when the server's SERVER.EXE program executes.

You've documented everything in sight and your fingers are cramping. Don't forget one last, very important, bit of documentation. In your LAN Log, place a copy of the file server's AUTOEXEC.BAT, CONFIG.SYS, AUTOEXEC.NCF, and STARTUP.NCF files. Record the file server's name and describe its contents. The information you should include is:

1. The size of the DOS partition
2. The contents of the DOS partition
3. The NetWare partition size
4. A list of the groups on the file server and a description of each group
5. The users on the network and their usernames
6. The users in a group
7. The names of the volumes on the server and a description of their contents
8. The directories within each volume and a description of their contents

For each application, you'll want to record its serial number, identify where the documentation is kept, keep information on the number of software licenses to the application you have purchased, and list any maintenance or technical support numbers if pertinent. You'll need to record the application's warranty period, the date of purchase, and information in the event you need to upgrade the software (see Figure 3-3 on p. 33).

Tip

Create a diskette that contains copies of NET$OS.EXE or SERVER.EXE files, the disk or LAN drivers, and a copy of VREPAIR.

Tip

Keep these records current. Before you make changes to any of these files, copy them to another name such as AUTOEXEC.SAV. If you make mistakes, you'll always be able to fall back to the original version. STARTUP.NCF contains the commands that load the disk driver information the server needs to boot.

Application name ______________________ Version # ______________

Vendor name ____

Serial # ______________________ Date purchased______________

Method of licensure ❑ By file server ❑ By workstation

# of licenses available______________ Cost per package __________

Technical support # ______________ Site #______________

Bulletin board #______________

Board settings ______________ (i.e., 8,N,1,2400)

Minimum RAM required ______________ Minimum disk space ________

Directory path information

EXEs and COMs ______________________________

Data______________________________

Configuration files ______________________________

Startup directory and command ______________________

Other information______________________________

Rights, attributes, flags (users) ______________________________

____

____

Rights, attributes, flags (supervisor)______________________________

____

____

Search mappings ______________________________

Groups with access to______________________________

Upgrade information ______________________________

____

Figure 3-3. *Server software applications inventory.*

Cabling

The part of documenting the LAN that will give you the most reward is a description of the cabling and topology of the network. You should draw a map of the layout of the network, noting the speed of the network, the type of media used, and the location of each workstation on the network. Identify each device with the number you assigned previously. Include a description of all concentrators, hubs, and multistation access units (MAUs) on the network, and mark the location of each.

On all cables, label both ends so you'll be able to identify them, and note each of the ends on the network map. Number the wall plates the cables extend from with an indelible marker and note them on the map. Last, mark the length of each cable, note its installation date in your log, and label all the punch-down blocks and repeaters. On this map, also include the traffic pattern individual workstations use to reach the file server.

Other Devices

Once you've completed the bulk of your documentation work, you'll want to create the same type of worksheets and information for the printers, hubs, concentrators, tape backup units, modems, communication servers, and other devices on the network.

Inventory Packages

There are numerous packages that allow you to inventory the configuration of the devices on your LAN. These packages, available for either DOS or Windows environments, either install a terminate-and-stay resident (TSR) program on each workstation that will be audited or audit the workstation as it logs into the network. While the auditing of information during the login process can be time-consuming (up to 40 seconds per workstation), the information is more comprehensive than the information you can gather by hand.

These are some of the inventory packages available:

LAN Auditor from Horizons Technologies

LAN Directory from Frye Computer Systems

LTAuditor from Blue Lance

LAN Workstation from Saber Software
Brightworks from McAfee
Norton Administrator for Networks from Symantec

Other Packages

Bindview NCS

The LAN Support Group's Bindview NCS allows you to report on the directory structure of the LAN, the contents of the bindery, and perform a hardware and software inventory of its components. Bindview NCS is known for the completeness of its reporting. At present, it does not offer complete support for NetWare Directory Services (NDS).

MSD for Windows

A diagnostic utility included in versions of MS-DOS 6.0 and above and Windows 3.1 lets you obtain the physical contents of the machine you run it on. With MSD, you can either display information on screen or print it to a report to add to your LAN Log.

Implementing Changes

Changes on the LAN are inevitable. For each way of performing a task, there is always a better way. You can make change less stressful by providing a method for users to request changes. This method may be implemented via e-mail request or hard copy. You'll want to have change forms for adding new users and for deleting users who have left the company, for requests to use certain applications, and for access to devices. On the form you'll want to have the appropriate management signatures and the date the request needs to be performed by. You may want to set a policy that all changes will take "x" period of time. Some changes will need to be automatic, such as deleting a user who your company terminates, but other changes can wait and be performed by priority.

Plan your day around the changes you have to make to the LAN and prioritize all requests. Document in your log the changes you've made, if necessary, so you can answer responsibly to anyone who asks.

MAINTENANCE

One of the signs of a well-built LAN is how well it is maintained. LANs are sometimes installed in a hodge-podge fashion simply because no one took the time to think about the changes before implementing them. When maintenance is required or when you need to expand, justify the expense using your LAN Log and carefully plan the changes that take place. If required, get management permission to make the changes.

Have a Plan

Create a plan for your network that lists when maintenance is performed on a LAN device, whether the maintenance is time-and-materials or under contract, and the action performed. To the plan, add where you will get equipment from if you need to replace devices, and also detail step by step what you will do when hardware or software problems occur.

Analyze the equipment you have and consider buying extra devices (spares) in case one malfunctions. Then, while it is out for repair, you can insert the spare into the network and keep operating. Include in your plan a schedule to test the integrity of spare equipment.

What Does Maintenance Involve?

Regular maintenance of the LAN is important. Read trade journals and keep current with vendors so you will know when software or hardware revisions or new versions are available. Talk to other network administrators about the products they use. Join a user group so you can keep in touch with the latest happenings in the networking industry.

Know the characteristics of your LAN. Monitor it so you'll know when disk space is limited and you need more; keep your security profiles on each user up-to-date so you'll be able to respond quickly when something happens; and consider adding a menu interface. Users work from this menu interface, thus saving you time rounding up renegades who are working places they shouldn't be. Update the menus when new applications are added to the LAN, or when you change directories.

Most important of all, keep informed on the workstation shells you are using, so that you use the most up-to-date shells.

Packages are available that will help you monitor the operating system and file server utilization and help you gather statistics so you can optimize network performance.

Tip

Before you add new applications to the LAN, test them first either by yourself or with a few adventurous users. Testing will save you headaches in the end.

What Do I Do, and When Do I Do It?

So now that you have a long list of maintenance items that you need to perform, you're probably wondering when you will ever get the chance to do them all. We've itemized network changes needed daily, semi-monthly, monthly, annually, and as needed.

Daily

1. Upgrade and revise software
2. Solve problems
3. Perform backups
4. Check and maintain disk space
5. Watch network traffic
6. Prepare reports for management
7. Add users and groups
8. Delete users
9. Document the LAN
10. Evaluate software
11. Support users

Semi-monthly

Update your disaster recovery plan

Monthly

1. Conduct user training as necessary
2. Check your backup procedure

3. Check UPS integrity
4. Optimize performance
5. Review configuration

Annually

Review your LAN plan

As needed

1. Internetworking
2. Check spare equipment

People Backup

All too many network administrators forget a key element of network management—having a person back you up when you are absent from the office. Appoint someone, such as a supervisor-equivalent who knows how to fix the printer and is familiar with applications. Have this person back you up for lunch hours, vacations, times you're too busy, or when you're sick. Give him or her some training.

In addition, train your users, too, so they can solve many of their own problems with the network. Teach them about the printer and give them an overview of the printer utilities. Give a once-a-month training class if you can.

Disaster Recovery

Keeping a record of your backup procedure is a good idea if someone else ever needs to run it for you. Include the name of the backup software you are using, the location of the tape drive, the rotation schedule (which tapes to use and when), and the location of the off-site storage. While you're writing, put down your plan for fire and natural disaster recovery. This should include whether you have an uninterruptible power supply, its location, and sources for replacing equipment if it is destroyed.

The Survivor Syndrome

People who survive harrowing experiences many times develop the same personality traits. Administering a LAN can be considered to be one such experience you're likely not to forget. You'll develop tenacity, patience, curiosity, and determination. All these characteristics, plus an attention to detail, will help you out.

If you've documented everything diligently as we've explained in this chapter, you'll be on the right path to surviving your first year on the LAN successfully. You'll know where to look when trouble occurs, and most of all, your documentation will help you know what to do next. What you do will depend on the plan you have for the network and for problems when they occur. That's what we'll talk about in the next chapter of this book.

chapter 4

Plotting Your Course

The decision to network is a big one. Once you've settled on networking, you need to make the decisions about components that will make up the LAN. You have to consider what operating system to use, which network operating system to choose, and the type of workstations and file servers you will need.

After you've put all that together, your next chore is to decide how these workstations will be laid out, the access method they will use, and the type of media that will permit communications. Finally, the applications you will be using on the network will dictate the network operating system and the type of other components you use.

Choosing the Operating System

If you're like almost everyone who has PCs in their office, the operating system you use will be probably be DOS. DOS operates on 286-, 386-, and 486- or Pentium-based microprocessor–based machines. You may have a smattering of Macintoshes in the office and someone may have an OS/2 or UNIX machine.

Then you need to decide which user interface your LAN will have. Will you use a graphical user interface (GUI) such as Microsoft Windows, Saber LAN Workstation, or the Norton Desktop for Windows? Or, will you require your users to use a DOS-based menuing system that lists their applications in menu-like form?

If you choose DOS-based menus, a number of them are available, including WordPerfect Office, NETinc's NETMenu, and Marx Menu from Computer Tyme. Finally, you need to decide if all users are going to use the same interface and whether the interface works well with the network operating system you use. Administering some users working within Windows and some working from the DOS command line will complicate the support of these users—you'll need to know how each works.

The Network Operating System Is Next

Choosing the network operating system (NOS) you'll use depends on a lot of things. Of primary importance is whether the NOS supports all the network clients you have. Does it support OS/2, UNIX, and Macintosh users, as well as DOS users? What about that engineer in the corner who has a Sun workstation that runs the Network File System (NFS)? Does the network operating system work well with the user interfaces you have chosen? Last, you need to decide the applications you will be using on the network. Do they work with the NOS you choose? Can they be networked?

Next, you need to determine whether the NOS will support all the hardware platforms you have in the office. Will it work with the 286s, 386s, and 486s you have? What about Pentium-based machines? Will it operate with UNIX-based RISC workstations, as well as with NuBus-based Macintoshes?

If you are looking at the network to improve the security of files and data contained on the network, you'll want a system that provides a measure of security. Can you control security of both the files and the directories? Can you create individual user profiles for the workers on your LAN? Can you protect your LAN against intruders or unwelcome guests?

The list of features you need to look for is endless. Here are some of the more important questions you should ask yourself when you are looking for a network operating system:

1. Do you expect the LAN to grow so that some day you'll need to have two or more LANs to support all the users? Does the LAN allow internetworking? Is there a maximum size the network can grow to?

2. Do you need to communicate with mainframes, minicomputers, or other LANs? Does the network support gateways to these devices, and can information be routed to them easily?
3. Does the network have the administrative support that you want? Are there plenty of utility programs to let you administer the LAN, or do you have to learn arcane commands to do your work for you?
4. Last, is the network secure?

Choosing Applications

Your network will need to support all the applications you choose for your users. These applications will vary from word processing packages to spreadsheets to a particularly networkable product, e-mail. When you look for network applications, you should ask yourself several questions. These are some of them.

Is the application available in a network form, or do you need to buy a separate license for each user on the network? How is the application licensed? By the file server for use by "X" number of users or by the file server for all users?

Is the application a NetWare Loadable Module that runs on the file server? Is it a Value-Added Process that operates on NetWare v2.x? If you are using NetWare 4.x, has the application been tested on 4.x?

Does the application support a number of different clients? Will it work for OS/2 clients as well as DOS clients? Is there are version for Macintosh users?

How much space does the application take on the file server? Does it require a terminate-and-stay resident program at each workstation?

Choosing a File Server

Choosing a file server is one of the most important tasks of putting the network together. We've devoted an entire chapter to it. (See Chapter 5.) Here, though, we'll tell you that you should choose a vendor that is reliable and stable. You want to make sure that the vendor supports its product if something goes wrong. Also, you want to make sure that the machine you choose for the file server is Novell-certified. Novell maintains an extensive testing and certification program for everything from file servers to the NetWare Loadable Modules that run on them.

Next, make sure that the machine you choose is capable of supporting the amount of RAM you want to put into it. Does it support only up to 16MB as some clones do, or will it allow up to 2GB the maximum supported? Is the machine available in an EISA or Micro Channel bus configuration? Does it have enough expansion slots to accommodate all the devices you'll want to attach to it? Does it support more than one LAN adapter? What is the maximum number of adapters the machine can support?

You'll need to look at specialized servers. Will you be faxing from the network? Do you need a fax server? Will the database users cause the file server's performance to slow down? Do you need a database server? How are you attaching your printer to the network? Will you need to have a workstation for a print server?

Choosing Workstations

When you choose the workstations for your network, you should choose no less than 386-based DOS machines. If you choose a GUI interface such as Windows, you'll want to make sure that the machine has sufficient RAM (at least 4MB). These are some other things you need to determine:

1. Does the machine support the LAN adapters you want to use?
2. Do you want the machine to have diskette drives or do you prefer diskless workstations?
3. What bus type will the machine have? Will it be an ISA, EISA, or Micro Channel machine?
4. Is the machine capable of being upgraded in the future if your LAN grows?
5. Are there power users who need more capable workstations than other users?
6. Will you need to have hard disks on the workstations?

Choosing the Access Method

The network access method you choose depends on a number of characteristics of your LAN. Some of them are:

1. Is there media already installed? What types?
2. Which access method supports the media? Or, are you going to rewire the building with new media?
3. What is the size of the network you are building? Is it small or medium-to-large?
4. What type of traffic will be on the network? Will the traffic be bursty? Or do you need regular, guaranteed traffic delivery?
5. How much money do you have to spend?
6. Do you have to connect to IBM mainframes or minicomputers?
7. Will you be communicating with UNIX workstations?
8. How many users are on the network?
9. What type of growth do you expect?
10. Will you be doing any wide-area networking?

Choosing the Topology

When you choose the layout for your network you'll need to look at a number of factors, such as:

1. What access method are you using? What topologies does it support?
2. What is the size of your network? How many users are there?
3. What is the traffic pattern on the network?
4. Can you tolerate down-time in which all users may not get to work?
5. Is media already installed that dictates the topology?

Choosing the Media

The media you use for your LAN depends on a number of factors, including:

1. Is there media already installed in the building? What kind is it? What is its condition?
2. Will you need to install new media?
3. Where are all the workstations located? Are they located close together, or will your network span large distances?

4. What is the nature of the traffic? Does it consist of large graphics files, is it mostly database traffic, or is it light because most users are only doing word processing?
5. How much money do you have to spend?
6. Are you going to install the media in the walls? What about the ceiling?
7. Is there a high amount of electromagnetic interference (EMI) or radio-frequency interference (RFI)?
8. Will the media you choose allow network expansion?
9. Will you be running media between buildings?
10. Will you be forming a backbone of file servers to improve communications?
11. Are you worried about network intruders?

Choosing Your Dealer

One of the most overlooked factors in choosing a network is the dealer you work with. In considering a dealer, ask yourself these questions:

1. What do you know about the company from which you are buying your network components?
2. Do you know other people who have bought computers from this company?
3. Is the dealer authorized?
4. Does the dealer offer technical support?
5. Does it offer training services?
6. Does it do its own repairs?
7. How much does equipment cost at this dealer?
8. Does the dealer carry brand-name equipment?

Choosing Disk Drives

The drives that contain your LAN's data on the file server should be high-quality and capable of storing all the data you need to store. These are some of the factors you need to consider when purchasing your server's disk drives:

1. How many users do you have on your network?

2. What type of file server do you have?
3. Will you be adding additional devices to the file server?
4. Is high performance or high capacity a requirement?

Choosing Backup Devices

Once you've spent money on devices to store data on the network, you need to consider the equipment that will guarantee your network's data security. Among the factors in choosing backup devices for your network are:

1. How much data will you be backing up each night?
2. How fast does the backup need to be?
3. Is there already existing equipment for the backup?
4. Will you be backing up information from only DOS machines? Or will you be backing up Macintoshes, UNIX machines, and OS/2 workstations?
5. Is the tape device Novell-certified?
6. Does the tape backup software work with NetWare? Will it back up as well as restore the NetWare bindery?
7. If you are using NetWare 4.x, does the backup software you use support NetWare Directory Services?
8. Where will the backup device be located?
9. Where will you be storing the backup tapes? Have you arranged for off-site storage?
10. Can you automate the process, or will you change tapes when one is full and another is required?
11. Does the backup software include full reporting? Can you tell from the report which files did not get backed up or where problems occurred?
12. Is the software a NetWare Loadable Module (NLM)? Is it Novell-certified?

Choosing Printers

Printing is one of the primary reasons users give for installing LANs. The printer you choose will depend on a number of factors and on features you need. Some of these factors and features are:

1. What printing speed do you need?
2. Where will the printer be located?
3. How much do you have to spend?
4. Will you be using a print server, dedicated workstation, or will you attach the printer directly to the network or to the file server?
5. Can the printer be connected directly to the network?
6. What access method are you using?
7. What protocol will be running to the printer? Only IPX? Or will you be printing data from IP or AppleTalk networks?
8. Is the printer Novell-certified?

chapter 5

Making the Best of It
File Servers

What Am I Looking for and Why?

The file server is the heart of your network. It must perform smoothly and efficiently. If it doesn't, your entire network is worth no more than a high-priced boat anchor. While your workstations may be excellent machines, they don't serve as the primary storage for the network's applications or data. In a networked system like NetWare, most applications run on the workstation but are stored on the file server. Thus, since the file server is the most important component on your network, when you choose a file server you must take into account exactly what you need.

Let's first take a look at what the file server does. Its primary function is to respond to requests made by the devices on the network and to provide file or other services to them. That means that the file server stores files and makes them available across the network to users' workstations or devices when requested. When you run Microsoft Windows at a workstation, you request the program from the file server, but your workstation processes the program. The server does none of the processing.

Most file servers provide network print services. When you send a job to a printer, the file server stores the print file before sending it to the printer. Even if the print server or a remote printer on a workstation finally services the print job, the file server services it first.

The file server also performs other functions that require extensive computing power. It handles most of the network operating system's security and management features, performs integrity checks of data stored on its hard drive, and performs transaction tracking, in which the network protects data from loss in case of a file server failure. With the advent of NetWare v3.x and the NetWare Loadable Module (NLM), NetWare file servers have taken on a larger role.

Now the server can more easily serve other functions not related to simple file and print services such as network monitoring and database management. These services are integrated into the network operating system on the file server. As time goes on, the traditional file server takes on many more roles, but for now, its primary function still is servicing requests for data (data I/O).

Because the primary function of a file server is data I/O, the most important consideration when determining which file server to purchase is the throughput you can expect from it. In determining the throughput you can obtain from any given combination of hardware, you must remember that the total system is only as fast as its slowest component. In other words, you must be able to identify and eliminate components that may cause bottlenecks and slow the operations of the network. Bottlenecks can occur in several places. These areas are the most important:

1. The processor and bus type. Is the machine an 80386 or 80486 machine? Is its bus an Industry Standard Architecture (ISA), Extended Industry Standard Architecture (EISA), or Micro Channel? Is the bus a 16-bit or a 32-bit bus?
2. Disk I/O.
3. The amount and type of memory. Is there sufficient memory to process requests efficiently?
4. The type and speed of the network adapters. Are the adapters 16-bit or 32-bit adapters? Do they limit the flow of information from the workstation to the file server? Is the adapter in the file server powerful enough?
5. The workstations. Are your workstations 80286, 80386, 80486 or Pentium workstations? Is a slow workstation bogging down the rest of the network?

Processors and Bus Design

With NetWare v3.x (and higher-numbered versions), Novell took a giant step toward enterprise networking with a full multiuser, multitasking operating environment. Previous versions of NetWare took advantage of the Intel 80286 processor, and before that the Motorola 68000 processor. As such, NetWare has all the inherent limitations of the processor used for the file server. The 80286 processor has a 16-bit I/O port and processing, and is much slower than today's 80386 or 80486. NetWare v2.x operates on 80286 servers, in which a server is either dedicated to serving the network or nondedicated, in which case it can act as a workstation on the network as well as the server.

The 80386

The 80386 processor, used in many of today's file servers, has 32-bit data and address buses. It is capable of transferring 32 bits of data at a time across the bus, twice that of the 80286 processor. In EISA and Micro Channel-based systems, full 32-bit performance and I/O occur, while ISA buses limit the 80386's performance to 16-bit transfers.

The 80286 can address a maximum of 4,096MB of memory, while the 80386 can only handle 6MB. The 80386 can also emulate several 8086 processors and is fully compatible with software designed for the 8088, 8086, or 80286 processor. The 80386 also has enhanced memory features to speed up memory access. NetWare v3.x and 4.x require at least an 80386 processor.

The 80486

The 80486 processor is compatible with the 80386, and many of the 80386's features are integrated into the 80486. The functionality of the 80387 math coprocessor and the Intel 82385 memory cache controller are two of these features. For basic functionality of server-based applications or where a need exists for extensive file I/O processor speed, an 80486 processor is essential.

In addition to the processor, you must also consider processor speed. For instance, a 16-megahertz (MHz) 80386 processor can carry out approximately 4 million instructions per second (MIPS), while a 25-MHz processor can carry out 7 million instructions per second. An 80486 25MHz machine can carry out 8 to 40 MIPS, depending on configuration. As more processing power is necessary at the server, the demand for a faster 80386 or 80486 will increase.

As servers become more sophisticated and server-based database applications such as Microsoft's SQL Server or programs such as Lotus Notes become more prevalent, the need for more processing power at the server will grow. Vendor response may well be the multiprocessor system.

Multiprocessor Systems

Multiprocessor systems provide two or more 80386 or higher processors on the same machine, each dedicated to specific services. You would have one processor dedicated to handling data I/O and disk storage, and one reserved for other functions and server-based applications. NetFrame, Compaq, IBM, and Tricord have introduced multiprocessor superservers. These systems are optimized to provide fast throughput by placing additional processing when and where it is needed. Disk I/O increases from approximately 6 megabits per second (Mbps) for the fastest 80386 single-processor systems to almost 19Mbps for multiprocessor systems. As you might expect, the price tag jumps accordingly from $12,000 to upwards of $60,000.

Which Bus Do I Take?

Because data input and output from the network adapter to the hard disk is one of the primary functions of the server, one of the most important considerations you need to make is the type of I/O bus the server has. This is the highway data travels on. There are presently several PC bus types to choose from. However, there presently are only two you should consider for file server use. These are the various bus types:

1. The ISA bus
2. The EISA bus
3. The Micro Channel Architecture bus
4. The local bus
5. The PCI bus

ISA Bus

The ISA bus is characteristic of AT-class machines. It is an expansion of the original eight-bit PC bus, used in the original IBM PC. The ISA bus is a 16-bit bus architecture and is the standard in most 80286-, 80386-, and some 80486-class machines. The ISA bus is limited to 11 usable interrupts. Because interrupt sharing is rarely used in DOS machines, you can quickly become limited in the devices that can be installed on the machine. Further, the 80386 and higher processors use 32-bit instruction sets. By limiting the bus to 16 bits, you automatically reduce the speed and efficiency of the chip.

Tip

We will not discuss the eight-bit PC bus architecture even for use as workstations. If you have one of these PCs, attach some rope to it and use it as an anchor for your new boat. If nothing else, that is what its performance does to your network, not to mention the productivity of whatever user must cope with it.

The "standard" bus speed for ISA is limited to 8MHz, which greatly diminishes the speed of any processor. A 33-MHz processor quickly reaches the maximum capabilities of the I/O channel. Utilization is also a problem with any adapter that attempts high-speed data transfers across an ISA bus. In this case, the bus quickly becomes the bottleneck for information. Vendors have made attempts to increase the bus speed to 12, 16, and 32MHz. While these higher-speed implementations work well under many circumstances, a large number of interface adapters that were not designed to work with the faster buses fail to operate properly. If you must reduce the bus speed of a computer to compensate for timing problems, you lose much of the machine's functionality.

Tip

One of the hardest problems to identify and troubleshoot is an adapter-related bus-timing problem. The adapter appears to work well until it is placed under any load, at which point it causes network errors. Normally, an adapter receives its timing from the bus clock on the motherboard. However, many manufacturers attempt to compensate for odd bus-timing on faster buses by altering the timing. This change normally works well, but you should always check with the manufacturer if you suspect a problem.

ISA bus-mastering, which we will discuss in more detail in Chapter 17: What's This Driving Me Around, is also an extremely difficult proposition at best. For now, remember that bus-mastering is supported on ISA machines and can greatly increase throughput and reduce the overhead for the processor. ISA bus-mastering is not true bus-mastering, and with some non-Intel processors, problems will occur.

Tip

ISA bus-mastering can aid your server's performance, but you should attempt to verify that your motherboard supports bus-mastering before you purchase bus-mastering adapters. Bus-mastering must be implemented properly for ISA bus-mastering adapters to operate. If you suspect that this is the problem with your interface adapter, disable bus-mastering on the adapter. Most manufacturers allow you to disable this feature through a software driver or hardware switch.

Tip

When you use ISA bus-mastering adapters on NetWare v3.x and 4.x servers with more than 16MB of memory, the adapter cannot address memory over 16MB. This is a limitation of NetWare that you can avoid by allocating buffers below 16MB of memory or by disabling the extra memory. To allocate the buffers, place this line in your STARTUP.NCF file:

SET RESERVED BUFFERS BELOW 16 MEGABYTES = X

where X equals the number of buffers allocated. Your manufacturer should tell you in the product's documentation how many buffers to allocate and also of any parameters you need to set. You'll enable these parameters with the LOAD statement in the AUTOEXEC.NCF file.

EISA Bus

The EISA bus is used primarily for servers and high-speed workstations. We do not recommend that you use an ISA bus machine for your primary server or for a server on your network that must handle a large number of users. The EISA bus or Micro Channel bus is a better choice for those machines.

The EISA bus was designed by a consortium of computer manufacturers in response to IBM's introduction of the Micro Channel bus. EISA upgraded the ISA format to support existing formats and still provide efficiency increases. In EISA buses, there are two bus channels—one for I/O that remains at 8MHz to maintain compatibility with existing adapters, and one for memory that can provide up to 33-MHz access rates.

The bus path on an EISA machine is a full 32 bits. While EISA accepts and works well with standard ISA adapters, to take full advantage of the new bus you must use EISA adapters. To achieve its dual architecture, the EISA bus slot is deeper than the ISA slot. The EISA contacts extend below the ISA contacts. The top slot still accommodates ISA adapters. The standard EISA bus speed is still 8MHz, but EISA also has a burst mode that can temporarily transfer at least three times that rate.

EISA also supports true bus-mastering, which makes for much faster data transfer at lower CPU utilization. The EISA specification requires that adapters be software-configurable in the machine they are used in via a configuration program. This means that each EISA adapter ships with a configuration file named !XXXYYYY.CFG (where XXX is the manufacturer identifier and YYYY is the individual file identifier). Each adapter is configured for the individual slot in which it is used. The EISA configuration routine should set each adapter so that no conflicts exist with other devices in the server.

Tip

Configuration routines only apply to EISA adapters. If you are using ISA adapters in an EISA machine, you must be careful that you don't create a conflict. You can avoid this by configuring each adapter using a generic ISA configuration file that comes with the EISA configuration program. This action lets the configuration program set up the EISA adapters according to the configuration of the ISA adapters and avoid conflicts that may be caused. Some ISA adapters operate better after being set up in this manner. Using a configuration program to configure ISA adapters does nothing to the adapter, but provides the machine with needed information about the ISA adapters.

The EISA bus is the best all-around choice for your server. It provides the speed and reliability a good server needs. Its dual-bus format provides excellent bus speed for peripherals and even faster speeds for memory. Its compatibility with prior processor and bus designs provides some flexibility in emergencies.

Micro Channel Bus

Primarily for workstations or servers, the Micro Channel Architecture bus was developed by IBM to solve inherent problems with the ISA bus. It uses a single bus line for both I/O and memory, but multiplexes the bus into several channels that numerous different processes can use at the same time. The Micro Channel bus multiplexes the memory and I/O lines across the channel and is divided into 16- and 32-bit designs. The 32-bit Micro Channel adapters will fit into the 32-bit slots, while 16-bit Micro Channel adapters can be used in either. In speed, this architecture also exhibits a dramatic improvement over the ISA bus.

The Micro Channel bus also provides for automatic configuration of the adapter using a configuration program called the Reference Program. Each Micro Channel adapter must have a configuration file called an Adapter Definition File (ADF). The name of the ADF file is based on a registration number and appears similar to @64b6.ADF. When you put a new adapter into the Micro Channel machine, it requires you to insert the Reference Program diskette or run the Reference Program from ROM memory. You may then choose the option Automatic Configuration and let the computer configure the adapter or choose the option Set Configuration and configure the adapter manually.

Tip

Keep a copy of your Reference Program diskette. Make another copy of the diskette every time you add a new adapter to the server. That way you always have a Reference Program diskette that has all the ADF files you need. Nothing is worse than finding your backup, only to discover it does not contain the ADF for the adapter you installed three months ago.

The Micro Channel bus is also an excellent choice for your server. Its combination of bus speed and the inherent advantages of the architecture provide the power a server requires. The one problem you may have with the Micro Channel bus is that machines and peripherals are approximately twice as expensive as ISA or EISA adapters. This cost disadvantage may make you decide to purchase EISA servers.

As a result of the success of the EISA standard, vendors have introduced new bus options. Two of these, the VESA and local bus architectures, circumvent some of the problems with the ISA bus. They allow video adapters, disk controllers, and, at some point, network adapters to connect directly to the system processor bus. Three VESA and local bus slots are allowed per motherboard. Intel is developing PCI as a new bus standard that is more compatible with Intel microprocessors.

Who Is the Master of the Bus?

With the traditional network adapter, the CPU controls all I/O from the bus to system memory. This is true also of the EISA dual-bus architecture. This mechanism increases CPU overhead and prevents the CPU from being used to its full potential. To increase throughput and relieve the CPU of the responsibilities it has for bus control, some adapters have bus-mastering capability. In bus-mastering, the adapter manufacturer places a separate processor on the adapter. During a data transfer, the device signals the CPU that it intends to take over the bus. The adapter then sends data down the bus, which it now controls. It then relinquishes control of the bus. The main CPU is not interrupted to perform data I/O and thus is free to continue other operations.

The real pressure for bus-mastering comes in when more than one bus-mastering adapter is introduced into the file server. Then, bus-mastering requires an arbitrator to determine which device has control of the bus. On EISA adapters, a chip called a BMIC (Bus-Mastering Interface Chip) performs the arbitration. There is no such chip on ISA systems, so a principle called *fairness* must be implemented via LAN or disk drivers. On Micro Channel machines, each bus-mastering adapter must have its arbitration level set. The arbitration level determines the access to the bus when more than one device wants the bus at the same time.

Tip

On ISA machines, the drivers control arbitration. The driver must have fairness enabled. Most adapter manufacturers implement fairness by default, but some do not. The result is that some adapters may dominate the bus and not let other bus-mastering adapters have access. If this happens, see if the manufacturer has implemented fairness.

Did We Forget Memory?

Without exception, when dealing with a NetWare v3.x or 4.x file server, the more memory the better. It is essential that you have enough memory to handle all the server functions and enough to allocate buffer space for incoming packets and disk I/O.

The absolute minimum RAM required for NetWare is 2MB. However, even to have a chance of operating properly, you should start with 4MB. Memory under NetWare is divided among the network operating system, third-party NLMs that run as server applications, and memory allocated for buffers. Under NetWare v3.x and 4.x, memory is allocated dynamically by the section that needs it. Dynamic allocation is new to NetWare v3.x. To change the static memory pools in NetWare v2.x requires major changes to the network operating system. NetWare v3.x holds memory in a large memory pool that is allocated for cache buffers, unless other network processes need it.

Dynamic RAM

Memory is divided into two types—dynamic RAM (DRAM) and static RAM (SRAM). Most older computer systems use DRAM. Its operating speed is between 80 and 200 nanoseconds and its memory refresh cycle is 4 milliseconds. This is fine for any server that operates at 16MHz or less. However, 80386 and 80486 systems require SRAM for special uses, although both systems have DRAM and SRAM.

Static RAM

SRAM does not use a system of flip-flop circuits that hold the RAM in one state or the other. This means SRAM does not need to be constantly refreshed like DRAM. However, SRAM design is more expensive. Some manufacturers use SRAM as the cache memory between the processor and standard memory. Cache memory holds the instructions most used by the processor. Thus, a system has fast access to the information it requires most. Additional circuitry moves the information between cache and standard memory. Most systems that use SRAM take advantage of the Intel 82385 cache controller to control the flow of data between cache and standard memory.

More Is More

No matter what system you choose, you can increase its performance by adding as much memory as possible. NetWare uses RAM for its cache buffering system. It sets a common memory pool, and whatever memory is not used by other sections of the operating system is allocated as cache memory for buffers. NLMs, LAN drivers, disk drivers, NetWare utilities, and third-party utilities that run as NLMs receive memory from cache when necessary.

The memory other utilities use is returned to cache memory when it is no longer needed. As other areas of NetWare and utilities need more memory, cache memory is loaned. In NetWare v3.x, memory is allocated dynamically. The memory comes from the cache. As the cache decreases in size, NetWare's performance suffers. When memory drops too low, NetWare will warn of low memory.

The more memory you make available to NetWare, the better server performance will be. Start with no less than 8–12MB of memory. Since most memory is devoted to cache, the larger the disk drive, the better. NetWare uses cache memory to:

1. Cache the File Allocation Table (FAT) of each volume.
2. Cache part of each volume's Directory Entry Table.
3. Cache commonly accessed files.
4. Cache the directory hash table.
5. Provide buffer space for the Turbo FAT indexing tables for all open files that have 64 FAT entries or more and are randomly accessed. This use is generally limited to database files.

As you increase the disk space, cache memory is used for these other memory requirements. A file server with 1GB of disk space should have a minimum of 16MB of disk space. You should also require at least 12MB of RAM for each additional gigabyte of disk space.

Tip

These RAM requirements exceed the recommended minimums by Novell. However, experience has shown that these minimums offer a more realistic estimation of RAM requirements. Performance is critical to file servers, and the performance depends on adequate memory. Memory is inexpensive compared to inadequate performance.

LAN Compass

If you choose to calculate memory for the file server by Novell's methods, refer to the LAN Compass in the back of this book.

The Disks That Drive the System

Now that you have the proper motherboard and have enough memory for the server, you must decide on the proper disk drive to run the server engine. There are four disk interface standards for current server configurations:

1. The ST506 interface
2. The ESDI interface
3. The SCSI interface
4. The IDE interface

The ST506, originally designed and introduced by Seagate Technologies, uses the Modified Frequency Modulation (MFM) encoding technique or the Run Length Limited (RLL) encoding method when writing data to disk. As one of the first controller implementations, the ST506 was commonly used in 80286 and some early 80386 machines. It has not been used extensively since then. Data transfer is limited to approximately 5Mbps. This type of interface is not recommended for use in NetWare servers. It is simply too slow.

The ESDI interface stands for Enhanced Small Device Interface. It provides transfer rates of up to 15Mbps, can attach up to two drives per controller, and has a storage capability of 100MB or greater.

The Small Computer System Interface (SCSI) is a major departure from previous standards. It allows up to seven devices including hard drives, tape drives, and CD-ROM drives to share the same SCSI host adapter. The SCSI host adapter takes up only one slot in the system and provides a bus that the seven devices use. SCSI buses can be 8-, 16-, or 32-bits wide. The SCSI host adapter is a control device for the other intelligent devices on the bus. Variations of the SCSI system include wide SCSI and SCSI II, which provide even faster throughput than SCSI. The throughput of the SCSI depends on how many devices are attached to the SCSI bus and the type of system you are using. Since SCSI devices must contain their own control circuitry, they are generally more expensive than standard controllers.

The Intelligent Drive Electronics (IDE) interface was designed to be a hybrid interface that offered some of the advantages of ESDI at a much lower cost. IDE devices have control circuitry built into the device. Because control circuitry is built in, the controller adapter is generally inexpensive. By using a local bus (VESA) IDE controller, you can achieve 32-bit access for your IDE devices. IDE supports two devices per controller.

How Do I Use What I Have?

The decision which drive you use depends on what system you plan to use to write data to your server. The basic server has one controller with one disk attached to it. Novell provides data protection to this system by the Hot Fix feature. Hot Fix reserves a percentage of disk space set by the network administrator. When Hot Fix detects a bad section of the drive, it automatically flags this portion of the disk as bad and redirects the data to the Hot Fix Redirection Area. When the Hot Fix Redirection Area becomes nearly full, NetWare warns you. Hot Fix is a fine mechanism for the majority of small systems, or if you have information that is not mission-critical. However, if you need additional protection against disk failure, you should consider mirroring or duplexing your data onto multiple drives.

Disk mirroring and disk duplexing provide a means of fault-tolerance against data loss. In disk mirroring, two disks are placed on a single controller. The disks are used as a primary drive and a backup drive. Mirroring is set up through the NetWare INSTALL utility. During mirroring, each drive "mirrors" the other drive. Data is written to both drives simultaneously. If the primary drive fails, the backup can take over until the server is brought down and the primary drive changed. Then the backup drive remirrors the drives to a synchronous state. Mirroring requires that you use an IDE, ESDI, or SCSI drive.

Tip

It is not necessary to have identically sized drives to perform mirroring. However, NetWare mirrors to the smaller drive. The additional space on the larger drive is wasted.

Mirroring is fine as long as the controller does not fail. However, if the controller fails, you lose both the primary and backup drives. If you want to provide fault-tolerance for the controller, you should duplex the drives. In disk duplexing, you install multiple controllers and attach the primary drive to one controller and the backup drive to the secondary controller. NetWare then automatically writes the same data to both controllers at the same time.

Tip

It is possible to mirror and duplex drives at the same time. Put two drives on controllers and then mirror the drives on the individual controllers. This provides the best network fault tolerance short of SFT Level III.

In NetWare, the unit of storage is the volume. A single disk can be separated into multiple volumes or a volume can span multiple drives. Performance enhancements are realized by spanning a volume across multiple drives. Additional drives can be attached to a spanned volume without reformatting the volume.

Tip

If you are using a volume that spans multiple drives, then you should use duplexed drives to provide fault tolerance.

Standard disk drives are discussed later in Chapter 8: Disks, Data, Memory, and Organization.

Disk Arrays: Do I Need Them?

As your needs for server performance and fault tolerance increase, one way to achieve more performance from your system is to utilize RAID (Redundant Arrays of Inexpensive Disks). A disk array is a series of drives, the number depending on the level of RAID technology you use, in which data is written across the drives by a technique called *striping*. Typically, the disk array uses the SCSI drive type and controller.

The amount of fault tolerance you achieve depends on the level of RAID you use. These are the different RAID levels:

1. RAID Level 0. Data is striped over several drives without any redundancy.
2. RAID Level 1. Data is striped to an array of drives, and each drive is mirrored to a backup drive.
3. RAID Level 2. Data is striped at the bit level to all drives in the array.
4. RAID Level 3. Data is striped at the bit or byte level to all drives in the array except one. This final drive is the parity drive. RAID

Level 3 provides good protection, but is the slowest of the RAID systems.
5. RAID Level 4. Similar to RAID 3 except that data is striped in disk sectors instead of bits or bytes. Read times are improved.
6. RAID Level 5. Writes are in entire disk sectors like RAID 3, except parity information is written to all drives.

Most designers use RAID level 4 or 5. RAID technology allows for hot swapping of bad drives. With RAID implemented, you can remove a bad drive and replace it without downing the server.

Adapters: How Do I Get There From Here?

Now that you have the file server set, you need to determine the type of network adapter you will use. The server adapter, in many respects, is the most important adapter in the system. If an adapter in a workstation dies, you lose that workstation on the network, and in the case of thin Ethernet, you lose the segment to which the adapter is attached. With the server adapter, the workstations connected to that adapter will go down until you can get it replaced. The other consideration for a strong server adapter is one of performance.

Performance Is the Key

The key to a good server adapter is performance. The adapter in the server handles many more packets and sends out much more data than the average workstation adapter. It handles all the I/O operations for the server. Good network performance demands a high-performance server adapter.

If you have followed our advice so far, you have chosen an EISA or a Micro Channel computer. In either case, be sure that your network adapter takes advantage of the architecture's 32-bit bus. If you have chosen an ISA bus, the same holds true. Choose a 16-bit adapter. Get the adapter that best takes advantage of the bus you are operating in.

If you are operating on an Ethernet, token-ring, or FDDI network, be sure that you have a bus-mastering adapter. You should use bus-mastering for several reasons. First, the bus-mastering adapter provides faster I/O from the adapter to the CPU memory. Fast I/O is essential particularly for the server adapter. Bus-mastering provides you with faster I/O than non–bus-mastering adapters.

The other reason for choosing a bus-mastering adapter is CPU utilization. In NetWare v3.x and 4.x your server is not just a file server, but has many other tasks to perform. As network traffic increases, server utilization increases dramatically. A bus-mastering adapter reduces the overall server utilization by reducing the requirement for CPU intervention during an I/O cycle. Server utilization can be decreased further by installing multiple adapters in the server. Remember, though, that as the number of adapters in the server increases, the amount of server utilization will increase proportionately as well.

A portion of the performance enhancement you get from any adapter depends on the driver written for the adapter. Verify with the manufacturer that the driver and adapter combination you are using is Novell-certified.

Tip

Novell certification is essential if you run into trouble. Novell is not obligated to provide technical support for noncertified products. However, if you have a certified adapter and driver, you can more easily obtain technical support from Novell, who will probably have a working relationship with the manufacturer of your adapter. Further, since problems with devices are often interrelated, you can obtain more help from the Technical Support Alliance (TSA), a group of hardware and software manufacturers headed by Novell that agree to help each other with common problems.

Reliability

While reliability applies to almost any product in your machine, it is especially true of network adapters. Be sure you can get immediate technical support and replacements from the vendor. Have an extra server adapter in stock. Typically a network adapter from a reliable manufacturer is probably the least likely component of the server to go bad. It is also the one part that you cannot mirror or duplex. Thus, if your network adapter dies, you do not have an automatic backup in the machine.

Also, verify the manufacturer's policy on warranty replacements. Most manufacturers have two-to-five-year, or even near-lifetime, warranties on the adapters.

What You See and How You See It

The monitor on the file server is probably the one area of the machine where you can scrimp. You only need a monochrome adapter and monitor. Today, it is sometimes less expensive to purchase monochrome VGA than a straight monochrome adapter. You typically use the monitor only to view the MONITOR.NLM statistics or to bring the server up and down.

Tip
If you are using SFT III mirrored servers, be sure to get the same type of monitor and adapter for each machine. If you are not using identical types of video equipment, SFT III may have trouble mirroring memory and may thus fail.

Specialized Servers

The server discussion so far has been about file servers. However, there are several types of servers that you can have on the network. The type of server you plan to add determines the items you need. Specialized servers normally require less equipment than the file server. Here is an outline of the types of servers and what you typically need:

1. The database server
2. The print server
3. The facsimile server
4. The e-mail server
5. The login server
6. The modem server

Database servers have similar requirements to NetWare file servers. The database server stores your database and typically has a third-party database program running on the server as an NLM. The database server may contain larger amounts of I/O than the file server.

Further, although the files on a database server are generally larger, the average packet going to and from a database server is smaller. This means that your choice of network protocol is critical. Select a protocol that handles large packets efficiently and still handles the small packets that comprise a lot of the traffic. Since the database server handles your database or at least a part of it, you should be sure to use mirrored and duplexed drives. Also, adequate memory is critical for this type of server. The database server is an excellent candidate for SFT Level III mirrored servers. This is an expensive option, but for this critical machine, it is almost essential.

Print servers are generally workstations that run NetWare's PSERVER.EXE utility, and are used to direct print jobs to individual printers. Typically, the print queue is stored on the NetWare file server and services the queue. You don't need a hard drive, and the print server is a good candidate for remote booting. Four megabytes of memory is generally sufficient for this machine.

A facsimile server is similar to a print server in that it is a workstation that runs software on the network that intercepts faxes directed to the fax and holds the transmission in a queue until it can be transmitted. With this type of machine, you typically want it to remote boot as well. You might want to add a little more memory. The fax server must generally service its own queue and may need some additional memory to handle this operation.

E-mail servers are workstations that route e-mail between two networks or serve as an access point for internetwork mail. You may or may not need a modem on the e-mail server. As with the other specialized servers, you want the e-mail server to remote boot for security reasons.

The login server is a standard NetWare server that is the main login point for the network. Since login is a network-intensive operation, you will sometimes want to off-load the file server and use a separate machine for this activity. This machine can also be used as a first line of security if you have a large number of users who log in as GUESTs. You can put the applications they use on the login server and deny them access to the rest of the network servers. User login scripts and user directories are stored on the login server. Since this server may store critical user information, you may want to mirror or duplex the drives. The login server should have a fair amount of memory, approximately 8–10MB. At a minimum, the login server should be a midrange 80386.

A modem server is also another workstation that acts as a redirection point for the network. In this case, it is a workstation that has several modems attached for use by network users. In the modem server, I/O is critical. You want to spend additional funds on the adapters that are used to attach the modems. You also want this machine to be a remote-boot machine.

If Performance Is Key, How Do I Know When I Have It?

Network performance is the holy grail of the administrator. It is also the hardest factor to measure. We know one administrator who measures his performance by the number of mad people who call him. The fewer calls he gets, the better an indication he has of good network performance. In the end, keeping users content and working as they want is probably as good a performance monitor as any.

Network performance is a subjective feature. Almost all performance monitors sold measure individual network components, and none really measures the entire network.

A number of factors affect network performance. You should start measuring your network performance by evaluating your users. The number of users and the applications they use is the primary factor in determining network performance. For the average network, if you have more than 40 users on one adapter in the server, you should add a second adapter in the server and split the network into an internetwork. If you have a small group of users who make extensive use of the network, you should purchase a high-speed network and place those users on the separate network.

Tip

Some proprietary network adapters and the new 100Mbps Ethernet adapters can deliver exceptional performance at an extremely low cost. For a small number of users, a proprietary option that delivers the performance you need can be a cost-effective option.

Another matter to consider when you look at the users on your network is the quality of their workstations. Particularly with high-speed networks, you can increase your overall network performance by increasing the quality and speed of your workstation. Watch the type of machine you add a high-speed adapter to. An 80286 with an FDDI adapter doesn't process information any faster than before you put the high-speed adapter in it. By making that machine a 80486/66 with an FDDI adapter, you not only increase the productivity of the user, but you increase the speed of the network incrementally.

The Whole of Performance Is the Sum of Its Parts

We've seen that a network is only as fast as its slowest component. High-speed workstations with superservers and high-speed network adapters fall flat with only 4MB of RAM and a slow disk drive in the file server. When you measure performance, you measure throughput. Throughput reflects the amount of information you can get off the hard drive, on the wire, and into the workstation and back during peak traffic hours. When a system is up, you can evaluate the throughput and try to identify bottlenecks. A bottleneck is where the pipeline of data on your network is held up waiting for a component or resource to become available. The bottleneck can be the wire, disk drive, controller, network adapter, server, or workstation. In a system that is up and running, you spend a great deal of time identifying the bottlenecks and eliminating them.

There are several things you need to identify in order to eliminate bottlenecks. Here are some things to look for immediately:

1. Be sure you have enough RAM in your server. The difference in price between 8 and 16MB is approximately $300. Don't scrimp. Install a minimum of 12MB or 16MB.

2. Make sure you have a high-performance bus in your server. EISA and Micro Channel are currently the best choices. Look for PCI in the future.

3. Match your hard drive controller to your bus. If you have an EISA bus, don't buy an ISA controller. If you have a Micro Channel server, be sure to get a 32-bit controller and not a 16-bit controller.

4. Purchase an extremely high-speed, high-capacity hard drive.

5. Duplex your drives instead of mirroring them. The performance is incremental, but duplexing does help.

6. Purchase high-performance network adapters. Match your bus design to the server. If you have an EISA bus machine, use EISA

adapters. If Micro Channel, use 32-bit adapters. Always use bus-mastering adapters. Also, look for adapters with upgradable onboard memory, especially if your network is token-ring.

7. Use the fastest access method you can afford.
8. Use a high-speed access method for the backbone network. For interconnections between networks, use high-speed routers.
9. Do not have more than 40 workstations on an individual LAN segment or network adapter.
10. If you have more than four adapters in your server, add a second file server.

How Do I Find the Bottleneck?

The first place to look to identify the bottleneck is in the components you already have. If you have the fastest hard drive available, it is probably not the bottleneck. If you have only 4MB of RAM on the file server, it is probably at least part of the problem. Once you have worked on the obvious problems, then you can look for an analysis package to help you.

Start with a software-based protocol analyzer or a traffic monitor. A good protocol analyzer allows you to capture packets and identify them. It should also allow you to generate network traffic and watch how the traffic affects your network. There are several packages on the market. One of the best is Network Communications Corp.'s LANalyzer. Good software-based analyzers are available from Novell, Intel, FTP Software, and Triticom. They are much less expensive than hardware-based analyzers and sometimes are all you need.

Another good analysis tool is a network adapter analysis tool. Norton Utilities provides a Speed Index tool. Novell's PERFORM3, available on Novell's electronic forum on CompuServe called NetWire, measures the actual performance of the network adapters.

Tip

If you have slow network performance, but still get good performance numbers with PERFORM3, the problem is somewhere else on the network, probably in your hard drive. You can add workstations to the network and measure the actual amount of traffic on the network.

PC Week also distributes an excellent analysis tool for motherboard and hard disk performance, which you can receive from ZiffNet on CompuServe. This utility gives you a good idea of how fast the drive performs reads and writes to the disk.

Tip

You'll notice that you always have better performance when you measure reads from the hard drive. This is because writes take longer than reads. If you are measuring reads, remove the operations of the hard drive from the picture and you'll get a better measure of the performance your users are seeing.

Another good tool is one that inventories the hardware and software on the network. This helps you to identify drivers that may be out-of-date and affecting the performance of the individual workstations. Checking your network regularly to be sure all your software is up-to-date goes a long way toward maintaining peak performance.

Your choice of a file server is probably the hardest of all the network choices you'll need to make. It is also the most important. Make sure you have purchased the best available components for the server. Also, be sure you purchased enough for two to three years of network growth, and not just your present needs. Your network quickly absorbs the resources available to it. When the network is used beyond the capabilities of the individual components, network performance slows. You must keep a watchful eye to be sure you find the bottlenecks before they develop.

chapter

What About Workstations?

6

How Does My Workstation Attach to the LAN?

NetWare is a client–server form of networking in which a file server acts as the I/O engine and storage facility for the network, and PC workstations process information. Workstations are called clients—they make requests of the server for information. When you run applications on a workstation, the actual work is done on the workstation.

When you boot a workstation, you first bring up the operating system (DOS, OS/2, UNIX, or Macintosh). Then, you run programs that initialize the network adapter in your workstation and attach it to the network. Workstations have these two characteristics in common: they contain a network adapter that allows them to communicate with the rest of the network, and they load programs that let them communicate with other devices on the network.

Tip
In NetWare, the term "workstation" is often used interchangeably with "PC." In instances where a device on the network may be a printer, it is called a device or node. Workstations in NetWare may be DOS, UNIX, OS/2, or Macintosh machines.

As part of the process of attaching to the network in NetWare versions prior to v3.12, a program called the *shell* filters all requests to the

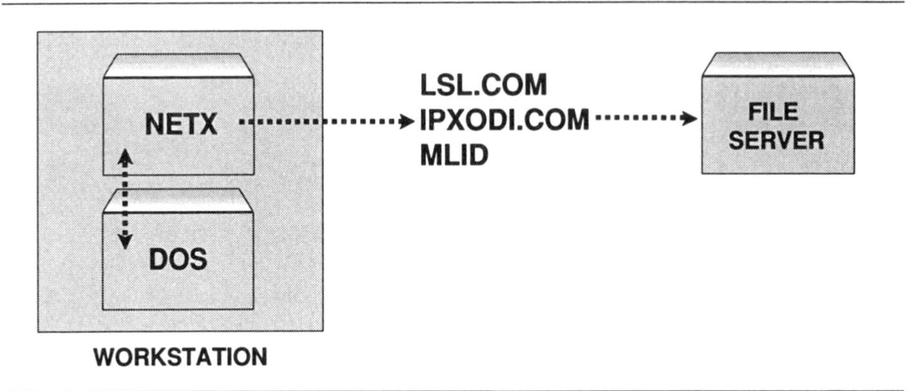

Figure 6-1. *The shell or requester functions as a traffic cop for the network.*

operating system or network operating system. The shell decides whether a request is for a device local to the workstation (such as drive A, B, or C) or for a device on the network (typically, drives F through Z). The shell then redirects the request to the appropriate device. (See Figure 6-1.)

In NetWare v3.12 and 4.0, a requester takes the place of the shell. All workstation requests are routed first to the network and, from there, to the proper local or logical network drive. OS/2 workstations on NetWare LANs use a similar requester program to handle their workstation requests in NetWare v2.x and v3.x.

When you log into the network, you attach to network devices that contain files and applications as a series of logical network drives, or to LPT or COM ports for network devices such as printers. Network devices are "mapped" to the network. Devices on the network are usually mapped with a NetWare command called MAP in the user's login script or in the system login script. The login scripts execute automatically when a user logs into the network. (See Figure 6-2 on the next page.)

Once devices are mapped to the network, and the shell or requester can identify which devices are local and which are attached to the network, the requests are routed to the file server or to the operating system.

How Does That Work Again?

Let's look at typing a letter in WordPerfect on a NetWare v3.12 network. You've logged into the network as JANE. Your login script maps

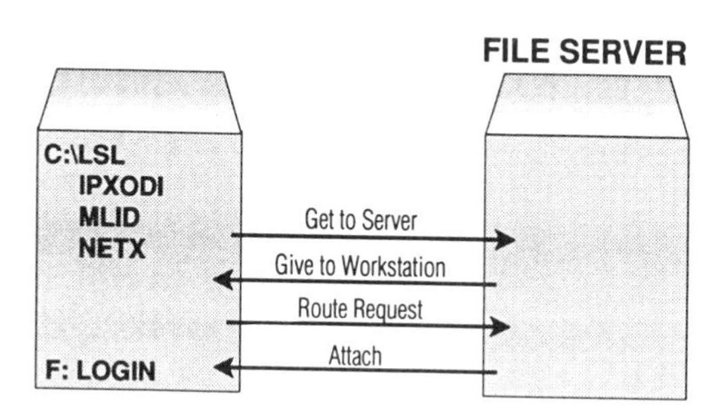

Figure 6-2. *The login process.*

the F: drive as your user or home directory (SERVER1\SYS:\USERS\JANE) and the G: drive as SERVER3\SYS:\APPS\WP51 (the location of WordPerfect on the network). Jane types G:, presses the Enter key, and types WP51. The requester (NETX.EXE) identifies G: as a network drive and routes the request to G: over the network adapter in Jane's workstation and out onto the media. The adapter in the server receives the request to provide the file WP51.COM to the workstation.

Each request is divided into a series of small pieces called packets. Each packet consists of a header, which contains information on the destination of the packet, a number that represents the total number of packets in the batch, the data, and a checksum at the end that indicates whether errors occurred during transmission. When her workstation receives the packets, it reassembles them into the entire file and executes WordPerfect on Jane's machine. When Jane finishes typing her letter, she saves it to diskette. The requester recognizes this as a local request and directs the file called RESIG.WP to the diskette drive. When Jane exits WordPerfect, or when she spell-checks the document, the workstation requests service from the file server.

If Jane had decided to print her resignation letter instead and had specified a network printer, she would have told WordPerfect to print to LPT3. In the login script, LPT3 is redirected to the print queue PROTEUS on server OPUS. The requester routes the output across the network and deposits it in the print queue. Jane then rushes to the laser printer down the hall to pick up her letter before her boss sees it and ruins the surprise.

This scenario illustrates how the process of requests and services works. The server is the repository of the files and queues, but most of the actual computing is performed in the workstation. This saves a lot of money by allowing you to use less expensive PCs and distributing the computing power where it is needed. Instead of having a large and expensive central computer that spends the same amount of power on a resignation letter as it would on a large, mission-critical database search, in NetWare, resources are placed where they work best. When you purchase workstations, remember this. You may purchase an inexpensive 386/33-megahertz machine for the marketing assistant who spends all his time writing client letters, and purchase an expensive 486/66-megahertz for the computer draftsperson who is designing the next new product for your company or for the person in accounting who does the month-end reconciliations. Tailor the computer power you need to the individual user.

How Do I Know What I Need?

A workstation contains a number of components, some which affect its processing speed on the network and others that determine which applications a person can use. These components are as follows:

1. The motherboard (80386, 80486, Pentium)
2. The case
3. The video adapter and monitor (VGA, EGA, monochrome)
4. The input devices (mouse, joystick, pen, keyboard)
5. The network adapter
6. The peripherals (printers and disk drives)
7. The memory (RAM and disk)

A lot of the decisions you make about the type of basic hardware for your network are based on how people use the network. Your workstations are much different for people using Windows than they would be if everyone ran DOS only. For example, Windows users definitely need a VGA monitor and adapter and at least 4MB of memory. If you have a design engineer on a PC using a computer-aided design program, he or she likely needs to have peripherals such as scanners, plotters, or input tablets attached to his or her workstation.

The first thing to do when deciding on workstations is some planning. Look at several things to determine what the basic workstation needs. These are the factors you'll need to decide on:

1. The network access method the network uses (Ethernet, token-ring, ARCNET, or the Fiber Distributed Data Interface)
2. The network's primary transport protocol (IPX/SPX, TCP/IP, UNIX, AppleTalk, or the Network File System [NFS])
3. The operating system (DOS, OS/2, UNIX, or Macintosh)
4. The user interface (Windows, a menuing system, or the DOS command line)
5. The application requirements (memory and devices required)
6. The performance requirements (how fast work needs to be done)
7. The primary use of the workstations (CAD/CAM, word processing, database management, or spreadsheets)

All these factors are interrelated and should be considered both individually and as a whole when you are looking for workstations that fit your users. You need to decide which items are more important than the others, and make your purchase decisions based on the best combination of factors.

Network Access Method

The network access method you use on your network depends largely on the type of media you already have installed in your network, the network operating system you choose, and the users' application needs. In some departments that have different network bandwidth needs, such as a group that does a lot of document imaging, you may need to change to an access method that operates faster for that data-intensive work. Or you may decide on an access method such as ARCNET because you already have RG-62 A/U coaxial cable installed in the walls of your building. If you have buildings arranged in a campus environment in which media needs to be strung between buildings, you may want to use fiber-optic media to link the unshielded twisted-pair (UTP) Ethernet LANs in each building.

The speed of each access method is also important in your decision. Say, for example, that you have 4 users who use a database application, and another 60 users who do word processing most of the day. You may choose to install 100Mbps Ethernet for the database users, and 10Mbps Ethernet for the remainder of the LAN. The decision to move to a faster network access method for your power users affects many other decisions as well. You may need to make cabling changes or add another adapter to the server to accommodate the additional access method, or change media from one type to another. You might require additional RAM or even a new file server.

Transport Protocol

Just as the network access method you choose for the workstation depends on your needs, so does the transport protocol. Transport protocols tend to consist of suites of protocols. One protocol performs its functions and relies on other protocols in the suite to perform the rest of the functions. In Novell NetWare, the protocol suite is the Internetwork Packet Exchange/Sequenced Packet Exchange (IPX/SPX). In UNIX networking, the common protocol suite is the Transmission Control Protocol/Internet Protocol (TCP/IP). In Macintosh networks, the protocol is AppleTalk.

NetWare v3.x and higher versions make use of a specification called the Open Data-Link Interface (ODI), which lets a single network adapter communicate with multiple protocols. Previously, an Ethernet user who wanted to communicate with a UNIX network and a NetWare network needed to have two adapters installed in the workstation and two drivers, one for each protocol. ODI allows you to bind (connect) multiple protocols to a single workstation adapter, saving time and money. This allows you to use IPX/SPX to communicate with your NetWare server and TCP/IP to correspond with someone on the Internet. However, the ability to add additional protocols to the workstation requires you to increase your workstation's RAM requirements.

You add protocols by purchasing the protocol as part of an application and installing it on your workstation. One common package is LAN Workplace for DOS, Windows, or OS/2. When you install this product, the installation procedure automatically makes changes to a workstation's NET.CFG file to handle packet addressing to both protocol stacks.

Operating System

The operating system you use on each workstation also impacts the workstation features you want. While DOS is the primary PC operating system, a multitude of other operating systems are available. In addition to DOS, you could use OS/2, UNIX or one of its variants, and Macintosh as the workstation operating system. The operating system you use dictates the amount of RAM, the amount of disk storage, and the type of video adapter you use. For example, if you decide to use OS/2, you need much more additional memory than if you used DOS. While it is possible to remote-boot OS/2, it is preferable to boot from the workstation. In the case of OS/2, you must have a hard drive on the workstation. OS/2 requires at least 15MB of disk space for best performance and should be allocated about 30MB for the operating system. NetWare supports all these operating systems in one fashion or another.

Tip

If you are planning to use OS/2, purchase workstations with at least 8MB RAM and 200MB hard drives. That gives you enough RAM and disk space to operate effectively.

If you decide to use operating systems other than DOS on your workstations, you'll need to change the file server's configuration. The file server must make allowances for the file systems of the other operating systems. Each operating system saves files in its own format. For instance, OS/2 allows longer file names than the standard DOS eight-character name with a three-character extension. NetWare supports these file variances with name spaces for OS/2, Macintosh, and NFS. Name spaces accommodate the translation of file names from one operating system to another. When you add name spaces to NetWare volumes, users can see their own files using its native operating system naming conventions and view other operating system files as well.

Tip

The term "native" refers to the operating system originally specified by the computer type. In PCs, the native operating system is DOS. For Macintoshes, it is the Macintosh Operating System, and for UNIX workstations, it is UNIX. We'll discuss DOS primarily.

LAN Compass

The addition of name spaces has no effect on the amount of RAM you need on the workstation. Name spaces do, however, require additional RAM on the file server. See the LAN Compass at the end of this book for suggestions on calculating file server RAM.

Application Requirements

The applications you use determine some of your workstation features. Applications sometimes dictate the type of monitor you need, the amount of RAM necessary for each workstation, and the network transport protocol and access method you use. You'll purchase most of the applications you use off-the-shelf, but some may be specially written for your company and have specific workstation requirements.

Performance Requirements

The user's performance requirements often have the greatest effect on the type of workstation you purchase. A user who constantly works with the company database requires a much faster machine than other users. Workstation performance enhancements can take many forms. A user who has large graphics requirements may want a video adapter with a large amount of on-board memory to improve the rate of video refreshes. The accounting department may require 486/66-MHz workstations to provide faster calculations. A programmer may require a fast machine with large amounts of memory to complete program compiles within a reasonable amount of time. Network performance requirements may require you to use a faster network access method or increase the workstation's RAM requirements.

Primary Use

The machine's primary use determines a lot of its requirements. A print server requires a much less powerful machine than a machine that is used for computer-aided design (CAD). The print server typically can be a DOS machine with a slow 80386 processor, or even an 80286 machine with a monochrome monitor, 2MB of RAM, and a couple of parallel or serial adapters. For a print server, you also want to use a boot ROM for the unit and remove any diskette drives. A CAD workstation should be a 486 DX 66 with 32MB RAM, a CD-ROM, a video adapter with 2MB of on-board memory, and a 21-inch monitor. The CAD workstation may operate on an FDDI segment, while the printer server remains on Ethernet.

What about RAM?

Obviously, we are worried about the amount of memory you have in your workstations. You should be, too. The typical user today uses some form of graphical interface, whether it is Microsoft Windows or any one of several menu programs. Any graphical user interface (GUI) requires as much memory as you can give it. In determining the amount of RAM you need, remember that in addition to the amount of RAM the GUI takes, you'll also be loading network and other programs into RAM. Be generous. Sufficient RAM can keep a workstation operating efficiently.

In DOS-based machines, three memory areas exist. The first 640KB of RAM is considered *low memory*. This is the area where programs load. You also have an area between 640KB and 1MB called *high memory*. You can use this area to create expanded memory if you have an 80286 or above processor. Beyond 1MB is the machine's upper memory, called *extended memory*. (See Figure 6-3.)

If you load your network adapter drivers in low memory (the first 640KB of RAM), you'll have approximately 500KB left for applications. Many programs today won't run in that memory size. If you are using an 80386 or above computer (which we recommend), you can take advantage of extended memory managers such as EMM386, QEMM, or 386MAX to use the memory above 1MB (the extended or *upper* memory). With these programs, you can load DOS, the network drivers, and other drivers into high memory. You can also use the memory manager to create expanded memory that some programs can use for paging memory.

Tip

If you are using a network adapter with shared memory, you must exclude the area of memory the adapter uses from the memory manager. For EMM386, this is done by adding the EXCLUDE command on the load line of the memory manager in the CONFIG.SYS file.

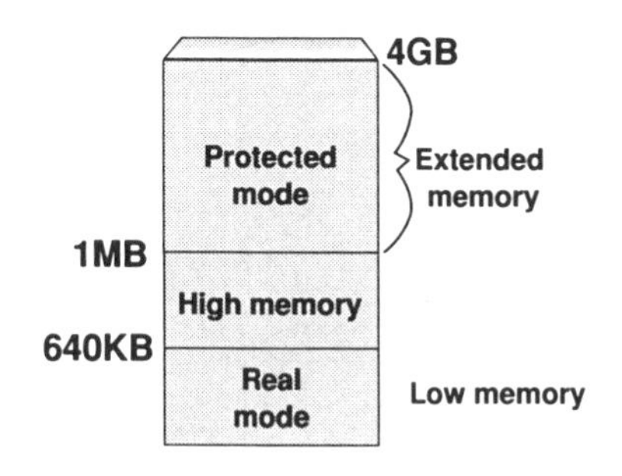

Figure 6-3. *The memory architecture of the 80386 computer.*

And Then There Was Windows

If Windows is your graphical user interface (GUI), your workstation memory requirements expand greatly. Windows extends your use of memory beyond the 640KB barrier and takes advantage of up to 16MB of RAM. It operates in Standard or Enhanced mode. Enhanced mode offers enhanced memory management and limited multitasking capabilities. Windows does not use the true multitasking mechanism OS/2 or UNIX environments allow, but it lets you quickly switch from task to task.

To take advantage of Windows' Enhanced mode, you must have a minimum of 2MB RAM. If you are using Windows on a network, we would recommend at least 4MB RAM. This amount greatly speeds Windows' performance. However, the more memory you can give Windows, the better.

Tip

Enhanced-mode Windows creates swap files to move currently unused programs on the Windows' desktop to disk. This creates more working space in memory. If you are running Windows from the network, which we'll discuss in Chapter 9, Don't Forget the Applications, you should add a small hard drive to your workstation that Windows can use for the swap file. Having this space available makes Windows run much faster and saves network disk space.

Windows offers many advantages for network users. The latest version, 3.1, takes advantage of the network—it is NetWare-aware. For example, the Windows' File Manager shows a different icon for network drives than it shows for non-network drives. Print Manager also works well with network printers. Network messages and warnings pop up Windows' dialog boxes. Novell also has a number of Windows-based utilities that help with simple network tasks such as adding network drives or connecting to network printers.

Tip

Refer to Chapter 9, Don't Forget the Applications, for configuring your workstations for Windows.

OS/2

If you are using OS/2 as your operating system, memory is even more important than it is with Windows or DOS. OS/2 requires 4MB of

RAM to boot, but you shouldn't consider running OS/2 in less than 8MB. OS/2 uses as much memory as your system allows, so 16–64MB may be advisable if the workstation allows it. Novell offers a NetWare Requester for OS/2 that lets you take advantage of OS/2's multitasking capabilities. With OS/2, you can log into the network as an OS/2 client, and then again as a DOS or Windows client, and set drive mappings to perform different functions and run different applications natively.

Start by Installing the Adapter

Through careful planning you have chosen several new computers. Now you need to attach them to your network. While it is possible to purchase computers with the network adapter already installed, chances are you have to install the adapter yourself and obtain the necessary software and media to attach the workstation to the network. First, verify that the area in which you'll place the new machine has a correct network drop cable. If it doesn't, you'll need to have one installed. Then, you need to install the adapter and configure it properly.

Install the Network Adapter

When you get your network adapter, open the box and verify it is what you thought you purchased. Nothing is worse than buying what you thought was a token-ring adapter, just to find out later that you received an Ethernet adapter. If you are installing a token-ring or Ethernet adapter, locate the node ID ROM and record the number in your LAN Log. Some of your applications may require that you know the node ID, especially if you are using a network monitoring application that requires you to associate a node ID with a NetWare user name. The location of the node ID ROM is shown in the adapter's documentation.

Tip

If you installing an ARCNET network, you must set the node ID before you attach the adapter to the network, and its node ID must be unique on the network. In ARCNET, there are 255 available node IDs, ranging from 1 to 255. You can set the node ID with switches or the Reference Diskette if the workstation is a Micro Channel or EISA machine.

After you've set the node ID, identify the peripherals in the workstation and the settings of each adapter. If you don't know what peripherals and settings exist in the workstation, you can use an application such as Microsoft's Diagnostic Utility (MSD) to inventory the computer and display the installed adapters and options. This utility tells you which interrupts, ports, and memory addresses are already assigned.

Typically the adapter's default settings work. If not, reset the switches on the adapter to the settings you want. Some ISA adapters come with programs that set the options on the adapter for you. With these, you must install the adapter and boot the workstation to run the setup application. The setup application may or may not verify the settings of installed adapters and reset the adapter accordingly. In any event, you need to check your LAN Log for the settings of other installed adapters.

LAN Compass

See the LAN Compass for a list of typical adapter interrupts, Direct Memory Access (DMA) settings, and base memory settings.

In EISA machines, the configuration routine tells you the settings of EISA adapters and ISA adapters that you have previously installed with an EISA configuration file. If you are installing an EISA adapter, you can simply install the adapter and let the EISA configuration routine assign the adapter's settings so they don't conflict with other devices.

Tip

Remember that ISA adapters installed in EISA machines don't appear in the configuration utility unless you have specifically assigned them a configuration file. This error can create havoc if the configuration utility sets up an EISA adapter that conflicts with the ISA adapter. Be sure to verify the settings of any ISA adapters in your EISA machine and set them up with configuration files when possible.

For Micro Channel machines, you need to locate the Adapter Definition File (ADF) and copy the file to the Reference Diskette before setting up the machine. The Micro Channel workstation performs an automatic configuration and sets up the adapter to work properly. You should always view the configuration and record the actual settings of each adapter in your LAN Log.

Tip

Even though all configuration information should be set up with the Reference Diskette or EISA configuration routine, some adapter manufacturers add jumpers for special options on their adapters. If you have an EISA or Micro Channel adapter with jumpers or switch settings, verify their operation prior to installing the adapter.

Finally, turn off the machine. Insert the adapter in a free bus slot, and turn on the machine. Many manufacturers ship their adapters with diagnostic programs. If a program is available for your new adapter, run the diagnostic program to verify proper operation. If the adapter passes the diagnostics the manufacturer provides, record the adapter settings and proceed to install your network software.

Installing the Network Software

Locate the disk that accompanied the adapter and also the DOSODI workstation diskette that ships with NetWare. At a minimum, the workstation needs four files to attach to and log into the network. They are as follows:

1. The Link Support Layer (the LSL.COM file)
2. The adapter Multiple Link Interface Driver (MLID)
3. The IPXODI.COM file (the NetWare protocol stack)
4. The NETX.EXE, NETx.COM, or VLM.COM files (the shell or requester)

LSL.COM is the Link Support Layer (LSL), an interface between the adapter driver and the various protocols including IPX/SPX and TCP/IP. You'll find this file on the NetWare Workstation diskette.

The adapter MLID is a driver that initializes the adapter and communicates with the adapter to assemble and send packets on the network. Each vendor writes an MLID for its adapters that conforms with ODI.

IPXODI is the name of the IPX/SPX transport protocol module.

NETX.EXE, VLM.COM, or NETx.COM (in which the lowercase "x" designates the DOS version of the workstation) represents the NetWare requester or redirector.

Tip

NETX.EXE, the current version of the requester for NetWare v2.x, v3.x, and 4.x networks, uses Virtual Loadable Modules (VLM). VLM.COM loads a series of programs that control network redirection.

2.2

In versions of NetWare previous to v3.x, the user needs to run a program called SHGEN or WSGEN to link the adapter driver to the IPX protocol stack. The resulting file is called IPX.COM. The process of creating IPX.COM is called "genning" and the file is called a "dedicated IPX." When a user wants to log into the network, he or she creates the SHELL.CFG file, which automatically runs much like the CONFIG.SYS file does in DOS workstations. Three shells exist—NETx.COM, EMSNET3.COM, and XMSNET3.COM.

Since the introduction of the Open Data-Link Interface (ODI) in 1989, genned shells are virtually obsolete. ODI drivers replaced dedicated IPX drivers, and a requester replaced the shell.

Virtual Loadable Modules (VLMs)

Netware v3.12 and 4.0 introduced the concept of Virtual Loadable Modules (VLMs) to load the DOS requester software. Managed by the VLM manager, you can load VLMs on the client workstation as you please, as well as unload them when you want. During workstation installation, a STARTNET.BAT file is created. The contents of this file include the LSL, the driver, the protocol stack (IPXODI), and the VLM.COM file. VLM.COM starts the VLM Manager, loads the required VLMs, and establishes the connection to the network. The VLMs are as follows:

AUTO.VLM (provides autoreconnect and retries to the requester)
BIND.VLM (bindery services)
CONN.VLM (establishes connections)
FIO.VLM (handles file I/O)
GENERAL.VLM

IPXNCP.VLM (IPX packet handler)
NDS.VLM (NetWare Directory Services)
NMR.VLM (diagnostic services)
NWP.VLM (multiplexer)
PRINT.VLM (printer redirector)
REDIR.VLM (the DOS redirector)
RSA.VLM (encryption and authentication)
TRAN.VLM (transport direction)

While the DOS redirector can connect up to 8 file servers, use of the DOS requester and VLMs can allow connections of up to 50 file servers, a number that may be more realistic when using a large internetwork.

The NET.CFG file

You configure each workstation driver by placing statements in the NET.CFG file, which you create in the subdirectory of the workstation that loads the other network commands. NET.CFG has a number of options, some of which you will use and some of which are uncommon. A typical NET.CFG file consists of several sections, each with its own commands (headers introduce these sections). The NET.CFG file may look like this:

```
Link Support
    BUFFERS 8

Link Driver TOKEN
    PORT A20
    SLOT 1
    MAX FRAME SIZE 4208
    PCMCIA
    FRAME TOKEN-RING

NetWare DOS Requester
    FIRST NETWORK DRIVE = F
    USE DEFAULTS = ON

SHOW DOTS ON
    PREFERRED SERVER = THUNDER_ROAD
    IPX PACKET SIZE LIMIT 16490
```

Tip

In the NET.CFG file, statement headers and NET.CFG commands are typed flush left. Statements are indented under a specific header, and none of the commands in the file is case-sensitive. In the example, the headers are Link Support, Link Driver, and NetWare DOS Requester. Link driver statement headers do not require the .COM extension on the driver name (i.e., LINK DRIVER TOKEN). A PROTOCOL section can also exist, in which you load other protocols and set information about them. The NET.CFG file is an ASCII text file that can be edited with any text editor such as EDIT from DOS version 4 or up, or with EDLIN from previous DOS versions.

Parameters for the LSL

The LSL.COM file, the interface between the MLID and the protocol stack, can be configured in the NET.CFG file under the Link Support heading. The configuration options are:

1. BUFFERS (number and size)
2. MAX BOARDS (number)
3. MAX STACKS (number)
4. MEMPOOLS (number)

The BUFFERS statement sets the number and size of receive buffers the LSL uses. Buffers must be large enough to hold the maximum packet. The default number of buffers is 0. The default buffer size is 1,130 bytes. The minimum buffer size is 628 bytes. The total buffer space and buffer number must fit into approximately 59KB. You can determine the total buffer space by multiplying the number of buffers by the size of the buffer. For example, if you wish to receive 4KB packets and use all the available space, you would enter the statement BUFFERS 14 4096. We recommend that you use all this space if you can afford it.

The MAX BOARDS statement configures the maximum number of logical adapters the LSL supports. Each LAN driver logical board uses one board resource. A logical board is used each time a FRAMETYPE is loaded. Since an Ethernet driver supports all four logical FRAMETYPES, the number of logical boards you are using is four. The default value for MAX BOARDS is four. From 1 to 16 logical boards are allowed in a workstation.

The MAX STACKS statement configures the maximum number of logical protocol stack IDs and the amount of resident memory the LSL can use. Each protocol stack uses one or more stack ID resources. The amount of memory the LSL uses is directly proportionate to the number of stacks. It ranges from 1 to 16. The default number of logical stacks is four. The amount of memory is fixed.

Tip

In most cases you never have to adjust the MAX STACKS number, because a workstation rarely contains more than one adapter. The only protocol that has four FRAMETYPES is Ethernet. If you are in a real memory crunch, you can adjust the MAX STACKS parameter to reflect the actual number of FRAMETYPES you are loading.

MEMPOOL lets you configure the size of the memory pool buffers the LSL maintains. NetWare's IPXODI protocol stack does not use MEMPOOL.

Normally, you can accept the minimum LSL.COM default settings. You should only change the defaults if problems occur and after you have talked to a technical support representative for the adapter you are using.

Adapter Driver Parameters (MLID)

The MLID is also configurable in the NET.CFG file under the Link Driver heading. The available settings are:

DMA (DMA channel number)	INT (number)
MEM (starting address)	Port (starting address)
Node Address (hex address)	Slot (slot number)
PCMCIA	FRAME (type)
Protocol (name, hex protocol, frame type)	SAPS (LAN Support Program only)
Link Stations (used in the IBM LAN Support Program)	Alternate (LAN Support)
MAX Frame Size (the maximum token-ring frame size of 16,490 bytes)	Double Buffer Off

For example, to load an NE2000 Ethernet adapter with an interrupt set at 3 and a base memory address of 300 hex, you would add these statements in the workstation's NET.CFG file:

```
Link Driver NE2000
   INT 3
   PORT 300
```

Not every adapter uses all the settings. Your adapter manufacturer has a complete list of the available options for the adapters you purchase. If you leave the adapter at its default settings, you may not need to have an adapter driver statement in the NET.CFG file.

Of all the adapter parameters, the FRAME statement is the most important. It corresponds to the frame type the driver uses for network communication. Remember that the frame type must be the same in both the source and destination devices for communication to take place. This means that if you are on a token-ring network, the FRAME statement in the workstation's NET.CFG file must correspond to the frame statement in the server's AUTOEXEC.NCF file. The allowable frame types for drivers under NetWare are outlined next.

For Ethernet:

1. ETHERNET_802.3 (used for versions of NetWare previous to v3.12)
2. ETHERNET_802.2 (used for NetWare v3.12 and 4.0)
3. ETHERNET_II (used for Digital minicomputers and AppleTalk Phase I)
4. ETHERNET_SNAP (used for AppleTalk Phase II and TCP/IP)

For Token-Ring:

1. TOKEN-RING (default frame type)
2. TOKEN-RING_SNAP (used for TCP/IP)

For ARCNET:

1. NOVELL_RX-NET

LAN Compass

See the LAN Compass for a list of FRAMETYPES.

3.x

In NetWare v3.x, the default Ethernet frame type is ETHERNET_802.3. In NetWare 4.x, the default frame type is ETHER-

NET_802.2. Be sure that you don't try to log into a v3.x server with drivers written for 4.x NetWare. Make sure that your frame types are correct.

If you are using TCP/IP, you use ETHERNET_II, ETHERNET_SNAP, TOKEN-RING_SNAP, or NOVELL_RX-NET frame types.

Via the Open Data-Link Interface (ODI), you can list multiple frames in the NET.CFG. The protocol you load first is bound to the first available frame. If you list the frames in the order you want them bound, you should load your protocols in the same order. Thus, if you list TOKEN-RING and TOKEN-RING_SNAP in your NET.CFG file, you should load IPXODI first and then TCPIP.

The frame type NOVELL_RX-NET is a Novell invention that allows multiple protocols to be bound to ARCNET. If you plan to use TCP/IP with ARCNET, or any of its variants, you must use the Novell product LAN Workplace for DOS to access the UNIX environment. There are some shareware packet drivers for ARCNET available at various File Transfer Protocol (FTP) sites, but if you plan to stick with a commercial product, LAN Workplace for DOS is the product to use.

IPXODI Parameters

The IPX protocol is highly configurable. When you want to change its parameters, you put them under the PROTOCOL heading. Its options include

Bind	INT64
INT7a	IPatch
IPX Packet Size Limit	IPX Retry Count
IPX Sockets	Maximum SPX Retries
SPX Abort Timeout	SPX Connections
SPX Listen Timeout	SPX Verify Timeout

IPXODI binds to the first adapter it finds in the NET.CFG file. If you want to bind the IPX/SPX protocol to a different adapter, you'll need to add the BIND statement to the Protocol section of the NET.CFG file. This action forces IPXODI to bind to a subsequent logical adapter.

The INT64 parameter allows applications to use interrupt 64h to access IPX services. The default is ON. You may need to use this option if your workstation locks up when using versions of NetWare previous to v3.11.

The INT7A parameter allows applications to use interrupt 7Ah to access IPX services. This parameter is only useful for specific applications that must use this interrupt. The default is ON. Like the INT64 parameter, you may need to use INT7A when you are using a version of NetWare previous to NetWare v3.11.

The IPATCH parameter allows you to patch any address in the IPX-ODI.COM file with any specified byte offset value. You should use this parameter only when an application specifies it.

The IPX PACKET SIZE LIMIT parameter reduces the maximum packet size. The default setting is the smaller of either 4,160 bytes or the size the LAN driver specifies. The range is 576 to 6,500 (bytes).

The IPX RETRY COUNT parameter sets the number of times IPX allows the DOS shell or requester and SPX to resend a packet. The default is 20 retries.

The IPX SOCKETS parameter configures the maximum number of sockets IPX can open at the workstation. IPX-specific programs may require you to increase this number. The default number of sockets is 20.

The MINIMUM SPX RETRIES parameter determines how many unacknowledged transmit requests are allowed before assuming the connection is bad. You should increase this parameter if an application that uses SPX loses its connection. The range for this parameter is 0 to 255.

The SPX ABORT TIMEOUT parameter adjusts the amount of time SPX waits without receiving any response from the other side of the connection. The value for this parameter is in clock-ticks (one clock-tick is approximately 1/18th of a second). The default value is 540 ticks, or approximately 30 seconds.

SPX CONNECTIONS configures the maximum number of SPX connections a workstation can have open at one time.

3.x

If you use RPRINTER.EXE for local printers on NetWare v3.x or 4.x networks, you need to increase this parameter to 60. The default is 15.

SPX LISTEN TIMEOUT sets the time that SPX waits without receiving a packet from the other side of the connection before it requests a packet from the other side to ensure the connection. The timeout value is specified in clock-ticks. The default is 108 clock-ticks.

SPX VERIFY TIMEOUT configures the frequency that SPX sends a packet to the other side of the connection to indicate that the connection is still alive. SPX sends the "alive" packet when no other SPX traffic is sent by the session. The value is measured in clock-ticks. The default value is 54 clock-ticks.

NetWare Requester Commands

You will spend most of the time configuring the workstation's redirector. The following is a complete list of the latest redirector parameters. We've noted parameters of import.

AUTO LARGE TABLE
AUTO RECONNECT
AUTO RETRY
AVERAGE NAME LENGTH
BIND RECONNECT
CACHE BUFFERS
CACHE BUFFER SIZE
CACHE WRITES
CHECKSUM
CONNECTIONS
DOS NAME
FIRST NETWORK DRIVE
HANDLE NET ERRORS
LARGE INTERNET PACKETS
LOAD CONN TABLE LOW
LOAD LOW CONN
LOAD LOW IPXNCP
LOCAL PRINTERS
LONG MACHINE TYPE
MAX TASKS
MESSAGE LEVEL
MESSAGE TIMEOUT
NAME CONTEXT
NETWARE PROTOCOL
NETWORK PRINTERS
PB BUFFERS
PBURST READ WINDOWS SIZE
PBURST WRITE WINDOWS SIZE
PREFERRED SERVER
PREFERRED TREE
PREFERRED WORKGROUP
PRINT BUFFER SIZE
PRINT HEADER
PRINT TAIL
READ ONLY COMPATIBILITY
SEARCH MODE
SET STATION TIME
SHOW DOTS
SHORT MACHINE TYPE
SIGNATURE LEVEL
TRUE COMMIT
USE DEFAULTS
VLM
WORKGROUP ID HIGH
WORKGROUP ID LOW
WORKGROUP NAME
WORKGROUP NET

The AUTO LARGE TABLE parameter enables AUTO.VLM, which allocates a table of 178 bytes per connection for bindery reconnects. The default setting is OFF. When disabled, the setting is 34 bytes per connection. If you use AUTO LARGE TABLE, the parameter BIND RECONNECT must also be set to ON.

The AVERAGE NAME LENGTH parameter reserves space for a table of NetWare server names based on the AVERAGE NAME LENGTH and the value of the CONNECTIONS parameter. By setting the length to a lower value, you can save memory. The default value is 48 characters. The range is 2 to 96 characters.

The AUTO RECONNECT parameter sets AUTO.VLM to reconnect a workstation to a NetWare server and rebuilds the workstation's environment prior to a connection loss. If you set this parameter to OFF, be prepared for whatever happens. The default value is ON.

The AUTO RETRY parameter sets the number of seconds AUTO.VLM waits prior to retrying after receiving a network error. When this parameter is set at 0, AUTO.VLM makes no retry attempts. The default time is 0. The range is between 0 and 3,640 seconds.

BIND RECONNECT automatically rebuilds the bindery connection and restores drives and printer connections. This parameter also requires AUTO RECONNECT to be set to ON. The default value is OFF.

CACHE BUFFERS designates the number of cache buffers the requester allocates for local caching of non-shared, non-transaction-tracked files. This parameter allows the DOS requester to cache one file. Increasing the number of cache buffers increases the speed of sequential reads and writes, but also increases memory use. The default is 5 cache blocks, with a range from 0 to 64 blocks.

The CACHE BUFFER SIZE parameter sets the size of the cache buffer. Increasing the CACHE BUFFER SIZE parameter increases network performance, but also increases memory usage. The parameter should never be set to a size larger than the MAXIMUM PACKET SIZE set for the network adapter driver. The default is 512 bytes, and the range is from 64 to 4,096 bytes.

The CACHE WRITES parameter may be set to ON or OFF. If the parameter is set to OFF, performance decreases, but data integrity increases. Setting the parameter to ON can cause data loss if the server runs out of disk space between writes. The default value is ON.

The CHECKSUM parameter forces the validation of NetWare Core Protocol (NCP) packets. There are various levels of security for this parameter:

0 = disabled
1 = enabled but not preferred
2 = enabled and preferred
3 = required

Setting the parameter to 2 or 3 increases data integrity, but decreases system performance. The default is 1. The FRAMETYPE ETHERNET_802.3 does not support checksums.

The CONNECTIONS parameter sets the maximum number of connections the requester supports. The range of values is 2 to 50. A value larger than necessary increases memory use without increasing performance. Setting the value to a number larger than 8 can affect NETx.COM or NETx.EXE compatibility. The default value is 8.

DOS NAME sets the name of the operating system the shell or requester uses. This value is used by the %OS variable in the login script to map search drives to the network's DOS directory. The requester automatically recognizes the names DR DOS and MS DOS without setting the DOS NAME parameter. Setting this variable turns off the auto-recognition feature. The maximum number of characters is five.

The FIRST NETWORK DRIVE parameter sets the first network drive letter when a connection is made. The default is the first available DOS drive found. The range is from A to Z. Only VLMs use this parameter.

HANDLE NET ERRORS determines the method for handling network errors. A network error is generated whenever the workstation does not receive a response from the server. If this parameter is set to ON, INT24 handles network errors. If this statement is set to OFF, a NET_REC_ERROR return is made on a network error. Some applications may not recognize a NET_REC_ERROR return.

LARGE INTERNET PACKETS determines the size of packets used when crossing bridges and routers. Previously, NetWare set the maximum packet size to 576 bytes when sending packets across bridges and routers. When set to ON, the NetWare server and workstation negotiate the packet size, even when crossing bridges and routers.

The LOAD CONN TABLE LOW parameter is used only with the initial release of NetWare 4.0 utilities. When set to ON, the connection table is loaded in low memory, which increases memory usage. The default setting is OFF, which loads the table in upper memory.

LOAD LOW CONN set to OFF loads the CONN.VLM into upper memory. This saves memory but decreases performance. The default is ON, which loads the VLM into conventional memory.

The LOAD LOW IPXNCP parameter sets where IPXNCP.VLM is loaded in memory. Set to ON, the VLM loads into conventional memory. Set to OFF, the VLM loads in upper memory, increasing conventional memory and decreasing performance.

LOCAL PRINTERS overrides the number of local printers determined by the system BIOS. Normally, the BIOS allocates one local printer for each parallel port. The default is 3, with the range from 0 to 9. In rare instances in older machines, you need to set this parameter to 0 to prevent the workstation from locking up.

The LONG MACHINE TYPE tells the requester the machine type when the %MACHINE variable is accessed from the login script. This variable is used to set the machine's search path to the correct version of DOS on the server. The default is IBM_PC.

MAX TASKS configures the maximum number of tasks that can be active at one time. The default is 31 tasks; the range is from 20 to 128 tasks. This parameter is extremely helpful for Windows and can help control memory usage. You may want to lower the number from the default.

MESSAGE LEVEL sets the amount of information displayed with load time messages. Each message level implies the previous level's message. The default is 1. The values are as follows:

0 = Always display copyright message and critical errors
1 = Display warning messages
2 = Display program load information for the VLMs
3 = Display configuration information
4 = Display diagnostic information

MESSAGE TIMEOUT sets the timeout in ticks before broadcast messages are cleared from your display without intervention. The default 0 requires you to clear the message. The range is from 0 to 10,000 ticks.

The NAME CONTEXT parameter allows you to set the current position in the Directory Tree Structure. This applies only to NetWare 4.0 networks. The default NAME CONTEXT is the root directory. Quotation marks are required for the name. The syntax is

NAME CONTEXT = "*name context*"

NETWARE PROTOCOL sets the network protocol that is bound to the adapter. Available protocols are

NDS	NetWare Directory Services for NetWare 4.x
BIND	NetWare Bindery for NetWare v2.x and v3.x
PNW	Personal NetWare

The NETWORK PRINTERS parameter sets the number of LPT ports the NetWare DOS Requester can capture. The range is from 0 to 9, with a default of 3. Setting the value to 0 specifies that the PRINT.VLM file does not load.

PB BUFFERS sets the number of packet burst protocol buffers. Packet burst is automatically enabled in the requester. Setting the value to 0 disables packet burst. The default is 3, with a range from 0 to 10. Setting the number to a higher value increases memory usage. Setting the value to 0 decreases memory usage and, in some cases, may decrease performance.

PREFERRED SERVER sets the NetWare v2.x or v3.x server to first attach if the server has a connection available. If both the PREFERRED SERVER and PREFERRED TREE parameters are specified, the first protocol to build an attachment successfully is used.

PREFERRED TREE sets the tree to connect to a NetWare 4.0 network environment if the tree specified has a server with a free connection. If both the PREFERRED SERVER and PREFERRED TREE parameters are specified, the first protocol to build an attachment successfully is used.

Personal NetWare

PREFERRED WORKGROUP sets the name of the workgroup for Personal NetWare to search for and attach to. This parameter is specific to Personal NetWare.

The PRINT BUFFER SIZE determines the size, in bytes, of the print buffer. The default is 64 bytes, and the range from 0 to 256. Increasing this value increases printing output and memory usage.

PRINT HEADER sets the size of the buffer that holds the information used to initialize a printer for each print job. This parameter should be used if print jobs with many instructions are used. The default is 64 bytes, and the range is from 0 to 1,024 bytes.

PRINT TAIL sets the size of the buffer that holds the information used to reset the printer after print jobs. The default is 16 bytes; the range is from 0 to 1,024 bytes.

READ ONLY COMPATIBILITY determines if a file marked read-only can be opened with a read/write access call. Prior to NetWare v2.1, a program could open a read-only file with write access without an error. To maintain compatibility with DOS NetWare v2.1 and above, READ ONLY COMPATIBILITY does not allow a read-only file to be opened for write access. Setting the parameter forces the shell or requester to allow the open request to succeed. The default is OFF.

SEARCH MODE changes the way the NetWare requester searches for .EXE and .COM files that are not in the current directory. Valid search modes are 0 to 7. In versions of NetWare previous to v3.11, the default drive has to be a network drive. The DOS requester searches all drives regardless of the current drive.

SET STATION TIME synchronizes the workstation date and time with the NetWare server to which the workstation initially attaches. The default is ON; setting the parameter to OFF disables synchronization.

SHOW DOTS shows the DOS directory entries for directories and subdirectories (. and ..). This setting is used with Windows 3.x to show the DOS dots for directory searches.

The SHORT MACHINE TYPE parameter is used with the %MACHINE_variable in the login script. The SHORT MACHINE TYPE is used specifically with overlay files. The default SHORT MACHINE TYPE is IBM and is limited to four letters.

SIGNATURE LEVEL sets the level of enhanced security support. The available values are

0 = Disabled
1 = Enabled but not preferred
2 = Preferred
3 = Required

Setting the option to 2 or 3 increases the level of security but decreases performance.

The TRUE COMMIT variable selects whether the commit NCP is sent on DOS commit requests. The option should be set to ON when processing critical data to guarantee integrity. Use of TRUE COMMIT also sacrifices performance over integrity. The default value is OFF.

USE DEFAULTS overrides the default VLMs that VLM.EXE loads. If USE DEFAULTS is set in the NET.CFG, then the DOS requester installs a set of VLMs to control NetWare services.

How Do I Get to the Network?

There are several ways for a workstation to connect to the network. You can copy the files to a hard drive on the local machine, or to a diskette drive and boot from a diskette. In either event, you want to create a batch file to load the commands. A batch file is an ASCII text file with the .BAT file name extension. This file lists the commands in the order you want them executed. You can write extremely sophisticated batch files. However, to get on the network you'll only need to create a very simple batch file. If you are creating the boot files from NetWare v3.12 or 4.x workstation diskettes, a file called STARTNET.BAT is created when you run the workstation installation. A typical STARTNET.BAT file looks like this:

```
STARTNET.BAT
NWLANGUAGE=ENGLISH
LSL.COM
```

NE2000

IPXODI.COM

NETX.EXE (or NETx.COM or VLM.EXE)

You may either use these commands in a STARTNET.BAT file or place them in the AUTOEXEC.BAT file. This is the batch file that runs every time your computer boots. You may also want to run the STARTNET.BAT file from the workstation's AUTOEXEC.BAT file. This method is probably the preferred way so that if for some reason you have to unload the network drivers, you can reload them easily.

Diskless Workstations

One of the easiest and most secure ways to attach your users to the network is by using a BOOT or Remote Program Load (RPL) ROM that is added to your network adapter. The chip contains instructions that will initialize the adapter, and send a request to the server to download the files necessary to boot the machine and log into the network when you turn on the computer. This is done by creating a boot image file and placing it in the LOGIN subdirectory.

Boot ROMs require no additional modules at the server. A RPL ROM, called an Enhanced boot ROM, follows the IBM Remote initial Program Load specification. When you use an RPL ROM, you must load an additional NetWare Loadable Module (NLM) on the server. This NLM must be bound to the adapter from which you want to boot. The commands should be placed in the AUTOEXEC.NCF file of the server and should appear as follows:

```
LOAD RPL
BIND RPL to TCTOKH
```

in which TCTOKH is the LAN driver.

The BIND statement is similar to binding a protocol to the adapter, except that you do not need to name a network. RPL.NLM opens an .RPL file that is found in the LOGIN subdirectory to send the instructions to download the boot files and complete the boot process. RPL.NLM and the associated .RPL files accompany NetWare and are copied when you load the SYSTEM and PUBLIC files. Under NetWare v2.x, a similar process is followed except that you load a value-added process (VAP) when the server boots. The VAP file must be obtained from Novell separately.

How Do I Set up the Boot Image File?

No matter what version of NetWare you are using, you must create a boot image file on the file server. The process for creating the boot image file is simple. First, prepare a diskette by formatting the diskette as a system diskette (FORMAT A: or B: /s.) Then, copy all of the files you need to the boot diskette. This includes all of the network drivers and any memory managers or other terminate-and-stay resident (TSR) programs you want to load.

Tip

The boot image file created will not read subdirectories, so don't use them.

Once you create your diskette, log into the server as SUPERVISOR from a machine that has a diskette drive with the disk you just created in it. Map the following drives:

MAP F:=SYS:SYSTEM

MAP G:=SYS:LOGIN

Type G: to log into the G drive. From G:, type DOSGEN. DOSGEN reads the diskette and creates a boot image file named NET$DOS.SYS. This is the generic boot image file you'll use for all workstations.

Tip

Be sure to use the FLAG command to flag the NET$DOS.SYS file as shareable read/write (SRW). To do this, type FLAG NET$DOS.SYS SRW from the LOGIN subdirectory.

The NET$DOS.SYS file works as long as the workstation configuration doesn't change. If it is necessary to boot a machine with different parameters, you need to create boot image files that correspond to the new configuration.

To create multiple boot image files, you must take some additional steps. Log into the network as SUPERVISOR. In the LOGIN directory, create a text file named BOOTCONF.SYS. This file contains a list of the node IDs of the remote booting workstations and their associated boot image files. A sample BOOTCONF.SYS file appears like this:

0x123,0001c8653def = TRBOOT.SYS

in which 0x123 is the network number and 0001c8653def is the workstation node ID. The resulting boot image file for this workstation is called TRBOOT.SYS. If you are creating BOOTCONF.SYS files for additional workstations, add their network numbers and node ID on separate lines following the first line.

Once you've created the BOOTCONF.SYS file, map your drives as if you were going to create a standard boot image file, and type the following instead:

F:DOSGEN A: [image file name]

F:DOSGEN A: TRBOOT.SYS

Tip

Be sure to include spaces between DOSGEN and A: and between A: and the boot image file name.

DOSGEN then creates the boot image file with the name you selected. When that workstation remote-boots, the ROM will first look to find its NODE ADDRESS and network number in the BOOTCONF.SYS file. If it does not find its NODE ID, it will then attempt to open and use NET$DOS.SYS.

chapter

7

Then There Are Printers

Why Are There Network Printers?

One of the primary reasons to have a network is to be able to share printers among users. Network printing is one of the most difficult parts of the network to understand, plan, and maintain. Yet, it is one function for which all network administrators will be responsible. Once you've learned how to set up your first network printer, you'll be far ahead. You can then worry about getting that PostScript printer to work, or managing printing to operate more efficiently.

The networking of desktop computers was the logical extension of buying a computer for everyone in your company. As companies began to depend more on the network for their day-to-day activities, sharing expensive resources such as printers became a large part of network activities. Without networking, printer cables were attached and unattached from one workstation to the next; in network printing, however, printers can be shared without going through a lot of hardware mumbo jumbo. The four basic reasons for print-sharing are as follows:

1. To spread out expensive printers among all your users
2. To use printers efficiently and keep them in use a larger portion of time
3. To ease maintenance and upgrade tasks for network administrators without affecting users
4. To increase printing choices and options for control over print functions

Share and Share Alike

In a non-networked environment, each user needs to have his or her own printer. Specialized users may require multiple printers attached to their computers. These are expensive propositions to say the least. With network printers, multiple printers can be distributed throughout the network, and users can access them when they need to. Users can print endless draft copies and other less important documents on a wire printer and switch to a PostScript laser printer when they need to print letters and special documents. Large reports can be printed on a line printer.

Let's All Get in a Queue

When a user requests that a document be printed, the application sends the print job to the file server, where it is placed in a storage area called a *queue*. In NetWare, printers are assigned to these queues. The software running on the server, or on a specialized device called a print server, takes the print job when it finishes being queued and sends it to the printer as fast as the printer can access it. Print jobs that finish queuing first will be printed first. In the meantime, the software the user is working with is ready for more work. The user doesn't have to wait until the printer has finished printing the job in the queue to get back to work. Even with fast printers, some of the larger and more complicated print jobs can take several minutes to print. By using a network printer, the user can almost always continue to work until his or her print job is ready to pick up.

Print queues efficiently handle the network printing needs. You can create one queue for all the printers on your network, or multiple queues with different priorities and functions to take advantage of the differing needs of the users. If confidential data that you don't want other people to see is printed on the printer, you can create a print queue for that printer and limit the users who are members of the queue.

Control over the printing functions is also streamlined. Printing can be administered by a Print Queue Operator, who the network administrator assigns to help with printing-related functions. Different print job definitions can be created for special printing functions. Definitions are instructions for the printer on how to print specific print jobs. You can add these instructions when the job is placed in the queue. When the specific print job is completed, the printer returns to its default state to wait for the next print job.

What Kind of Printers Do I Need?

Your choice of printers will vary greatly with the type of work your users do. The different printers include:

1. 9- or 24-pin dot matrix printers
2. Near–laser-quality ink jet printers
3. Laser printers
4. Laser PostScript printers
5. Line printers
6. Wax thermal printers
7. Plotters for mapping or design work.

For the standard office, you'll need only one or two printer types. You'll normally have one or two dot matrix printers and a laser or PostScript printer. PostScript printers, which use a language called the Page Definition Language to control their operations, are generally used for vector graphics and for applications that combine text with graphics.

Types of NetWare Printers

There are four methods you can use to attach NetWare printers to the LAN. The type of printer you purchase will often determine the NetWare or third-party software you will use to control the printer. In NetWare, printers can be connected to the network in these ways:

1. Directly to the server
2. Connected to a remote print server
3. Connected directly to the network like any other remote device
4. Connected to a nondedicated workstation

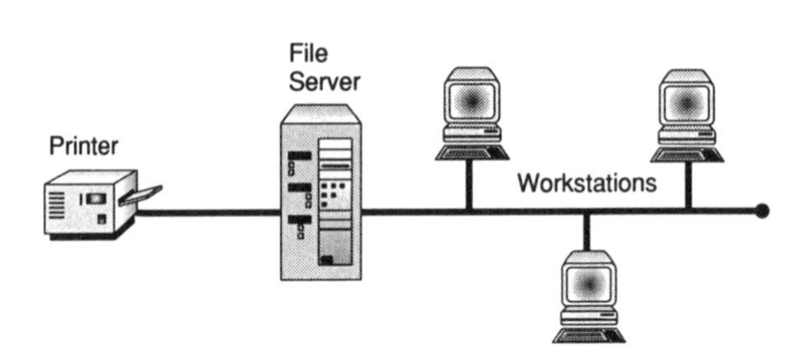

Figure 7-1. *A printer attached to the file server.*

File-Server–Attached Printers

Printers connected directly to the file server are the most common type of network printers. These printers use NetWare's PSERVER.NLM to control print functions. You should use server-attached printers only if your server has extra memory and CPU capacity to handle the additional chore of printer control. You must realize also that since these printers are close to the file server, the file server is also accessible to users. (See Figure 7-1.)

2.x

If you are using NetWare v2.x, you will load a value-added process called PSERVER.VAP on the file server. PSERVER.VAP will load every time the server loads. Since PSERVER.VAP cannot be unloaded from the server's memory, if you need to define another print server, you must bring down the file server after making your changes and then restart PSERVER.VAP.

Print-Server–Attached Printers

Remote printers connected directly to a workstation or specialized print server devices use the NetWare utility PSERVER.EXE to control print functions. These connections have the advantage that you can locate printers in areas where they are most accessible. You also have better access control over the file server by using remote printers. However, you also need to add the extra expense of dedicating a work-

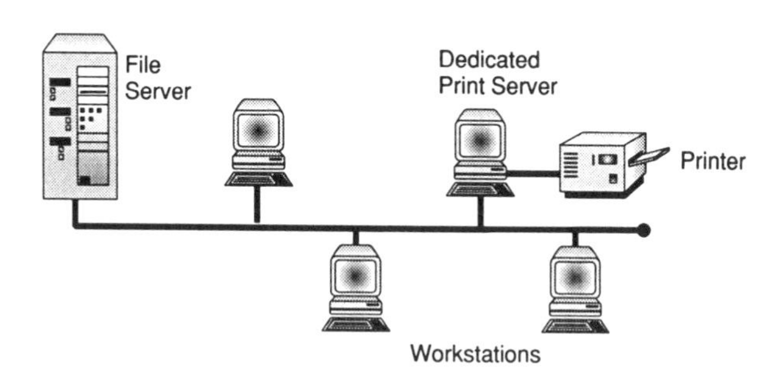

Figure 7-2. *Typical print server configurations.*

station to the job of printer control. (See Figure 7-2.) Any 80286 or higher workstation can be used as a print server. Specialized print servers are available from companies such as Digital Products, ASP Computers, and Emulex.

Tip
If you use PSERVER for remotely connected printers, you must add the following statement to the printer server's NET.CFG file:

```
SPX CONNECTIONS = 60
```

Network-Attached Printers
Some printers are equipped with built-in Ethernet or token-ring connections. Others, like the HP LaserJet III, allow you to add a printer adapter to the printer's optional I/O slot. These printers have ROM memory that runs third-party software similar to NetWare's PSERVER.EXE. With these printers, you don't need to dedicate a workstation—you simply connect the printer to the media as if it were another workstation. (See Figure 7-3 on the next page.)

Nondedicated Workstations as Print Servers
A printer running RPRINTER.EXE can be connected to users' workstations as a remote printer. While this is an economical way of adding

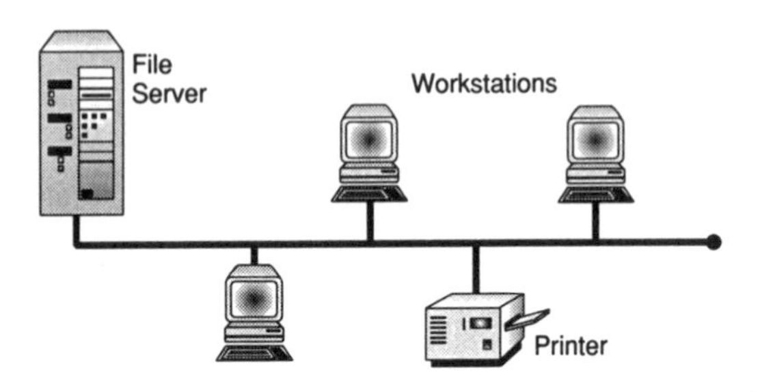

Figure 7-3. *A network-attached printer.*

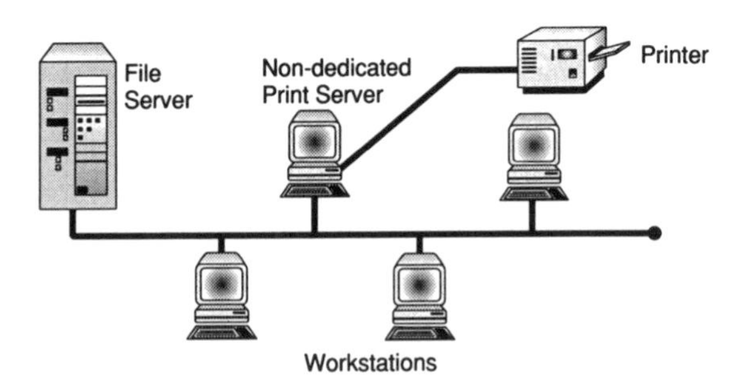

Figure 7-4. *A nondedicated workstation that can be used as either a workstation or a print server.*

printers to the network, it can cause the user's workstation to run slowly if the printer is used very often for network printing. (See Figure 7-4.)

Printer Control

Just as there are a number of ways to connect network printers, each method uses a different control program. NetWare's printing control programs are:

PSERVER.NLM
PSERVER.EXE
RPRINTER.EXE

PSERVER.NLM

PSERVER.NLM is a NetWare Loadable Module (NLM) that allows printer control, supports up to 16 local or remote printers, and can service queues on up to eight file servers. The number of printers that can be placed local to the server is determined by the number of available printer ports on the server.

PSERVER.NLM requires 128KB of RAM, plus 10KB of RAM for each defined printer. PSERVER.NLM is loaded only once per server. If you need more than 16 printers on your network, you must use another NetWare utility, PSERVER.EXE or PSERVER.VAP, on an 80286 router. Be sure that you allow for the additional RAM requirements for your server. PSERVER.NLM automatically loads when you copy SYSTEM and PUBLIC files over. It is located in the SYS:SYSTEM directory.

PSERVER.EXE

PSERVER.EXE must run on a dedicated workstation. You do not need to be logged into the network as a user. Only NETX.COM or VLM.COM will need to be loaded. Like PSERVER.NLM, PSERVER.EXE will support up to 16 locally or remotely connected printers and can service queues from 8 file servers. PSERVER.EXE requires a minimum of 256KB of RAM plus 10KB of disk space for each printer. You can use older 80286 workstations as print servers.

Tip

If you do not log into the server as a user, you must copy the following files over to a diskette or to the hard drive you'll use to boot the print server:

PSERVER.EXE
IBM$RUN.OVL
SYS$ERR.DAT
SYS$HELP.DAT
SYS$MSG.DAT

Otherwise, you can copy the files to the SYS:LOGIN subdirectory, which any attached workstation has access to.

Figure 7-5 shows PSERVER's main status screen, which lists the first eight printers. When you depress any key, the menu will show the next eight printers. Each printer will list one of the following status messages:

Not Installed—No printer is defined for this slot.
Waiting for Print Job—The printer is ready and waiting for the print server to service a job.
Not Connected—A remote printer is defined but is not connected.
Out of paper—The printer is out of paper or not connected to the port.
Printing—The printer is currently printing a job. This status message will also list the name of the server, the queue the job is being printed from, the job number, and a description of the job.
Ready to go down—The print server has received a request to terminate and this printer slot has already stopped servicing the queues.
Mount form—The printer needs a form change before the next job will be printed.
Off-line—The printer has been taken off-line.

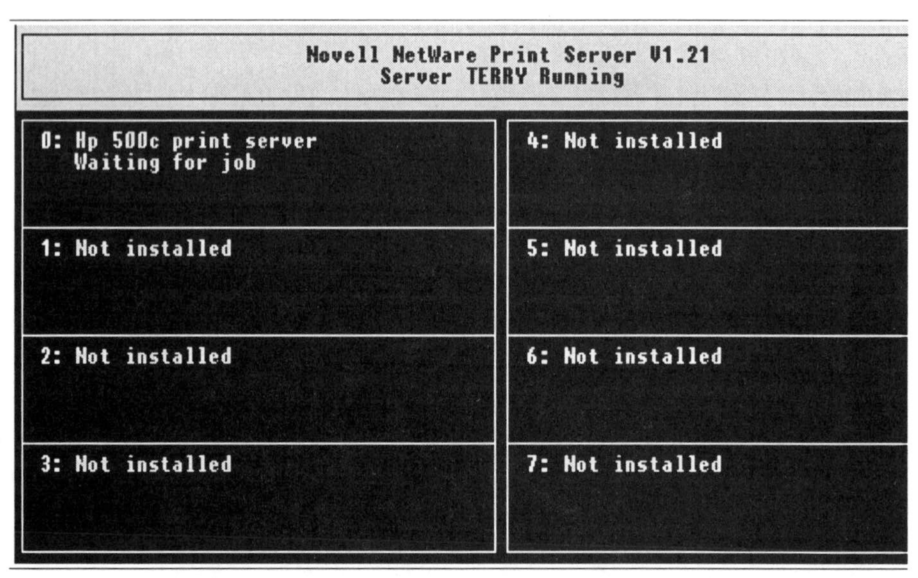

Figure 7-5. *PSERVER's Main Status Screen*

Paused—The printer has received a request to pause from PCONSOLE or PSC.

Stopped—The printer stopped due to a request from PCONSOLE or PSC.

RPRINTER.EXE

RPRINTER.EXE allows a printer local to a dedicated or nondedicated workstation to be used as a network printer. The utility consists of a terminate-and-stay resident (TSR) program that runs on the workstation. RPRINTER.EXE requires 9–13KB of RAM and an additional 3–4KB for each printer attached to the workstation. It communicates with PSERVER.NLM (or .EXE) to send the print jobs to the remote printer. RPRINTER.EXE does not create a print server itself; it allows the workstation to accept data from PSERVER and send it to the printer. Users of nondedicated workstations will see performance decreases when the printer is servicing a print job.

To run RPRINTER.EXE, you need to add the following line to the workstation's NET.CFG file:

SPX CONNECTIONS = 50

Like PSERVER.EXE, RPRINTER.EXE uses several files that are located in the SYS:PUBLIC directory on the file server. Those files are:

IBM$RUN.OVL

RPRINTER.EXE

RPRINTER.HLP

RPRINT$$.EXE

SYS$HELP.DAT

SYS$MSG.DAT

SYS$ERR.DAT

You can run RPRINTER without being logged into the network. If you choose to use this method, copy these files to the workstation's local diskette or disk drive. You can load RPRINTER from the command line at that workstation by specifying the print server name and the slot assigned in PSERVER.EXE to this printer:

RPRINTER printserver printernumber

For example, the print server name is OPUS, and the slot in the workstation is number 0 (the first slot available).

Alternately, you can run RPRINTER from the command line. You'll see a list of printer names and numbers. Highlight the appropriate printer, and press the Enter key. This will initiate RPRINTER on the workstation.

Installing the Hardware for Printers

There are two types of printer connections: *serial* and *parallel*. The serial port is the slower of the two, but it allows you to place the printer farther away from the file server or the workstation that is acting as the print server. The parallel printer is a faster printer connection, but it requires that the printer be relatively close to the computer.

Serial Printers

When you set up a serial printer, you must supply the following information:

Baud rate—The rate is in bits per second. NetWare supports 300–9,600 bits per second.

Data bits—This number represents the number of data bits in the communications sequence. Novell supports 5–8 data bits. Most printer connections use either 7 or 8.

Stop bits—This number represents the number of stop bits required to end the printing sequence. Novell supports 1, 1.5, and 2. The usual number is 2.

Parity—This parameter represents the bit used to check parity. Novell supports Even, Odd, or No Parity. Most printers use No Parity. Parity is represented as E, O, or N.

Use X-ON, X-OFF—This parameter sets hardware or software flow control. Novell supports either X-ON or X-OFF. Hardware flow control is generally considered the best.

Parallel Printers

If you are using a parallel port, you will need to know the interrupt number the printer uses to receive data. Printers can be configured to use interrupt-driven or polled processes. Interrupt mode requires a hardware interrupt and is generally faster than polled processing. The polled process uses the CPU to poll the port. In a file server, the polled process is more reliable, but will decrease server performance. If you are configuring a workstation with RPRINTER, you must use the interrupt mode. If you are using PSERVER.EXE, you can configure the printers either way, but it is best to use the interrupt mode.

Tip
To select interrupt or polled mode, use the NetWare utility PCONSOLE. From the Printer Configuration menu, select the Interrupts field and type a Y or an N. If you enter Y, you must move to the next field and enter an IRQ number.

The following interrupt assignments are standard:

LPT1 - IRQ 7

LPT2 - IRQ 5

COM1 - IRQ 4

COM2 - IRQ 3

LPT3, LPT4, COM3, and COM4 do not have standard assigned ports. You will need to look at the documentation to see which port is available for configuring these ports.

LAN Compass
Check the LAN Compass in the back of this book for a list of the common interrupts devices use.

Installing Printers on NetWare

You install printers on NetWare LANs via the PCONSOLE utility. This utility is DOS-based in NetWare versions previous to 4.0. You use PCONSOLE to assign queues and queue operators, and to create print servers. (See Figure 7-6.)

To create a print server, highlight Print Server Information in the Available Options menu. Press the Insert key to create a new queue. Insert the print server name and press Enter. The print server name can be up to 47 characters in length and can contain spaces. Assign a name that is easy to remember and that, perhaps, will tell you the location of the printer, such as HP_2ND_FLR.

Once you've created the print server, you must define a printer. You also use PCONSOLE to define printers. Highlight Print Server Configuration and press the Enter key. Then highlight the Printer Configuration option. Select the printer slot you want to define, and press the Enter key. The configuration will input a default printer of the name PRINTER X, where X represents the slot number. You can then highlight the name, change it to a more descriptive name, and press the Enter key. Continue to the Type field and press the Enter key. A list of

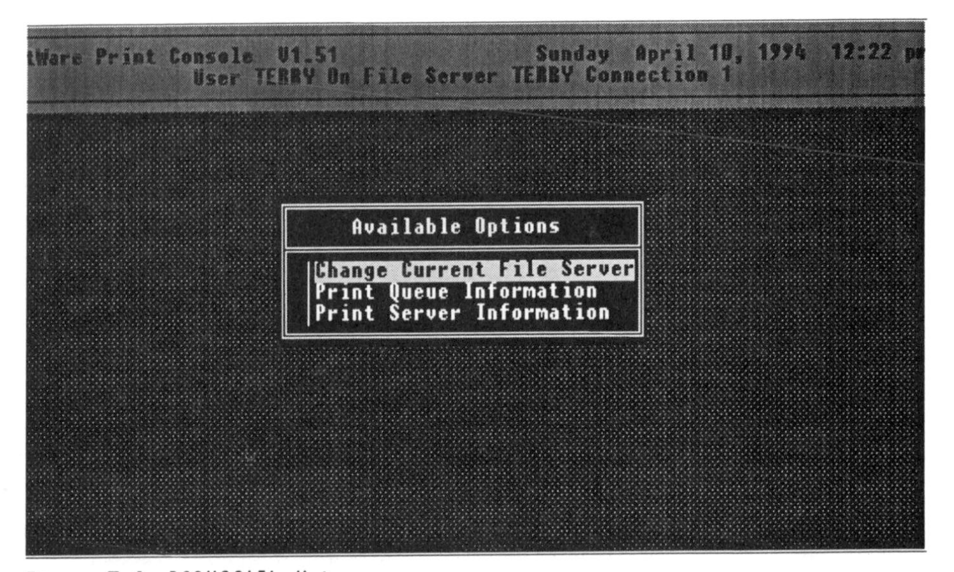

Figure 7-6. *PCONSOLE's Main menu.*

available printers appears in Figure 7-7. Select the type of port you want, either serial or parallel.

Tip

If you use RPRINTER and select the printer port when you load the software, select Remote Other/Unknown for the printer port.

The next step is creating a print queue. Load PCONSOLE. Select Print Queue Information from the Available Options menu. Enter the queue name and press the Enter key. The queue name can be up to 47 characters long. To rename the queue, highlight Print Queues from the Available Options menu. Press the Enter key.

Next, you need to add users and groups to the Print Queue as Queue Users or Print Queue operators. At the Print Queue Information menu,

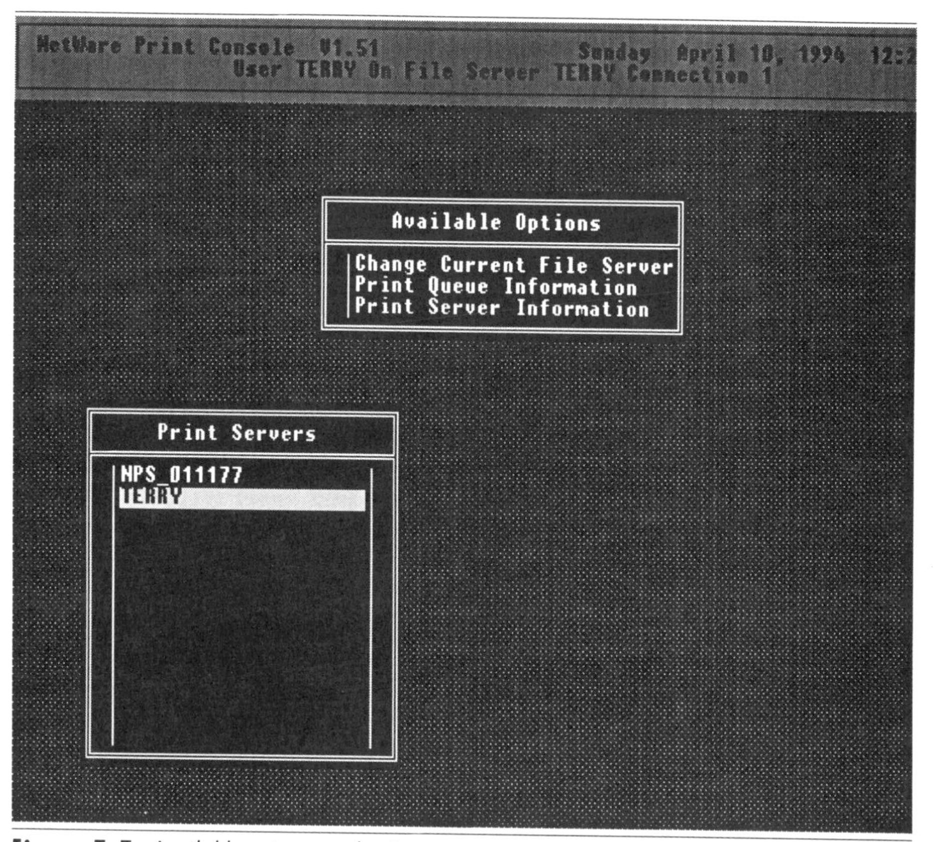

Figure 7-7. *Available printers selection.*

highlight Queue Operators or Queue Users and press the Enter key. Press the Insert key. Highlight the user or group you want to add to the queue, and press the Enter key. It is easier and faster to add queue users by their group membership than by individual user.

You can delete users or groups from queues by entering the Information menu and highlighting Queue Operators or Queue Users. Position the cursor at the user, group, or queue operator you want to delete, and press the Delete key. You may use the F5 key to mark multiple users to delete.

Tip

A command-line utility called PSC, which is a companion to the menu-based PCONSOLE, also exists. PSC lets you start and stop printers, mount forms, and determine the current status of the printer.

Printer Definitions and Forms

A printer definition is a list or database of printer functions that can be sent to a specific printer to tell it to perform specific functions. By using escape codes you can command the printer to change many of its functions, including the page orientation and the fonts that are used. Each printer is defined as a print device. Multiple devices can be defined for each printer. Each definition contains functions for the printer to print in the required manner.

You can also define the printer definition database as a list of printer forms. When you use one of two NetWare command-line utilities, NPRINT or CAPTURE, and request the form by number or name, the print job configuration uses the form name and must be in the printer definition database. Printer forms are a way for the print server to determine which form it needs to mount on the printer for the particular job. Using different forms for each type of print job allows you to print on different kinds of paper without worrying about printing on the wrong paper. Form definitions apply to all printers serviced by the print server.

Printer Modes

You can also define printer modes. Printer modes define a specific operation for a printer. Modes are created with the NetWare menu utility PRINTDEF. Each printer has a default mode that can be changed at the start of a new print job. When the print job completes, the mode returns to its default state. Escape sequences are placed at the beginning of the print job to put the printer in the new mode. Additional special escape sequences are placed at the end of the print job to return the printer to the default mode.

How PRINTDEF Works

PRINTDEF lets the supervisor or supervisor-equivalent define forms, print devices, printer modes, and functions. Modes are the methods of printer operation, and functions are the escape sequences that place printers in a particular mode. Device modes are made up of a number of device functions.

Use PRINTDEF to select the particular functions from a list, and then save the functions as a mode in the database. The database is located in the SYS:PUBLIC directory. You must have SUPERVISOR or equivalent rights to modify the database with PRINTDEF, although any user can read and use the database for printing operations. The CAPTURE and NPRINT utilities make use of the database.

Novell ships NetWare with a list of predefined printers and printer modes. These files end in a .PDF extension. These PDF files are written for most of the major printers on the market today. The files predefine the major functions for each of the listed printers.

Configuring Print Jobs

Once you've defined the printer, assigned users to queues, and assigned Print Queue Operators, you can begin to define the configuration of individual jobs. This is accomplished through the DOS-based menu utility PRINTCON. PRINTCON uses the printer definition database commands you create in PRINTDEF to set up individual print jobs.

Job configuration allows you to set up the mode of operation of the printer and to define settings you would normally need to specify if you were using the NetWare utilities NPRINT or CAPTURE and manually entering characteristics.

The PRINTCON database is stored in each user's SYS:MAIL directory. PRINTCON allows the supervisor to copy print job definitions between users. The database printer definitions are saved in the PRINTCON.DAT file.

Tip

For ease of administration, you can set up the PRINTCON database in the SYS:PUBLIC directory. You must then use the SMODE (Search Mode) parameter on all programs that will use the database. To do this, log in as SUPERVISOR. Then type the following:

```
SMODE SYS:PUBLIC/NPRINT.EXE 5
SMODE SYS:PUBLIC/CAPTURE.EXE 5
SMODE SYS:PUBLIC/PCONSOLE.EXE 5
SMODE SYS:PUBLIC/PRINTDEF.EXE 5
```

There is a drawback to this method: SMODE will search in the proper directory, but if you use PRINTCON, it will still save a new configuration to the user mail directory. This is fine for the individual user, but if you are attempting to maintain the shared database, you must remember to copy it from your mail directory to the common PUBLIC directory.

CAPTURE and NPRINT

CAPTURE and NPRINT are NetWare printing utilities. CAPTURE allows you to redirect normal parallel port output from your applications to the NetWare print queues. NPRINT allows you to print a file from a copy of the file that has been saved on disk. If you have NetWare-aware applications like WordPerfect or Microsoft Word, you will not need to use these NetWare-specific redirection programs.

CAPTURE and NPRINT allow you to make changes to the default job configuration as you need. A CAPTURE must be ended with either a specific ENDCAP (end capture) or AUTOENDCAP statement.

Tip

Remember that until you use ENDCAP, you are taking up disk space on the server by holding the print job open.

You can use the following parameters with CAPTURE and NPRINT:

Capture Flag	NPRINT Flag	Configuration
copies	Copies	Number of copies
NoTabs	NoTabs	File contents
Tabs	Tabs	Tab size
No form feed	No Form Feed	Suppress form feed
NOTify	NOTify	Notify when done
Form =	Form=	Form name
NoBanner	NoBanner	Suppress print banner
Local	N/A	Local printer
Autoendcap	N/A	Autoendcap
TI=	N/A	Enable timeout
TI=	N/A	Timeout count
Server (S)	Server (S)	File server name
Queue (Q)	Queue (Q)	Print queue name
N/A	Print Server	Print server name

With these parameters you can change the print job configuration to whatever you need currently. For example, to print two copies of a file without a banner page to the print queue MARKETING on the server MCKENNA, you would type:

```
CAPTURE COPIES=2 NOBANNER SERVER=MCKENNA QUEUE
    = MARKETING AUTOENDCAP
```

LAN Compass

The LAN Compass in the back of this book contains a list of CAPTURE parameters.

Since many applications are not NetWare-aware, you will need to add CAPTURE statements to the system login script. If individual users want access to printers other than the main printer, place CAPTURE statements to these printers in their user login scripts.

So What's the Order?

You might be wondering what you do first, next, and last. Here is a quick list that gives you the steps through the printing jungle.

Flash List

1. Find out what type of printers you have and where they are located.
2. Decide the best way to attach them to the network.
3. Create the print server.
4. Define each printer.
5. Create queues for each print server.
6. Add printers to the queues.
7. Assign users and groups to the queues.
8. Assign Print Queue Operators.
9. Create any forms you need.
10. Document the printer configurations in your LAN Log.

With the exception of a little practice, you should have a good overview of how printing on the NetWare network works. You should also have a better idea of the difficulties that printing can bring to your network. It is best to work with the utilities to get an overall idea of how they work together before attempting to install printers on your network. The basic printing techniques are fairly simple. Also, most of the applications are now network-aware, but a good understanding of how network printing works is essential.

chapter 8

Disks, Data, Memory, and Organization

Hard Drives and What Do I Do With Them?

The three most important components, after the motherboard of the server, are the hard drive, its disk controller, and the server's use of memory. Novell has added many disk management features to NetWare to ensure that you can retrieve data from disks or memory as quickly as possible with a high degree of reliability. Use of memory and choice of hard drives and controllers will determine the speed and reliability of your network.

NetWare divides the disk drive into a NetWare partition and a DOS partition. Partitions provide logical sections of the disks for later use in disk duplexing or mirroring. Each partition may be divided further into volumes, where data is stored. Volumes may span multiple partitions. We'll discuss partitions and volumes in more detail later in this chapter.

NetWare divides the partition into two block types: disk allocation blocks and directory entry blocks. Disk allocation blocks can be configured as 4-, 8-, 16-, 32-, or 64KB blocks. The default size under NetWare v3.x is 4KB. The default under NetWare 4.x depends on the size of the hard drive and will be discussed later. All blocks on the same volume must be the same size. NetWare uses these blocks to store information. If a file consists of more than one block, these blocks may not be stored adjacent to each other. When a file is stored in multiple blocks, entries in the File Allocation Table (FAT) record their locations in the order of the blocks' placement on the disk so that the blocks can be put back together later.

Directory entry blocks (DET) always consist of 4KB blocks, regardless of the size of the disk allocation blocks. The DET is divided into one or more blocks that store directory entries. When a volume needs to add another directory block to its directory table, the server allocates another block. Each directory entry block can hold up to 32 entries of 128 bytes. The maximum number of directory blocks per volume is 65,536.

NetWare Enhancements to Hard Drive Reliability

In NetWare 4.x, Novell moves closer to true client–server computing in which the server is a seamless part of the network. The NetWare server remains the source of file storage and retrieval. In many respects, the hard drive and disk controller in the NetWare server is the largest single investment in your computer, not for the hardware itself, but in the value of the data that can be stored on it. Novell's main focus in its enhancements for the hard drive have been to be ensure that the data reaches the users as fast as possible and that the data is as fully protected as possible.

In pursuit of reliability, Novell built a number of features into NetWare, including:

Hot Fix (System Fault Tolerance I [SFT I])
Drive mirroring and duplexing (SFT II)
Duplicate directories (SFT I)
Duplicate File Allocation Tables (FAT) (SFT I)
Read-after-write verification (SFT I)
The Transaction Tracking System (TTS) (SFT I)

SFT Level I

NetWare's SFT I consists of several mechanisms. They are Hot Fix, duplicate directories, duplicate FATs, read-after-write verification, and TTS.

Hot Fix

NetWare has three types of fault tolerance, called *System Fault Tolerance I through III*. Hot Fix is a member of SFT I. In a file server with Hot Fix running, a specific user-definable section of the hard drive is set aside during disk setup. When NetWare detects a bad portion of the disk during a read, write, or write-after-verify operation, it will mark the section of the disk as bad and transfer the data to an area called the *Hot Fix Redirection Area*. When the Hot Fix redirection area becomes full, a warning is sent to the SUPERVISOR account. This warning does not warn of impending disk failure, but rather that the redundancy Hot Fix built into the system is close to failing.

When installing NetWare, the supervisor can enable or disable Hot Fix. Typically, two percent of the disk drive should be assigned to the Hot Fix Redirection Area. (See Figure 8-1.)

Duplicate Directories

NetWare creates a duplicate of the root directory structure at the end of the hard drive, which is used as a backup if the main directory structure is corrupted. NetWare will automatically use the backup directory and alert the supervisor.

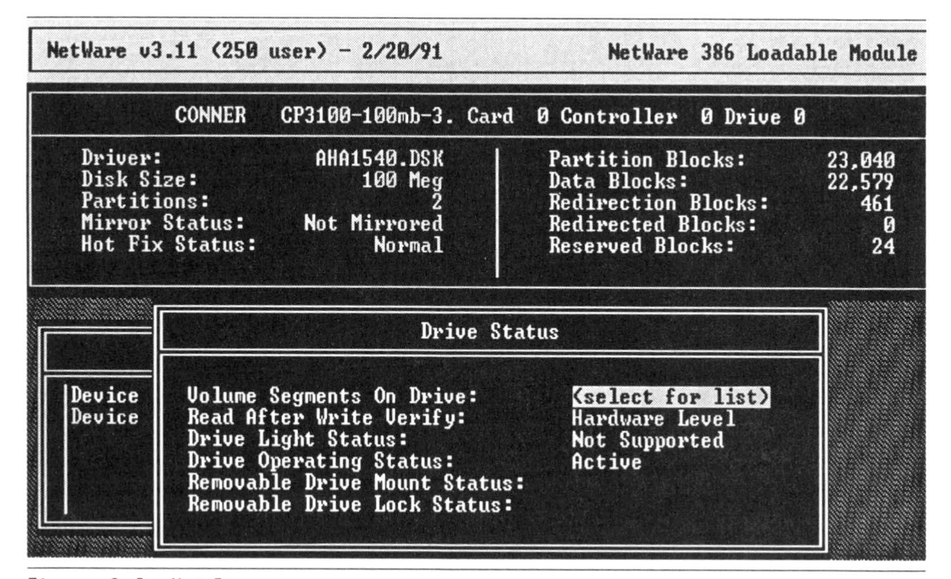

Figure 8-1. *Hot Fix.*

Tip
If this happens, reformat the hard drive and allow it to remirror or restore from the backup directory.

Duplicate FATs

NetWare maintains a duplicate of the FAT. If the FAT is corrupted, you can still access the hard drive through the duplicate FAT. Remember, as occurs with the duplication of the root directory, if it is necessary to access the drive by reading the duplicate FAT, you should reformat the drive and allow it to remirror or restore its contents from tape.

Transaction Tracking System (TTS)

TTS protects database files and transactions from incomplete writes. An incomplete write can occur when a user is accessing a file and attempts to write to the disk when the server goes down. When the server comes back up, TTS will roll back the incomplete database edits to the last complete transaction. Files are returned to the condition they were in before the transaction began. The application in use needs to support record locking. Also, incomplete edits are deleted.

During installation, you need to specify the volume size and location for the TTS work files.

2.x
In NetWare v2.x, you can install NetWare with or without TTS when you run NETGEN.

3.x
In NetWare v3.x, TTS is automatically installed each time you bring up the server.

Read-After-Write Verification

NetWare uses read-after-write verification to ensure data integrity each time the disk completes a write operation. When NetWare completes a write to the disk, it maintains the data in memory. It will then read the data from the disk and compare the data read from the disk to the data in memory. If the data compares properly, NetWare will flush the memory and move on to the next operation. If the data does not compare, Hot Fix will mark the sector as bad and move the data to the Hot Fix redirection area.

Tip

You can turn off read-after-write verification to improve performance. If you do, you will increase performance, but you will also risk data loss and limit Hot Fix's ability to maintain disk integrity.

Disk Mirroring

Mirroring and duplexing were built into NetWare as SFT Level II (SFT II) and enabled with the NetWare INSTALL utility. These features provide redundancy by allowing two disks to be installed, with the contents of one disk mirrored to the other. Both disks share a controller. When NetWare does a disk write, the data is automatically written to each disk. If a disk becomes bad, the server can be brought down at a convenient time and the disk replaced. When the server is brought up again, the disks will automatically remirror.

When disks are mirrored, the two disks are connected to one hard disk controller in the server. This can only be accomplished with a hard disk system such as IDE or SCSI, that allows multiple disks attached to the same controller. Mirroring slows server performance marginally.

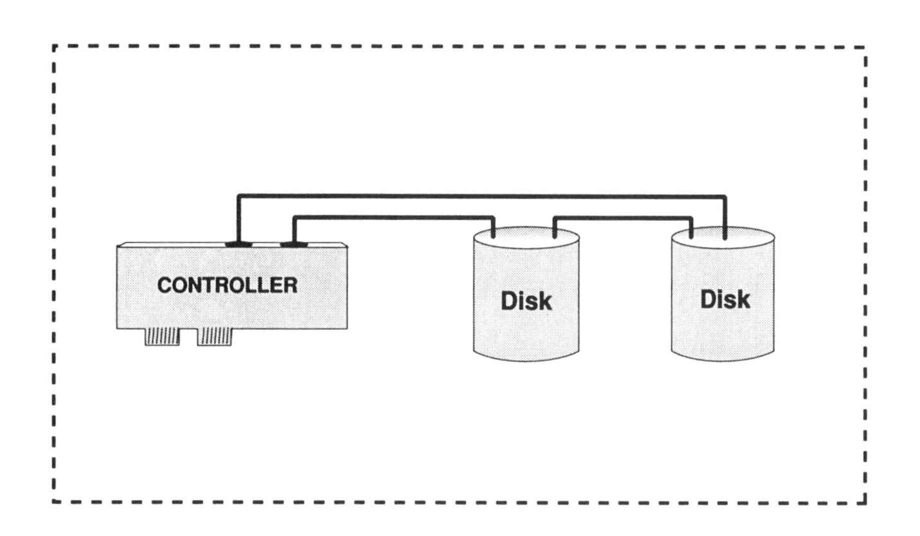

Figure 8-2. *A mirrored file server.*

The disadvantage to mirroring is that if the controller fails, the server fails. (See Figure 8-2 on the previous page.)

Disk Duplexing (SFT II)

The problems of mirroring are overcome by disk duplexing. In duplexing, two controllers are placed in the server. One disk is attached to each controller and the contents of the two disks are mirrored. The two disk channels provide redundancy for the controller and increase performance. However, duplexing is a costly venture, but the performance increases you will see are significant.

In duplexing, the system can direct reads to either controller concurrently, in which read requests are split between the disk channels and answered by whichever disk is free first. This process is called split seeks.

During installation, you can add further redundancy by combining mirroring and duplexing. This is accomplished by adding a second drive to the duplexed drives. You then mirror the contents of the two drives on each controller. (See Figure 8-3.)

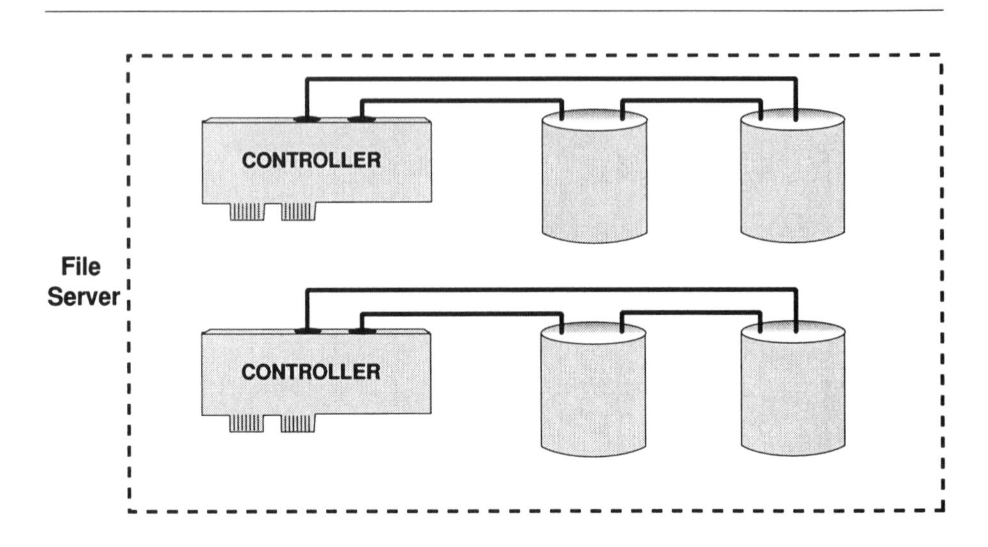

Figure 8-3. *A system that has been mirrored and duplexed.*

Mirrored Servers (SFT III)

The ultimate logical step is mirrored servers, which is available as SFT III. In this fault-tolerant method, two servers are set up and the hard drives and memory are mirrored via a high-speed connection called the *Mirrored Server Link* (MSL). Artisoft/Eagle, Plaintree Systems, and Thomas-Conrad Corp. offer MSL adapters. For those who need the ultimate protection for mission-critical information, SFT III is an excellent option.

Mirrored servers also allow other advantages. If you need to upgrade the server software, you can update it on one server, while network operations occur on the other.

The MSL consists of two 100megabit-per-second (Mbps) Ethernet or Thomas-Conrad Networking System (TCNS) adapters, one placed in each server. Novell recommends that the servers be 386/33-MHz or 486/25-MHz machines with a minimum of 12MB of RAM, and the same video adapter and monitor.

Tip

When installing SFT III, be sure that you use machines that are identical. If you have machines that have different VGA adapters, problems can occur.

SFT III is available for NetWare v4.1.

NetWare Enhancements to Hard Drive Performance

To increase the performance of your hard drive, Novell developed the Universal File System. Within the Universal File System, NetWare uses these features to increase performance:

Elevator-seeking

File caching

Background writes

Overlapped seeks

Indexed File Allocation Table (Turbo Fat)

Directory caching

Directory hashing

File compression (available in NetWare 4.x)

Block suballocation (available in NetWare 4.x)

Elevator-Seeking

NetWare prioritizes disk read requests based on the location of the disk's read/write head. This means that the disk head glides across the disk platters in an orderly fashion, minimizing its head travel. This action is similar to the way that an elevator operates in a large building. The elevator will not jump from floor 2 to 10 and then back down to floor 5. It will go up from 2 to 10, picking up floor 5 on its ascent. This means that some disk read requests will be placed ahead of others, depending on the location of the request on the disk. Elevator-seeking decreases the overall time for disk reads and reduces the wear and tear on the disk drive's mechanical parts. In systems that do not use elevator-seeking, the disk's read/write head is said to "thrash" as it attempts to read and write data in a random fashion.

File Caching

One of NetWare's most powerful features is file caching. In file caching, the most often used files are stored in the system's cache buffers, where they can be read quickly. Reading files from cache reduces the amount of disk access that must be made for files that are used. The files that are used less (called least-recently used) are released from memory in favor of newer files.

Tip

In most cases, the file caching should be left at its defaults. However, in NetWare v3.x and 4.x, SET parameters can be added to the server's AUTOEXEC.NCF file to control file and directory caching. These are:

Minimum file cache buffers
Maximum concurrent disk cache writes
Dirty disk cache delay time
Minimum file cache buffer report threshold

Of these SET commands, minimum cache buffers and maximum concurrent disk cache writes are the most frequently used. While most available memory is given to cache buffers, other tasks and modules will take memory. You should set the minimum number of buffers or disk cache writes available to prevent the OS from giving the memory to other tasks. Be careful that you do not set the minimum too high, or modules you need may not load. The number of minimum cache buffers ranges from 20 to 100. If the number of dirty cache buffers exceeds 70 percent, you should raise the number of concurrent disk cache writes. The range is from 10 to 100.

Background Writes

NetWare separates disk reads from writes. This allows NetWare to schedule disk writes to background operations. Because NetWare gives priority to disk reads, overall network performance is higher.

Overlapped Seeks

If you have two or more hard disks and each is connected to its own controller, NetWare will access both controllers simultaneously, allowing each hard disk to function independently and improve performance. If both hard disks are attached to the same controller, they are accessed one at a time.

Indexed File Allocation Table (Turbo FAT)

The Turbo FAT indexes the File Allocation Table of all files over 2MB in size. This gives the user instant access to the files. The locations of the segments are indexed and available without reading the FAT.

Directory Caching

Directory caching copies the NetWare Directory Entry Table (DET) and File Allocation Table into server RAM. When a request is made for data, the file server reads the location of the data from the tables stored in memory. Reading the location from memory rather than retrieving the data from the hard disk allows much quicker location of needed data.

Directory Hashing

Directory hashing indexes the memory-stored Directory Entry Tables (DET). Directory hashing is similar to alphabetizing the entries in a telephone book. It makes finding the entry much easier. Directory hashing allows NetWare to locate file entries much easier. This process reduces disk I/O by approximately 30 percent.

File Compression (NetWare 4.0 only)

NetWare 4.x allows you to designate file compression. With NetWare compression routines, you can increase disk space by approximately 63 percent. You can set each file for compression or noncompression.

Block Suballocation (NetWare v3.12 and 4.0)

NetWare v3.12 and 4.x will take partially used disk blocks and divide them into 512-byte sub-blocks that can be used for storing smaller files. Suballocation also saves disk space.

NetWare Memory Use

One of the advantages of NetWare over other networking operating systems is the way NetWare optimizes server memory. NetWare uses memory dynamically—it takes memory when it needs it and releases it when it is done with it. Memory is stored in pools, most of which can be dynamically allocated to different resources as needed. This dynamic allocation of memory saves you from having to set specific memory requirements for each area of the operating system. Allocation also reserves memory for file caching and releases memory to other resources only as needed.

Memory Buffers

NetWare stores information in buffers. These buffers are as follows:

File cache buffers

Directory cache buffers

Packet receive buffers

File Cache Buffers

File cache buffers are blocks of RAM where files are temporarily stored. These buffers are the main use of file server memory and make up the File Cache Buffer pool. Cache buffers consist of blocks of memory. The default block size is 4KB, changeable to 8KB or 16KB. You can view the number of buffers allocated in NetWare's MONITOR utility in the entry for "Total Cache Buffers."

Tip

The Cache Buffer Block size should never be larger than the smallest disk allocation block size on all volumes. For example, do not use an 8KB cache buffer with a 4KB block allocation. The volume will not mount.

Minimum file cache buffers are manipulated with the SET command in this manner:

SET MINIMUM FILE CACHE BUFFERS = xxx

in which the default is 20 and the range is from 20 to 1,000. The maximum number of file cache buffers is a function of the total amount of memory and the amount required by other memory pools.

Directory Cache Buffers

The directory cache buffer is a section of the file server memory that contains the entries for the DET. NetWare allocates directory cache buffers as needed until the maximum number is reached. The maximum and minimum numbers can be set with the SET command at the server prompt or in the AUTOEXEC.BAT file. The number currently allocated can be viewed in the MONITOR utility in the entry for "Directory Cache Buffers." You use SET commands like this:

SET MAXIMUM DIRECTORY CACHE BUFFERS = xxx

in which the default is 500 with a range of 20 to 4,000, or

SET MINIMUM DIRECTORY CACHE BUFFERS = xxx

in which the default is 20, with the range from 10 to 2,000.

Tip

Remember that the minimum directory cache buffers can actually be larger than is needed for most small networks. The directory cache buffers are taken out of the file cache buffer memory pool. In many cases, it is a better use of memory to reduce the minimum to a smaller value. NetWare will allocate more memory as needed, but it will never go below the value set as the minimum. Use the MONITOR utility to view the number of buffers currently allocated. If the number rises above 20 percent, it is probably a good idea to reduce the number of buffers.

Packet Receive Buffers

The packet receive buffers are the area of memory set aside for the receipt of packets from the network adapter. These buffers hold data until the server can process it. The size of the packet receive buffer is a function of the Maximum Physical Receive Packet Size. The larger the Physical Receive Packet Size, the larger the buffer. Your network access method determines the Physical Receive Packet Size. The approximate sizes by access method are

ARCNET—512 to 4,096 bytes on NetWare v2.x or v3.x, and 16,384 bytes on NetWare v3.12 and 4.x

Ethernet—1, 512 bytes on NetWare v2.x or NetWare v3.x and 4.x

Token-ring—4,096 bytes on NetWare v2.x, v3.0, and v3.1, and up to 24,576 bytes on NetWare v3.12 and 4.x

FDDI—4,096 bytes on NetWare v2.2, v3.0, and 3.1, and up to 24,576 bytes on NetWare v3.12 and 4.x

Two SET commands control the number of buffers. They are

SET MINIMUM PACKET RECEIVE BUFFERS = xxx

in which the default is 100 and the range is 100 to 300, and

SET MAXIMUM PACKET RECEIVE BUFFERS = xxx

in which the default is 100 and the range is 100 to 2,000.

Tip

In NetWare v3.x, the minimum number can only be set in the STARTUP.NCF file, and the maximum number can only be set in the AUTOEXEC.NCF file.

Packet receive buffers are taken from the File Cache Buffers Memory pool. You should set the minimum to the minimum you actually need. Some high-speed adapters may require more than the minimum. NetWare will dynamically allocate the buffers up to the maximum set.

Memory Pools

NetWare v3.x allocates memory via memory pools. (See Figure 8-4.) NetWare v3.x requires 4MB of memory to boot the operating system. Memory that is not required for the operating system is given to the File Cache Buffer or Main Memory pool. NetWare allocates file cache buffer memory to other NetWare functions as follows:

1. It loans cache buffer memory to NetWare Loadable Modules (NLM) that return the memory when completed.
2. It allocates buffers to cache for the File Allocation Table (FAT).
3. It allocates buffers to cache for the Directory Entry Table (DET).

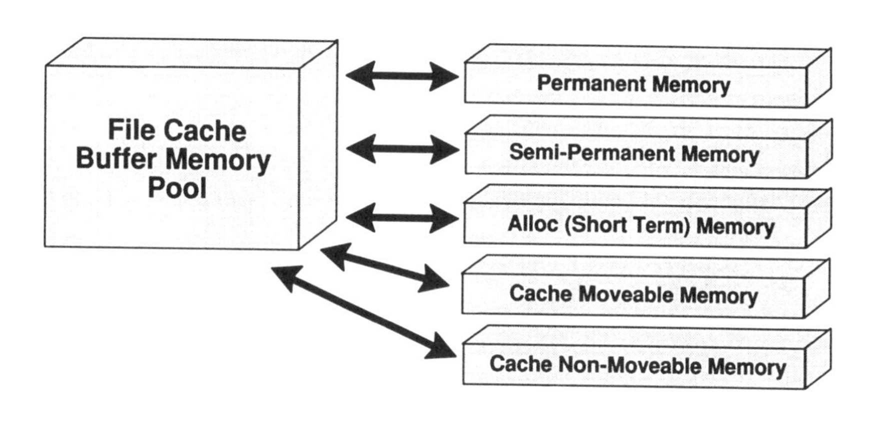

Figure 8-4. *NetWare memory pools.*

4. It uses cache buffers for files that users want to access.
5. It allocates memory to build hash tables for all directory names.
6. It allocates cache buffers to build the Turbo FAT indexes.

The File Cache Buffer Memory pool is also used to distribute memory to the other memory pools. These pools include:

Permanent memory

Semipermanent memory

Alloc (short-term) memory

Cache movable memory

Cache nonmovable memory

Permanent Memory

The permanent memory pool is the source of memory for the semipermanent memory pool and the alloc short-term memory pool. The operating system uses long-term memory for long-term memory needs such as permanent tables, directory cache buffers, and packet receive buffers. NetWare allocates as little memory as possible to the permanent and short-term pools. It will allocate memory dynamically to these pools as they need it.

Semipermanent Memory Pool

Semipermanent memory is a subset of permanent memory used for NLMs that you expect to use the memory for a significant amount of time. Semipermanent memory is also used for LAN drivers and disk drivers.

Alloc Short-term Memory

Alloc short-term memory is used for services that don't require memory for an extended period of time. (See Figure 8-5.) For instance, NLMs that use pop-up window messages use alloc short-term memory to store the previous menu information. This memory is returned to the main memory pool when no longer needed. Alloc short-term memory is also used for:

1. Drive mappings
2. Service requests
3. Open and locked files
4. Service advertising
5. User connection information
6. Messages waiting to be broadcast
7. Loadable module tables
8. Queue manager tables

Cache Movable Memory

Cache movable memory is taken from the cache buffer memory pool. The contents of this memory block move around to optimize memory usage. This stops the fragmentation of the main memory pool. The cache movable memory pool is used by the system tables such as Directory Entry Tables (DET) and File Allocation Tables (FAT). Hash Tables also use this memory. The pool grows dynamically as tables need more memory. As memory is no longer needed, it is returned to the main memory pool.

Cache Nonmovable Memory

Cache nonmovable memory is used to load modules into memory and to allocate large memory buffers. Memory no longer needed by the pool after allocation is returned to the main memory pool. NLMs also use cache nonmovable memory for loading. It is also used to list memory buffers that are reallocated to programs temporarily.

How Much Memory Do I Need?

NetWare v3.x uses memory dynamically. It pays to understand the basic memory requirements of your server. To calculate memory requirements, you should consider the following:

1. The minimum amount of memory needed to boot NetWare
2. The memory NLMs and adapter drivers need
3. The hard disk and volume sizes
4. The block size
5. The directory entries
6. Memory caching

The amount of memory for each DOS volume is calculated as follows:

M(emory) = .023 times VOLUME SIZE (in MB) divided by the BLOCK SIZE

The memory for each volume with an added name space is:

M(emory) = .032 x VOLUME SIZE (in MB) divided by BLOCK SIZE

The total server memory calculation is:

M(emory) = SYS: VOLUME SIZE plus 1ST VOLUME SIZE plus 2ND VOLUME SIZE plus ANY OTHER VOLUMES plus 2MB

This figure should be is rounded to the next highest megabyte. Remember, 4MB is the minimum RAM to boot NetWare.

LAN Compass

The LAN Compass in the back of this book will help you determine file server memory.

4.x

In NetWare 4.x, there is only one memory pool. Memory is allocated to optimize all resources and to ensure that when a service no longer needs the memory it is returned to the main pool.

Memory resources are also structured to ensure that different processes do not use the same memory. Memory is allocated in 4-KB memory pages and assigned to domains. NLMs are loaded into individual domains. Segments are created within domains for code and data. A descriptor is assigned to each domain to protect the NLM running in it.

To protect the operating system from stray or misbehaved NLMs, NetWare 4.x has established privilege levels called protection rings. There are four protection levels numbered 0–4. You can test suspect NLMs in ring 3. When you prove the NLM stable, it can be moved to a lower-level ring.

Tip
When you buy a new NLM for your 4.x server, test it in ring 3. When you find that the NLM works dependably, you can move it to ring 0.

Which Hard Drive Should I Use?

There are several types of hard drives for you to choose from. The type you purchase will depend upon your needs and budget. Some of these hard drives are as follows:

1. ST506
2. ESDI
3. SCSI
4. IDE interface

The ST506 Interface

The ST506 was originally designed by Seagate Technologies. It uses Modified Frequency Modulation (MFM) encoding when writing data or Run Length Limited (RLL) encoding. As one of the first methods, ST506 was commonly used in 286 and early 386 machines. The ST506 interface has not been used extensively since then and is not recommend for file server use because of its limited capacity and speed. Transfer is limited to approximately 5Mbps. While the ST506 is a slow interface for file servers, it allows users to add two drives to each controller. This capability makes the ST506 a good choice for a mirrored system where absolute speed is not essential, such as in a backup system or login server.

ESDI Disk Systems

ESDI is an extension of the ST506 and stands for the Enhanced Small Device Interface. Used as an interface in early file servers, it provides transfer rates of up to 15Mbps. An ESDI disk controller can attach up to two drives per controller. ESDI drives generally have a storage capability of 100MB or greater.

SCSI Systems

The Small Computer System Interface (SCSI), pronounced *scuzzy*, is a major departure from the ST506 or ESDI disk subsystems. Most popular for file servers, SCSI allows up to seven devices including hard drives, tape drives, and CD-ROM drives to share the same SCSI host adapter. The SCSI host adapter takes up only one expansion slot in the system and provides a bus that the seven devices use. The SCSI bus can be either 8, 16, or 32 bits wide.

Variations of the SCSI system include wide SCSI and SCSI II, which provide even faster throughput than SCSI. SCSI's throughput depends on the number of devices connected to the SCSI bus and the type of SCSI you are using. Since SCSI devices must contain their own control circuitry, they are generally more expensive than standard devices. SCSI drivers perform at a minimum of 300Mbps.

SCSI drives are connected to a host adapter with a 50-pin connector. Each disk attached to the controller is numbered 0 and 1. If you install multiple controllers, the SCSI ID for each controller will be 0 and 1.

If you are using the SCSI system as a RAID system, NetWare will see it as a single unit. With a RAID system, it is not necessary to mirror or duplex the drives. RAID mirroring consists of a hardware mirror that is typically faster and more efficient than NetWare's software mirroring.

IDE Drives

The Intelligent Drive Electronics (IDE) interface is a hybrid that offers some of the advantages of the ESDI system at a much lower cost. Ideal for workstations, IDE devices have control circuitry built onto the device. Because the control circuitry is built onto the device, the controller adapter is generally inexpensive. By using a local (VESA) IDE controller, you can get 32-bit access for your IDE devices. IDE supports only two devices per controller.

Generally, IDE interfaces are directly attached to the motherboard and are capable of attaching two drives via a 40-pin connector. Make sure that you set the boot drive as the master drive and the second drive as a slave drive. You set the drives as master and slave with jumpers on the drives.

Tip

NetWare does not allow mirroring IDE drives. Duplexing is supported.

Tip

Be sure to check the NetWare v3.x release notes for compatibility with the IDE.DSK driver. You can also use the ISADISK.DSK driver.

Tip

If you are mirroring or duplexing drives with different size drives, NetWare will only allow you to partition the drives to the size of the smallest drive. That means that if you have a 200MB and a 150MB hard drive, you can only mirror 150MB. The remaining 50MB is unused and useless.

Setting Up the Drives

Once you have chosen the drive and have installed it, you are ready to install the remainder of the equipment that will go in your server. Bring up the server and run the diagnostics utility to make sure you have no conflicts with other devices. Many new machines ship with their own diagnostics utilities. EISA or Micro Channel machines have their own setup programs for this purpose. If you are using an ISA machine, use a utility such as CheckIT LAN or Microsoft's Diagnostic Utility (MSD) for this purpose.

Prepare the Drive

If you are installing NetWare v3.x or 4.x for the first time, you should set up your primary drive with a 5MB DOS partition and leave the remainder as free space. Use the DOS utility FDISK to format the DOS partition as a bootable DOS drive. Use this partition to boot the server. With a 5MB partition you should have room for the NetWare files that need to be stored in the DOS partition and for any DOS files.

Tip

Do not use any DOS-based disk compression utilities such as STACKER to enlarge the DOS partition.

Tip

You should set the server's AUTOEXEC.BAT file to load SERVER.EXE automatically. It allows the system to reboot into NetWare automatically without your intervention.

Store SERVER.EXE, the VREPAIR.EXE utility, any files with the .DSK extension, and the INSTALL utility in the DOS partition. You can also store LAN and new hard drive .DSK files in the DOS partition.

Tip
You should be sure to store VREPAIR.EXE and associated files on the DOS partition. If your SYS volume refuses to mount, you can load VREPAIR.EXE from the DOS partition and repair the volume.

Boot the Server
To bring up the file server, type:

SERVER

to load SERVER.EXE. Enter the server name and an IPX internal net number.

Load the Disk Driver
Locate the appropriate disk driver. This file ends with the .DSK extension. NetWare automatically will look in the DOS partition of the server for the drivers. Common disk driver names are the following:

Bus Type	Controller Type	Driver
ISA	ST506 or ESDI	ISADISK.DSK
ISA	IDE	IDE.DSK
ISA	NOVELL SCSI	DCB.DSK
Micro Channel	ESDI	PS2ESDI.DSK
Micro Channel	MFM	PS2MFM.DSK
Micro Channel	IBM SCSI	PS2SCSI.DSK
EISA	ST506 or ESDI	ISADISK.DSK
EISA	IDE	IDE.DSK
EISA	EISA	Vendor-specific

Tip
Many disk controller and hard drive manufacturers write their own drivers. Check to see if NetWare includes the driver for your controller. EISA controllers generally use vendor-specific drivers. Also, make sure you have the latest driver.

When you load the driver from the console prompt (:), you must include the interrupt, slot, and memory address the controller will use:

LOAD ISADISK INT=X PORT=XXX

or

LOAD AHA1742 SLOT=3

Place the LOAD statement in the STARTUP.NCF file when you create the file later in your server installation. STARTUP.NCF is similar to a CONFIG.SYS file and runs automatically when the server boots.

Partition the Drive

Load the INSTALL utility from the DOS partition on drive C. Select the Disk Drive option, and set the partition's size. If you let NetWare automatically set the partition, it will assign the remaining space on the disk as the partition size. You should use the largest size partition possible. If you have multiple disks, you must create a separate partition for each disk.

Of the total NetWare partition, NetWare will set a default size of two percent as the Hot Fix redirection area. If you add multiple partitions to a drive, each will require space for Hot Fix. The INSTALL utility allows you to change the Hot Fix size, but not disable it.

Duplexing and Mirroring Drives

If you are duplexing with only one drive on each controller, NetWare will assign the drive numbers as 0 for the DOS partition, 1 as the NetWare partition on the first disk, and 2 as the NetWare partition on the second disk. Remember that you can only mirror the exact partition size. Be sure that disk 2's partition size matches disk 1's size. You will need remaining used space equal to the size of your DOS partition on disk 1. (See Figure 8-5 on the next page.)

If you are duplexing multiple drives, the partition numbers are sequential. For controller 1, the DOS partition is 0. The rest of disk 1 is partition 1. The entire second disk on controller 1 is partition 3. The second disk on controller 1 will have a small unused portion to match the partition size of the first disk on controller 1. The NetWare partition on disk 1 of controller 2 will be 3. The NetWare partition on the second

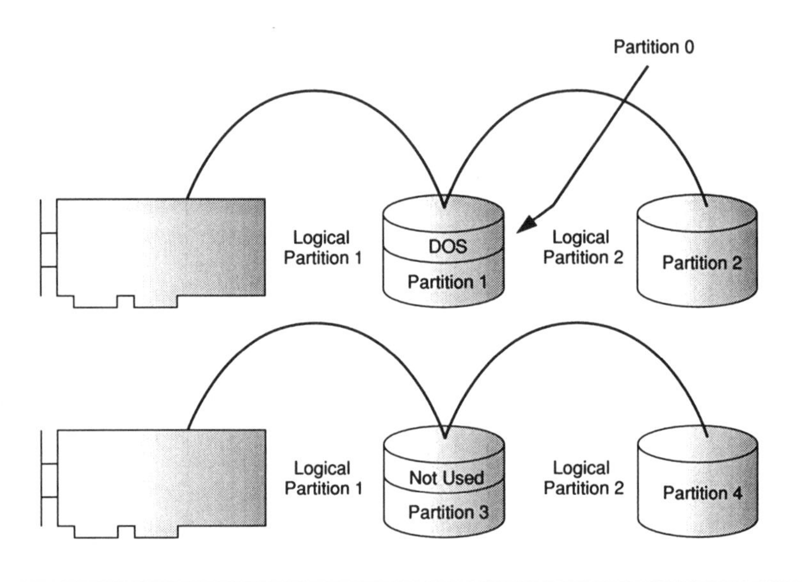

Figure 8-5. *Disk partitioning on a duplexed drive.*

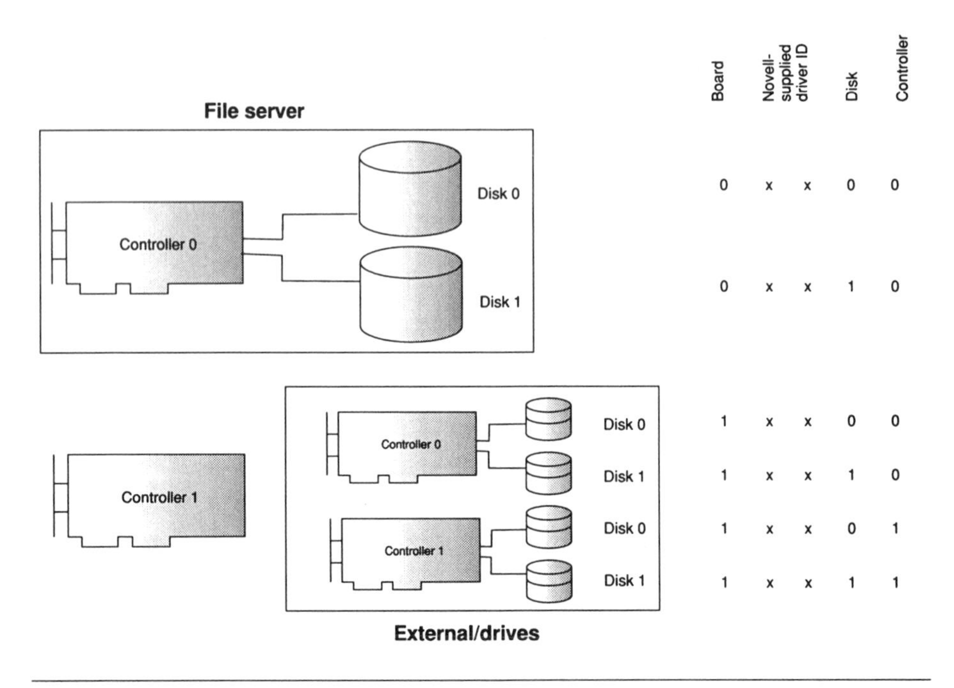

Figure 8-6. *Drive partitioning with multiple drives.*

disk 1 of controller 2 will be 3. The NetWare partition on the second disk will be 4. (See Figure 8-6 on the previous page.)

When the drives have been partitioned, move back to INSTALL's main menu and select the option Disk Mirroring. After selecting the option, press the Insert key. A list of NetWare partitions will be displayed. Select the first disk. In a two-disk duplex or mirror, you have only two choices. Select both. In a multiple disk situation, be sure to select one partition number for each controller.

Tip

Remember to record the mirrored partition numbers in your LAN Log. You'll need that information if something goes wrong.

Creating Volumes

NetWare volumes store network data. You may have more than one volume for each server. SYS is the first volume on any NetWare server. It will be created on the first NetWare partition on the first disk drive. Remember, in the case of duplexed drives, it will be duplicated on the mirrored drive as well.

The volume SYS is the primary volume on the server. It contains all the NetWare files. NetWare recommends that you leave the SYS volume for only NetWare system files and NetWare Loadable Modules (NLMs), and create separate volumes for your data and NetWare PUBLIC files. Volume names can range from 1 to 15 characters. This method offers the following several advantages:

1. It is easier to organize and back up the drive.
2. It takes less time to restore the volume SYS if a failure occurs. To bring up the server, VOL SYS must be able to mount. It takes less time to VREPAIR a small VOL SYS than a large volume.
3. Security is improved by granting access only to the supervisor to VOL SYS.
4. If a disaster happens, you need only restore VOL SYS without disturbing your valuable data.

2.x

In NetWare v2.2, the maximum size of a volume is 255MB.

3.x

In NetWare v3.1, the maximum volume size is 32 terabytes (1,000 gigabytes) and can span multiple drives. Spanning drives increases performance. The advantage of a large volume size is that it can store files that are over 226MB in size. The disadvantage of spanned volumes is that in a disk failure the entire volume fails. To prevent this, always duplex drives that have spanned volumes.

Once you create the SYS volume, you should organize the remainder of your partition. In most cases, it will be best to have only one volume per partition. NetWare allows a volume to span multiple partitions, and there are significant performance enhancements in having one volume on the rest of the partitions.

To assign volumes, go to the Volumes option in the INSTALL utility. You will see a menu of volume parameters. The only other parameter you need to set is the block size. The name of the first volume automatically is SYS. NetWare does not store files in space that corresponds to the actual file size. Instead, it allocates blocks and uses them to store the data. If the size of the data does not match the block size, the remaining block space is left as unused. The default block size is 4KB. If you have large files, you might want to increase that size to save disk space.

3.x

In NetWare v3.12, you can increase the block size of large files and conserve memory. The down side of this is that when small files exist you waste memory.

4.x

NetWare 4.x will assign a default block size based on the volume size as follows:

Up to 32MB	4KB
33-150MB	8KB
151-500MB	16KB
501-2,000MB	32KB
Above 2,000MB	64KB

With 4.x you also have additional parameters for file compression and block suballocation that will allow NetWare to collect the unused portion of blocks and write small files to them. NetWare 4.x allows data migration, which writes seldom-used files to an optical storage device. You must enable data migration during the installation process.

After installation, the SYS volume contains four directories: MAIL, LOGIN, SYSTEM, and PUBLIC. The MAIL directory contains the user's personal login script, any print job definition files created with PRINTCON.DAT, and a subdirectory that contains mail information for each user on the network.

The LOGIN directory contains the LOGIN.EXE file, which the user types to gain access to the network, and SLIST.EXE, which lists the file servers on the network. PUBLIC contains NetWare command-line and menu-based utilities, as well as printer definition and overlay files. SYSTEM contains supervisor utilities and NetWare system files.

Name Spaces

NetWare allows you to add name spaces for OS/2, Unix, NFS, and Macintosh to volumes, which handle the proper storage of these files on a NetWare file server. If you are going to use these operating systems on your workstations, you might create additional volumes specifically for these users. Be sure to designate the volumes you will be using as namespace volumes. Once the volume for a name space is created, you must recreate the volume to remove it.

If you add name spaces after installation, you risk fragmentation of data and resulting decreases in performance.

You add name spaces from the file server console prompt by typing:

```
LOAD MAC
```

Then assign the name space to a volume by typing:

```
ADD NAMESPACE MAC TO VOLUME xxxx
```

in which xxxx is the volume name. You must add name spaces only one at a time. NetWare autoloads NAMESPACE each time it mounts the volume.

Organizing the Data

Creating data on the hard drive is only the first part of network organization. Organizing the data once it is on the hard drive is one of the largest jobs of the network administrator. There are several rules to follow:

1. Organize users' home directories in a separate subdirectory by department or group.
2. Organize applications in a separate subdirectory. Assign each application to a group of similar applications (e.g., SPREADSHEETS).
3. Organize the remaining data so you can control and organize it.
4. Subdirectories can only be created 25-layers deep.

When you are finished, you should have a server that looks similar to that in Figure 8-7 on the next page.

Flash List

Here is a suggested order for installing and configuring the hard disks in your file server.

1. Select the hard drive(s).
2. Select the disk controller(s).
3. Install the hard drive and controller(s).
4. Run DOS's FDISK to partition the disk.
5. Leave the remainder of the disk as free space.
6. Format the DOS partition as bootable.
7. Copy over the DOS files.
8. Copy NetWare disks 1 and 2 to the DOS partition.
9. Run SERVER.EXE.
10. Enter the server name and the internal network number.
11. Load the disk driver.
12. Run the INSTALL utility.
13. Set the NetWare partition size.
14. Establish mirrored drives.
15. Establish the volume size.
16. Establish additional volumes.
17. Exit the INSTALL utility.

```
SYSTEM:
    PUBLIC
    LOGIN
    MAIL

ENTERPRISE:
    USERS\
      ACCOUNTING\
          \CHEATEM
          \HOWE
      SALES\
          \INSIDE SALES
              \MARY
              \SALLY
              \ROBERT

          \OUTSIDE SALES
                \JAMES
                \DEAN
                \ROGER
      MANUFACTURING\
            \GEORGE
            \BELINDA
      EXECUTIVE\
          \DENA
          \GINA
          \JOHN
    APPLICATIONS\
      \WINDOWS
          \WORD
          \ACCOUNTING
          \MACOLA
      \DOS
        MAHJONG\

    MARKETDAT
    ACCTDAT
    MANUDAT
```

Figure 8-7. *In this example, two volumes exist. SYS contains the directories NetWare automatically creates. ENTERPRISE contains the user directories, application directories, and data directories.*

18. Load the name spaces.
19. Add the name spaces to the volume.
20. Continue with the installation.

When Disaster Strikes Your Disk

At some point in your server's life, you will have the ultimate problem hit your drive. The volume will refuse to mount because of a FAT error. Your only solution is the Novell utility VREPAIR. VREPAIR can repair FAT errors in your hard drive.

Starting VREPAIR

VREPAIR consists of these files:

VREPAIR.NL

V_MAC.NLM

V_OS2.NLM

V_NFS.NLM

V_FTAM.NLM

VREPAIR.NLM is the initial program that you will load. The additional NLMs repair errors in the name space files for Macintosh, OS/2, NFS, or Unix machines. If you install your hard drive properly, you will have copies of VREPAIR and its associated NLMs in the DOS partition of the server's hard drive.

In most cases the server will not be operating when you need to use VREPAIR. Bring the server up until you get to the console prompt. If volume SYS will not mount, you will be prompted to enter the server's name and its internetwork number. Enter any valid name and network number at this point. It will not matter later. If the SYS volume is up, your problem is with another volume. Dismount the volume by typing the following:

DISMOUNT volume name

Then load VREPAIR with the following command:

LOAD C:VREPAIR

VREPAIR Options Menu

VREPAIR loads with default settings. You can set the following options:

Remove Name Space—The default option is to quit VREPAIR if the namespace NLM is not loaded. Remove name spaces only if you have no name space data stored.

Write All Changes to Disk—The default option is to write only changed information to disk. The alternate option is to write ALL changes to disk. In most cases, the default option is appropriate.

Write Changes Immediately—The default option writes changes to disk when they are complete. The alternate option is to write changes immediately. The default option allows VREPAIR to operate more quickly.

Purge Deleted Files—The default option is to retain deleted files. The alternate option is to purge all deleted files. If you want to retain deleted files, keep the default option. Choosing the alternate option will delete recoverable deleted files and increase the performance of VREPAIR.

Tip

When you go to the options menu, you will see the alternate options. You may think you are changing the options shown. Instead select the option by number. When you are finished, type 0 to return to the main menu.

To start VREPAIR, select 1 from the options menu. Pressing F1 at any time during the repair process will pause VREPAIR and enter the selections menu. There are three available VREPAIR options, as follows:

Stop Pause—The default option will stop VREPAIR when it finds an error. VREPAIR will run much faster if you choose the alternate option.

Option Log—Specifies a log text file for errors. Errors are written to a log file and assigned the name you specify.

Stop Volume Repair—Stops volume repair.

When VREPAIR is complete, you will receive a message that includes the number of repairs made. If you select the option to retain repairs in memory, VREPAIR will request to write changes to disk.

Tip

It is a good idea to run VREPAIR until no errors are found at least twice in a row. Sometimes VREPAIR will miss errors on the first pass.

chapter 9

Don't Forget the Applications

What Are Network Applications?

Not every program that you run from the network is a network application. There are three classes of programs. Many programs you run from a local drive or from a user directory on the file server are designed to be standalone applications—to be used by one person at a time and licensed for use on a single computer. A game is an example of this kind of application.

The second class of programs are written to be run on a network, from the network file server. They have network installation procedures and are designed to be used by multiple users. These applications will have features that allow them to take advantage of some aspects of the network, including record locking and transaction tracking. Record locking ensures that the file can be used by one user at a time. Transaction tracking maintains the integrity of database applications. An example of this type of program is a network version of WordPerfect or a database program with network capability.

The final class of programs are those that are known as "NetWare-aware." These programs are not only designed to be multiuser, but they also take advantage of network services. These applications use record and file locking and transaction tracking. Users of these applications will be recognized by their login names; the application will take and use other bindery information such as rights available to the user to make decisions as to what the user can do; and users take advantage of other NetWare applications on the network such as Novell's Message Handling Service (MHS). An e-mail package and event control software, which allows network task scheduling, are examples of this class of programs.

Where It All Begins

Before looking in detail at NetWare applications, you must know what it takes to get most applications to work. You must define the environment the user will use for any applications on the network. On a DOS machine the environment is controlled by the CONFIG.SYS and AUTOEXEC.BAT files. When you add NetWare, the environment is additionally controlled by login scripts.

What Are Login Scripts?

Login scripts are designed to establish the working environment for the user, his or her home directory, the DOS environment, the servers he or she can attach to, a series of drive mappings to network devices, messages for users, and menus. Login scripts are unique to each file server and are called *system login scripts*. Users also have login scripts called *user login scripts* that operate after the system login script. If a user attaches to more than one server during the day, he or she should have only one login script on the primary server.

Tip

By using the PREFERRED SERVER statement in the NET.CFG file or on the DOS command line, you will force the user to attach to the server that contains his or her login script. The syntax for PREFERRED SERVER is:

PREFERRED SERVER Enterprise (from the DOS command line)

NET.EXE ps=Enterprise (from the NET.CFG file)

There are three types of NetWare login scripts, the System Login Script, the User Login Script, and in NetWare 4.x, the Profile Login Script. The System Login Script sets the operating parameters for all the users on the network. Only the supervisor or supervisor-equivalent can modify the System Login Script. The User Login Script modifies the structure defined in the system login script and individualizes the network for each user. The user can modify the login script as he or she desires using the NetWare utility SYSCON or the LAN Compass in the back of this book. The login script for each user is stored in the user's mail directory on the SYS volume.

LAN Compass

Use the LAN Compass in the back of this book to edit the Supervisor or User Login Script.

Tip

If you do not want the user to be able to modify his or her login script, move the NetWare utility SYSCON to the SYS:SYSTEM directory. Make sure that users do not have Read and File Scan rights to the SYS:SYSTEM directory.

4.x

The theory behind login scripts changes with 4.x. You no longer log into the server, but to the entire network. As a result, your login script changes. The script is written and stored on one server and replicated on the other servers on the network. In 4.x there are three login scripts; the System, the Profile, and the User Login. The Profile Login Script applies to a group.

Using SYSCON to Create and Change Login Scripts

You create or modify login scripts using SYSCON. SYSCON allows the supervisor to change a number of the NetWare environments, including login scripts. To create or modify the System Login Script, select Supervisor Options from SYSCON's main menu. Then select System Login Script. For users, select User Information from SYSCON's main menu. Then select the user whose script you want to change. Once you select the user, another menu appears. Select Login Script from that menu. (See Figure 9-1 on the next page.)

Once you select the login script you want to modify, you'll see the login script appear in the editor window. The NetWare editor is similar to most other ASCII text editors. The following keystroke commands are available:

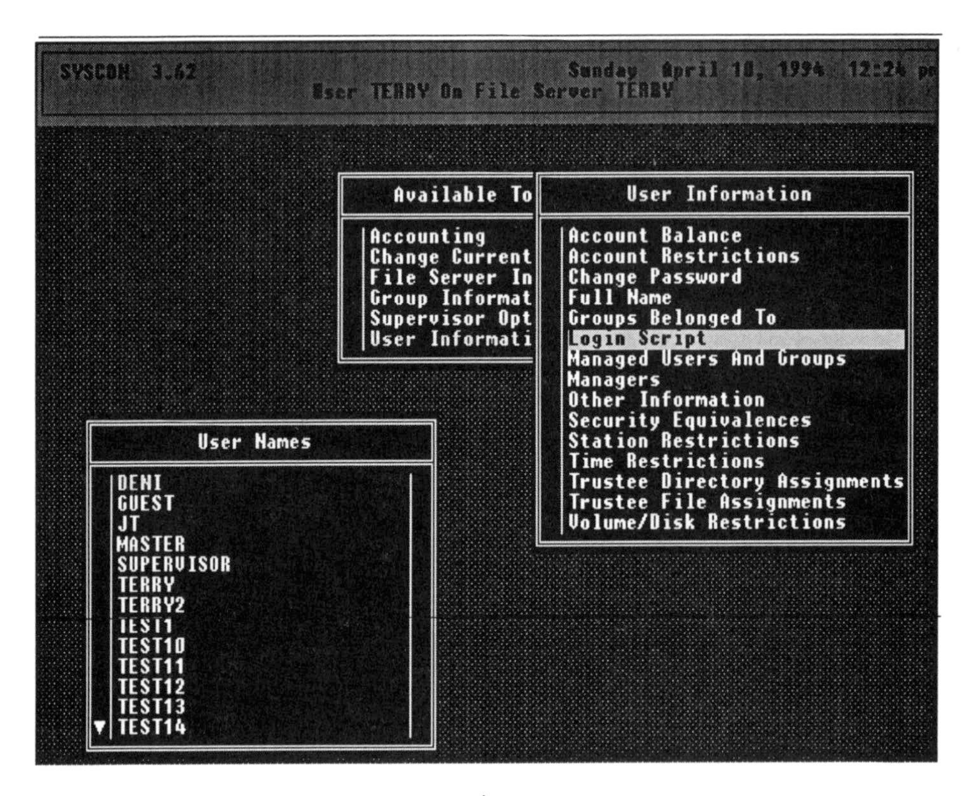

Figure 9-1. *SYSCON's User Login Script selection.*

HOME

END

DEL

INS

ARROW

F5—Marks a block of text for deletion. Once you mark the text, use the arrow keys to highlight the text area. Deleted text can be placed elsewhere by using the Insert key.

Other rules for the login scripts are

1. Login scripts have a specific command set, which is listed on the next page.
2. DOS commands in login scripts must be preceded by a pound (#) sign.

3. The maximum length of a command in the login script is 150 characters. The window size is 78.
4. One command is allowed per line. (This does not include conditional statements.)
5. The command must be the first statement (WRITE, FIRE PHASERS, etc.).

Help is available by pressing the F1 key. When you are finished editing, use the Escape key to save your work and return to the previous menu.

Login Script Variables

Login scripts use a variety of statements to obtain existing operating parameters from the system. These statements are called variables because they change for each login. Many of these variables are previously set by NetWare or by the NET.CFG or SHELL.CFG file. For instance, the SHORT and LONG MACHINE NAME variables are set in the NET.CFG file when the configuration file runs. TIME is set by the server. When the user logs in, the login script uses the previously set variables to execute specific commands in the script. The login script variables are as follows:

Variable	Description
SECOND	Holds current second
MINUTE	Holds current minute
HOUR	Holds current hour
HOUR24	Holds current hour in military time
AM_PM	Holds day or night
GREETING_TIME	Holds morning, afternoon, or evening
DAY	Holds current day as number
NDAY_OF_WEEK	Holds day of week in word format (Sunday)
MONTH	Holds current month as number
MONTH_NAME	Holds current month as full name
YEAR	Holds year in full form (1996)
SHORT_YEAR	Holds year in short form (96)
LOGIN_NAME	Current user's login name (BJOHNSTO)
FULL_NAME	Current user's full name (Belinda Johnston)
USER_ID	Number assigned at login
STATION	Holds station number of login workstation
P_STATION	Holds the node ID (12-digit hexadecimal number of adapter)
MACHINE	Holds the LONG MACHINE TYPE from the NET.CFG file
SMACHINE	Holds the SHORT MACHINE TYPE from the NET.CFG file
NETWORK_ADDRESS	Holds the network number assigned in BIND statement

Variable	Description
FILE_SERVER	Name of the file server
OS	Holds the operating system (OS) the workstation uses (PCDOS, CPQDOS)
OS_VERSION	Holds the version number of the OS (3.1, 5.0, 6.2)
< >	Used to hold DOS environment variable
ACCESS_SERVER	Returns TRUE if an access server is available
ERROR_LEVEL	A value is registered for errors; 0 indicates no errors
MEMBER OF "group"	Returns true if user is member of a group

LAN Compass

Refer to the LAN Compass for a list of login script variables.

Login Script Commands

All variables in a statement are preceded by a % sign. The variables are used in conjunction with login script commands, especially the WRITE command or with conditional statements. Each command is explained with examples below.

Tip

Now we are now getting into some of the fun stuff in NetWare that carries severe consequences for individual users if done improperly. Review this section carefully before attempting to use some of the statements.

ATTACH connects the user to another file server. The syntax for the command is

ATTACH *servername/username; password*

If you do not include the variables when you are writing the login script, you will be prompted for them. If you plan to use the ATTACH command in the System Login Script, include only the servername. Do not include the username or password. In a user login script, include the username and password. For security reasons, you might not want to include the password since it will be entered automatically, compromising the network security.

BREAK ON/OFF allows the script to be terminated with the CTRL-BREAK or CTRL-C keystrokes. It may be necessary to allow the user to stop termination of specific portions of the login script. To allow breaks, use BREAK ON. When BREAK ON is used, input in the keyboard buffer is ignored. To stop the user from breaking out of the login script and returning to DOS, use BREAK OFF. You can use these commands several times within each script.

COMSPEC specifies where the user's COMMAND.COM file is stored. Some applications require that COMMAND.COM be deleted from active memory during execution. When the program is finished, the system must be able to locate a version of COMMAND.COM. This is similar to the same command in DOS. The syntax of COMSPEC is

COMSPEC = *drive*:COMMAND.COM

The drive designation can be replaced with the search drive number or a specific directory.

DISPLAY and FDISPLAY print large blocks of text to the screen for the user to read. DISPLAY shows all text including formatting characters such as carriage returns and line breaks. FDISPLAY attempts to exclude the formatting characters. To create messages, use an ASCII text editor that does not include format characters. The syntax is

DISPLAY *path/filename*

The DISPLAY and FDISPLAY commands can be used in the same statement with other commands such as the IF-THEN statement, which only displays information or a text file when specific conditions are met. For example, you could inform the sales group of a party. The path can be a full path name or a mapped drive letter. The syntax is

IF GROUP = "SALES" THEN DISPLAY SYS:\PARTY.TXT

Tip
It is a good idea to create a separate directory for the files that need to be displayed. This makes management much easier, and you can limit access to the messages that are displayed.

DOS BREAK ON/OFF allows the user to break out of DOS commands. It is similar to the BREAK command.

DOS SET creates variables that DOS batch files use after the login script executes. The syntax for the DOS SET command is

DOS SET name = "value"

The "name" is the login script or DOS variable you want to use, and the "value" is the variable's contents. Quotation marks must enclose the value if it is a DOS variable. If you use NetWare variables, do not enclose them in quotes. DOS SET can be used to set a username for programs that are not NetWare-aware such as:

DOS SET USER = LOGIN_NAME

or

DOS SET PROMPT = "pg"

DRIVE switches the user to a specific drive. This command is used at the end of the login script to switch the user to his or her home directory. The syntax is

DRIVE *n*:

in which "n" is the drive letter.

EXIT stops login script execution. It is used as part of a conditional statement to stop execution of the script for certain users, such as those who are members of a specific group that does not need the remaining portions of the script. By adding a file name in quotes at the end of the statement, you can exit the login script and execute a program or batch file. EXIT's syntax is

EXIT

or

EXIT *"filename"*

Replace "filename" with the program name you want to execute or the DOS batch file name that should run.

The pound sign (#) denotes external program execution. It is similar to the EXIT command, but allows the login script to continue after the program completes. The syntax for the command is

path/command parameters

This command is very useful for running programs that need to execute whenever a user logs in.

FIRE PHASERS creates an attention-getting sound. Use it during the login process to alert users to notices they must see. FIRE PHASERS can be used outside the login process as well, for instance, to alert for incoming mail. The syntax is

FIRE PHASERS *n* TIMES

Tip

Some people find the noise FIRE PHASERS generates annoying. Use it only when necessary. Continued use of the command could cause your co-workers to contemplate murder.

IF THEN ELSE is a command sequence that allows you to place conditional statements in the login script. The syntax for the command is

IF *conditions* {AND;OR;NOR} THEN *command* ELSE *command*

or

IF *condition* THEN BEGIN

commands

commands

END

The statements AND;OR;NOR allow additional conditions to branch to the response. The ELSE statement allows branching to a secondary command. Thus, IF condition 1 exists, THEN *command* occurs. If the condition does not occur, the command after the ELSE statement executes. You can add conditionals that IF condition 1 exists AND condition 2 exists, THEN *command 1* executes. If neither condition exists, ELSE executes. Or IF condition 1 exists OR condition 2 exists, THEN *command 1* executes, ELSE *command 2* executes. Finally, IF neither condition 1 NOR condition 2 exists, THEN *command 1* executes, ELSE *command 2* executes. For example:

IF DAY_OF_WEEK = "MONDAY" AND MEMBER OF "MANAGERS" THEN FDISPLAY SYS:NEWS\FIRELIST.TXT

In the above example, the day must be Monday and the user a member of the group MANAGERS for the notice in the file

FIRELIST.TXT to be displayed. The IF THEN ELSE command set evaluates six relationships between conditions:

1. Equal to
2. Not equal to
3. Greater than
4. Less than
5. Greater than or equal to
6. Less than or equal to

INCLUDE executes the script commands contained in a separate ASCII text file. The syntax for the INCLUDE command is

INCLUDE *path\filename*

You can nest up to 10 levels of statements in a login script, and the user must have Open and Read rights in the directory where the INCLUDE text file is stored.

MACHINE sets the machine name of the workstation logging in. The name may be up to 15 characters in length. The syntax of the MACHINE command is

MACHINE = *"name"*

MAP specifies true drives or search drives for the user and is similar to the DOS ASSIGN and PATH commands. It specifies a drive letter for a specific subdirectory or subdirectory to search automatically when looking for a program. The syntax for MAP is

MAP P:=USERS:APPS

Maps drive P to volume USERS and the APPS subdirectory.

MAP ROOT Q:=SYS:PUBLIC\WIN31

Maps drive Q to volume SYS and the PUBLIC\WIN31 subdirectory. MAP ROOT also makes the application think it is located on the root of a drive.

MAP S3:=SYS:WINDOWS

Maps search drive #3 to volume SYS and WINDOWS subdirectory.

MAP INS S2:=SYS:PUBLIC\APPS\ACCESS

Maps search drive #2 to volume SYS and the PUBLIC\APPS\ACCESS subdirectory. It also keeps the current search drives and increments existing search drives S2 to S3.

MAP DEL Q:

Deletes the drive mapping for drive Q.

MAP DEL S3:

Deletes the drive mapping for search drive #3.

Mappings during login script execution can be displayed to the user. The commands to display the mapping functions are

MAP DISPLAY OFF

Displays drive mappings during login script execution.

MAP ERRORS OFF

Doesn't display mapping errors during login script execution.

MAP DISPLAY ON

Displays drive mappings during login script execution.

MAP ERRORS ON

Displays drive mapping errors during login script execution.

Tip
Drive mappings, like many of the commands in login scripts, are not restricted to use in login scripts and can be used at the DOS command line. MAP is one of the commands you may use many times each day.

PAUSE temporarily stops login script execution. Use it after a message is written to the screen to pause the display so users can read the message:

WRITE "Engineering meeting at 2:00"

PAUSE

Striking any key continues login script execution.

PCCOMPATIBLE designates the machine as a PC-compatible if the EXIT command doesn't work properly. This can occur if the LONG MACHINE NAME has been changed in the NET.CFG file. The syntax is

PCCOMPATIBLE

EXIT

REMARK places comments in the login script text. The script ignores the text following the statement and does not display it. Use REMARK to make descriptive or explanatory comments on the script's action. The syntax is

REMARK text

REM text

* text

; text

Tip

REMARK can be used in any ASCII text file NetWare uses, including the AUTOEXEC.NCF and STARTUP.NCF files, to make it easier to understand what you are doing. We recommend using remark as a way of documenting files you create.

WRITE displays text to the display and may be used in combination with other variables to display text to groups or certain individuals. Its syntax is

WRITE "text" ; variable

or

WRITE "text %VARIABLE"

When you include a variable in a text string, you must precede it with a % sign, include it in quotation marks, and capitalize it. Additional strings can be added, such as:

\r	Forces a carriage return
\n	Forces a new line
\"	Embeds a quotation mark
\7	Beeps when executed

A typical write command appears like this:

WRITE = "Good % GREETING_TIME, %LOGIN_NAME"

Novell Menu System

NetWare includes a menu system that allows a user to create custom menus from which to select applications, tasks, or operating system commands. Menus consist of ASCII text files that contain commands and variables that allow menu execution. Each menu may call an additional submenu, and system security can be maintained by restricting users to only the applications they should be using. NetWare's menu system is one of many menuing programs that make workstations easier to use. Users can be asked for input before performing an action. Menus can also be called from the System or User Login Script if desired. Novell's MENU system is not limited to use on network workstations. It can be used on standalone computers as well.

MENU Files

NetWare's MENU system uses several files that are stored on the file server during installation. They are the following:

MENU.EXE
MENUPARZ.EXE
MENUPARZ.HLP
IBM$RUN.OVL
SYS$MSG.DAT
SYS$ERR.DAT
SYS$HLP.DAT

How MENU Works

MENU uses many standard Novell overlay and data files to give it the look and feel of a NetWare utility. However, the actual menu items are based on your design. In writing the menu interface, you'll use an ASCII text editor to create a list of menu titles, commands, responses, and variables. Menus will require planning on your part and a modicum of knowledge on how to write in the required syntax.

There are four basic menu parts. They are as follows:

MENU TITLES—A percent sign indicates a main menu title. The display position on the screen and the menu colors are specified at the end of the title. You will indicate the horizontal and vertical positions and the color palette with numbers.

MENU SELECTION—Individual menu items are left-justified under the menu title. MENU sorts the items in alphabetical order and numbers them sequentially. If you want specific numbers or a

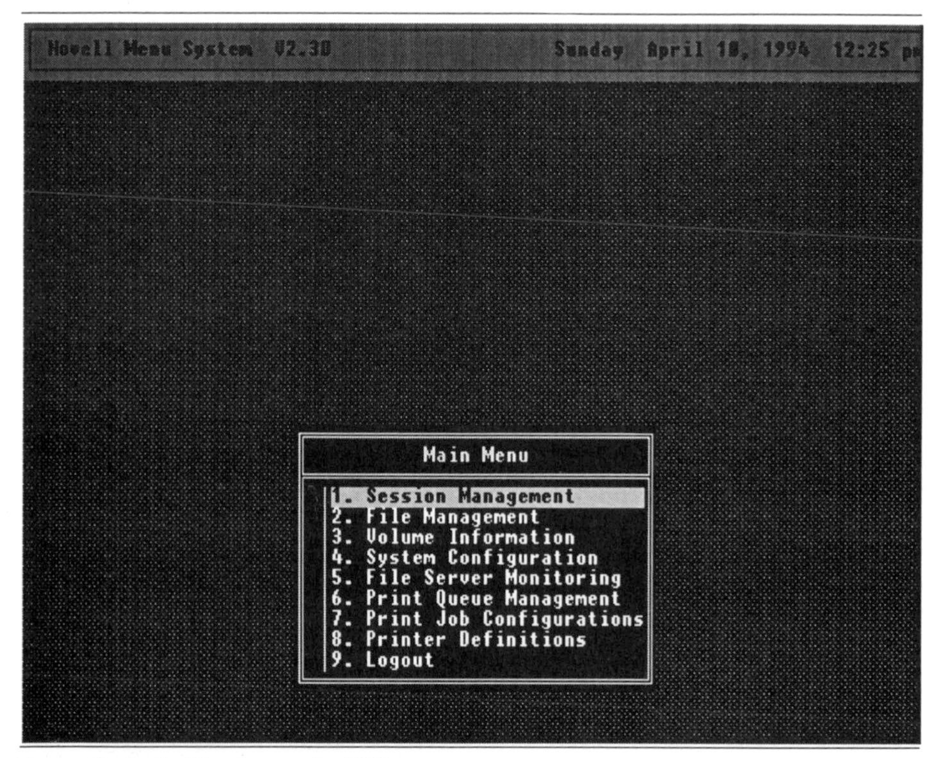

Figure 9-2. *NetWare's sample MAIN menu.*

nonalphabetical order, place the items in the list with a number preceding the menu choice.

COMMANDS—Commands are indented from the left margin and placed directly under the menu item. Any command directly under the menu selection is treated as a command unless it is preceded by a % sign.

SUBMENU—Placed under a menu selection and indented and preceded by a % sign. The indentation and % sign indicate a submenu.

Each MENU file you create must have the extension .MNU. To run the menu, type MENU and the file name, such as MENU MAIN. NetWare's sample MAIN.MNU is shown in Figure 9-2 on the previous page.

Creating Menus

The first step in creating menus is to plan them carefully. Decide which users will be using menus and tailor the menus to the users' needs. If you are using menus as a security device as well, include ALL the programs and commands that the user will need to use. Here is a list of possible menus you can create:

SUPERVISOR—The supervisor probably doesn't need a menu.

New users—Menus for new users could be vital for users who are unsure of themselves on a network.

Temporary users—You don't want them to have free reign on the network.

Groups—Consider menus for groups of users who do the same thing or are in the same department.

Individual—Individual users will probably use many of the same programs, but may also need individual attention and specific programs designed around their work.

After you decide which users or groups need menus, you need to plan the menu structure. You should group programs and other menu items in a logical order. For example, if a person in marketing also performs customer service activities, group his or her marketing activities in one part of the menu and the other activities in another. You may want to create a submenu for each.

Screen Placement

When you plan the screen placement of the menu, you must remember to leave room for submenus and user input. You can use the following formulas to determine the horizontal and vertical positions for screen placement:

> the number of menu lines divided by 2 plus the distance to top of screen = the vertical placement, or
>
> 12 / 2 + 6 = 12
>
> the number of menu columns on the screen divided by 2 plus the distance to left of the screen = the horizontal placement, or
>
> 30 / 2 + 20 = 35

These figures yield the following statement in the menu title:

%Menu Title,12,35,0 (where 0 is the color scheme)

Choosing Colors

The menu color scheme is designated in the IBM$RUN.OVL file, which all NetWare menu utilities use. You can change this scheme by using the COLORPAL utility. The default color palette is as follows:

Palette 0 is for lists, menus, and normal text.

Palette 1 is for main headers and screen backgrounds.

Palette 2 is for help screens.

Palette 3 is for error messages.

Palette 4 is for exit and alert menus.

Additional Considerations

When you are using variables, follow these rules:

1. The @ sign requests a numbered variable (numeric input) from the user.
2. Statements are typed in quotation marks following the variable. Statements will display in a box or screen.
3. The total length of any command statement is 100 characters including remarks.

Be sure to test your menus before you release them to users. A faulty menu system is frustrating. Also, be sure that the user has the appropriate rights and attributes to perform the menu items you have selected.

OTHER APPLICATIONS

Many applications are designed to be run by many network users from a single, shared copy of the application, or are truly "NetWare-aware" and take advantage of the network.

Tip
A word about software application licensing. A networked program does not mean you need to buy only one copy of the program and place it on the network for everyone to use. You must purchase enough licenses to cover each person who will be using the product. Many vendors will allow you to purchase group or network licenses that cover all your users. Applications are available that let you maintain proper application licensing.

Microsoft Windows and Windows Applications

Windows is probably the most popular application running on your network. Novell and Microsoft have teamed up to make Windows more NetWare-aware and extremely easy to set up and use on a network. Many of the additions to Windows are available on Novell's CompuServe forums, NetWire.

Tip

The Windows tools enhancements from Novell extend Windows' functionality and provide a graphical user interface (GUI) for many network functions including attaching network drives, printing, and sending network messages. These tools also provide a mechanism from within Windows to receive network broadcast messages or turn them off. The programs that accompany the NetWare Windows tools are NWUSER, NWPOPUP, and new Windows drivers. Some of the new functionality is only available when you use the VLM.EXE program in place of the NETX.EXE program. Virtual Loadable Modules (VLMs) are the new standard for v3.12 and 4.0 network redirection.

Network Setup on Windows

Microsoft Windows includes a network setup option that allows you to have a single copy of Windows that is shared by all users on the network. The majority of the files in this configuration are maintained in a common, shared directory. The files specific to an individual user, including his or her .INI and .GRP files, are maintained in the user's home directory.

Microsoft provides an administrative setup option that copies Windows to a shared directory on your server. To copy the files, first log into the network as SUPERVISOR. Then, create a subdirectory for the shared copy of Windows.

This is a good time to plan your subdirectory structure. You may want to place this subdirectory off the SYSTEM\APPS subdirectory or SYSTEM\WINAPPS subdirectory. Use the SETUP program with the /A switch to install Windows on the network. This switch copies and expands Windows files. After running SETUP /A, flag these files read-only (RO).

Tip

You can set up Windows' groups that will be used by many users. Create a group with the Windows' Program Manager, and copy the .GRP file to the common directory for Windows. Then include this group's name in the PROGMAN.INI file for each user.

Individual users should be set up using the SETUP /N or SETUP /H option. SETUP /N is the standard Windows network setup for users and should be run from the Windows shared subdirectory. SETUP /N copies WIN.COM and the users' individual files to the users' Windows' subdirectory. SETUP /H lets you create setup batch files that have an .SHH extension.

Setting up a workstation is as easy. Microsoft provides NetWare-specific files that are installed when you select the Novell Network option during installation. Although you are encouraged to use VLMs, you can still use NETX.EXE. To do this, modify the NET.CFG file as follows:

SHOW DOTS ON—Places .. and . in the Windows' directory selection boxes.

FILE HANDLES 60—Sets the number of open files allowed. The minimum for Windows is 60.

Tip

Remember that when you set up Windows with a LAN adapter that uses shared RAM, you must exclude the area of memory the adapter uses. If you are using an extended memory manager, you have probably already excluded this memory. If you are only using HIMEM.SYS, you will need to exclude the area in the 386ENH section of the SYSTEM.INI file. The syntax is

EMMEXCLUDE=D000-D3FF

This statement will work for a 16-kilobyte memory address beginning at D000 hex.

Windows for Workgroups

An enhancement to standard Windows is Microsoft's Windows for Workgroups. It allows peer-to-peer network capability that lets a user share his or her individual hard drive with others in a workgroup (department). In a peer-to-peer network, you won't normally find a server that is responsible for all file access. The redirector in the workstation will accept calls from other components on the network and make calls through the network adapter to others workstations on the network. This type of network is excellent for small groups. However, each user must have a hard drive and an individual copy of Windows for Workgroups (WFW) running on the workstation.

WFW works with Network Driver Interface Specification (NDIS) from Microsoft or with Open Data-Link Interface (ODI) LAN drivers. As a result, the package is almost seamless with NetWare. In WFW, you can have simultaneous connections to Novell and WFW, Microsoft

Windows NT, or LAN Manager servers. To make these connections, you need to run ODI drivers and connect to the NetWare LAN normally. Then, when you run WFW, your workgroup connection will operate over NDIS. This takes advantage of the multiprotocol aspects of the ODI driver.

Tip
Novell offers products similar to Windows for Workgroups called Novell DOS 7 and Personal NetWare, which accomplish the same functionality without using NetBIOS as the network transport protocol. They also offer the same seamless integration with NetWare.

Windows-based Applications

Microsoft markets a package of products called Microsoft Office. This package includes Word for Windows, Excel, Powerpoint, and Microsoft Mail. All these packages operate in a network environment and take advantage of the network printing components in Windows. Once you set up the network printer in Windows, it will handle the printing for any program that runs in Windows.

Tip
Windows' printing component does not apply to DOS applications running in a DOS compatibility box. These applications print out of their own print setups and need to be individually set up for network printing.

Most of the applications in Microsoft Office, with the exception of Mail, are network programs, but are not truly NetWare. The majority of their network functionality comes from Windows. A shared copy of each program is placed in a common directory. A setup program individualizes a copy for each user on the network. The users' .INI and other files are maintained in the users' home directories or a program subdirectory.

Tip
Make the shared copy of the programs for Microsoft Office Read-Only (RO) and grant users Read and File Scan rights unless the program requires additional rights. Do not store any of the individual users' .INI or .CFG files in the common directory. The program runs from that directory and will pick up the users' initial-

ization files from their home directories.

Many vendors have created Windows-based applications including WordPerfect Corp, Borland, Computer Associates, and Lotus Development Corp. All these applications must comply with the programming requirements of Windows, which provides a common look and set of controls for the majority of the program functions. The Windows interface also gives these programs access to the Windows enhancements for NetWare.

Windows is a very sophisticated user interface designed to give the user a way of choosing programs, controlling the various components of the computer, and resetting the workstation's environment. As such, it combines a menu system with extremely powerful DOS controls. The NetWare enhancements provide easy access to a networking environment.

DOS-based Menu Systems

There are a large number of DOS-based menuing systems, including WordPerfect Office, Saber Software's LAN Workstation, NETinc's NETMenu, and Computer Tyme's Marx Menu. One of the simplest of these menu systems and one of the most commonly used is WordPerfect Office. It combines a large number of WordPerfect Products into a common menu system that can be tailored for each user by the system manager or by the user himself. WordPerfect Office's major drawback is that it is not NetWare-aware. It depends on the system manager to create and maintain an additional user database. This database sets up the initial user environment and establishes the mail system for WordPerfect Mail.

DOS-based menuing systems are variations of the Novell MENU system. They are generally more elaborate than Novell's MENU. However, they all depend on some knowledge and ability in basic batch language programming. The more powerful the menu system becomes, the more ability it requires from the administrator. However, these menu systems can provide a very clean, efficient interface for the user. If you are willing to invest the time, you will see that your troubles are rewarded.

Mail Systems

Choosing the electronic mail (e-mail) system you'll use on the network is probably one of the single most important software choices you'll make. Mail systems can connect you with all users on the network and with the rest of the world at a fraction of the cost of conventional postage.

In 1990, Novell announced the Message Handling Service (MHS), which is compliant with the Open Systems Interconnection (OSI) X.400 mail standard. The MHS system is a store-and-forward messaging system format that is capable of sending messages to and from a variety of systems. In store-and-forward systems, messages are stored in an area on the messaging server and forwarded to their destination at a convenient time. MHS has four basic components. They are as follows:

The Directory System (DS)—Contains a complete list of names and addresses of network users. Depending on the size of the network or internetwork, this database can be large.

The Message Store (MS)—The storage area for messages that are waiting to be transferred to users.

Message Transfer Agent (MTA)—Controls message routing from the user to other MTAs on the internetwork.

User Agent (UA)—Used to create and prepare messages for routing on the network. It uses a lookup table to find the names and addresses of other users.

MHS and X.400 are the standards that Novell has chosen as its internetworking mail standard. If your mail system is compliant with MHS, you automatically have access to a central mail hub you can use to contact Novell or other MHS users. Novell is at present establishing a large internetwork of mail users based on its MHS standard. The mail package you choose for communications within your network should be capable of working with MHS or some other mail standard such as the Simple Mail Transfer Protocol (SMTP) if you want to communicate with companies that are not on your local mail system.

Whether you will communicate with outside networks, the mail package you choose should have local and internetwork capability to allow it to communicate messages to all the LANs in your company. It should also require as little administration as possible. A large variety of mail packages are available, including Microsoft Mail, WordPerfect

Mail, DaVinci E-Mail, ExpressIT, BeyondMail, and cc:Mail. The packages require you to set up a separate system for routing the messages across the network. The mail will be routed to the central system and across the network to a connected machine. The mail router may require a dedicated machine. As your network traffic grows, you may want to dedicate a machine, even if the mail package you use doesn't require it.

The other issue to consider in implementing your mail system is the username convention you will use. If your network is small enough, you may simply need to use the first name of the user as his or her mail username. Other mail packages will require a user's full name.

Tip
If your package requires a username and is not NetWare-aware, it is still a good idea to use the NetWare username when establishing the mail username. Doing so will prevent confusion for you and your users.

Packages such as Microsoft Mail are NetWare-aware and will establish a mail directory using the NetWare username. This saves administration time. For Internet messaging, the standard for usernames is to use the first initial of the first name followed by last name, up to a maximum character length of eight letters. Sometimes you will be required to use a different scheme, depending on the user's name in your system.

Tip
For instance, we know of at least three users in the same network named JOHNSON. As such we have an SJJOHNSO, RJJOHNSO, and SCJOHNSO. This naming convention is not an absolute.

Whatever naming convention you decide to use, stick with it. Your users will find it extremely easy to address mail based on user names if they have standard names to use. Some mail packages, including Microsoft Mail, have an aliasing capability that allows the user to enter the user's full name and the mail package then translates the name.

Miscellaneous Applications

Along with a menu system and mail system for your users, you will need to consider other applications such as word processors, spreadsheets, accounting packages, and database management packages. Plus, you'll want to get some programs for yourself that will help you administer the network.

In choosing a word processor, it is important for you to have a version that is NetWare-aware. If you use a standalone word processor on the network, you'll need to include the CAPTURE statement in the login script to allow your users to print. Most word processors, including Microsoft Word, WordPerfect, and AMIPro, have network versions available that recognize network printers and print appropriately on them.

The CAPTURE command captures data sent to the printer port and routes it to the network print queue. To invoke CAPTURE, simply type CAPTURE and press the Enter key. A number of options are available for CAPTURE. They are as follows:

SH (show) is used to view the file server, queue, and printer the local port is captured to.

NOTI (notify) tells you when a print job is complete.

NNOTI (no notify) stops notification if a print job has been preconfigured for notification.

A (autoendcap) sends data to the network only when the application is exited.

NA (no autoendcap) cancels a previously configured AUTOENDCAP.

TI=n (timeout) enables the time-out feature. Replace "n" with the number of seconds from 1 to 1,000 that you want to wait from when printing is initiated to the time it is sent to the queue.

S= (server) designates the server the print job is sent to.

J= (job) designates a predefined print job that has been established using PRINTDEF.

Q= (queuename) specifies the queue name to send the print job to.

F= (form) specifies a form that is defined in PRINTDEF.

C= (copies) equals the number of printed copies.

T= (tab) sets the number of TAB spaces and is used only if the application does not have a print formatter.

NT= (no tabs) is used only if the application does not have a print formatter.

NAM= (name) specifies a username that will be printed on the document's banner. The banner separates and helps identify printed jobs.

B= (bannername) replaces the username on the banner when printing.

NB= (no banner) stops the banner from printing.

FF (form feed) produces a form feed after the job has printed.

NFF (no form feed) stops a previously defined form feed in a predefined job.

CR=filename (create) sends the print job to a disk file instead of a printer.

K (keep) is used when the workstation crashes. This switch is used when the CAPTURE may take several hours. If the workstation crashes, the job is sent to the printer 15 minutes after the server no longer hears from the workstation.

Database Management Systems

Database management systems are particularly well suited for use on NetWare. Novell provides support for two database systems developed and marketed by Btrieve Technologies, Inc., called Btrieve and NetWare SQL. NetWare provides a built-in protection for databases called the Transaction Tracking System (TTS), which provides integrity for database transactions in the event that network errors occur. Databases that make use of Btrieve or NetWare SQL automatically take advantage of TTS; others may not. Btrieve is a key-indexed record manager that supports high-performance handling for several data management systems and is implemented via a NetWare Loadable Module (NLM). NetWare SQL is also a NetWare Loadable Module that provides back-end support for applications such as Lotus 1-2-3, version 3.0.

Event Control Systems

Event control systems (ECS) allow you to schedule specific jobs at times the network is not busy or to optimize network operations by using unused workstations. Task-scheduling activities may include network backups, large print jobs, or database reindexing that can take hours and slow the network down. ECSs often run as NLMs on the file server or require a dedicated workstation as an event control server and a terminate-and-stay resident (TSR) program running on the workstation. Job schedules consist of sophisticated script files that load the applications on a specified workstation, and leave the application when the job is completed. Several vendors, including Knozall and Vinzant Systems, make event control systems.

Inventory Packages

Inventory packages allow the network administrator to collect information about the hardware and software on the network. Some packages operate as NLMs on the file server and require a TSR on the workstations being audited. The inventory package can constantly monitor the network or inventory the network during off hours. It will alert the administrator to changes on the network if requested. Inventory packages are extremely valuable tools in keeping track of your current hardware inventory. Several vendors, including Symantec, Intel, Frye Computer Systems, Saber Software Corp., and Horizons Technology Inc., market software and hardware inventory packages.

Software Metering Packages

Software metering packages monitor the license requirements of the software you have purchased and lock out unauthorized use or use in excess of the number of current licenses. They generally run as NLMs on the server and may require separate TSRs on the workstation. Software metering packages such as McAfee's SiteMeter, Integrity Software's SofTrack, or Blue Lance's LAN Auditor help you maintain the software inventory and licenses and alert you to the need to purchase additional licenses.

IN CONCLUSION

Applications, when properly set up on the network, can make operations a breeze. Plan to spend most of your time supporting users, but remember that an application that is installed correctly on the network will save you time and your company money.

chapter

10 Protecting Your Data

Why Back Up?

NetWare features and utilities seem to come in groups of three. You have three levels of system fault tolerance and three types of login scripts, but only one in three network managers backs up the data on his or her LAN. The important statistic here is that nearly two thirds of the LANs are not being backed up. No protection exists for the files users create, and in the event of a disaster, countless dollars may be lost.

Backing up the network is like an insurance policy you buy against floods, fire, and earthquakes. But it is more than that. It protects against the accidental deletion of files, data corruption caused by viruses, data loss through power outages, and disk crashes.

One of the more mundane tasks you'll perform on the network, backing up the data, files, and programs on the LAN, is also one of the most important tasks you will do. You'll want to make sure that you have mechanisms in place so that you can back up your LAN every day, thus protecting your job and the livelihood of your company.

Data protection is expensive, but not as expensive as the components of your LAN and the cost of data loss. Consider having to replace and recreate all the files and applications for all the users that could be lost if something happened to the network. Imagine asking the data entry clerk to reenter all the sales orders that had been placed in the previous day, and telling customers why they hadn't received what they had ordered. Not only would this be time consuming, but revenue from customers could disappear, some data would be impossible to replace, and users might lose confidence in the network and its network manager.

Most data on the network is lost through operator error, not natural disasters such as floods, earthquakes, or even power outages caused by lightning. Users accidentally delete or copy over files they need. They erase subdirectories, make changes to files they didn't intend to, or simply can't find a file when they need it. Changes to configurations can cause application and network errors. Programs can corrupt data.

In a network, the majority of the data is located on the file server's hard disks. It is easy to protect this data. Other data that is located on users' local disk drives, on near-line storage devices, and on other file servers may be harder to replace. Backup software and hardware are available that can provide protection for all these forms of storage and all circumstances—the problem is selecting the type of data protection you need most, and deciding how much data you want to back up each day.

Storage Forms

Three types of data storage exist: online storage, near-line storage, and off-line storage. Online storage comprises the data that is instantly retrievable, used almost everyday, and stored on the file server's or workstation's hard disk. Online storage consists of data and applications you need to be most aware of backing up to off-line storage. Near-line storage consists of data that is accessible, but not as readily available as online storage. A networked CD-ROM drive that contains an encyclopedia or universal telephone directory is a common example of near-line storage. Off-line storage consists of data that is not needed immediately and often must be mounted to the network before it is available to users. Two types of off-line storage are available: backup storage via magnetic tapes, and archived data that needs to be retained for company records.

Types of Backup Media

The most common type of off-line backup storage, tape backup, is also the easiest to implement. Tape backup comes in several formats, useful for backing up different amounts of data and achieving various backup speeds. The common tape types are quarter-inch cartridge (QIC), digital audio tape (DAT), and 8-mm tape. These methods are used most often as the primary form of backup and archiving for the network's critical daily data and rarely, if ever, for near-line storage.

In addition, several forms of storage are available for near-line or off-line data storage, the data that is rarely or less frequently accessed. They are CD-ROM, optical jukeboxes, write once, read many (WORM) drives, and magneto-optical drives.

Quarter-Inch Cartridge (QIC)

Quarter-inch cartridge, developed in the 1980s by the 3M Corp., has storage capacities ranging from 20MB to 2.1GB and a data transfer rate of 30Kbps to 800Kbps. Most QIC tapes have a 10-year shelf life, provide for error-correction, and support data compression. QIC drives use a variety of interfaces to the backup computer's bus, including the machine's diskette controller, the parallel port, or higher speed SCSI controllers, which allow the attachment of multiple devices. QIC drives support several physical tape formats that are based on the size of the cartridge. The capacities vary according to the physical format.

In the QIC technology, data is written in a serpentine fashion along the length of the tape. Several tracks of data can be written.

Digital Audio Tape (DAT)

Digital audio tape (DAT) is 4 millimeters wide and fits in a tape cartridge the size of a cigarette package. DAT uses helical-scan technology, in which data is written to the tape in diagonal stripes. It supports Quick File Access (QFA), which allows the user to find data quickly, and is available in two formats: DataDAT and Digital Data Storage (DDS). The preferred type is DDS.

The interface to DAT is the SCSI bus. DAT supports storage of 1.3GB to 2GB and allows error detection and correction, as well as compression. The use of data-grade tapes in DAT systems is highly recommended.

Eight-mm Tape

Eight-millimeter tape is based on the cassettes commonly used as videocassettes. Like DAT, 8-mm tape drives use the helical-scan method of writing data to the tape. 8-mm drives support from 2.5GB to 5GB of data and QFA.

CD-ROM and Other Media Forms

Three other forms of backup exist that have nothing to do with tape and are rarely used for network backups. They are CD-ROM, a read-only technology used for near-line storage, WORM (write once, read many), and magneto-optical, which combines laser technology with magnetic recording methods. Each of these technologies is useful for storing information such as encyclopedias or other compendiums of information.

Backup Components

Backing up the network requires several components: a tape backup unit, a controller, backup software, and media to back up data to. It also requires a plan. A wide variety of vendors make tape backup devices, using Adaptec or Bustek controllers most commonly. To allow communication between the tape backup device and the network, each controller also ships with an adapter, which facilitates communications.

Tape backup devices range in capacity from 20MB to 5GB of storage.

NetWare Requirements

In NetWare, it is critical to back up other data than just the data applications generate. The backup software you choose needs to be able to back up the NetWare bindery, which contains the users' rights and attributes, information on the other devices on the network, and the NetWare directory structure, which defines the organization of the server's hard disk. Some backup systems are capable of backing up all the file servers on an internetwork and the users' local disk drives, if desired.

One of the most important requirements of a backup system is that it not only back up data, but also that it can correctly restore the data you back up. The software will need to accommodate files that are open and being used when the network is backed up, and be capable of backing up all the network data or just incremental quantities of the data. If data is not backed up or if problems occur, you will need reporting capabilities to alert you. You'll need to look at the software's ability to compress data if you need to save space, the time the software takes to restore data or single files, and the speed of the backup unit. If you manage an internetwork, you'll need to buy software that will allow you to back up data over bridges or routers.

In planning your backup needs, you need to decide how much data you'll need to back up each day. You may have time to back up all the network data, or only the data that has changed. A number of rotation schedules are available for backing up data and ensuring that all data is backed up on a regular basis.

You'll also want to make sure that the backup software you choose will back up all the NetWare files, and not just DOS files, but OS/2, Macintosh, and UNIX files as well. When you purchase software, make sure that it supports these name spaces.

Because you don't want to have to sit and watch the network being backed up, you'll want to automate the backup process. Tape changers and autoloaders are available that will back up a larger network.

These are some other decisions you will need to make when you purchase the tape backup unit for your network:

1. Where will you locate the tape backup device? Will it attach directly to the media, to the file server, or to a dedicated workstation?
2. Will you need to back up data from database servers or specialized servers?
3. Can you restore files on a file-by-file basis? Or does the software only perform an imaging backup?
4. Does the tape backup unit support the data capacity you need?
5. Can you automate the process so that you don't need to be there to change tapes when one tape fills and another one is needed?
6. What type of error handling do the device and software have?
7. Is the software easy to use? Software that is difficult to learn and use will discourage regular use.
8. Does the software have security features that allow only the supervisor or other specified person to back up the network?
9. Does the software support unattended backups?
10. Is the vendor reliable? Does the vendor have a responsive technical support department? What hours for telephone support does

the vendor support staff offer? Does the company have a bulletin board system (BBS)?

The Backup Schedule

In many small LANs, it is possible to back up all the LAN's data and applications when users are not using the LAN. In circumstances where a sufficient backup window does not exist, you will want to consider partial, or incremental, backups of network data. For example, on Monday through Friday, you may want to back up only the data that changed that day, and do a complete backup of all data and applications on Saturday night. Or, you may want only to back up data and the configuration files created by the applications on a regular basis. If lost, the applications may be restored from their original diskettes.

How large is your window of opportunity for backing up data? Here are some questions you'll need to ask:

1. What time do most of the users log out of the network?
2. What time do most of the users log into the network?
3. Is there any range of time when all users are logged off the network?
4. Do you have employees that work after normal business hours?

Once you've determined these factors, you'll need to decide how much data should be backed up each day. If you decide to back up the entire server disk, the amount of data is equivalent to the amount of space used on the disk in all the volumes. If you decide that you want to do incremental backups, you can determine the volume of files that have been created or modified during that day.

Tip

If you have organized your directories so that data and applications are in separate directories, the server will be easier to back up. You can back up the data daily, and the applications less frequently.

A variety of methods exist for rotating the tapes you use in a daily backup. The most common are Grandfather-Father-Son (GFS) and the Tower of Hanoi. In the GFS method, which is used for incremental or full backups, you will have a total of 20 tapes. For each workday,

Monday through Thursday, you will use a different tape. On Friday, you will use a weekly tape. Each month you'll use a monthly tape. Here's how it works:

Monday	Daily tape	
Tuesday	Daily tape	
Wednesday	Daily tape	
Thursday	Daily tape	
Friday	Weekly tape	Monthly tape

In each year, there are 52 weeks, or 13 four-week intervals. You will use a weekly tape for the first three weeks of each four-week interval, and a monthly tape for the fourth week in the interval.

The Tower of Hanoi method uses each tape set a varying number of times. For example, tape set 1, consisting of a tape each for Monday through Friday, will be used every other week. Tape set 2, also consisting of five daily tapes, will be used every 4 weeks. Tape set 3 will be used every 8 weeks, and so on. Week by week, you will use these tape sets:

Tape set 1 = every other week
Tape set 2 = every 4 weeks
Tape set 3 = every 8 weeks
Tape set 4 = every 16 weeks
Tape set 5 = every 32 weeks (5 is the new tape set)

Week 1	Set 1
Week 2	Set 2
Week 3	Set 1
Week 4	Set 3
Week 5	Set 1
Week 6	Set 2
Week 7	Set 1
Week 8	Set 4
Week 9	Set 1
Week 10	Set 2
Week 11	Set 1
Week 12	Set 3
Week 13	Set 1
Week 14	Set 2
Week 15	Set 1
Week 16	Set 5

Week 17	Set 1
Week 18	Set 2
Week 19	Set 1
Week 20	Set 3
Week 21	Set 1
Week 22	Set 2
Week 23	Set 1
Week 24	Set 4
Week 25	Set 1
Week 26	Set 2
Week 27	Set 1
Week 28	Set 3
Week 29	Set 1
Week 30	Set 2
Week 31	Set 1
Week 32	Set 6 (a new tape set)

Tip

Remember to label all your tape sets clearly.

Backup Performance and Placement

A number of factors influence backup speed. They are the placement of the backup device, the type of file server or workstation you use, the type of network media installed, and the verification made on data written to the backup system.

Performance Considerations

In choosing the speed of the backup process, you need to consider some of the following things. You may not be able to change some of these factors in your setup, but each factor contributes to network backup speed.

1. The backup machine's CPU and bus type. The faster the CPU and bus used as a backup workstation or server, the faster the backup.

2. Traditionally, slow access methods such as ARCNET at 2.5Mbps can hamper speedy backups. Many networks use ARCNET or Ethernet for normal network communications and add a high-speed access method such as FDDI or one of the high-speed proprietary methods between the file server and the backup workstation.
3. The media the network uses can hinder the network's backup ability. Twisted-pair media is susceptible to electromagnetic interference and will perform more slowly than fiber-optic media, which is immune to electromagnetic interference. Fiber-optic media also supports higher speed access methods such as FDDI.
4. The amount of traffic on the network at the time you are trying to back up the network will directly impact the backup performance. Open files or applications or servers that are being used after hours hamper successful, complete, and efficient backups.
5. In a situation where the data being backed up must travel from the file server to a separate, workstation-based backup device, the size of the data packet transmitted will affect performance. An access method that supports a larger packet size will be more efficient than one that supports only small packet sizes.
6. The amount of error correction the backup software and hardware perform affects backup performance.
7. If the backup software is capable of compressing data for transmission to the backup device, performance increases. In like fashion, the caching and buffering capability of the software affects performance.
8. If your backup device supports QFA, files can be retrieved faster.
9. Using software options that verify data written to tape and compare the data to the original data sent can decrease performance, although these options increase data integrity.

Positioning the Backup System

The location of the backup device on the network will depend on a number of factors, including network speed, availability of the file server to back up the network, and the number of file servers and amount of data you need to back up.

Network backup can take place on a workstation attached to the file server, on the file server itself, or on a backup device such as Intel's StorageExpress that attaches directly to the network media.

File Server-based Backup

File server-based backup, while faster than workstation backup because the data doesn't need to travel across the wire to be backed up, also may tax an otherwise busy file server. File server-based backup systems offer higher security than workstation-based backups because the file server is located in a secure area. If your internetwork has two file servers, you can increase backup performance by placing the backup device on the backbone between the servers.

Workstation-based Backup

In workstation-based backup, the process may be slowed by the access method the network uses. At least one vendor, Thomas-Conrad, offers a high-speed solution called TCNS that allows you to create a separate backbone between the file server and the workstation that functions as the backup server. Workstation-based backup can pose a security threat to the rest of the network if it is left unattended during the backup process.

Directly Attached Network Backup

Backup devices, like print servers, can be attached directly to the network media without an intervening file server or workstation. The most predominant implementation, integrated with Novell's Network Management System, is Intel's StorageExpress. Devices such as these save the cost of a dedicated workstation.

BACKUP STANDARDS

In 1993, Novell developed its specification for storage on NetWare LANs. Called *Storage Management Services (SMS)*, the specification aims to ensure compatibility between different backup devices and software, as well as provide backup capability to client workstations of any type. SMS is independent of NetWare changes. It consists of several parts: the Storage Management Engine (SME), the Storage Management Database Engine (SMDE), the Storage Device Interface (SDI), the Storage Management Data Requestor (SMDR), and the Target Service Agent (TSA).

The Storage Management Engine is the vendor-supplied software that provides backup capability. It is linked to the Storage Management Database Engine, which contains information about the data to be backed up or archived. The SDI sits between the SME and the backup unit's driver and allows data to be transmitted between the two devices. The SMDR allows the TSA to communicate with the SME and the SDI. Each device to be backed up, including the file server, loads a TSA and the SMDR. The TSAs allow communication with the file systems, their applications, and files a user is backing up. (See Figure 10-1.)

4.x

NetWare 4.x supports optical disk jukeboxes via the High Capacity Storage System (HCSS). HCSS is used for archiving seldom-used files. When a file is saved to an optical drive, it is called *migration*. When the file is recalled from the drive, *demigration* occurs.

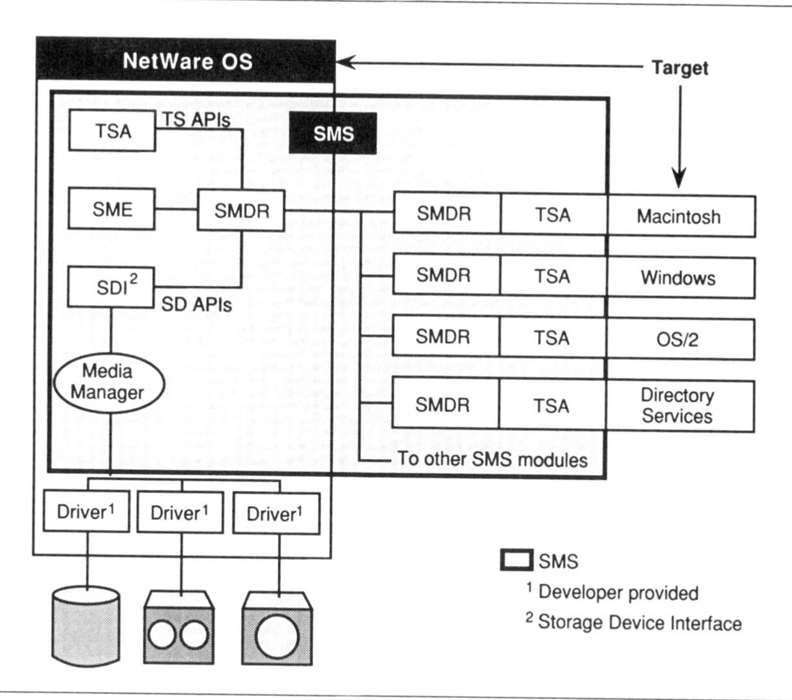

Figure 10-1. *NetWare's SMS architecture. Figure adapted from graph by Shane Weaver in "SMS Compliance," Jim Spicer, NetWare Solutions, March 1994.*

NetWare Backup Utilities

While we recommend that you spend money on specialized tape backup software because of its added functionality, Novell provides two utilities that allow you to back up data. They are NBACKUP and SBACKUP.

2.x

NetWare v2.x networks can use NBACKUP to back up the NetWare bindery and the file server. NBACKUP provides an unattended mode and only backs up DOS or Macintosh files to DOS-only devices.

Tip

NBACKUP will not back up v2.2 hidden and system files.

3.x

NetWare v3.x uses SBACKUP, a NetWare Loadable Module (NLM), for backing up the file server and NetWare bindery from a workstation to a device attached directly to the file server. SBACKUP backs up DOS and OS/2 files. SBACKUP uses a strategy of a host and its targets. The host, a NetWare file server, initiates the backup and orders the backup of the target service agents (TSAs)—other file servers. The files operating on the host are the SBACKUP NLM, a requester called SIDR.NLM, and the device driver for the backup interface, called the driver.NLM, in which the driver name is the name the interface vendor supplies. The target modules include the TSA NLM and the TSA-311.NLM.

You use NBACKUP to back up data on the file server and workstation local drives to DOS-based tape drives, floppy disk drives, or optical drives attached to a workstation. To back up the file server, the user must be the supervisor or have supervisor-equivalence. NBACKUP is located in the SYS:PUBLIC directory, from which users can easily access it. To back up local drives, a user must have File Scan and Read rights.

Tip

The tape sets you use in SBACKUP are not interchangeable with NBACKUP tapes.

4.x

NetWare 4.x uses SBACKUP to back up both file servers and workstations. It supports QIC, DDS DAT, and 8-mm tape drives and will back up DOS, OS/2, Macintosh, Sun Microsystem's Network File System (NFS), and the Open Systems Interconnect's FTAM.

Tape Care

Part of ensuring backup integrity is continual care for the media you use. If you take care of your network backup system as you do the file server, you'll have data available when a disaster occurs. The following list details the essentials of tape care.

1. Clean the tape drive you use regularly with a special cleaning kit made for tape drives. Do not use cotton swabs or cotton balls—they leave small fibers on the tape that may interfere with writing data.
2. Use a clearly defined rotation method and stick with it. Introduce new tapes on a regular basis and rotate out old tapes.
3. Store the tapes you use in a fireproof, secure area. Fireproof file cabinets are not adequate—the heat from a fire is enough to destroy tapes. Hire a courier service to pick up tape sets daily.
4. Retension the tapes you use regularly. Like audio tapes, backup tapes become loose. To retension them, place a pencil in one of the gears and turn to tighten.
5. Test your backup and restore procedure regularly.
6. Check your tape log daily to make sure that all the data was backed up on schedule.

chapter 11

NETWORK SECURITY

HOW IT WORKS

WHAT IS SECURITY AND WHY DO I NEED IT?

Most of us would agree that leaving our offices without locking a filing cabinet full of customer files is unthinkable. Yet we leave a computer system full of the same files completely unprotected when we leave the office for the day. In fact, it is much easier to leave your office with a diskette full of files tucked in a shirt pocket than it is to leave with any hard copy of the same information. Just ask anyone who has taken files home at night to work on them.

Many data files become lost or corrupted, though, not by intentional espionage, but by thoughtless, although unintentional acts. Users make changes that can affect the way your network runs. People can get into files that aren't theirs.

Protecting and securing the data on your LAN is of paramount performance. Security for the LAN falls into three categories: hardware security, file-level security, and network security. File-level and network security generally involve assigning attributes to a file that don't allow it to be modified or deleted, using password protection that keeps files from snooping eyes, and restricting user accounts to keep users from data that isn't theirs. In addition to watching these areas where security breaches can occur, you'll need to adopt measures to keep your computer safe from computer viruses and protected from environmental factors such as dust or moisture that can destroy data.

HARDWARE SECURITY

Keeping your network secure begins with making sure that the network (file server, workstations, and other devices) stays where it is supposed to and also that the information contained in the system can be used as it should be. The level of security you choose to implement will depend entirely on your needs and those of your users. You may want to lock up payroll information on a separate file server or at least in a separate directory, so no one except accounting personnel can get to it. Alternately, you may choose to leave a group scheduling package unprotected so that everyone can modify it, scheduling and rescheduling meetings as they please.

When choosing the level of security you have on your LAN, keep three concerns in mind. First, the file server needs its own special security measures. Second, the workstations and other devices such as printers need to be secured. Finally, the network cabling and some other safety factors will need to be watched in some networks.

Keep Your Server Secure

The file server, with the exception of some NetWare Lite and Personal NetWare installations, is the heart of your network. The file server is the repository of most of your applications, data, and network files. Keeping the file server and related backup equipment free from both intentional and unintentional physical harm should be your primary concern. Someone tampering with the server or accidentally spilling coffee on the motherboard can cause as much damage as taking a drill to the file server or hauling it away.

Basic file security calls for placing the server in an area where you can control access. This may be a separate locked room to which only you have a key, or may be a section of your office (with a door you can lock when you leave). A secured file server does not always require a room to itself if it is off the traffic path and safe from a janitor unplugging the power cord to vacuum or from someone's child playing with the ON/OFF switch. You may assume you know the characteristics of the people you work with, but you'll be better off if you don't leave anything to chance. You risk other people's data, which is expensive to replace.

The file server should also be secured when no one is there to watch it. If you do place it in a room by itself, be sure that you have adequate ventilation for the computer and that the room is relatively dust-free. The heat the file server generates probably will require additional air conditioning, especially if the file server is placed in a small room. If you plan to keep your system in an open environment, be sure to secure the system to an object or furniture that is not easily moved, and consider removing the monitor and locking the keyboard when you are not using them. You might also consider removing the keyboard and display permanently and controlling the server remotely via NetWare's RCONSOLE utility.

One of the best ways to implement file server security, however, is via means inherent in Novell NetWare. These mechanisms are disk mirroring, disk duplexing, and NetWare System Fault Tolerance Level III (SFT Level III), which ensure different degrees of fault tolerance. In disk mirroring you duplicate disk drives (or mirror them) within the file server so that data written to one disk drive is duplicated on the second disk drive. Mirrored disks share the same disk channel (including the disk controller) though, so if a problem occurs with the disk controller or another part of the disk channel, the problem will manifest itself on both disk drives.

Tip

Calculate what a day of down-time will cost your company. If the cost of the down-time is more than adding disk mirroring to your network, then you know what you should do.

Disk duplexing, on the other hand, doubles not only the disk drives, but the entire disk channel as well. This ensures that information will have every chance of being duplicated from one disk to another except during a disaster that affects the file server as a whole.

Novell's newest technology, SFT Level III, solves the limitations of mirroring and duplexing by duplicating data across two file servers. The two servers operate together with all memory and disk access mirrored from one server to the other via a high-speed data link connecting the two computers. This hardware/software link consists of cabling that joins a special LAN adapter in each machine. In SFT Level III, disk drives and LAN adapters are mirrored between the two systems. If one server goes down, the other will take over automatically. With SFT Level III, your system is protected from any single hardware failure or malicious act. (See Figure 11-1 on the next page.)

SFT Level III is a more expensive option than duplexing and mirroring, but it does allow for complete recovery if a disaster strikes that disables only one file server. When you plan for an SFT Level III file server

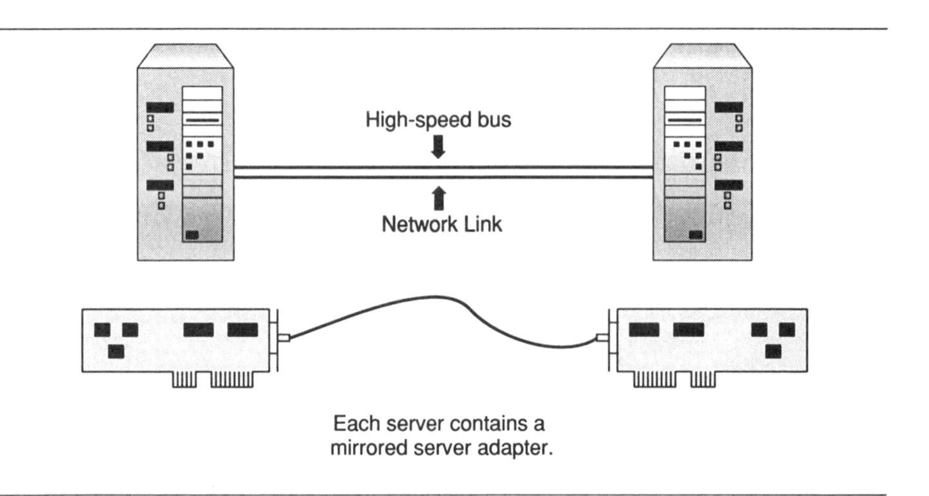

Figure 11-1. *SFT III.*

system, locate the file servers at a distance from each other—at the very least, in separate rooms and on separate power systems. If possible, locate the systems as far away from each other as the media and adapters will allow. The minimum configuration for SFT Level III is a 386- or 486-based workstation with 12MB of RAM.

Tip

NEVER locate SFT Level III servers together or on the same power system. By doing so you eliminate many of the features of the fault-tolerant system.

Personal NetWare

NetWare Lite and Personal NetWare users should remember that you are now working on a peer-to-peer network. As such, you no longer have a single file server or a workstation that holds all the important applications and data you'll need. The data and applications are spread among the workstations that serve as Desktop Servers. This makes your security problems closer to those of standalone workstations. You should be sure to protect the individual machines as much as possible. Find a reliable company that sells lock-down security devices for all of your hardware. To do so, try to limit the machines that will act as servers to only those where access control can be maintained and information can be backed up. Don't make the machine in the lobby or in other areas accessible to the public a server on which you store confidential data and applications. Keep data you want to protect on machines that can be locked in offices. This way, even if no other network safeguards are in effect, no one will be able to access the data directly from the server nor obtain it across the network unless authorized.

Be Wary of Your Workstations

Workstation hardware security is a more difficult matter than file server security. By definition, workstations must be located where people can access them. Further, with the advent of notebook computers that can be easily moved, hardware-based security problems can exist. Many devices on the market will secure both standard PCs and notebook computers to the user's desktop and yet allow them to be moved easily when necessary. If your company is lucky enough to have a full-time security team in its reception area, implement a policy that no machines leave the office unless security personnel sign them out at the front desk.

File, Application and Directory Control

Another area of workstation security is the control of files and applications that can be copied to or from the network. This area has implications for virus protection as well as for software licensing. Users who have hard disks and standard disk drives can introduce unknown software or viruses to the network simply by copying information onto the network or taking information off. They also can copy licensed software and important data from the network, a violation of your software licensing agreement that you'll want to avoid.

One of the best protections for the problem of data moving on and off the network is to remove the drives from the workstation and boot the machine directly from the network. By placing a chip called a *boot ROM* on the network interface adapter, you can boot the machine directly from the network. (See Figure 11-2 on the next page.) The ROM will initialize the adapter and send a request to the network to send the files required for booting the computer and logging it onto the network without the intervention of a diskette drive. The disadvantages of boot

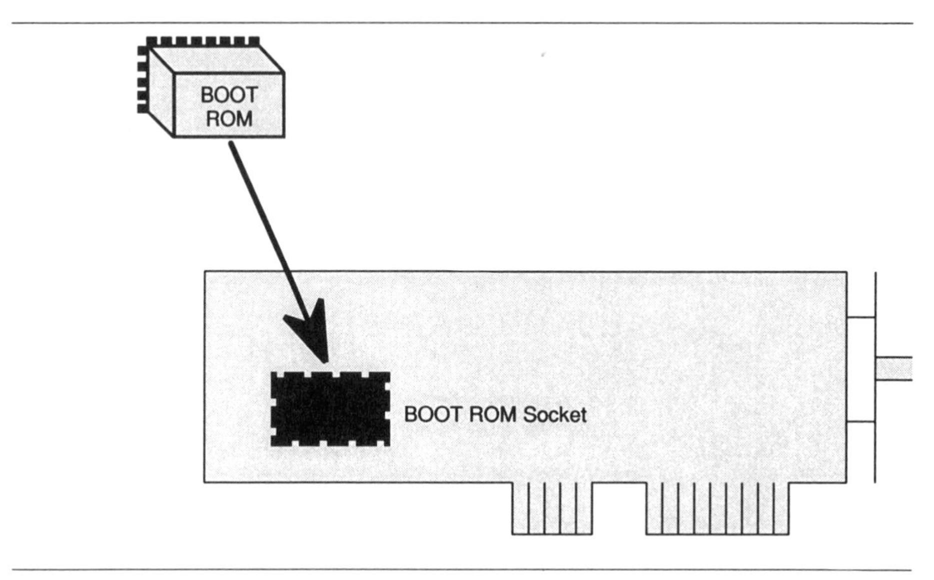

Figure 11-2. *A boot ROM in position.*

ROMs and diskless workstations are that if the file server is not available, the workstation isn't, and if Novell changes NetWare, you'll most likely need a new boot ROM.

By eliminating the drives from the workstation, you prevent the user from copying files to and from the network and you secure the network from many forms of tampering. Boot ROMs, which cost about $40 each, can save money by reducing your cost for diskette drives.

For more information on implementing boot ROMs and the advantages and disadvantages of doing so, refer to Chapter 6, What about Workstations?

Cable Security

In areas where high security is essential, the network manager must also be conscious of cable security. For the majority of networks this is not an issue because cable tampering is more difficult than entry through the server or workstation. However, remember that all activity on the network travels on the cable and that means can be employed, especially in non–fiber-optic networks, that can breach network security. Someone with access to the cable itself; and the network connections hardware such as hubs, concentrators, and multistation access units (MAUs); or the termination points such as the terminators on an Ethernet network, can easily capture data directly off the wire by adding a workstation or other device.

If you feel you need to be concerned with cable security, you can take a few steps to guard against this problem. First, secure all connecting hardware such as hubs and concentrators in areas where you have access control. It is generally best to conceal these devices in wiring or other locked closets. Make sure that all cable runs are installed where necessary in conduit or within the walls. Finally, do not add cable drops where you don't need them. At best, screw the connectors and cables securely to the machine. If you get really serious about network security, high-end cable monitors are available to alert you of cable breaks.

Software Security Measures

Some software alternatives exist to help you maintain the hardware security of your network. NetWare provides the MONITOR utility that lets you lock and password-protect the file server's console to protect it. For file servers that are left in the open, this is an excellent alternative.

Workstation screen blankers with NetWare password protection also are available from vendors such as Citadel Systems. Some token-ring, Ethernet, and ARCNET management packages will monitor the network for unauthorized nodes and alert the network manager if one exists. Finally, packages exist that will monitor the actual network, inventory the hardware on the network, and notify the administrator of changes. These packages can be helpful in detecting unauthorized nodes on the network and configuration changes.

The best protection for the workstation, however, is to insist that people log off the network when they leave their desks, and if that is not possible, always to log off at the end of the day.

NetWare Security

Once you are sure that your physical network is secure, you must begin to consider the security aspects of your network file system. The level of security you require will depend on your individual circumstances. Network security generally takes the form of account and attribute restrictions on files and directories. You will also need to be concerned with virus protection. NetWare Lite has some special security considerations that will be discussed in this section as well.

Usernames and Password Security

Before a user can attach to the network, that person must have an account. The network account consists of an entry placed in a database, called the NetWare *bindery* under NetWare v2.x and v3.x, that holds information about the user including the user's password, file and directory permissions, and network restrictions. NetWare identifies the user account with a name (called the *username*) the system administrator assigns to identify the user to the network.

When a user wants to use the network, he or she logs on using the assigned username and a password, if required. NetWare looks up the name in the NetWare bindery. If the username is present, the user is granted access to the network based on the profile information that accompanies the account and that is assigned when the account is created. If the username is not in the database or if the password the user enters is not correct, he or she is not granted access to the network. After several unsuccessful attempts to access the network, the user may be locked out for a period of time. This is called *intruder detection*. We'll talk more about it later.

In NetWare v3.x the password is sent across the media in encrypted, rather than clear-text, fashion.

Supervisory Access

When you first install NetWare, it creates two accounts automatically—the SUPERVISOR and GUEST accounts. You are the supervisor of the LAN. The SUPERVISOR account controls the entire network and has the following characteristics:

1. It can never be deleted.
2. It has all rights to all directories.
3. It can create and delete all user accounts except for the SUPERVISOR account.

4. It can create and delete all groups. Groups are collections of users controlled by a group account used to provide access to applications all users will use in common.
5. It can create and delete workgroup managers. Workgroup managers manage groups of people with common skills, such as all the personnel in the Marketing Department.
6. It can create and delete print queues.
7. It can assign console operators. Console operators have access to the file server console to view or perform maintenance operations on the server.
8. It can create and modify the system login script. The system login script controls the users' process of logging into the network, automatically creating paths to network drives and access to print queues. (For help modifying the system login script, use the LAN Compass in the back of this book.)
9. It can create default user account restrictions that limit and control users' access to the network.
10. It can set intruder detection parameters, which help prevent intrusion on network resources.

When NetWare creates the SUPERVISOR account, the account initially has no password. One of the first things you should do, which many users forget, is set the SUPERVISOR password with the NetWare menu utility SYSCON or with SETPASS, which runs from the DOS command line.

Tip
If you forget the supervisor password, utilities are available that can change it for you.

Tip
You should create at least one other user with the same security equivalence as the supervisor. These users are called *supervisor-equivalents*. This account should have a username that an intruder may think is an actual user but that does not make it stand out. Bob is a good name if there are no Bobs on your network. Whatever you do, don't name the supervisor-equivalent something obvious like Super. We know people who do; playing on their networks is always fun.

Supervisor-equivalents also may be actual users who help manage the network. If nothing else, one supervisor-equivalent account will create a back door if the SUPERVISOR account is disabled for some reason, locked out by intruder detection, corrupted by a virus, or if the password is forgotten or compromised.

4.x

In NetWare 4.x, the SUPERVISOR account is called ADMIN. Also in 4.x, you can delete the ADMIN account. Don't.

Tip

To ensure security, create a separate account with normal user rights that you'll use when you need to work on network applications.

The other user NetWare creates during installation is GUEST. This account is generally designed for printing or for visitors to the network who need LAN privileges. If a user is logged into another server in the network and attempts to use a print queue assigned to a server he or she doesn't have an account on, the CAPTURE or NPRINT commands will attempt to log in that user as GUEST. The GUEST account has the same network privileges as members of the group EVERYONE, which means that it has access to everything the group EVERYONE has. At a minimum, these are the SYS:PUBLIC and SYS:MAIL directories, which contain NetWare utility programs, users' e-mail files, and print queue information. If you do not want the GUEST account to have access to this information, simply delete GUEST from the group EVERYONE. If you still want user accounts to have printer access, add the user GUEST as a queue user with the NetWare command-line utility PCONSOLE, and limit access to the SYS:PUBLIC and SYS:MAIL directories.

Personal NetWare

For NetWare Lite and Personal NetWare users, the SUPERVISOR is the only account NetWare creates at installation time. The SUPERVISOR account should be protected, and one or two other users should be given privileges similar to the SUPERVISOR. This action will provide a convenient back door to the network if needed.

Creating Users

Virtually only the supervisor or supervisor-equivalent can create or delete users. For a person to use the network, he or she must have a user account. Users can be created with the following NetWare utilities:

1. SYSCON
2. MAKEUSER
3. USERDEF

SYSCON is a menu-driven utility that allows the supervisor or supervisor-equivalent to create and delete user accounts, assign rights, and apply restrictions to various user accounts. A user can use SYSCON to change his or her password, modify his or her login script, or view account restrictions. SYSCON is used most often to change existing accounts, create a single account, assign additional file and directory rights, and make trustee assignments.

MAKEUSER, a menu-driven utility that runs from the DOS command line, is designed to allow the supervisor or supervisor-equivalent to create users and login scripts in bulk. The supervisor creates an ASCII script file within MAKEUSER that contains instructions to NetWare that will create user accounts. Using this utility saves the tedious task of creating individual users and assigning the trustee rights separately to each user. Instructions on MAKEUSER are included in the NetWare documentation. If you are creating numerous users that have the same account restrictions and file and directory access, use MAKEUSER.

USERDEF is similar to MAKEUSER in allowing the supervisor to create user accounts in bulk. It differs from MAKEUSER in allowing you to assign disk space limitations to multiple users and create print job configurations for new users.

Regardless of the method you use to create users, the result is a group of accounts with specific rights and restrictions that enforce many network security options. These options include the password requirements such as a minimum length, trustee assignments and associated rights, and account restrictions. Only the supervisor or a user with equivalent rights can change the assignments and restrictions once they are in place.

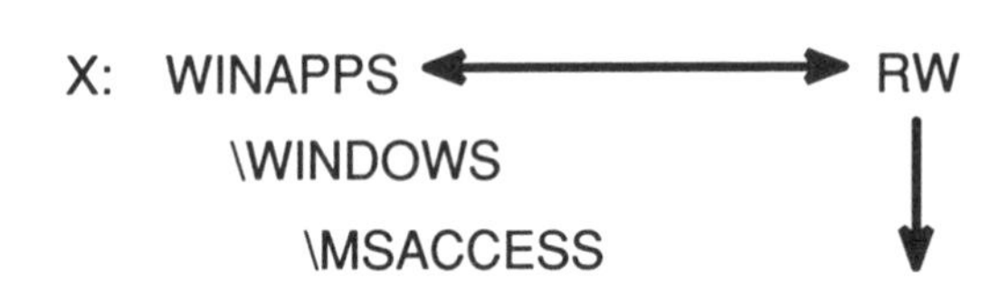

Figure 11-3. *Inheritance characteristics of NetWare LANs.*

Personal NetWare

In NetWare Lite, the NET.EXE utility lets you create users. This all-inclusive, menu-driven utility allows those users with supervisor privileges to create users and assign directories and print queues. The real security in NetWare Lite is the restrictions on directory access. When you first install NetWare Lite, you must decide which directories will be shared and which directories will be private. Remember that by sharing a directory you also share ALL subdirectories under it. Rights in NetWare flow down the directory tree. For example, if a user has access to the directory WINAPPS, he or she will also have access to all the subdirectories under WINAPPS, such as WINDOWS and MSACCESS. (See Figure 11-3.)

Once a directory has been made shareable, the supervisor may grant full or read-only rights to the directory. Therefore, care should be taken to assign rights to only those directories that need to be shared. Subdirectories that contain applications should be granted read only rights to all but the supervisor and the owner of the machine. (Those two users should have full access.) Full rights should also only be granted to subdirectories where the user must write data. In a well-organized LAN, applications are kept in a directory separate from the data directories if possible. If corruption occurs on the file server, you may need only to restore data files from backup tapes or to copy executable program files from the original diskettes to recover the data you've lost.

Personal NetWare

Personal NetWare uses the menu-based utility NET ADMIN to create users and assign directories and print queues. Only the supervisor or the owner of the machine will have the right to use many of the features of this utility. As with NetWare Lite, care must be taken when assigning shared directories and granting rights to users in those directories. The first level of security is the decision to share a directory with the other users on a network. By sharing a directory, you also share all subdirectories under it. This means that if you decide to share the ROOT directory (C:\), you will share your entire machine with the rest of the network.

You may want to grant full or read-only (RO) rights to directories users need to access. As with NetWare Lite, you should take care to separate applications and data and to assign cautiously the rights to individual users of the Desktop servers. You should grant full rights only to those subdirectories to which the user must write data.

Tip
For NetWare Lite and Personal NetWare users, NEVER share the ROOT directory with the rest of the users on the network. This will grant access to all the subdirectories on your machine, including your DOS directory. Remember that you have a file server; create the directory structure on your machine so that it is easy for all users to use. This will mean that you create subdirectory names that users will recognize. Create an application's subdirectory off the root of the drive. Place only those applications you want to share with other users.

Group Accounts

Instead of managing a number of individual users who share similar application use, the supervisor can create and manage a large number of users by creating a group. Individual users are then assigned to the group. Users can be members of multiple groups, and any number of users can be in any group. The supervisor can then change directory assignments for the group and change the assignments for all the individual users within that group in one step rather than many.

The group EVERYONE is automatically created when NetWare is installed. As we said, this group grants directory rights to the SYS:PUBLIC and SYS:MAIL directories. You can create additional groups through SYSCON. For example, you may want to have a group for every user who uses Microsoft Word (call it MSWORD) and another group for every user who uses Lotus 1-2-3 (call it LOTUS). To create a group, select Group Information from the main SYSCON menu. Press the Insert key and type the name of the new group. Then, using SYSCON, you can assign users to the group, add Trustee Assignments, and assign rights. Managing just one or several groups instead of individual users will make your job easier.

Workgroup Managers

Obviously, managing a large network is more than enough work for one person. To alleviate this problem, Novell created the concept of workgroups and workgroup managers. The supervisor creates a workgroup manager with SYSCON. Then the workgroup manager can handle the management of users within his or her designated workgroup. Typically, when the supervisor creates a workgroup, he or she will also assign a specific volume or directory to the workgroup and give the workgroup manager all rights, including access control, to the directory or volume.

The workgroup manager has limited rights in SYSCON, MAKEUSER, and USERDEF to create, delete, and manage user accounts assigned to him or her.

In NetWare, user account managers can also be created to manage groups and perform a limited set of functions for users, such as changing passwords.

Personal NetWare

Personal NetWare also allows you to create workgroups. In workgroup management, the supervisor creates workgroup managers, or users who may act as supervisor for a group of users that share similar applications. If the supervisor creates several workgroups within an organization that use a number of Personal NetWare Desktop Servers, then he or she should assign a workgroup manager for each of the workgroups. These managers will be responsible for setting up individual users within the workgroup and assigning shared directories and print queues to those users.

Security Equivalence

When a user account is created, it has the security equivalence of the group EVERYONE. When you add a user to a group, the user gains the security equivalence of the group you add it to. This means that the

Equivalence is one way

A=B	Just Because	It doesn't mean
B≠A	A=B	B=A
A=B		
B=C	A=B and B=C	C=A
C≠A		

Figure 11-4. *Equivalence is one way.*

user has the same directory rights as the group. You can also grant the security equivalence of individual users to the group.

Equivalence is unidirectional. If user A is granted the equivalence of user B, then user B does NOT necessarily have the equivalence of user A. Also, the equivalence is only single-depth. Thus, if user A is equivalent to user B and user C is made equivalent to user B, it does not necessarily follow that user C is equivalent to user A. This prevents a group from obtaining supervisor-equivalency. (See Figure 11-4.)

Passwords

The NetWare password is the first level of network security most users encounter. It is also the most important and most abused feature of NetWare. Each user should have a unique password that he or she is required to change on a regular basis. Password restrictions are added by using the SYSCON utility. From SYSCON the supervisor can:

1. Force password use.
2. Require a minimum password length of 1–20 characters (the default is 5).
3. Allow the user to change passwords.
4. Force periodic password changes.
5. Require that a user's password is unique from the previous eight passwords used.

NetWare passwords can range from 1 to 127 characters in length. The problem with most passwords is that the user will use something familiar to avoid forgetting the password. This is not a good idea, because if you can remember it, it is likely that one of your co-workers can guess it. You should encourage your users never to use their spouse's names, street address, children's names, birthdate, or first, last, or middle name.

Tip

People have a penchant for passwords that are familiar but that they think are unique and unknown. This can yield surprising results. For instance, as a big George Lucas fan, I used a password I thought was unguessable. Our IS technician discovered in about 10 seconds when she needed to get into my mail one day. The password was THX1138. There are packages on the market to generate random nonsense passwords. If you are wise, you'll use them.

Require your users to maintain their own passwords, but require them to change their passwords at least once per month. Further, require a minimum password length of at least five characters. This is the default for NetWare passwords and is also just about the maximum length any user can remember on a regular basis. Five characters for your passwords will still provide effective security if administered correctly.

If you have multiple servers on your network, NetWare will allow you to synchronize the passwords between the servers. This is generally a good idea as it will facilitate the login process and require the user to enter only a single password to gain entry to the network.

Tip

If you are combining NetWare v3.x servers with NetWare v2.x servers, you must add the following line to the AUTOEXEC.NCF file on the v3.x server: "SET UNENCRYPTED PASSWORDS = ON." This statement will allow the user who logs in from the v2.x server to log into the v3.x server as well.

Remember that not all accounts should require a password. When you are setting up remote print servers, you must set up each printer as a user on the network. You don't want the print server to have a password. If the machine reboots after a power outage, you do not want to have to wait to have someone enter a login name and a password for each print server in your network. Remember that printer accounts need almost no additional rights beyond those to the SYS:PUBLIC and SYS:MAIL directories, assigned automatically to the group EVERYONE. This account will need access to the print server software, conveniently located in the PUBLIC directory, and access to queue information stored in SYS:MAIL. This rule is generally also true of mail and fax servers.

Personal NetWare

NetWare Lite and Personal NetWare users have a similar structure for passwords. However, the maximum password length with these network operating systems is 15 characters. If you are combining a NetWare Lite and standard NetWare network, you must log in separately by providing your username and password to the NetWare Lite network.

For Personal NetWare, your login name and password will grant you access to any Novell v2.x, v3.x, or 4.x network. This single password login is unique to Personal NetWare and its new Personal NetWare client software. If you combine a NetWare Lite network with a Personal NetWare workgroup, you must log in twice, once to the workgroup and once to the NetWare Lite network.

Tip

For users of Microsoft Windows on the network, it is a good idea to log out of the network whenever you leave your desk. Windows provides an extra measure of security if you forget. When setting up your Windows' screen saver, you have the ability to password-protect your workstation with a unique non-NetWare password. This means that you can set up a password that is required to be entered before the screen saver will switch to Windows program. You should take care when you use the screen saver, though. First, the screen saver will not come up if you are using a DOS program from the Windows MS-DOS box. Second, you should not make your login password the same as your screen-saver password. You should have different passwords for each application you use. Be aware, however, that in Windows, the screen-saver password is stored encrypted in the CONTROL.INI file and is accessible to intruders.

Account Restrictions

NetWare provides several other security restrictions you can place on user accounts. These restrictions are designed to prevent unauthorized access during times or in places when the user should not have access to the network. The supervisor can set these restrictions in SYSCON. When you run SYSCON, select the Account Restrictions menu. These restrictions include

1. Time of Day
2. Station Restrictions
3. Concurrent Connections
4. Password Changes and Unique Passwords
5. Account Disabled and Expiration Date
6. Limiting Grace Logins
7. Volume Restrictions

The Time of Day restriction lets the supervisor limit the users' authorized access to the network to specific hours and days. This limitation is especially useful for shift workers who would not be expected to be using the network during off-work hours.

Station Restrictions are set in the User Information menu of the SYSCON utility. This option allows the supervisor to limit the workstations from which the user can log into the network. Restricting workstations will prevent users from logging in from an unsupervised workstation or will force them to log in from a diskless workstation that is assigned to them.

The Concurrent Connections options sets the number of simultaneous logins the user can have. Typically, the supervisor will want to limit users to only one login at a time. Only under special circumstances should a user have more than one login. For example, Joe writes software documentation and uses two machines, one to look at the program and the other to write about it, and thus may need two concurrent connections.

As previously discussed, the supervisor can force the user to maintain a password, force password changes, and require that the password be unique for up to eight login periods. Password protection is one of the major security flaws in any network. Forcing the user to change his or her password periodically and requiring minimum lengths is the best way to maintain security.

Using the Account Disabled and Expiration Date option is a good way to maintain user security when someone is granted a leave of absence or goes on vacation. Assigning this option to a user account prevents the use of the account while the user is absent, and the account will remain inactivated until the user returns. By placing an expiration date on an account, you will force the account to be disabled after a certain time period. This is especially useful for temporary employees or for visitors who need access to the network.

By using the Limit Grace Logins option, the supervisor can limit the number of times a user can log in with an expired password. This will give users time to think of and implement a new password. The default is six. Take our advice and tell your users to change their passwords the first time the system asks them to.

The Volume Restrictions option is also located in the User Information screen in SYSCON. To limit the amount of disk space the user is allowed, select Volume Restrictions from the User Information screen. If you answer Yes to the Limit Disk Space option, you must then select the amount of disk space allowed per user. Once this restriction is in place, the user cannot exceed the selected amount of disk space usage in his or her home directory. A good rule of thumb is to start with the amount of disk space you have free on the file server, divide it by two, and then divide the remainder of the disk space among the users. The disk space you set per user is a highly variable number that depends on the applications a user has, the swap files Windows uses, and any temporary files an application might use.

Another security measure available in SYSCON is the Intruder Detection and Lockout feature. Intruder Detection will count the number of times an attempt is made to enter an invalid username or password combination during a specific amount of time. If the number of attempts set in Intruder Detection is exceeded, the username is locked out of the network for a specified amount of time. This feature is available under Supervisor Options in SYSCON. After turning Intruder Detection on, you must select the number of unsuccessful attempts NetWare will accept before locking a user out, the time period the attempts must be made in, and the amount of time the user will be locked out of the network. Remember to set the number of attempts high enough to allow for typing mistakes.

File System Security

Once a user has logged into the system, he or she comes under the security the file system provides. This takes the form of three features:

trustee rights, the *Inherited Rights Mask*, and *file rights*. These rights, in combination, determine the directories users will see and their ability to manipulate files within those subdirectories.

Trustee rights are access rights to particular subdirectories. The rights must be granted by a supervisor, supervisor-equivalent, or work-group manager. The rights that are initially given will then continue to subdirectories below the directory in the tree unless blocked by the Inherited Rights Mask. These rights can be invoked or deleted by NetWare's GRANT and REVOKE commands as well with SYSCON and NetWare's menu-driven FILER utility. You can remove a user from the Trustee List or from a group by using the REMOVE command.

Rights that are initially granted to a user are inherited by the user to subdirectories below the directory for which the rights are granted unless they are blocked by the Inherited Rights Mask. The mask is implemented by the ALLOW command and FILER utility. The supervisor or equivalent can override the mask by granting specific trustee rights in the subdirectory.

To determine your specific rights in a particular subdirectory, you must verify the trustee rights and the Inherited Rights Mask. The rights you have are based on variables called your *effective rights*. The Inherited Rights Mask is used to determine rights for all users, while trustee rights are generally used to grant specific rights to a user in a particular directory. The easiest way to determine a user's effective rights is to determine his or her trustee rights in the previous directory and then remove the rights revoked in the Inherited Rights Mask. The default Inherited Rights Mask grants all rights.

Tip

You can determine what your rights are by using the RIGHTS command at the DOS prompt. You can view the trustees of a directory by using the TLIST command.

Tip

The rights for NetWare v2.x, v3.x, and 4.x, NetWare Lite, and Personal NetWare are different. The rights variables here are for NetWare v3.x. In a mixed environment, the results you can expect may be different. Be sure to consult the documentation for NetWare v3.x and 4.x. The ability to change rights under NetWare Lite and Personal NetWare are limited to those who have full or read-only rights.

Trustee and inherited rights are based on the NetWare system of rights. These rights are different from file attributes. They are the rights that can be assigned and revoked with trustee rights and the Inherited Rights Mask.

The trustee rights NetWare uses are:

1. A—Access Control
2. C—Create
3. E—Erase
4. F —File Scan
5. M—Modify
6. R—Read
7. S—Supervisor
8. W—Write

The access control right allows the user to determine who may have rights to a directory. This will give the user complete control rights within a subdirectory. It can be blocked by the Inherited Rights Mask.

The create right lets the user create new files and subdirectories below the directory.

The erase right lets the user delete files and subdirectories.

The file scan right lets the user list the files in a subdirectory. It does not grant the right to view the files individually, however.

The modify right allows the user to change the name and attributes of a directory and the subdirectories below it.

The read right gives the user the right to open and actually read a file within a directory.

The supervisor right is similar to Access control in that the user has complete ability to control the directory, including granting other users rights. However, this right cannot be removed by the Inherited Rights Mask.

The write right grants the user the right to open and write to files in a subdirectory.

Tip

To run most applications, the user needs only file scan and read rights. Some applications create files that may require create and write rights.

Tip

When using the GRANT command you have one more option, ALL, with which you can GRANT users the same rights other users have in the directory. You cannot GRANT more rights than what you have.

File and Directory Attributes

Our earlier discussion shows a complex group of rights and their usage. However, any of your rights to a directory or a file within that subdirectory can be modified or eliminated by NetWare features called *File and Directory Attributes*.

The Directory attributes for any particular directory can be modified by someone either having modify rights or owning the directory. Directory attributes are modified by using the FLAGDIR command. The available directory attributes are as follows:

1. DI—Delete Inhibit will prevent a user from deleting a directory or subdirectories even if he or she has Erase rights.
2. RI—Rename Inhibit will prevent a user from renaming a directory even if he or she has Modify rights.
3. H—Hidden will hide a directory to all users in a normal directory search. Further, the directory cannot be erased. However, if a user with File Scan rights uses the NDIR command, he or she will be able to see the directory.
4. P—Purge causes the system to purge deleted files immediately.
5. S or SY—System identifies the directory as one used by the system. It will not appear in a normal directory search, but will appear if a user with File Scan rights uses NDIR.
6. V—Visible only applies to volumes that have both the Macintosh name space loaded and Macintosh files stored.

Tip

Be very careful with the Purge attribute. A file that has been purged cannot be recovered using the SALVAGE utility.

File attributes are similar to directory attributes but affect only those files to which they are specifically applied. These attributes are applied using the FLAG command. The File attributes are analogous to DOS attributes, but are much more extensive in scope. They are as follows:

1. A—Archive is set by NetWare only if the file has been modified since the last backup. This bit is scanned and used during incremental backups.
2. CI—Copy Inhibit restricts Macintosh users from copying a file even if they have Read and File Scan rights.
3. DI—Delete Inhibit stops users from deleting a file even if they have erase rights.
4. X—Execute Only prevents an EXE or COM file from being altered or copied. Be careful with this attribute. If the file is not NetWare-aware, it may cause damage or lock up the file. Only the supervisor can assign this attribute.

Tip
Flag.EXE and .COM files execute only when you install them. Remember that once you have set the Execute Only attribute, you cannot remove it. If the file is corrupted, you may have to reinstall it from the original distribution diskettes.

Some applications such as WordPerfect need to write to the executables. Look into this before you mark these files execute only. Virus checking may also fail if .EXEs or .COMs are marked execute only. Last, do not use execute only on Windows files.

5. H—Hidden will not allow the file to be viewed using a DOS DIR command. It also prevents the file from being erased.
6. I—Indexed causes the file's FAT entry to be indexed for faster access. This is performed automatically if the file exceeds 64 FAT entries.
7. P—Purge automatically causes the file to be purged after it is deleted.
8. RA—Read Audit keeps track of when a file is accessed when the NetWare Audit trail system is in place. This is the companion attribute to the WA or Write Audit attribute.

9. RO—Read Only causes the file only to be read. It cannot be written to even if the user has erase rights. It automatically invokes the Delete inhibit and Rename inhibit attributes.
10. RW—Read Write is the companion to Read Only and is the default attribute.
11. RI—Rename inhibit prevents a file from being renamed.
12. S—Shareable is used to denote that a file can be used by more than one user at a time. Normally NetWare will not allow shareable access. This is especially important to databases and files used to boot diskless workstations.
13. SY—System hides a file to DOS directory searches. It will appear to NDIR listings. It also prevents a file from being copied or deleted.
14. T—Transactional denotes that the file is protected by the Transaction Tracking System (TTS).
15. W—Write Audit is used in conjunction with Read Audit and is used by NetWare's Audit Trail System to track writes to the file. This allows continuous backups to be made as well.

Tip
A user who has modify rights may modify a file or directory to remove or modify any of these attributes. Thus, a user with modify rights could remove a copy inhibit attribute from a file, copy the file, and then replace the copy inhibit attribute. Therefore, grant modify rights with caution.

What about the Phone Lines?

So far we have discussed the threat to your network's security from those who would attempt to access the files from within the confines of your office. One of the more dangerous threats to the network comes from the outside. Today's LANs must have access to the outside. Whether it is in the form of a dial-up server for your outside salespersons, a direct connection between two servers across the country, or the boss who has Carbon Copy installed on her machine and wants to dial in from home at some time, you will have to connect the LAN to a public telephone line via a modem.

When you connect your LAN to a phone line via a modem, you leave the LAN open to anyone who has a modem and discovers the phone number. The key to security in this scenario is access control. You must be sure that only those with proper authority can gain access to your network.

First and most obvious, limit the number of modems in the system to as few as possible. A very good idea at this point is installing a modem server that will allow users access to a modem without putting a modem on each workstation. This will limit access and allow control over the way in which the modems can be used.

Second, keep tight control on how dial-up systems are used. Most dial-up software has authentication checks that require, at the very minimum, a password to access the computer on-site. Some more sophisticated systems have a call-back feature that will dial the user back at a predetermined phone number. The system will not allow a direct connection but must call the user back to establish the link. If the user is not at the predetermined phone number, however, he or she cannot access the system. This is not very helpful for users who must call in from many different numbers. In any event, be sure and use the security that is provided by the dial-up software.

Finally, remember that once the user gains access to the system through whatever dial-up software you choose to use, he or she still is subject to all of the NetWare procedures in place to prevent unauthorized access. Enforce the password protections available to you. Further, be sure to change the passwords on the dial-up software often, and delete the user accounts of those who have left the company as soon as they leave. A former user who no longer works for the company, but still has an active account and knows the dial-up passwords, can cause a large number of problems.

Tip

Whenever anyone who has had dial-up access leaves the company, be sure to change the password on the dial-up software immediately.

So What Do I Do First?

Now, that you know about NetWare's security, you're probably wondering which steps to take first. Here's a list that will guide you:

Flash Points

1. Assign the SUPERVISOR account a password.
2. Create a supervisor-equivalent. Assign it a password.
3. Create the users on the network.
4. Create their account and login restrictions.
5. Create groups.
6. Assign rights to the groups.
7. Assign users to groups.
8. Assign file attributes.

Do I Really Need All This?

By now it should be obvious that Novell thought long and hard about how security on a NetWare LAN should be implemented. However, security is only as good as those who run the system want it to be and are prepared to work at. The LAN needs to be monitored often for problems with security. Users accounts must be monitored and maintained properly for the security to work.

Remember that deletion of the company database is just as devastating when done accidentally as it is when done maliciously. Security is not a matter of lack of trust in your employees, but is rather a way to prevent the unforeseen accident from destroying the LAN.

Security does not happen by accident—it takes planning. You must plan from the beginning of the LAN to look at security issues. Where and how the physical layout is made, the number of hard drives, and how they are arranged, down to the individual structure of the volumes—it all needs to be planned. Plan where each application is going to be placed on the network. Once set up, a well-run network normally does not require administrators to worry about security.

part

All the Beasts in The Jungle

II

Which Access Method Do I Use?

The network access method (sometimes referred to as the data-link protocol) you use depends in large part on the applications and work you are doing on your LAN. Your decision is also based on the media that is already installed in the walls or ceilings of your building, and on the environmental and physical requirements of the installation. In many cases, you will inherit an existing network access method or wiring scheme and must work within its limits. If that is true, although you don't have to decide which access method to use, it is useful to know the requirements and limits of the access method you already have.

There are currently four major LAN access methods and a host of implementations of each. These four are ARCNET, Ethernet (IEEE 802.3), token-ring (IEEE 802.5), and the Fiber Distributed Data Interface (FDDI). Of these access methods, Ethernet is most prevalent. Token-ring follows Ethernet in popularity. FDDI is the third most popular, followed by ARCNET.

chapter 12

Protocols, Access Methods, and Media

What Are Communication Protocols?

The manner in which PCs communicate with each other is as important as the fact that they can communicate at all. Each PC uses sets of rules called *protocols* to compose data, envelope and package data in proper containers, and transmit data from one device to another. Protocols communicate with other protocols, forming assembly lines that organize the data into packets for transfer, so that the packets can be sent across the cabling, or media. In networking, much like the operation of sending a letter to Aunt Mary via the postal system, one protocol relies on another or many others to complete data transmission. Multiple protocols that work together are often called *protocol suites,* much like the postal system's network that employs workers, each with different tasks.

Included in a protocol are rules that specify the format of data (the order of its bits), its sequence (the order of its transmission), and the error checking that must take place to ensure data integrity. You can compare protocols to the international rules of diplomacy, in which each diplomatic member is governed by certain rules common to his or her station. The content of this communication and the method by which the diplomat communicates with other members, or with his or her peers, is governed by certain well-defined rules.

In data communications, you have several types of protocols that not only determine who communicates, but the manner in which they communicate. You have routing protocols, which determine how messages get from one network to another, and e-mail protocols, such as Novell's Message Handling Service (MHS), which govern how e-mail is distributed across an internetwork.

To communicate with each other, workstations need to share the same protocol. As with the telephone system, both participants need to speak the same language. Speaking French to someone who speaks only Russian doesn't improve communication. The two parties need to agree on the language they will speak so that each will be able to get his or her message across. The protocol then, the network's way of speaking, may be the Transmission Control Protocol/Internet Protocol (TCP/IP) in government computer installations that use a large number of different computers, or it may be AppleTalk, the common language that Macintoshes use to talk to each other.

In NetWare, the protocols used for network communications are the NetWare Core Protocols, the Internetwork Packet Exchange protocol, the Sequenced Packet Exchange protocol, the Routing Information Protocol, and the Server Advertising Protocol. Since acronyms are so popular and also easier to say, we'll provide you with a string of them—NCP, IPX, SPX, RIP, and SAP. That's not nearly enough—there's also the Watchdog protocol. We'll discuss them more later after we give you a stronger foundation for understanding network communications.

Let's Talk

Network communication in the file-server–based world of NetWare consists of multiple machines called *clients* that request information from a central processor called the *server.* Communication flows roughly according to a model called the *Open Systems Interconnect (OSI) Model.* To simplify communications between two workstations, consider the last letter you wrote from your house near Richland, Michigan, to your Aunt Betty in Boston, Massachusetts:

1. You had some information you needed to communicate. It was, "Thanks for the hand-knit red, orange, and purple argyle socks you made me for my birthday."
2. You choose to write a letter rather than use the telephone because Betty is hard of hearing.

3. Since you live in the United States and she does too, you write the letter in English so that your Aunt in Boston will understand it.
4. Then, you sign the letter, put in an envelope, and seal the envelope so the contents won't become lost.
5. You address the letter to your Aunt and you put a stamp on it so that the post office will pick it up. You also write your return address on the envelope so that if something goes wrong, you will get the letter back and will be able to resend it.
6. You carry the letter down the driveway to the mailbox and put it in. You raise the flag on the mailbox to tell the postman you have something to send.
7. The next morning, if it is one of the regular delivery days, which means it's not Sunday or a holiday, the postman picks the letter up and delivers it to a central sorting area where someone makes sure that the envelope has a stamp on it and that the address can be read. If they can't read the destination address because you haven't written it clearly enough or you forgot a zip code, they return the letter to you using the source address you supplied.
8. If the post office can read the address, the postal carrier puts it in a bin designated for Betty's neighborhood, so the letter can be delivered to Betty.

That's how the communication on your end takes place. This is how Betty finally gets the letter.

1. The letter is delivered by some transport means to the post office in Boston. This transport method may be by automobile, train, or plane, depending on what you specified on the outside of the envelope. If you marked it with a $.29 cent stamp, it will be delivered by car. If you marked it express mail, your letter will be delivered by plane. Of course, everyone knows the post office doesn't really work that way, but you're tempted to think so sometimes.
2. If the transport method is an automobile, the letter travels from your mailbox down the rural road to Richland, where it is taken by country road to Battle Creek, and then by interstate highway to Kalamazoo, where it is routed by plane to Boston. At each point in the transfer, someone looks at the envelope and notes its destination before passing it on to the next vehicle for transfer.
3. Once the post office in Boston gets the letter, a postal worker sorts it by address.

4. A carrier traveling by a proscribed route delivers it to the mailbox labeled for Aunt Betty.
5. Aunt Betty checks her mailbox regularly to see if any letters have arrived. She receives your letter. The envelope is intact, her name is spelled correctly, and the contents are preserved.
6. Betty opens the envelope, removes the letter, unfolds the paper, discards the envelope, and starts to read the letter.
7. When she finishes, she gets out paper and pen and writes a letter to you: "Dear Sonny, I'm glad you liked the socks. I'll make you some more."
8. She sits down, gets out her knitting needles, and with purple, green, and yellow yarn, starts to knit. When she gets done, she'll have another package to put in the mail.

This letter-writing scenario illustrates several things about data and communications in general. First, information that needs to be sent somewhere must exist. This is called the *data.* Second, the data must bear an address, so that the delivery mechanism will know where to deliver it. Third, the data must be contained in standard packaging so the delivery mechanism will know how to deliver it. In this case, the socks (data) are enclosed in a box with wrapping paper (packet), addressed and packaged according to standard rules for package sending (protocol), and delivered from post office to post office by several means of transportation until it reaches its destination. Betty, on the receiving end of the transmission, acknowledges she got your letter by preparing her response.

In NetWare, three protocols working in concert with the operating system, application program, user, and media, make sure that every bit of data is delivered intact. These protocols are NCP, IPX, and SPX.

NCP

The NetWare Core Protocol (NCP) is responsible for all network actions. These include print services, file access, security, resource allocation, communications, and event notification.

IPX

The Internetwork Packet Exchange (IPX) is similar to a protocol called *XNS (Xerox Network System)*, which was developed at the Xerox Palo

Alto Research Center (PARC) in the 1970s. The majority of communications on the network use IPX. It is a connectionless protocol that does not offer guaranteed delivery of data. It resides at the Network Layer of the Open Systems Interconnect (OSI) Model. It relies on other mechanisms at different layers of the model to verify the correctness of the data and to acknowledge message receipt.

IPX also creates and maintains connections, addresses data packets, routes packets to their destination, reads addresses, and directs data to the proper area.

SPX

The companion to IPX, the Sequenced Packet Exchange Protocol (SPX) resides above IPX at the OSI Transport Layer. SPX is a connection-oriented, guaranteed-delivery protocol that requires the acknowledgment of data. (See Figure 12-1.)

SAP

The Service Advertising Protocol (SAP) is responsible for server broadcasts. Each server on the network uses SAP to advertise its presence

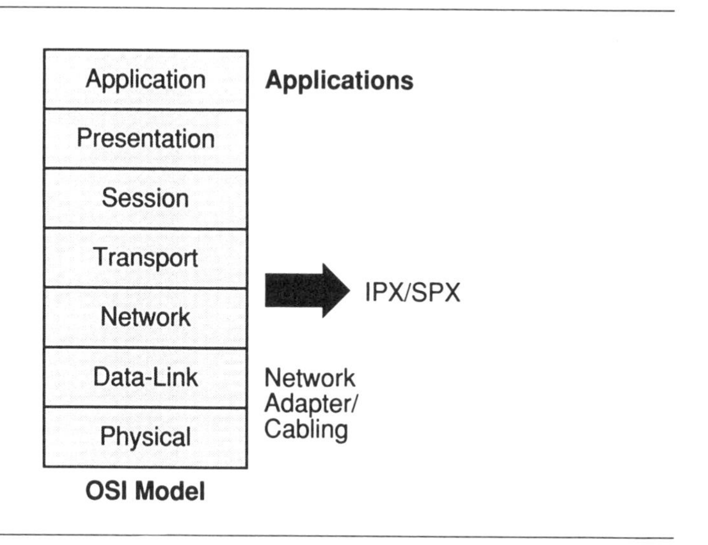

Figure 12-1. *IPX and SPX correspond to the Network and Transport Layers, respectively, of the OSI Model.*

and its ability to service requests. The packet the server generates to advertise that it is available to service requests contains the server's name, the type of service it provides, and its network address. Servers issue SAP packets every 60 seconds.

OSI Model

The OSI Model, a seven-layer protocol suite, defines the rules for interconnecting machines, the structure of the data that will be communicated, and timing issues that make sure the data gets where it needs to go. OSI was defined by the International Standards Organization (ISO) as a means to let machines of all kinds communicate. The OSI Model, a reference model, also serves as a point of departure in explaining how protocols interact with each other. The seven layers of the OSI Model are as follows:

The Application Layer

The Application Layer represents the interface between the user application and the network.

The Presentation Layer

The Presentation Layer converts data it receives from the application layer to the proper syntax for communication with another device. It also handles the encryption and compression of data, if necessary.

The Session Layer

The Session Layer is responsible for establishing the connection between two devices that want to communicate.

The Transport Layer

The Transport Layer prepares data for transmission, segments the data, and creates a checksum that will test the integrity of the data. This layer is also responsible for the quality and reliability of the transmission.

The Network Layer

The Network Layer is responsible for routing data and creating packets from the segments it receives from the Transport Layer.

The Data-Link Layer

The Data-Link Layer packages and unpackages data it sends or receives. It also confirms that the checksums on the packets are correct. The Data-Link Layer is divided into two sublayers: The Media Access Control Layer (MAC) is responsible for transferring packets to their destinations; the Logical Link Control Layer (LLC) receives packets from the Physical Layer and hands them to the MAC Layer.

The Physical Layer

The Physical Layer is the interface to the network. It is responsible for the electrical and physical characteristics of the transmission and controls how the network adapter gets access to the cable.

TRANSPORT REFERS TO ACCESS METHODS

Although the manner in which communication takes place has been established, unless you have a form for transmitting it, nothing will happen. The mechanism responsible for the transmission of data to the network media and the specific information that accompanies it are left up to the access method.

Access methods determine how packets, which are built according to the rules of protocols, access the network media. Access methods correspond to the Physical and Data-Link Layers of the OSI Model. Network adapters and their associated drivers exist for each of the access methods.

Two types of access methods are common: Carrier Sense Multiple Access with Collision Detection (CSMA/CD) and token-passing. In a CSMA/CD network, workstations contend for access to the media rather than waiting their turn for an indication that they can communicate. In token-passing, workstations communicate in an orderly manner, according to whoever has the "token" that gives them permission. Of the four major access methods, three of them use token-passing; only one uses CSMA/CD.

The four common access methods are: Ethernet, ARCNET, token-ring, and the Fiber Distributed Data Interface (FDDI).

ARCNET

Developed in 1977 by Datapoint Corp. in San Antonio, Texas, ARCNET is a token-passing access method that operates at a speed of 2.5 megabits per second (Mbps). ARCNET is cabled in a bus, star, or distributed-star topology and has an overall network distance of 20,000 feet, depending on the media used. ARCNET supports up to 255 workstations on a single network and operates on RG-62 A/U coaxial cable, unshielded twisted pair (UTP), or fiber-optic cable.

ARCNET implementations are common on 16-bit adapters that fit in ISA machines. Eight-bit adapters, which are used in 8088-based machines, are also available although not recommended even on a workstation, as are Micro Channel and EISA versions.

While ARCNET has a rated speed of 2.5 megabits per second, you will rarely see ARCNET adapters that operate faster than 200 kilobytes per second (Kbps). Adopted by many users in small to medium-sized businesses as a low-cost but stable and reliable technology, ARCNET's use has fallen off in recent years. Presently, there are approximately six million ARCNET nodes installed. Of the three predominant access methods—Ethernet, token-ring, and ARCNET—ARCNET is the least commonly implemented.

ARCNET has a maximum packet size of 512 bytes, much smaller than that of Ethernet or token-ring. Because ARCNET is a token-passing access method, it is reliable and deterministic, and is well-suited to moderate LAN traffic.

Alternate forms of ARCNET are available. One, ARCNETPlus, developed by Datapoint in 1989, is a 20Mbps version of ARCNET that has never gained much popularity. In ARCNETPlus, standard 2.5Mbps and 20Mbps nodes are allowed to interoperate on the same physical cable, but so far the cost has been more expensive than ARCNET and its counterparts, Ethernet and token-ring.

An extension of the ARCNET family is Thomas-Conrad's TCNS (Thomas-Conrad Networking System). A token-passing technology that allows up to 255 nodes on a star-wired network with an overall network distance of no more than 17,600 feet, TCNS operates at a speed of 100Mbps. The speed of TCNS makes it resemble the performance characteristics of FDDI. TCNS is popular for backbone operations, as a link between the file server and a backup workstation, and in database and imaging applications where large amounts of data must flow across the network in a short time.

ARCNET networks consist of several components: the LAN adapter, the media, BNC connectors, T-connectors, BNC terminators, and the ARCNET active or passive hub. The adapter is available for most bus implementations.

When an ARCNET workstation joins the network, it identifies itself to the rest of the network. A token that passes from workstation to workstation determines when the workstation gets to communicate. When an ARCNET node receives the token, it generates its request and sends it across the media to its destination. All workstations on the network hear the transmission, but only the workstation the request is destined for receives and stores the request. The destination workstation then acknowledges that it has received the request. The sending workstation relinquishes the token to the next logical workstation on the network (the workstation with the next higher node ID). That workstation can now communicate. (See Figure 12-2.)

ARCNET can be wired in either a star or a bus topology. In the bus topology, which is limited to coaxial media, a central trunk cable attaches all the workstations to the network.

In this configuration, you have several components—the adapter, the media, the hub, and the connectors. This hub may be either passive or

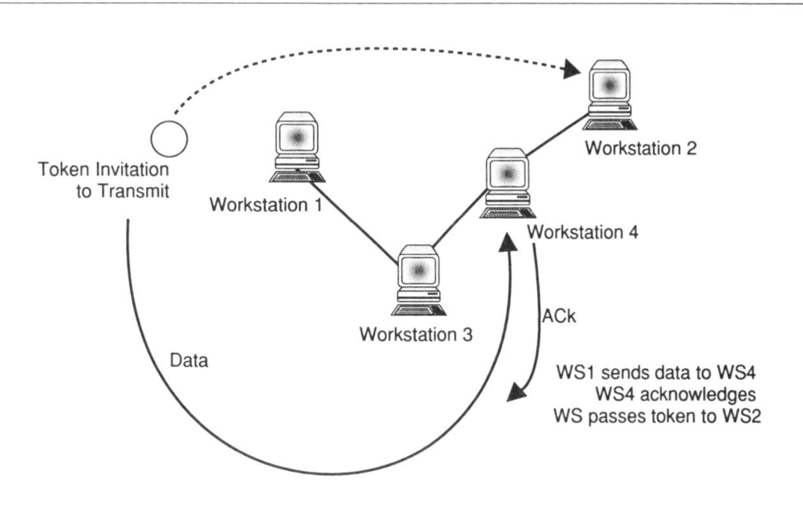

Figure 12-2. *How ARCNET works.*

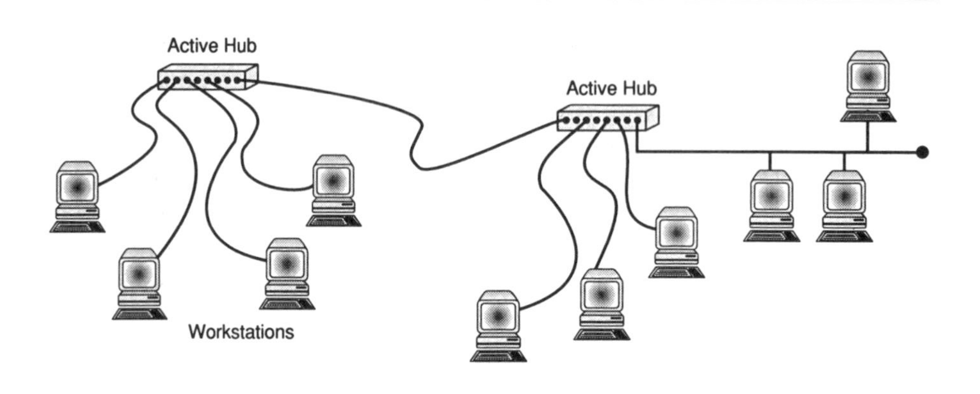

Figure 12-3. *A distributed-star ARCNET network.*

active. Passive hubs do not boost the signal over distance when it weakens. Active hubs do.

In a star topology, common to UTP, workstations radiate from a central hub. Hubs may be daisy-chained together, and a combination of bus and star topologies can be used. (See Figure 12-3.)

Read Chapter 13, Implementing ARCNET, for details on implementing ARCNET networks.

Ethernet

Ethernet is a collision-based access method with 10Mbps communication. Two Ethernet standards exist: the Ethernet II standard developed by Digital, Intel, and Xerox in 1980, and the IEEE's 802.3, specified in 1985. The packets in these standards differ by one field. Ethernet II uses a type field, which is assigned by Xerox and represents the manufacturer of the adapter. The IEEE 802.3 Ethernet uses a length field, which specifies the length of the data.

Versions of NetWare previous to v3.12 used IEEE 802.3 Ethernet. Versions v3.12 and 4.0 use 802.2 Ethernet. 802.2 Ethernet divides its Data-Link functions into two layers: The Logical Link Control Layer (LLC) establishes, maintains, and terminates logical links; The Media Access Control Layer (MAC) is responsible for media access.

Four implementations of Ethernet are available that are based on the media they use and the topology. They are 10BASE-5 Ethernet (called *thick Ethernet*), 10BASE-2 Ethernet (called *thin Ethernet*), 10BASE-T Ethernet, which uses UTP, and 10BASE-F (fiber-optic Ethernet).

The components of an Ethernet LAN vary depending on the implementation and topology. All Ethernet LANs operate at 10Mbps and are baseband access methods. At present, several specifications for 100Mbps are seeking attention. Because Ethernet is a collision-based access method, network throughput will slow as more nodes join the network. In general, however, Ethernet is easy to install, well known, inexpensive, and appropriate for networks with bursty traffic.

10BASE-5

10BASE-5 Ethernet was the first Ethernet implementation to be used. It uses RG-8 150-Ohm coaxial cable and is commonly referred to as thick Ethernet. Thick Ethernet contains these components: the adapter, a transceiver (repeater) that allows segment distances to be increased, the transceiver cable, trunk cables, N-series terminators, and barrel connectors. Thick Ethernet cable is unwieldy and heavy. It is being replaced by thin Ethernet or UTP Ethernet. Thick Ethernet uses a bus topology.

10BASE-2

10BASE-2 Ethernet or thin Ethernet uses RG-58 A/U, 150-Ohm coaxial cable. Its components consist of the adapter, the transceiver (repeater), the media, BNC connectors, T-connectors, barrel connectors, and terminators. 10BASE-2 Ethernet uses a low-cost bus topology.

10BASE-T

Ethernet based on UTP cable is becoming the most common Ethernet implementation. The two-paired UTP wire, which is 22, 24, or 26 gauge, is light, easy-to-pull, small, and flexible. It does, however, have a low tolerance for noise. 10BASE-T Ethernet is a star-wired topology in which individual nodes radiate from a central hub or concentrator. 10BASE-T Ethernet consists of the adapter, the hub, a transceiver, a transceiver cable, punch-down blocks, and wall plates. The implementation uses UTP media with RJ-45 connectors.

10BASE-F

10BASE-F, the latest implementation of Ethernet, is based on fiber-optic media and is resistant to electromagnetic interference (EMI) and radio-frequency interference (RFI), and allows longer segments because of the characteristics of fiber.

Token-Ring

Four-Mbps token-ring was developed by IBM in the early 1970s and was followed by 16Mbps token-ring in 1988. Both versions are token-passing access methods that were adopted by the IEEE as IEEE 802.5. Token-ring consists of several components: the adapter, the lobe cable, the multistation access unit (called a MAU or hub), media filters, patch cables, RJ-45 or hermaphroditic connectors, and patch panels.

The adapter is responsible for retiming and generating the signal it receives from the workstation, for generating the token, and for providing error checking. The lobe cable connects the workstation to the MAU. The MAU consists of a 4-, 8-, or 16-port device that is responsible for network reconfiguration when errors occur when workstations enter and leave the network. MAUs enhance network reliability because they mechanically bypass components in the workstation that fail. MAUs can be passive or active. Passive MAUs do not regenerate, retime, or boost the signal when signal weakening (attenuation) occurs. Active MAUs do. (See Figure 12-4 on the next page.)

Token-ring is a star-wired ring topology in which a token passes from one physical node to another. It operates on shielded media or UTP. Shielded media is called Type 1 cable; UTP is called Type 3.

Token-ring is a deterministic access method, in which each node on the ring has a reasonable expectation that it will receive the token within a defined period of time. It has extensive recovery routines for when problems occur. The access method is well suited for integration with IBM mainframes or minicomputers, large-scale environments, LANs with heavy-duty traffic, or any network where dependable, high-speed communication is necessary.

FDDI

The third of the token-passing access methods is the Fiber Distributed Data Interface (FDDI). FDDI is cabled in a ring topology and can consist of a single ring or a double ring. On the double ring, called *dual counter-rotating*, traffic on each ring moves in the opposite direction. FDDI is commonly used for backbone-based LANs and for internet-

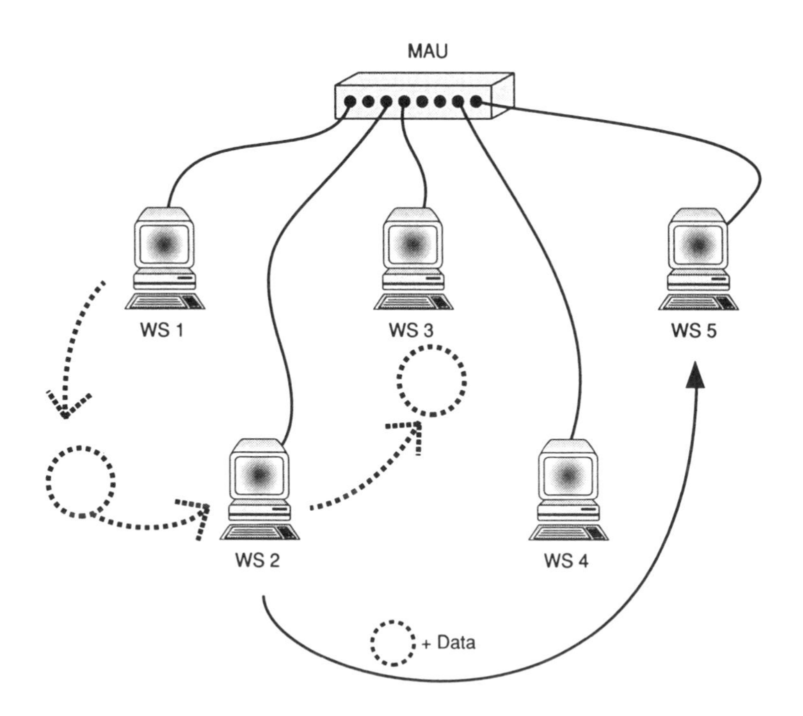
MAU
WS 1
WS 3
WS 5
WS 2
WS 4
+ Data
WS 2 receives the token from WS 1
WS 2 appends data to the token and sends to WS 5
WS 5 reads in data, releases data and token
WS 2 receives the token + data, strips the data, and releases the token to WS 3

Figure 12-4. *A typical token-ring configuration.*

working. Its speed is 100Mbps, and it allows an overall network distance of 68 kilometers and up to 500 active nodes per segment.

Variations of FDDI exist, both proprietary and standards-based. The first of these is CDDI, the Copper Distributed Data Interface, which uses shielded twisted-pair or unshielded twisted-pair as its media. Nonproprietary, 100Mbps contention-based methods exist, but their performance, like Ethernet's, will decrease as more nodes are added to the ring. Thomas-Conrad's ARCNET-like TCNS also operates at 100Mbps and, according to the International Data Group, outsold FDDI adapters by two-to-one in 1992.

CABLING

Media is the pathway that all data crosses. Various types of media are available, but the most common types are coaxial media, unshielded and shielded twisted-pair media, and fiber-optic media. Each media has advantages such as cost, extended distances, or immunity to electromagnetic interference.

All media share some common characteristics. These characteristics are attenuation, capacitance, crosstalk, and resistance, or lack of, to EMI and radio-frequency interference (RFI).

Attenuation

Attenuation is a decrease in signal strength over distances caused by electrical losses in the media's sheath and conductor.

Capacitance

The capacitance of a cable is the amount of energy it stores between its conductive materials. It is the measure of the media's ability to store electrical charges and withstand voltage changes. Capacitance can cause distortion of the signal.

Noise

In cabling, noise consists of unwanted signals that disrupt transmission. Noise can be caused by EMI or RFI. Examples of devices that cause EMI are fluorescent lights, vacuum cleaners, light dimmers, and fans. Coaxial ARCNET is tolerant of noise.

Crosstalk

Crosstalk occurs when the induction of one line is coupled into that of another line. Simply stated, the lines' magnetic fields cross. It is most common in twisted-pair media. To avoid crosstalk, cables should be kept as far from sources of noise such as fluorescent lights, fan motors, or radio transmission as possible.

Coaxial

Coaxial cable consists of several layers of material surrounding a central copper core. It is less flexible than twisted-pair cable, but is EMI-resistant and excellent for backbone use. Three types of coaxial cable are used in networking. 10BASE-5 Ethernet uses RG8 50-Ohm media, otherwise known as thick Ethernet. 10BASE-2 Ethernet uses 50-Ohm RG-58 A/U or CU, and is also known as thin Ethernet. ARCNET uses RG-62 A/U 93-Ohm media.

Shielded Twisted-Pair

In twisted-pair cabling, two wires are twisted across the length of the cable. The twisting minimizes crosstalk between the pairs. Shielded twisted-pair (STP) is represented by IBM Type 1 and Type 6 media. STP cable is susceptible to crosstalk, capacitance, and attenuation, but less so than UTP.

Unshielded Twisted-pair

Unshielded twisted-pair is 22–24 gauge, 150-Ohm media that is inexpensive, flexible, reliable, and excellent for short distances. ARCNET, Ethernet, and token-ring all use unshielded twisted-pair. UTP is susceptible to crosstalk, capacitance, and attenuation.

Fiber-Optic

Fiber-optic media consists of a central glass core surrounded by a shielded cladding. Fiber-optic is excellent for high-speed communications and is immune to EMI and RFI. It is also more expensive than its companion media.

Wireless

In the last two years, LANs have been introduced that use radio waves or infrared signals to transmit data. These LAN implementations are at an advantage both in areas where pulling cable is impossible and over limited distances. Wireless adapters are expensive. NCR and Motorola both have implementations.

We'll talk more about installing these access methods and media in later chapters of Part II, All the Beasts in the Jungle.

chapter 13

Implementing ARCNET

Characteristics

Of the four access methods, ARCNET was the first developed and is still one of the most reliable. While not an IEEE standard, ARCNET finally became an ANSI standard in 1992 (ANSI/ATIA 878.1). ARCNET is a baseband-modified, token-passing access method that is physically wired in a bus or star-topology and works as a logical ring. The transmission speed of ARCNET is 2.5 megabits per second (Mbps).

ARCNET Basics

ARCNET has some terms that you will need to understand prior to working with the access method. The terms are as follows:

Active hub—A central wiring device that actively repeats and retimes the data signal, allowing longer distances.

Bus topology—Connection of the adapters in a linear topology using T-connectors. The beginning and end of the bus require 93-Ohm termination with a terminator or a star-topology ARCNET adapter.

Distributed-star—A wiring scheme that combines the star and bus topologies to create a free-form wiring design.

Frame—The data and additional information required to transmit the data to the proper node on the network. A frame is also called a packet.

NIC—Network Interface Card. The NIC or adapter handles communications in the computer.

Packet—The data and additional information required to transmit the data to the proper node on the network. A packet is also called a frame.

Passive hub—A wiring device that simply splits the signal in several directions. Up to four devices may be connected to the passive hub.

Star-topology—Connection of the adapters to the central wiring device called a hub. The hub can be an active device or a passive device.

Token—In ARCNET, the token is called the invitation-to-transmit frame. It grants a node permission to transmit on the network.

Token-passing—A deterministic protocol that requires a node to possess a token that grants it permission to transmit. The token and data pass from adapter to adapter in turn.

How ARCNET Works

In ARCNET, a token passes sequentially from node (workstation) to node based on the nodes' IDs. The token passes from the lowest node ID (1) to the highest node ID (255) and from there, back to the lowest. The token, also known as an invitation-to-transmit (ITT), grants a node the right to transmit data on the network. Once a node receives the token, it sends a packet called a Free Buffer Enquiry (FBE) to the node it wants to transmit to. The receiving node (called the destination node) transmits either a negative or positive acknowledgment, which indicates whether it has room to receive data. If the destination node sends a positive acknowledgment, the transmitting node (called the source node) sends its data packet. The destination node sends an acknowledgment when it receives the data. If the source node receives the positive acknowledgment, the transmission is complete, and the source node releases the token to the next sequential node ID.

Nodes entering or leaving the ARCNET network cause the network to enter a "reconfiguration mode." The reconfiguration stops all activity on the network. Nodes, beginning with highest node ID first, send an ITT to the next sequential node ID. When that node receives the ITT, it continues the process until all nodes are accounted for. The network then starts normal transmissions again.

The network depends on the node ID to configure itself properly. Node IDs are individually set for each adapter. On ISA adapters, a series of eight hardware switches on the adapter set the node ID. EISA and Micro Channel adapters are normally set in software by running a configuration program that ships with the adapter. As stated, ARCNET node IDs can range from 1 to 255. Node ID 0 is reserved for broadcasts, which consist of data packets intended for all nodes.

Tip

If you are installing Macintoshes in an ARCNET network, you cannot use node ID 255, which is reserved for AppleTalk.

Tip

Since the system administrator sets the node ID, it is extremely important to keep careful records of assigned node IDs. A duplicate node ID can cause the network to reconfigure itself constantly, which disrupts all network services.

In 1992, Datapoint introduced ARCNETPlus, a 20Mbps variant of standard 2.5Mbps ARCNET. ARCNETPlus uses the same cabling ARCNET does and has the same distance limitations as ARCNET. It also interconnects with standard ARCNET on the same physical network. ARCNETPlus is not an ANSI standard.

How to Set Up the Network

Many users consider ARCNET a slow access method. However, because it is a token-passing access method, its performance is deterministic. When you add the second to last ARCNET node to the network, you know what your performance will be. Network throughput does not degrade as you add nodes to the network. With 20 or so nodes, you quickly realize that a well-tuned ARCNET network can be nearly as fast as an Ethernet network with the same number of nodes.

The simplicity of ARCNET carries over to its setup. ARCNET networks are wired as star, bus, distributed-star, or combination bus-star topologies and use various kinds of cable.

The Bus Topology

A bus topology in an ARCNET network consists of a series of network adapters cabled from one adapter to another in a linear fashion. Bus-topology ARCNET networks can be wired with RG-62 A/U coaxial cable or unshielded twisted-pair (UTP) media. In a coaxial bus ARCNET network, a 93-Ohm connector, called a *terminator*, is placed at each end of the cable (bus). T-connectors on each adapter continue the media from node to node. Up to eight adapters can be placed on a bus, and the network can have a 1,000-foot maximum bus length. (See Figure 13-1.)

The Daisy-Chain Topology

In a twisted-pair bus implementation, up to 10 nodes can be placed on the bus, with a minimum of 6 feet between each node and an overall

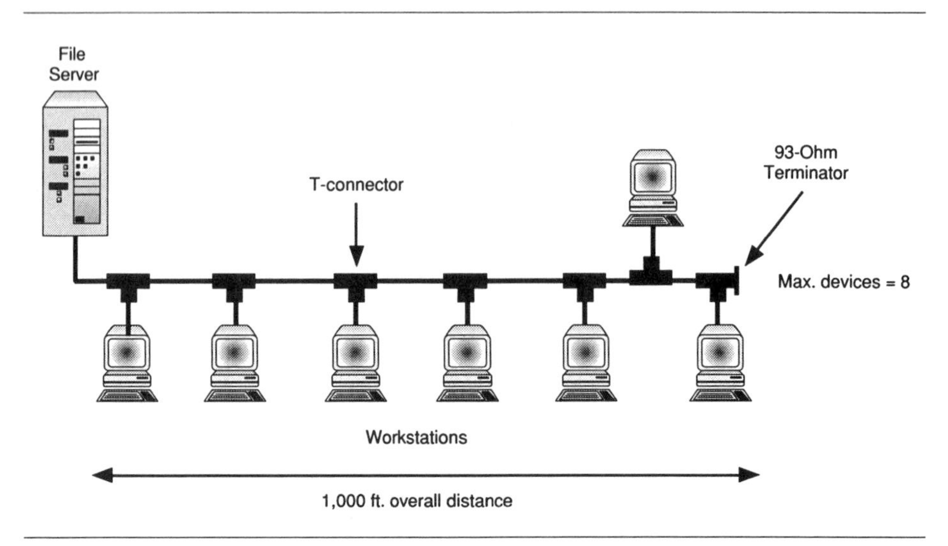

Figure 13-1. *An ARCNET coaxial bus network that shows the distance limitations.*

network length of no more than 400 feet. Twisted-pair bus ARCNET adapters contain two RJ-45 jacks on the end of the adapter. One jack receives media from the previous node; the other connects the media with the next node. For workstations on the end of the twisted-pair bus, it is necessary to terminate the unused ports.

The Star-Topology

A star-topology ARCNET network requires an additional piece of equipment called an active or passive hub. The active hub is a wiring center that retimes and retransmits the signal to all nodes attached to it. Workstations radiate from the hub via their media connections. The data a workstation receives first flows through the hub. Data the workstation sends passes from the workstation to the hub. Passive hubs, which are less expensive than active hubs and less commonly used, merely split the signal between each of its four ports and allow workstations to radiate from them.

Active hubs, which normally consist of 8 to 16 ports, one for each workstation connection, can be daisy-chained with media to create larger networks. Terminators are not used on a star-wired network. The overall distance of a star topology ARCNET network is 20,000 feet. Up to 2,000 feet can separate a node from the active hub. Daisy-chained active hubs can be placed up to 2,000 feet apart.

If a passive hub is connected to an active hub, up to 1,000 feet can separate the two hubs. If the network uses passive hubs, the distance is restricted to 100 feet between the nodes and the passive hub. Figure 13-2 on the next page displays an ARCNET star topology, its distance limitations, and its use of hubs. Passive hubs cannot be connected to other passive hubs. If you are using passive hubs, always terminate the unused ports.

Tip

ARCNET operates like a logical ring, not a physical ring. Although it operates like a ring, you cannot connect the hubs or adapters together so that they are able to loop back to form a complete ring.

The Distributed-Star ARCNET Network

ARCNET allows you to use both bus and star topologies in the same network. Called a distributed-star topology, active hubs are connected

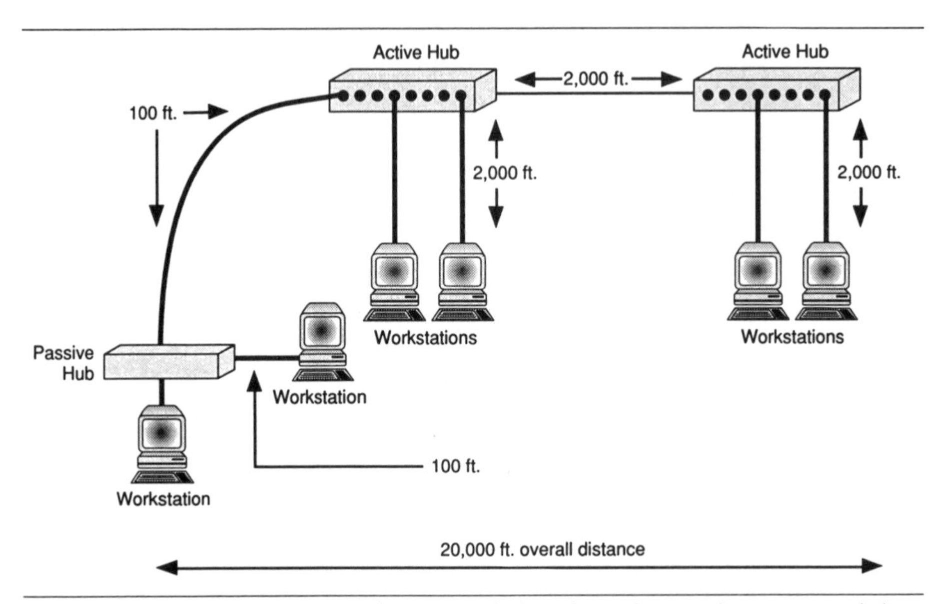

Figure 13-2. *An ARCNET star-topology network that shows distance limitations and the use of active and passive hubs.*

together by linking one of the ports on the first active hub to an empty port on the second active hub, and so on. You can also run a bus of nodes from each port of the active hub. In an active hub with 8 nodes, it is possible to bus up to 64 nodes in this manner. Each port on the active hub acts as the terminator to one end of the bus. The maximum length of each bus is still limited to 1,000 feet, and the last node on the bus must be terminated.

You can also place a passive hub off the active hub and radiate nodes from it as long as you remember the 100-foot distance limitation. The distributed-star topology makes the cabling of ARCNET extremely flexible.

The total cable distance for an ARCNET star-wired or distributed-star network is 20,000 feet with default retiming and adapter configuration settings. Some manufacturers of ARCNET adapters allow you to change adapter settings to increase the overall network distance. The distances vary depending on the timeouts you set.

Tip

If you change the timeouts to extend the total network distance, you must make the same change on all nodes on the network. This action is not recommended unless you need to have a single, large network. If you need additional distance, it is better to divide the network into two or more networks and connect the segments via the internal router in the NetWare server.

ARCNET Cabling

ARCNET networks use the following media:

1. RG-62 A/U coaxial cable
2. Category III or higher unshielded twisted-pair (UTP) cable
3. Fiber-optic cable

Cabling with RG-62 A/U

RG-62 A/U cable is a coaxial cable similar to the type used with cable television. It consists of a solid copper core surrounded by a sheath of nonconductive material. The ends use standard lock-mount bayonet (BNC) connectors. (See Figure 13-3.)

Most ARCNET adapter manufacturers require that you use a different adapter for a coaxial bus connection than for a star connection. The star-topology adapter is self-terminating at 93 Ohms; the bus adapter requires a separate 93-Ohm termination. Some manufacturers sell a more expensive adapter that works in either a bus or star configuration.

In addition, the wire that connects the adapter with the bus requires a T connector, which makes the connection between the incoming and outgoing bus cables. (See Figure 13-4 on the next page.)

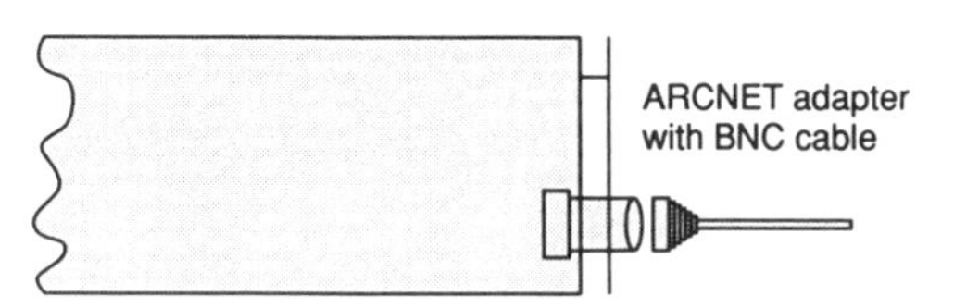

Figure 13-3. *A cable with a BNC connector and an adapter with female BNC.*

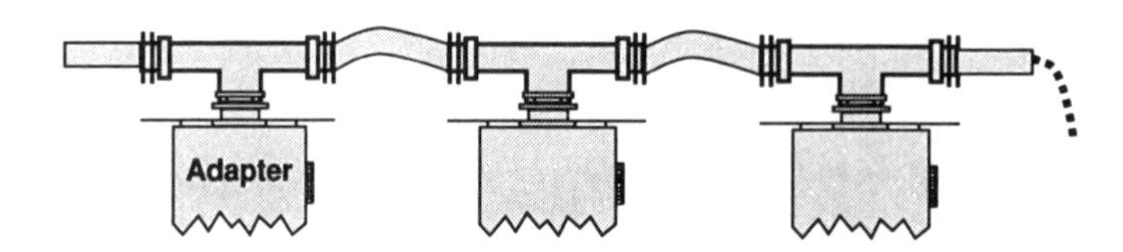

Figure 13-4. *A T connector with a terminator used in a bus configuration.*

Tip
In a pinch you can use a bus adapter on a star-wired network by attaching a T connector to the adapter media, placing a terminator on the end of the adapter, and plugging the cable into the T connector. Likewise, as long as the workstation is placed on the end of the bus, you can use a star-topology adapter in a bus-topology network. In that case, you do not use a separate terminator and T connector for the star-topology card.

The following are the cabling distances for RG-62 coaxial cable:

For a star-topology network with active hubs:
- 2,000 feet between two adapters if only a two-node net work exists
- 2,000 feet from the adapter to the active hub
- 2,000 feet between active hubs

For a star-topology network with passive hubs:
- 100 feet from an adapter to the passive hub
- 100 feet from an active hub to the passive hub

For a bus-topology network:
- 1,000 feet from the first adapter to the last adapter in the bus

Cabling with Unshielded Twisted-Pair

Unshielded twisted-pair consists of two or more pairs of 22 to 26 gauge single-strand wire in which each pair is twisted around the other and the total pairs are surrounded by a protective sheath. Most adapter manufacturers recommend the use of at least Category 3 unshielded twisted-pair (UTP) cable for ARCNET networks, which requires that the cable have a minimum of 2 to 3 twists per foot and support 100–110 Ohms.

In UTP, ARCNET uses only one pair of wires. One of the wires in the pair has a solid color and the other has to be the same solid color broken with a white stripe. The wires are designated as Blue, Blue/White, Orange, Orange/White, and so on. To connect the media to the adapter, you can use either an RJ-11 four-conductor connector or an RJ-45 six-conductor connector. (See Figure 13-5.) In either case, you will use the two center conductors and wire the connection straight through to the other end without crossing the wires.

Tip

To verify your connections, place the two connectors side by side. Read the color coding of the wire across the two connectors. They should be the same. Also, check the ends of the connectors to be sure you can see the copper end of the wire on all of the wires. If you can't, recable the end.

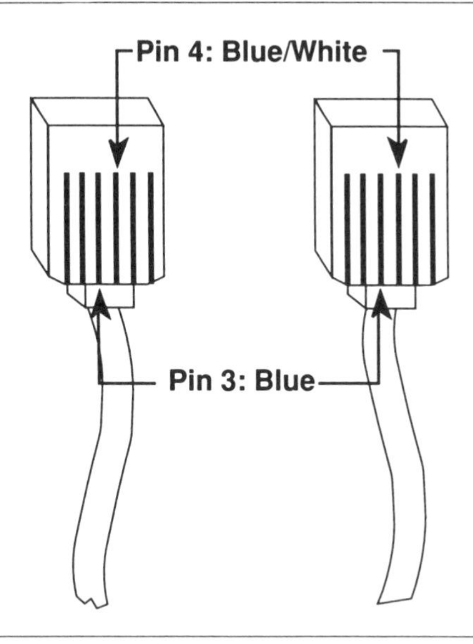

Figure 13-5. *Two RJ-45 connectors placed side by side showing the wires connected.*

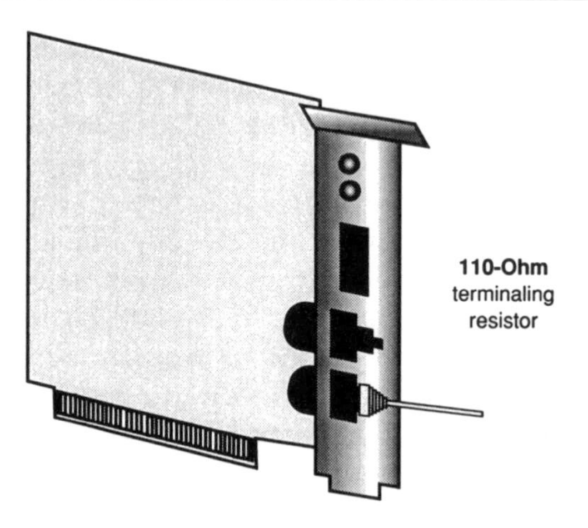

Figure 13-6. *The 110-Ohm terminating resistor.*

UTP ARCNET has two RJ-45 or RJ-11 connectors on the end of the adapter. With these adapters, you can use the adapter in either a star or a bus configuration. The adapter is supplied with a terminator. The UTP terminator is an RJ-45 or RJ-11 connector with a 110-Ohm resistor. (See Figure 13-6.) In a star configuration, the terminator is placed in the unused port. In a bus configuration, you will terminate the first and last adapter in the bus, and daisy-chain the cable from one adapter to another.

Tip

Do not under any circumstances try to use cable called *flat satin* or *silver satin cable*. Silver satin is the connection cable between your telephone and the wall outlet. It is not unshielded twisted-pair cable.

In a star-wired UTP ARCNET network, these distances apply:

400 feet between two adapters if only two nodes exist
400 feet from the adapter to the active hub
400 feet between active hubs

In a bus-wired UTP ARCNET network, different distances apply:

400 feet total distance on the bus
6 feet between nodes

Tip

Thomas-Conrad produces an extended distance ARCNET UTP card, which increases the distances in a bus- or star-wired network to 800 feet and allows up to 23 nodes on a bus-wired topology. However, this enhanced form of ARCNET UTP does not interconnect with an existing UTP network and must be routed to other ARCNET networks by placing an additional ARCNET adapter in the file server.

Tip

Do not use UTP or coaxial cable for outdoor wiring or wiring between buildings. Copper cable uses the building's earth ground. Different buildings can have different ground potentials. Ground potential is the amount of voltage on the ground line. This difference in ground potentials can scramble the signal or generate additional voltages on the network line that can either stop network traffic or damage your network adapters or other equipment.

Fiber-Optic Cabling

ARCNET also uses dual-stranded, multimode fiber-optic cable as a transmission medium. A fiber-optic adapter has two ports, one for data transmission and the other for data receipt. Fiber-optic ARCNET can only be wired in a star topology. However, two adapters can be networked without a hub.

Fiber-optic ARCNET uses two different connectors. The first connector is a screw-on connector called an SMA connector. The other connector is a bayonet-type connector called an ST connector. Before choosing connectors, be sure to find out which connector is on your adapters. The cost of changing the connectors if you get the wrong ones can be enormous.

Tip

In configurations using an active hub, the cables must be reversed between the adapter and the active hub, so that the transmitter on the adapter is linked to the receiver on the active hub, and vice versa. The best way to figure out which cable transmits and which receives is to connect the adapter transmit and receive cables. Then, turn on the computer, which powers up the transmitter on the adapter. The transmit cable shines light out the unattached cable end. Connect that end to the receive port of the active hub.

ARCNET cable distances vary depending on the type of fiber-optic cable you use. Fiber-optic cable size is designated in microns as a two-number set in which the first number represents the size of the inner core and the second number represents the size of the cladding that surrounds the inner core. ARCNET uses the following fiber-optic cable sizes:

62.5/125 microns

50/125 microns

100/140 microns

Most ARCNET manufacturers suggest the use of 62.5/125-micron cable because it yields a distance of approximately 8,000 feet between active devices. Other cable types can yield longer distances. You should consult your adapter manufacturer to determine the type of fiber-optic cable you use and the distances it supports.

Fiber is the most expensive of the cabling methods. The cost, including the cost of terminating the fiber, is approximately $1.00 per foot. However, fiber's immunity to electromagnetic interference (EMI) and radio-frequency interference (RFI) makes it the only choice in some circumstances. Fiber should always be used between buildings or where there is a potential for interference.

ARCNET Troubleshooting

ARCNET has few potentials for problems. When a problem exists on an ARCNET network, the network constantly reconfigures itself, or recons. These recons alert the user to possible network trouble. When you troubleshoot a problem with an ARCNET network, look for the following:

1. Verify that you do not have any duplicate node IDs. A duplicate node ID can bring down an ARCNET network.
2. Check for unterminated ends on passive hubs or bus segments. Also, check for bad cable connectors or terminators.

3. Be sure you are using bus and star adapters appropriately.
4. Be sure you have not violated any cabling rules such as the number of nodes on a bus or the distance a cable extends.
5. Check the diagnostic LEDs on the hubs and the end of the adapters to find an adapter that may be causing a problem. Recons will cause the red LED to flash.
6. Bring down the entire network. Take all nodes off the active hub or disconnect all the nodes on a bus and terminate the first and second adapters. Then, bring up the server. Attach the other nodes in succession, until you can recreate the failure. When you start to see recons after attaching a node, you will probably have found the problem adapter. Replace the adapter and add it back to the network.

In configuring ARCNET adapters for installation, you will need to set a base memory address, an I/O port address, and an interrupt. A conflict at any one of these points can cause the adapter to fail to initialize or cause it not to be able to find the network. The default settings of an ARCNET adapter are a base memory address of D000, an I/O port of 2E0h, and an interrupt of 2 or 9.

To troubleshoot these settings on an ARCNET adapter, perform the following actions:

Flash List

1. Verify that there is not a port address conflict. Use a diagnostics program such as CheckIt LAN or MSD from Microsoft to verify that you do not have more than one adapter using the same memory, I/O port address, or interrupt. Although Micro Channel and EISA computers may allow interrupt-sharing, most adapters don't.
2. Look for a decoding conflict. This problem occurs mostly with 16-bit adapters. Adapters send information to the CPU in 16-bit or 128-kilobyte (KB) segments. Adapters such as C000-Dfff that use a memory space in the same 128KB area must decode information in the same manner. If they are different, you won't be able to initialize the network adapter. The conflict usually occurs with video adapters that use the C000-C7ff address space. Sixteen-bit ARCNET adapters now have a decoding jumper to change the decode block size.

3. Look for bus-timing conflicts. If you can reduce the speed of the bus of the computer, try changing it to reduce the speed. Some ARCNET adapters come with jumpers that allow you to adjust the bus timing on the card.
4. If you are using a memory manager, verify that you have specifically excluded the memory address space the adapter is using. While many memory managers scan for the adapter using address space and exclude it, this generally doesn't work with network adapters. The adapter does not begin using address space until the adapter's driver is initialized. This occurs long after the memory manager has examined the adapter.
5. Verify that the computer is not using the address space used by the adapter to shadow video or RAM into the high-memory area.

chapter 14

Implementing Token-Ring

Characteristics

In the 1980s, International Business Machines (IBM) developed the token-ring network. IBM's token-ring was adapted by the IEEE (Institute of Electronic and Electrical Engineers) as the 802.5 standard. The Logical Link Control portion of the token-ring protocol (the upper sublayer of the Data-Link layer) uses the 802.2 standard. Later, Texas Instruments (TI) announced an agreement with IBM to develop a chip set that became the TMS380 chip set. This chip set was enhanced and became the TMS38C15, which accommodates 16Mbps token-ring. Recently TI announced a new token-ring chip set that uses the TMS380C26 chip. IBM also developed the Token-Ring Protocol Interface Controller (called TROPIC) chip set. The TROPIC chip set is marketed by National Semiconductor and is used by various manufacturers including Madge Networks, Proteon, Thomas-Conrad, Standard Microsystems Corp., Cabletron Systems, and 3Com to produce adapters that are register-compatible with IBM token-ring adapters.

Tip

Adapters based on the TI chip sets generally allow more adapter settings and enhanced driver capabilities than IBM adapters do. The TI chip set also supports bus-mastering, giving it a speed increase over IBM's 16/4 adapters. To counter the speed difference with TI-based adapters, IBM introduced its own bus-mastering Micro Channel adapter in 1993.

Token-ring started as a 4Mbps token-passing network. Later, 16Mbps token-ring was developed and supported by a number of manufacturers. The development of 16Mbps token-ring and the explosion in the number of adapter manufacturers has led to a large increase in the number of networks using token-ring.

Token-ring was originally designed to provide IBM mainframe and minicomputer users with a way to connect PCs to the mainframe or minicomputer environment. As a result, it has built-in ring diagnostics that ring management programs such as IBM's NetView can use.

Tip

Although the IBM and TI chip sets are both IEEE 802.5- and 802.2-compliant and operate on the same network without error, they do operate slightly differently. In some IBM-specific environments, only the TROPIC chip set, or an original IBM token-ring adapter, will operate properly. These environments include some Systems Network Architecture (SNA) and System Application Architecture (SAA) environments. Versions of Novell's NetWare for SAA prior to version 1.3 require an IBM or TROPIC-based adapter in the server.

Token-Ring Basics

The following terms are used commonly in token-ring networks:

Active MAU—A multistation access unit (hub) that actively retimes and retransmits the signal, allowing for greater distances.

DB9 connector—The DB9 connector, a D-shaped 9-pin adapter, connects the adapter to the network's lobe wire. The DB9 connector end is a female connection; the adapter connection is male.

Frame—The data and additional information required to transmit the data to the proper node on the network. Also called a packet.

Hermaphroditic connector—The hermaphroditic connector cannot be characterized as either male or female. This connector joins the lobe wire to the multistation access unit (MAU).

Lobe wire—The lobe wire joins the adapter to the MAU.

MAC frame—Media Access Control frame. These are the packets that are relayed between the adapters to provide information and management functions to the ring.

Main ring length—The total amount of wire in the MAUs plus the wiring between MAUs and the longest lobe length from a MAU to an adapter.

Maximum lobe length—The longest length of cable from an adapter to the MAU. This distance is a function of the main ring length.

MAU—The multistation access unit is a central device that connects workstations to the network.

Media filter—A media device integrated into an adapter or a separate device that allows media changes from Type 1 to Type 3 and vice versa.

Packet—The data and additional information required to transmit the data to the proper node on the network. Also called a frame.

Passive MAU—A MAU that does not actively retime or retransmit the signal. This is the general method of connecting token-ring cards. The device can be powered to reset the relays in the MAU when a card leaves the ring and to provide diagnostic LEDs. IBM and some other vendors' MAUs require a reset tool to reset the relays.

Relay—Each MAU contains a relay in its ports, which opens when a workstation inserts into the ring and remains closed for inactive or faulty nodes.

Ring—The electrical path of the network. The packet travels from adapter to adapter until it reaches the transmitting adapter, where the packet is removed.

Ring In/Ring Out—Each MAU contains a pair of Ring In/Ring Out (RI/RO) ports, which allow daisy-chaining of MAUs.

TIC—Token-Ring Interface Card—Used to designate the adapter card in an AS/400 minicomputer or a front-end processor (FEP) for a mainframe computer.

Token—A data packet that when held by a workstation gives that workstation permission to communicate on the LAN.

Token-passing—A deterministic protocol that requires a node to have permission to transmit by sending a single token around the network addressed to each adapter in turn.

How Token-Ring Works

Token-ring is most easily thought of as a physical star in topology and an electrical ring in operation. It uses a baseband signal that is encoded with the Differential Manchester encoding method. In token-ring networks, adapters are wired to a central wiring center called a multistation access unit (MAU) that is equipped with relays that automatically open when the token-ring adapter sends voltage (called a phantom voltage) across the media connecting it to the MAU. The media between the adapter and the MAU is called the lobe wire. (See Figure

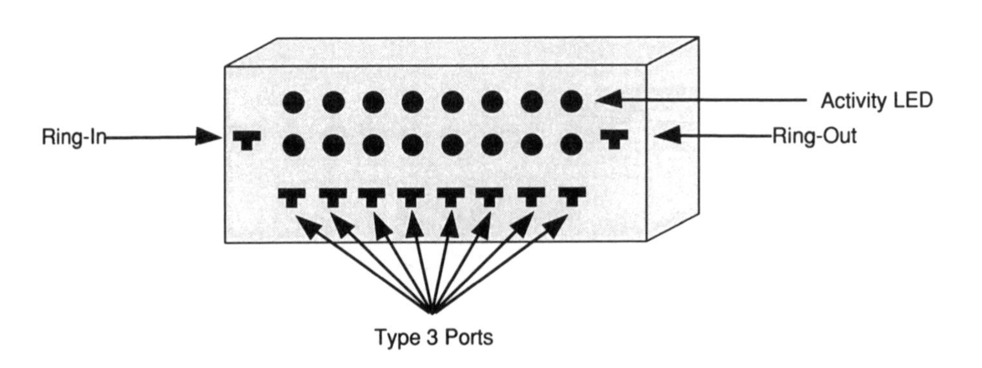

Figure 14-1. *A typical token-ring MAU.*

14-1.) Otherwise, the ports on the MAU remain closed, which allows the signal to bypass the port.

Originally, a MAU was a passive device such as the IBM 8220 eight-port MAU. In recent years, powered active MAUs, such as those made by Proteon and Madge Networks, that extend network distances have replaced passive MAUs.

Fiber-optic repeaters may be used to extend token-ring distances. (See Figure 14-2.)

In a token-ring network, a token determines which node has permission to transmit data. As Figure 14-3 on the next page shows, this token passes around the ring in physical node order. When a node receives the token, it appends its data to the token and sends the frame to its destination. The destination workstation reads the data frame, copies it to memory, and then releases it. Other workstations, realizing that the frame is not destined for them, read the frame and immediately release it. When the source workstation receives the data frame back, it checks to determine whether the destination workstation received the frame. If the destination workstation has received the data, the source node strips the data of the frame and releases the token to the next workstation in the physical ring.

To transmit a signal, the transmission flows into and out of each adapter on the network. (See Figure 14-3 on the next page.) Each node on the ring repeats the signal. In token-ring, the transmitting (source) node must receive the packet back in order to complete the transmis-

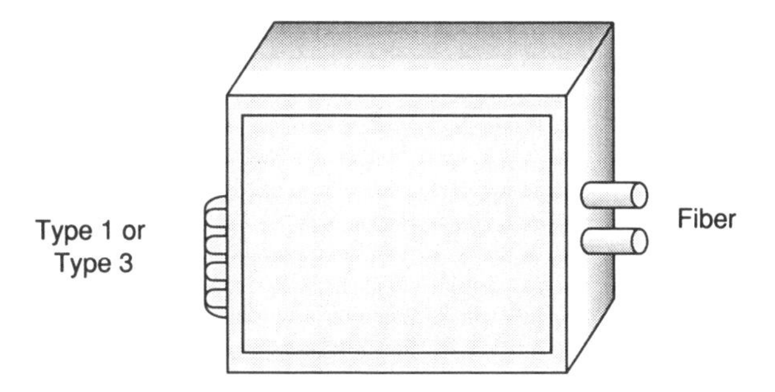

Figure 14-2. *A fiber-optic repeater.*

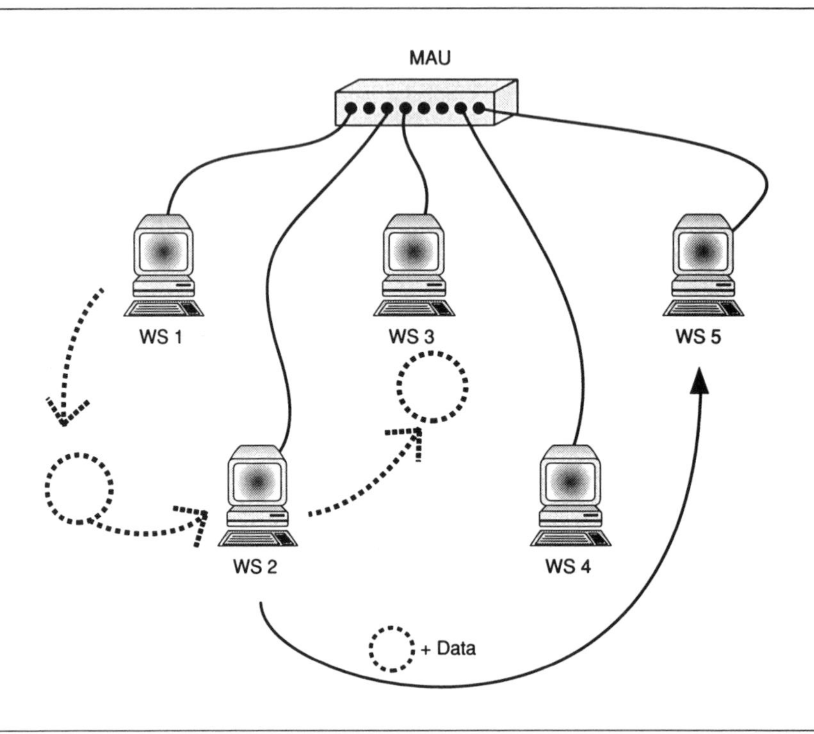

Figure 14-3. *Typical token-ring transmission.*

sion. To work properly, the ring must be closed. An open ring can cause an error.

Token-ring is divided into two sublayers. These sublayers are responsible for different aspects of the token-ring protocol. The Media Access Control (MAC) layer is responsible for controlling access to the transmission medium and has the following functions:

Frame formats—The MAC layer defines the token, a MAC frame for management and error recovery and reporting, and the Logical Link Control (LLC) frame for data transmission.

Error control—Generates the frame check sequence (FCS).

Ring maintenance—The MAC layer determines ring monitors, error recovery, and ring management.

The second sublayer, the LLC layer, defines the virtual data paths including multiple links to multiple logical entities. These virtual paths are called link service access points, or LSAPS. They allow one adapter to provide communication services to both IBM's NetBIOS and the Systems Network Architecture (SNA). In token-ring, LSAPS are used as a connection-oriented service in which frames are transmitted sequentially with acknowledgments between the frames. These are also known as Type 2 services.

Error monitoring under token-ring is one of the access method's strongest points. The majority of token-ring errors, connection, and recovery is built into the MAC layer of the token-ring protocol. The first node to enter the ring becomes the active monitor. If the active monitor leaves the ring, the other nodes on the ring enter a contention process, in which the device with the highest node ID becomes the active monitor. The other nodes on the ring become standby monitors. There are three additional monitors on a token-ring network. They are the following:

The *ring error monitor* (REM) collects error reports from the adapters, the active monitor, and the standby monitors. Management applications use the REM to monitor and control network functions.

The *configuration report servers* (CRS) collect the current network configuration and control adapter parameters such as access priority.

The *ring parameters server* (RPS) assigns operational parameters to the adapter at the time of its insertion into the ring.

These monitors use a series of different frames to provide information on the data they collect. These frames include the following:

The *claim token* is used to start the monitor-contention process if the active monitor is no longer present.

The *ring purge frame* is used to establish the ring after a monitor-contention process is completed or after the active monitor detects a token error condition. The ring purge is repeated by all nodes until the active monitor receives it again without error. Then, the active monitor generates a new token.

The *neighbor notification frame* allows all stations to determine the MAC layer node address of its nearest active upstream neighbor (NAUN) and to generate a list of node IDs for the configuration monitor.

The *beacon frame* alerts a downstream neighbor of a hard network error. This frame also informs the downstream neighbor of the type of error. The upstream neighbor automatically enters a self-test mode and may remove itself from the ring.

The *transmit forward frame* relays information around the ring to test communications.

The *hardware error frames* are generated whenever a wire fault, frequency error, or signal loss is detected.

The *soft error frames* are a listing of network errors that degrade performance but don't cause a failure.

The *active monitor present frame* is transmitted by the active monitor every seven seconds or after a ring purge to indicate that the active monitor is present.

The *standby monitor present frame* is transmitted in response to an active monitor present or to a standby monitor present frame.

The *lobe media test frame* is transmitted during the first phase of ring insertion to test the media from the MAU to the node and back.

The *duplicate address test frame* verifies the uniqueness of the entering node's ID.

The *request initialization frame* consists of a transmission to the ring parameter server (RPS) to request initialization parameters.

The *initialize ring station frame* is transmitted by the RPS in response to a request initialization frame.

The *report neighbor notification incomplete frame* indicates that the station has not received a transmission from its upstream neighbor during the neighbor notification process.

The *report new monitor frame* is transmitted by the winning station at the end of the claim-token process.

The *report stored upstream address* (SUA) Change Frame is used to report a change in the stations stored upstream address from information gathered during the neighbor notification process.

The *remove ring station frame* is sent by the configuration report server frame to force a station to remove itself from the ring.

The *change parameters frame* allows the configuration report server to adjust the ring parameters.

The monitoring features of token-ring make it the obvious choice for networks where network management is of primary importance. Several products on the market take advantage of token-ring's features, including IBM's LAN Network Manager, Proteon's NetView, Cabletron's Spectrum, and Thomas-Conrad's Sectra.

Token-Ring Cabling

Token-ring networks use three media types—shielded twisted-pair, unshielded twisted-pair, and fiber-optic media.

Shielded Twisted-Pair (Type 1)

Type 1 22-AWG shielded, twisted-pair token-ring uses four wires. They are transmit+, transmit–, receive+, and receive–. The media is terminated with a DB9 connector. Type 1 media supports 16Mbps transmission with up to 260 workstations per network.

Five other shielded twisted-pairs variants exist. The specific cable types are:

Type 2—Consists of two 22-AWG shielded, solid twisted-pair wires and four solid twisted-pair 26-AWG wires. Only the 22-AWG gauge pairs are used for the token-ring connection.

Type 3—Consists of 22- to 24-AWG unshielded twisted-pair wire. Supports transmission at 4- or 16Mbps with 72 stations and a distance limitation one third that of Type 1 cable.

Type 5—Consists of 100/140-micron fiber-optic cable, used for fiber repeaters.

Type 6—Consists of 26-AWG stranded, shielded twisted-pair media. Type 6 media supports a distance limitation of two thirds that of Type 1 cable. This cable is generally used as the patch cables between MAUs or from a wall plate to the adapter or wall plate to MAU.

Type 9—Consists of 26-AWG shielded, solid core, twisted-pair. Type 9 is approved for plenum installation. It carries a distance limitation that is two thirds that of Type 1 cable.

Tip

A series of wiring charts and documents is included here for your reference and convenience.

Cabling with Type 1 Cable

Type 1 cable and its variants use two specific cable ends. Connections between MAUs and on wall plates use a hermaphroditic or Type 1 connector. (See Figures 14-4 here and 14-5 on the next page.) The connection to the adapter uses a DB9 connector. The specific pinouts are as follows:

Signal Lead	Pinout Type 1 Connector	Pinout DB9
Receive+	Red (R)	Pin 1
Receive–	Green (G)	Pin 6
Transmit+	Orange (O)	Pin 9
Transmit–	Black (B)	Pin 5

Tip

The Type 1 connector is designated as hermaphroditic because it is not gender-specific—it has no male or female end. The connector is self-shorting when not in place. This allows for some adapter

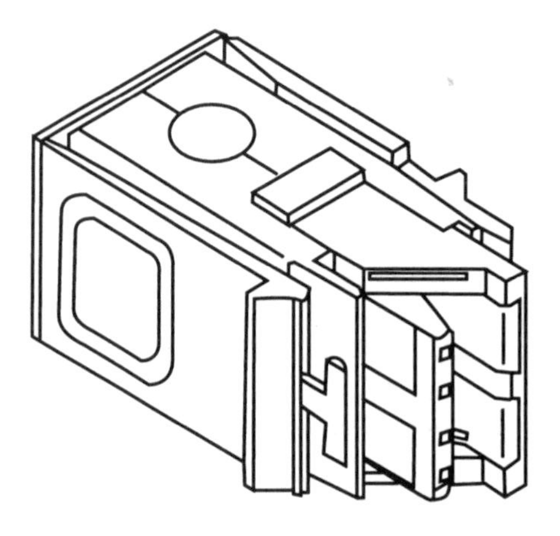

Figure 14-4. *A type 1 hermaphroditic connector.*

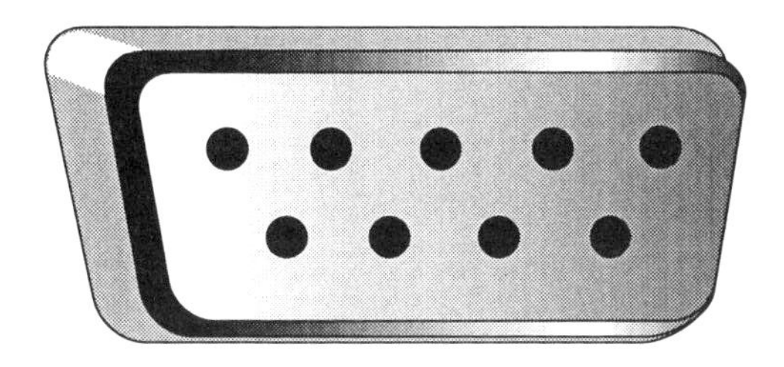

Figure 14-5. *A DB9 connector.*

diagnostics prior to placing the adapter on the ring and allows you to check the cable between the adapter and the wall. Placing the pins of a Volt-Ohm-Meter across the transmit+ (Pin 9) and transmit– (Pin 5) or the receive+ (Pin 1) and receive– (Pin 6) should yield zero Ohms, or a short condition. If it does not, the cable is probably bad.

Type 6 patch cables, which link MAUs to each other, use the hermaphroditic connector on each end of the cable. The wiring is straight-through—it is wired the same way on both ends. Patch cables are connected to the Ring Out port on one MAU to the Ring In port on the next MAU. They can also be used between a Type 1 patch panel and a MAU.

Cabling with Type 3 Cable

While Type 1 cable offers greater distance and a larger number of nodes on the network, it is generally difficult and bulky to work with. Most installations prefer working with Type 3 cable. Type 3 uses an eight-position RJ-45 jack at both ends of the cable. Type 3 cable, in this context, is unshielded twisted-pair cable. This cable is divided into several grades or categories. Of these grades, 3, 4, and 5 are most commonly used in token-ring networks.

Category 3—Also known as Level III cable, this is the most common Type 3 cable. Category 3 cable is 22- to 24-AWG UTP cable that complies with the standards set by the Electronic Industries Association/Telecommunications Industry Association (EIA/TIA) 568 Commercial Building Standards Guide. Category 3 cable is designed to carry 4Mbps token-ring traffic with up to 72 nodes per ring.

Category 4—Also known as Level IV, this is also a 22- to 24-AWG unshielded twisted-pair cable that complies with the EIA/TIA standards set in Technical Bulletin PN-2841. Category 4 cable is designed to handle 10Mbps Ethernet and can handle 16Mbps token-ring for short distances.

Category 5—Also known as Level V, this is 22- to 24-AWG UTP wire that complies with the Category V standards set in EIA/TIA Technical Bulletin PN-2841. Category 5 is designed to handle 100Mbps traffic over UTP. It easily handles 16Mbps token-ring traffic.

Tip

A Category 5 cable plant requires that you have all Category 5 components and that they are all installed properly. Expensive, improperly installed Category 5 components don't yield the proper results.

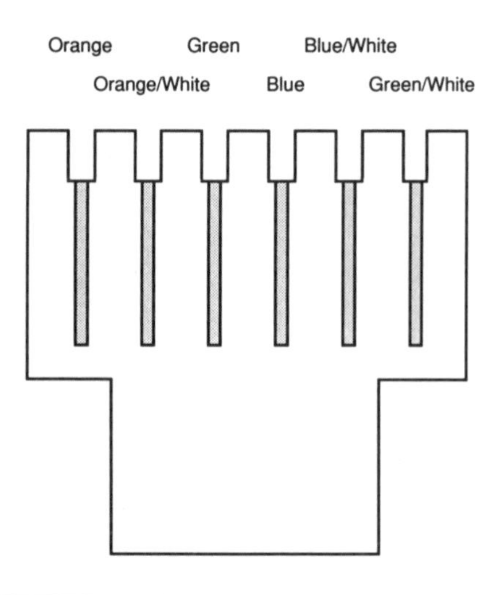

Figure 14-6. *The pinouts for a six-position jack.*

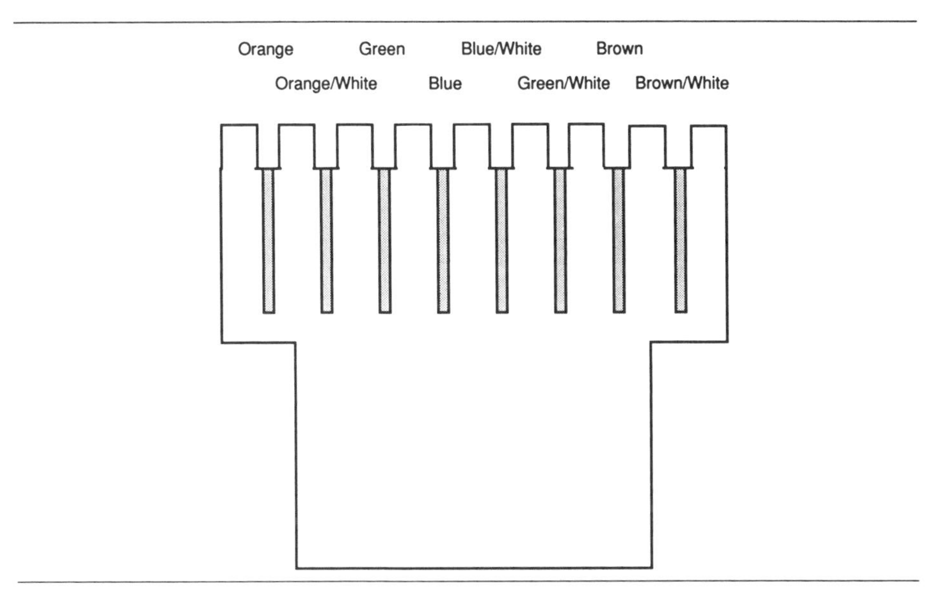

Figure 14-7. *The pinouts for an eight-position jack.*

The Type 3 RJ-45 connector uses the inner two connectors for one pair and the next outer two for the other. These are pins 3, 4, 5, and 6. Pins 1, 2, 7, and 8 are not used. A 60-pin RJ-11 connector can also be used. In that case, the pins you would use are 2, 3, 4, and 5. The connections appear as shown in Figures 14-6 on the previous page and 14-7 here.

As you can see from the figures, the inner two connectors are the receive pair and the outer two are the transmit pair. The original and second-generation TI-based adapters have both connectors on the adapter. You switch between the connector types with one or more jumpers. Newer TI-based adapters should contain circuitry to select the media automatically. IBM and TROPIC-based adapters come with only a DB9 connector. Some newer IBM and TROPIC-based adapters also have automatic media-selection capabilities. With adapters that only have the DB9 connector, you can still use Type 3 cable by installing a media filter.

Tip

The old saying that you get what you pay for is particularly true when it comes to media filters. If you are attempting to use media filters with 16Mbps token-ring, purchase the best one you can find. A poor or unstable media filter causes unending problems that are almost impossible to track down. The same is true for the quality of the cable you use. Category 3 works for 4Mbps and 16Mbps token-ring LANs if you keep the distance short. For most 16-bit applications, use Category 4 or 5 cable.

Token-Ring Rules and Distances

Token-ring cabling is straightforward in concept but difficult to install and maintain in practice. It uses six different types of cables and two different types of connectors. The basic cabling limits are determined by the following formulas:

Type I cable formula:

16Mbps (nonpowered MAUs)
The node distance = 600 feet – (2 feet * the number of ports on the MAU) – (the sum of all RI/RO cables – the length of the shortest RI/RO cable)

4Mbps (nonpowered MAUs)
The node distance = 1,200 ft – (2 feet * the number of ports on the MAU) – (the sum of all RI/RO cables – the length of the shortest RI/RO cable)

Type III cable formula:

16Mbps (nonpowered MAUs)
The node distance = 250 feet – (2 feet * the number of ports on the MAU) – (the sum of all RI/RO cables – the length of the shortest RI/RO cable)

4Mbps (nonpowered MAUs)
The node distance = 500 feet – (2 feet * the number of ports on the MAU) – (the sum of all RI/RO cables – the length of the shortest RI/RO cable)

Tip
If you are going to be using powered MAUs, check with the manufacturer to determine the correct distance calculations for its

MAUs. Fiber and copper repeaters generally are excluded from this calculation.

TROUBLESHOOTING TOKEN-RING NETWORKS

One of the blessings of token-ring is that diagnosis is sophisticated. The best place to start is with operator error. The first two basic troubleshooting tips are

1. Be sure all cables are plugged in securely.
2. Be sure that the adapter is set to the proper ring speed.

After you've determined that the cables are secure and that the adapters are operating at the correct ring speed, you must determine where the fault is occurring and isolate a fault domain. This is a fairly simple process, particularly if you have a simple token-ring management software such as Proteon's TokenView Plus or IBM's LAN Network Manager. Remember that the adapter reporting the error is not the adapter at fault. The adapter that reports the error is the NAUN of the adapter that has the error. The NAUN generates a beacon frame that alerts the rest of the network that there is a problem. Most token-ring management products can decode the beacon frame to give you the address of the adapter reporting the beacon and its downstream neighbor. The fault domain is the area including the adapter reporting the error, the media, and the adapter's downstream neighbor. Remove the adapter downstream from the beaconing adapter, and verify its operation and cable.

You'll find that the majority of your problems with token-ring involve cable problems. With that in mind, you should invest in a good cable tester. Depending on how much you wish to spend, you can run the gamut of testing devices. Certainly, however, you should at minimum have a good VOM to test cables. From there you can look to a tester from companies such as Microtest that make a wide range of cable testers for all budgets. Also, keep in mind your cable distance and the node number limitations. Do not exceed these recommendations without expecting errors over time.

Beyond the basic hardware ring problems are other token-ring problems are related to protocol. These are generally related to traffic patterns or malformed packets. For this type of problem, a protocol analyzer beyond the basic network management tools is necessary. There are several good protocol analyzers on the market, including LANalyzer for Windows from Novell, LANWatch from FTP Software, and LANdecoder/TR from Triticom, that can help decode frames on the network and discover protocol problems.

Troubleshooting Token-Ring Adapters

The majority of problems with token-ring adapters are related to either a conflict with another adapter or a bus-timing issue. Another source of trouble with TI bus-mastering adapters is a problem related to priority within the system.

Cards based upon the TROPIC chip set and IBM chip set use the following system features:

I/O port
shared memory address
interrupt request line (IRQ)

Cards based upon the TI chip set use the following system resources:

I/O port
DMA channel
interrupt request line (IRQ)

In token-ring adapters that exhibit a conflict with another system resource or fail to load the LAN driver, look first for a conflict with the interrupt request line (IRQ). The default is IRQ 2. TROPIC-based adapters use IRQs 2, 3, 6, and 7. TI-based adapters use a variety of interrupts.

Tip

TI-based adapters used with the IBM LAN Support Program are restricted to the settings that an IBM adapter uses. This reduces the ability of the adapter to work in areas where it must use an interrupt or I/O setting that is not available to the IBM or TROPIC adapters. The restrictions include using I/O ports A20 or A24 and IRQs 2, 3, 6, and 7. TI-based adapters do not use a shared RAM address. If you encounter a problem with a TI-based adapter running IBM's LAN Support Program, look at your shared RAM address first.

After interrupt conflicts, the majority of problems TROPIC-based adapters have are with the shared RAM address the adapter uses. The settings can range from C000h to DC000h. This address range can conflict with a variety of adapters and memory managers. Programs such as CheckIt LAN or MSD can be useful in verifying problems with shared RAM. Shared RAM problems most often appear with video adapters, SCSI controllers, or system shadowing.

TI-based adapters encounter problems with other adapters that use DMA channels and especially with those that use bus-mastering. The adapters that are most likely to cause DMA conflicts are:

SCSI controllers
CD ROM controllers
sound cards
other network adapters

One of the hardest token-ring problems to diagnose involves two bus-mastering devices on an ISA machine. They may both be at different DMA addresses, but they can still conflict with each other. This is based on the problems related to bus-mastering priority. In bus-mastering, the DMA controller on the adapter takes over the entire bus until it is finished with the data transfer or until the CPU completes a memory refresh cycle. The problem appears when two controllers want to control the bus at the same time. The problem is usually solved by the DMA channel number. The adapter with the lowest channel number has priority. This is similar to the idea of interrupt priority with IRQs. To prevent one adapter from keeping the bus when others need it, a concept known as fairness was developed. Some device drivers implement fairness, while others do not. If a device driver does not implement fairness, the best idea is to place it at the highest DMA channel available to it. This usually solves the problem.

Token-ring networks can be complicated to install and difficult to maintain. However, in the IBM world of mainframe and minicomputer connections, token-ring is practically a necessity. A well-maintained and well-installed token-ring network will bring years of use, reliable performance, and regular, deterministic operations.

chapter 15

Implementing Ethernet

Characteristics

Ethernet was originally developed in the early 1970s by Digital, Intel, and Xerox. Since then, it has gone through several permutations and has become the most prolific access method in the world today. Also called IEEE 802.3, Ethernet is a CSMA/CD (Carrier Sense with Multiple Access with Collision Detection) protocol.

The current Ethernet implementation is 10 megabits per second (Mbps), although 100Mbps Ethernet-based networks are being developed. The final IEEE specifications have not yet been promulgated for these higher-speed Ethernet implementations. For simplicity, we will discuss only the following types of Ethernet:

10BASE-2—thin Ethernet

10BASE-5—thick Ethernet

10BASE-T—unshielded twisted-pair Ethernet

10BASE-5 was the first Ethernet implementation, followed shortly afterward by 10BASE-2. 10BASE-T is a recent development.

Ethernet Basics

A discussion of Ethernet requires the use of some terms you may not be familiar with. These terms include

10BASE-2—Also known as thin Ethernet. The 10 stands for transmission speed, BASE stands for baseband, and 2 stands for the maximum length of a segment in hundreds of meters. (This figure is close to the actual length of 185 meters.) Thick Ethernet uses RG-58U as the transmission media.

10BASE-5—Also known as thick Ethernet. The 10 stands for the transmission speed, BASE stands for baseband, the 5 stands for the maximum length of a segment in hundreds of meters. Thick Ethernet is limited to an overall segment distance of 500 meters. It uses a double-shielded, .04-inch diameter coaxial cable as the transmission medium.

10BASE-T—Ethernet over unshielded twisted-pair (UTP) media. The 10 stands for the transmission speed, BASE stands for baseband, and the T stands for UTP. 10BASE-T uses Category 3, 4, or UTP media.

AUI—The attachment unit interface, used with 10BASE-5 networks, is the method of connecting the adapter or other device to the media. The AUI uses a DB-15 connector as its cable interface.

Bus—The cable segment to which workstations or repeaters are attached.

Collision—When two adapters attempt to transmit at the same time, the signals interfere with each other or collide. When a collision occurs, each station stops transmitting and waits a random amount of time based on a timing algorithm. After waiting, the workstations begin to listen again to see if the wire is clear before they transmit.

Concentrator—A central wiring device for 10BASE-T and 10BASE-2 networks, similar to an ARCNET active hub, which retimes and retransmits the signal.

Inter-repeater Link (IRL)—The segment between two repeaters. The IRL does not contain any workstations or other attached devices and is also known as an unpopulated segment.

Jabber—A signal on a 10BASE-T network that is out of specification and that disrupts network traffic.

MAU—Medium attachment unit. A wiring device that provides the physical attachment between the cable and the network device. Also known as a transceiver. MAUs allow 10BASE-2 adapters to operate on 10BASE-T networks.

Repeater—On 10BASE-2 and 10BASE-5 networks, the repeater is a device that regenerates and retimes the signal to increase the distance a signal can travel over a particular cable segment. Repeaters can be intelligent and perform network management, or they can simply connect dissimilar media segments together.

Segment—A length of cable on 10BASE-T, 10BASE-2, and 10BASE-5 networks. Workstations, transceivers, or concentrators connect to it.

Transceiver—On a 10BASE-5 network, a device used to connect the adapter or other network device to the media. Can also be used on 10BASE-2 or 10BASE-T networks to attach a device via the AUI port to the network.

Trunk—A cable segment on a 10BASE-2 or 10BASE-5 network.

Vampire tap—A device that cuts directly into the media and attaches to 10BASE-2 and 10BASE-5 cable to allow an attachment without splicing the cable or using a T connector. Many 10BASE-5 transceivers come with a vampire tap to make connections to the cable easier.

How Ethernet Works

Ethernet is a nonrooted, branching bus topology in which each adapter attaches to a central cable segment. Cable segments can be connected to each other with MAUs, repeaters, or concentrators to form longer segments or to branch existing segments.

The bus segments follow a wiring rule known as the 5, 4, 3 rule (see Figure 15-1 on the next page) in which no more than five segments can separate any two workstations on the network; no more than four repeaters can be placed between any two workstations; and no more than three populated segments can separate any two workstations.

This 5, 4, 3 rule is based on the propagation delay of the Ethernet signal and should not vary. Violate this rule at your own risk.

Tip

Even the 10BASE-T network, in which workstations radiate from the concentrator, is a bus configuration electrically. The media 10BASE-T uses makes it appear as a star topology, but the connections still operate as if they are on a bus. 10BASE-T is subject to the 5, 4, 3 rule. However, since it is impossible for 10BASE-T to violate the rule that calls for no more than three populated segments between two workstations, unless you are in a mixed environment with 10BASE-2 or 10BASE-5, you can ignore the rule.

In Ethernet, only one station may transmit at a time. Each adapter listens on the network for traffic. If the adapter detects no traffic, the workstation will begin a transmission. When more than one station transmits at the same time, a collision occurs. This collision stops all network traffic and destroys the two transmitted packets. When the stations that sent the packets do not receive an acknowledgment of the successful receipt of the packet, they assume a collision has occurred and back off a random amount of time before attempting to transmit again. The stations then listen for a free period on the wire and retrans-

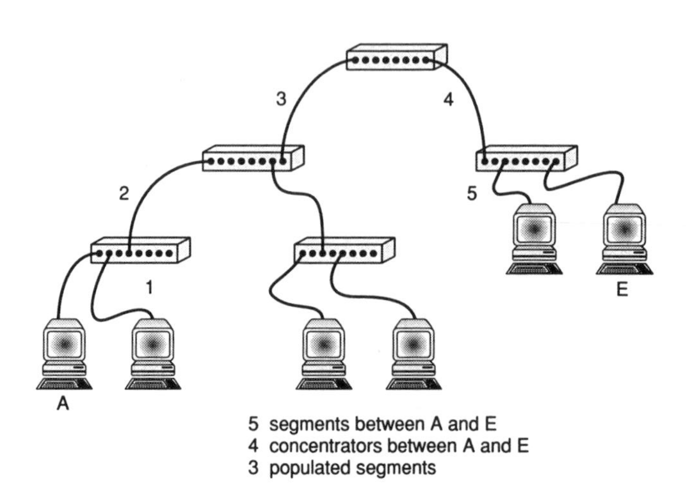

Figure 15-1. *A diagram illustrating the 5, 4, 3 rule.*

mit their packets. This communication method makes Ethernet extremely efficient for smaller networks. However, as the number of nodes on your network grows, the efficiency of the protocol falls dramatically as the number of collisions increases.

Remember, a collision stops all network traffic for a short period of time. 10BASE-T managed hubs will make this contention less noticeable, but you can still see delays on the network. The realistic cutoff point for Ethernet is about 40 workstations per segment.

There are a variety of Ethernet adapters and chip sets. Manufacturers include 3COM Corp., Artisoft/Eagle, IBM Corp., Olicom, Proteon, Standard Microsystems, Thomas-Conrad, and Ungermann-Bass. Of these adapters, the Novell NE2000 adapter and its clones are the most popular. NE2000s are based on the National Semiconductor ATLANTIC chip set, which combines a number of components to allow the manufacturer to make a less-expensive Ethernet adapter. One of the failings, however, of the ATLANTIC chip set and its implementation in the NE2000 is the limited number of IRQ settings available. For workstations, the NE2000 adapter is ideal. File servers, however, need higher performance. Manufacturers have responded with a large number of adapters that transfer the data on and off the CPU bus more quickly. These adapters include EISA and bus-mastering ISA adapters, which can increase your total network throughput dramatically.

New 100-Mbps adapters, or fast Ethernet adapters, are presently under development. Although the standards for these adapters are not completely formed, several manufacturers are experimenting with what they believe will be the resulting standard. The 100Mbps Ethernet adapters are based upon the IEEE 802.3 Ethernet and will not interconnect with standard 10Mbps Ethernet adapters. However, for high-performance needs such as CAD/CAM, these faster adapters can be useful.

10BASE-2 Cabling

10BASE-2 Ethernet uses RG-58U cable. This cable is similar to the RG-62 A/U cable used by ARCNET, but is slightly smaller in diameter. The maximum cable segment for 10BASE-2 is 185 meters (607 feet) per segment. An additional standard called *extended length* increases the maximum segment length by 20 percent. This method requires that all nodes on the segment have the extended length capability, including the transceivers that are used to connect cards of different media types. The maximum cable length for extended length is 925 meters.

In 10BASE-2 Ethernet, the maximum number of nodes per segment is 30. The maximum number of nodes on all segments cannot exceed 1,024 nodes. Each cable must be terminated by a 50-Ohm terminator attached to a T connector at the end of the cable. One end of the cable must be grounded. The leg of the T connector is connected to an adapter. The minimum distance between each adapter is .6 meters (1.5 feet). The adapters and T connectors use a BNC-style (bayonet) connector. A BNC connector joins each adapter to the media. The transceiver can be separated from the adapter. The maximum cable distance from the adapter to the transceiver is 50 meters (164 feet). (See Figure 15-2.)

10BASE-5 Cabling

10BASE-5 Ethernet uses a 50-Ohm, 0.4-inch-diameter coaxial cable. In 10BASE-5, the maximum cable length is 500 meters (1,640 feet). The ends of the cable are terminated with 50-Ohm terminators. One end of the cable must be grounded. A transceiver connects the adapter or device to the main network cable or trunk segment. Transceivers must be placed a minimum of 2.5 meters (8 feet) apart. The maximum network distance is 1,500 meters (4,920 feet). A total of 100 transceivers can be placed on any segment. (See Figure 15-3 on the next page.)

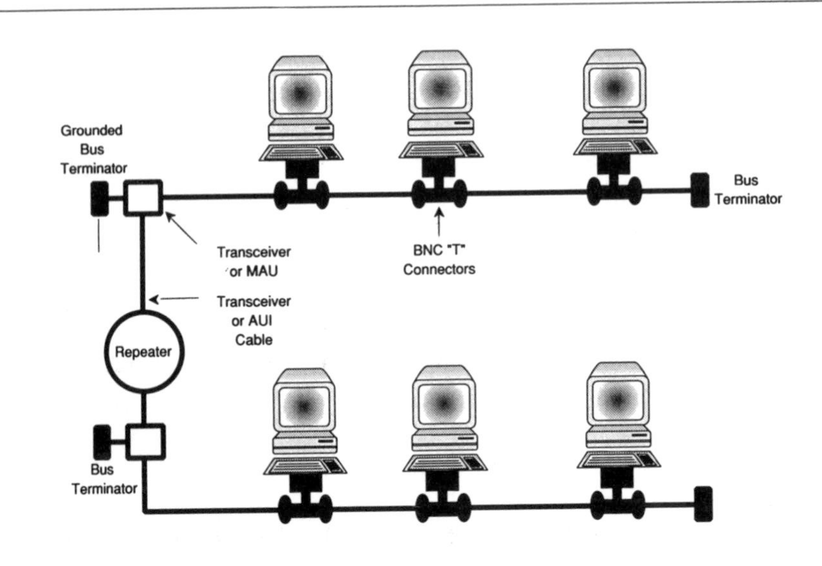

Figure 15-2. *Typical 10BASE-2 cable connections with distances.*

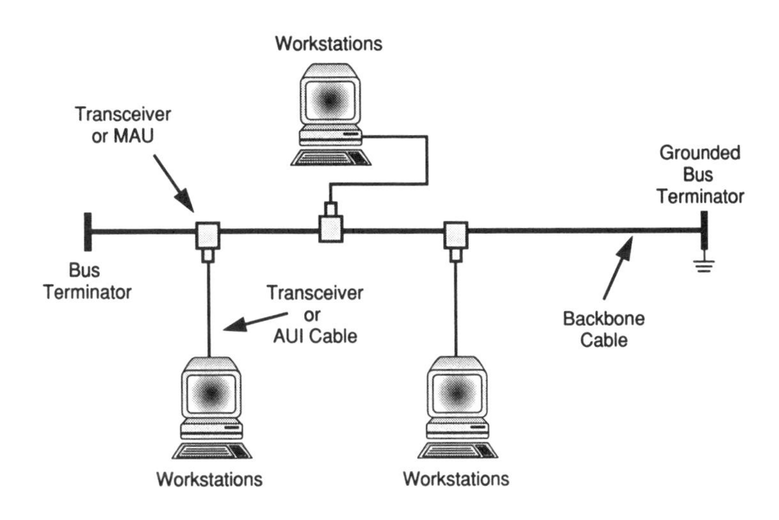

Figure 15-3. *A typical 10BASE-5 cable connection.*

Transceivers are normally connected to the media using a vampire tap. (See Figure 15-4 on the next page.) This connector pierces the cable and makes the electrical connection without having to cut the cable and splice a connector in place. Vampire taps are much less expensive and faster than splicing a connection.

The connection on the transceiver and adapter is a DB-15 or DIX connector. The cable is a 50-Ohm cable that is generally more flexible than the main trunk segment The maximum cable length between the transceiver and the adapter is 50 feet. (See Figure 15-5 on the next page.)

Fifty-Ohm 10BASE-5 media is generally difficult to work with and more expensive than 10BASE-2 media. As a result, it is rarely used. However, there is a large installed base of 10BASE-5 media, which makes a working knowledge of this type of cable essential.

10BASE-T Cabling

Because of its ease of use, 10BASE-T media is becoming the fastest growing Ethernet market segment. The UTP cable 10BASE-T uses is Category 4 or 5 unshielded twisted-pair. While you can use Category 3

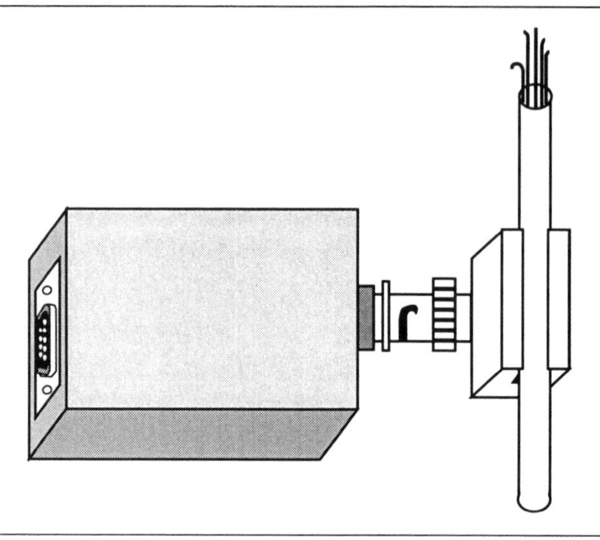

Figure 15-4. *Vampire cable connection with transceiver.*

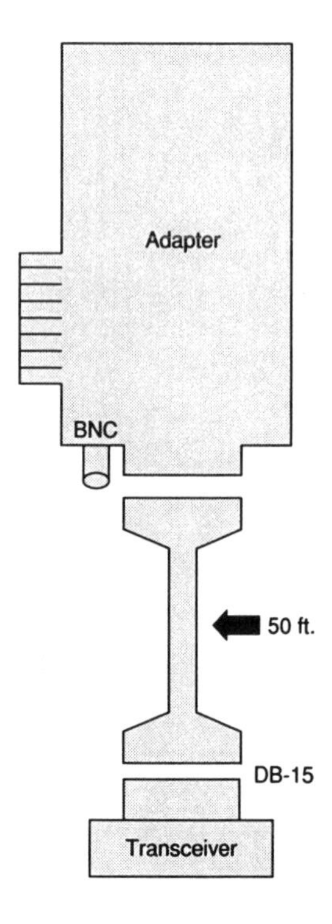

Figure 15-5. *Transceiver and adapter with cable showing connectors.*

(which is standard telephone wire), it is not recommended and will generally cause problems. Unlike 10BASE-5 or 10BASE-2, 10BASE-T uses a star-wired topology, which makes the connections much easier to install and troubleshoot. Users who are changing over from ARC-NET or UTP-based token-ring networks will find few wiring changes are required.

On a 10BASE-T network, each connection between the adapter and concentrator is considered a populated segment. The maximum distance between the concentrator and adapter is 100 meters (130 feet). This is also true of interconnections between concentrators. When concentrators are joined together with media, it is called daisy-chaining. (See Figure 15-6.)

As a result of the limitations of the 5, 4, 3 rule, daisy-chaining concentrators in a 10BASE-T network is not necessarily the best way to connect a large group of concentrators. For a large group it is best to use a 10BASE-2 bus with 10BASE-T segments radiating off it. Since concentrators are collectively considered as one device on a 10BASE-2 network segment, you can easily bus them by using the concentrator's onboard AUI port. Connect 10BASE-2 transceivers on the AUI ports and use T connectors to place the concentrators in a bus topology. (See

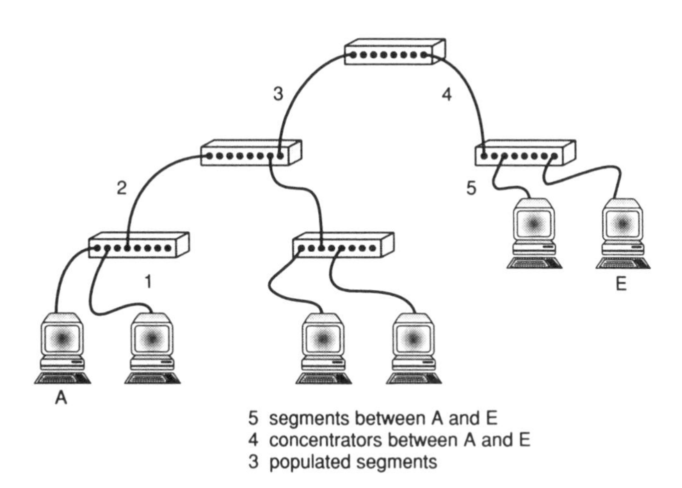

Figure 15-6. *Daisy-chaining concentrators and the 5, 4, 3 rule as it applies to 10BASE-T.*

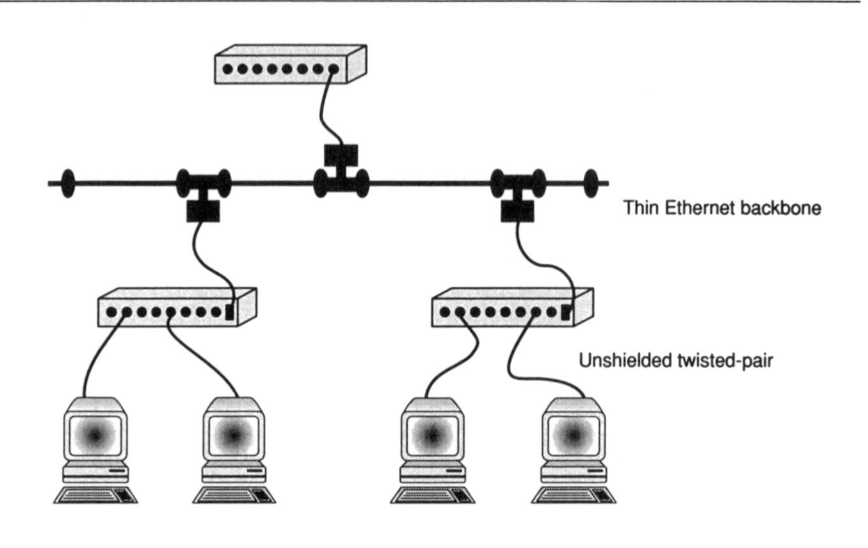

Figure 15-7. *Using a mixed-media network.*

Figure 15-7.) This configuration allows you to have up to 30 concentrators on a segment.

Tip

Do not under any circumstances use flat satin (silver satin) cable. Silver satin connects your telephone with the wall outlet. It is not UTP.

Concentrators

Concentrators are at the heart of the 10BASE-T network. All wiring is in a star configuration to the concentrator. The concentrator also has unique wiring diagnostics. It will inform you of a reverse polarity cable. A light on the concentrator should either illuminate or change color if a reverse polarity cable is plugged into the concentrator. It will also provide a link integrity light. Under the 10BASE-T specifications, the adapters and concentrators monitor the receive pair of wires for a special electrical signal that should be present on the wire. If it is present, the device assumes a good pair of wires and lights its link polarity light. Finally, a 10BASE-T network is susceptible to jabber, which is a corrupted signal on the wire that is out of specification. This signal will corrupt network traffic. It can be caused by a bad adapter or cable. If the concentrator detects a segment that is jabbering, it will automatically remove that node from the network and inform you by lighting its auto removal light.

Tip
Be sure to check BOTH ends of the cable (adapter and concentrator) for link integrity. The device monitors only its receive pair, and you must verify both ends to be sure you have a good cable.

Media

The UTP connection utilizes an RJ-45 connector at each end. Four wires are used to make the Ethernet UTP connection. (See Figure 15-8.) The connector uses pins 1 and 2 and pins 3 and 6 as the pairs. The pin configurations are shown in Table 15-1 on the next page.

The general UTP cable will have a straight-through wiring scheme. In a straight-through connection Pin 1 is connected to Pin 1 on the other end. The UTP cables may need to be wired in a reverse polarity connection. A reverse polarity wiring reverses the transmit and receive pairs such that transmit positive on one end will go to receive positive on the other, and the transmit negative will go to receive negative. (See Figure 15-9 on the next page.) Thus Pin 1 will go to Pin 3, and Pin 2 will

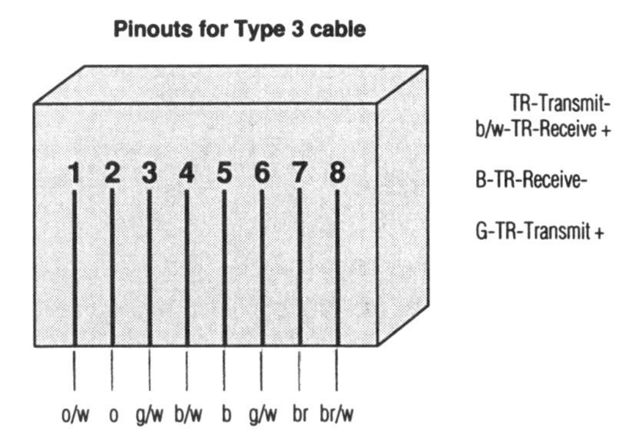

Figure 15-8. *RJ-45 wired for 10BASE-T.*

Pin	Color	Signal
1	**White/Orange**	**Transmit Positive**
2	**Orange**	**Transmit Negative**
3	**White/Green**	**Receive Positive**
4	Blue/White	Not Used
5	Blue	Not Used
6	**Green/White**	**Receive Negative**
7	Brown	Not Used
8	White/Brown	Not Used

Table 15-1. *Pin configurations.*

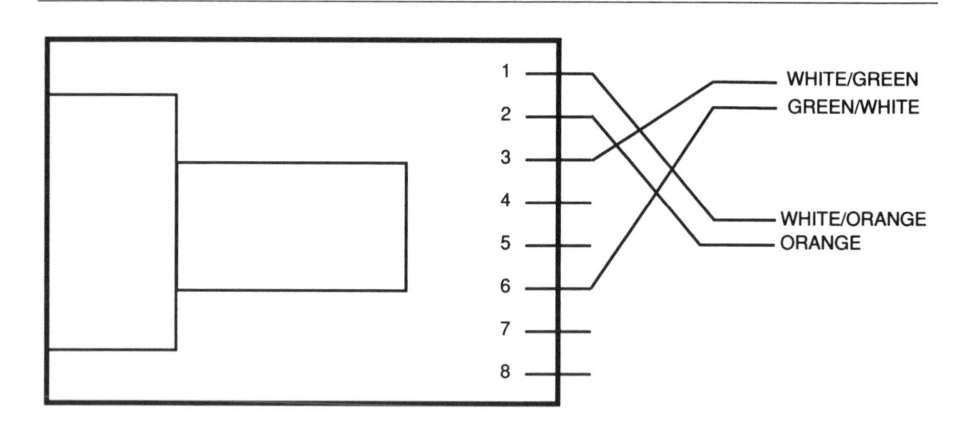

Figure 15-9. *Reverse polarity wiring scheme.*

go to Pin 6. The requirement for a reverse polarity cable will depend on the type of equipment you have. Concentrators that follow the 10BASE-T specification will have a series of ports labeled MDIX that have an internal crossover and utilize straight-through connections. Other ports are labeled MDI and do not have an internal crossover. This port is designed to connect between concentrators, but can be used for connections with adapters as well. Connections to this port require that reverse polarity cable be used.

If you are going to be using twisted-pair cables, it is a good idea to invest in a cable scanner. The connections on twisted-pair cable are troublesome and require a good connection. Using a pair scanner on all new and suspected cables can save a lot of trouble later on. It will spot problems with a cable and warn of bad crimps or reversed cables.

If you have a large Ethernet network, particularly in a mixed-media environment, the best consideration is an intelligent wiring device or managed hub. You can centralize your wiring into fewer devices and make troubleshooting and managing the network much easier.

Basic Ethernet Troubleshooting

Troubleshooting Ethernet is in many ways a difficult and demanding chore. As with most network problems, the majority of the problems will be related to cable. If a problem occurs that you suspect has to do with cable, look for:

1. Broken or miscrimped connectors.
2. Missing or broken terminators on 10BASE-2 or 10BASE-5 networks.
3. A broken cable or bad adapter on 10BASE-2 or 10BASE-5 networks. This will generally take down the entire Ethernet segment. To isolate the problem, remove all nodes from the segment and place the terminator from one end of the cable on the T connector after the first station. Determine that it works. Then, add stations one at a time until you find the adapter or cable segment. Move the terminator with each adapter you add.
4. Inadvertent violations of the 5, 4, 3 rule.
5. Violations of the maximum distance rules of the implementation you are using.
6. Nodes that exceed the maximum number of nodes per segment.
7. Reverse polarity cabling on 10BASE-T networks. Most concentrators should warn of a cable that has reverse polarity.
8. LEDs on concentrators and some adapters that don't show link integrity. When the cable is connected to both the concentrator and the adapter, and the workstation is powered on, the lights should be lit. If they are not, you probably have a bad cable.
9. An adapter the concentrator has automatically disabled because of jabber.

Tip

On 10BASE-T networks, the concentrator retimes and resends the signal, so you do not have to worry about generally taking down the entire network. The concentrator helps you isolate the problem quickly to a particular adapter or concentrator.

Tip

Intelligent wiring devices on any topology will provide much better troubleshooting capability than devices that are attached directly to the media.

Card-Level Diagnostics

After determining that the cable is not the culprit, you should look at the adapter. Ethernet adapters use an I/O port and an IRQ setting. Bus-mastering Ethernet adapters and some nonstandard Ethernet adapters will also use a direct memory access (DMA) channel. The default settings for these settings follow:

I/O port: 300

IRQ: 3

DMA channel: 5 (DMA is not used for most adapters)

The majority of problems with Ethernet adapters will be the result of conflicts with other devices in your computer. There are several steps you can take to diagnose adapter problems. They are

1. Verify whether or not the LAN driver will load. If the driver does not load, the conflict is either in the I/O port address or IRQ.
2. If the driver loads but gives an incorrect node ID or incorrect I/O setting, then the problem is most likely a conflict in the I/O port address.
3. If the driver loads but does not find the file server, check to see if you have an IRQ conflict or a timing problem.
4. IRQ 2 is generally reserved for COM2. Verify that you do not have another adapter that is using COM2. If you do, change the IRQ.
5. Verify that you are using the proper Ethernet frame type. Ethernet uses four frame types: ETHERNET_802.2, ETHERNET_802.3, ETHERNET_II, and ETHERNET_SNAP. Be sure that you match the frame type on the server adapter with the frame type on all workstations.

6. Most adapters available now have a transmission LED on the back of the card. Verify that the LED flickers when you attempt to log in. If it does not, you probably have a conflict.
7. Many Ethernet adapters also have timing switches or jumpers. If you are using a fast bus machine (12MHz or above), try changing the timing on the adapter.
8. Bus-mastering adapters may conflict with other bus-mastering adapters.

Bus-Mastering Problems

One of the hardest problems to diagnose involves a bus-mastering device on an ISA bus machine. Even though both adapters may both be at different DMA addresses, there can still be a conflict. Conflicts occur based on problems related to bus-mastering priority. In bus-mastering, the DMA controller on the adapter takes over the entire bus until it is finished with the data transfer or until the CPU must complete a memory refresh cycle. The problem comes in when two controllers want to control the bus at the same time. The problem is usually solved by the DMA channel number. The adapter with the lower number has priority. This is similar to the idea of interrupt priority with IRQs. To prevent one adapter from keeping the bus when others need some time, a concept known as fairness, was developed. Some drivers implement fairness, while others do not. If a driver does not implement fairness, the best idea is to place it at the highest DMA channel available to it. This will usually solve the problem.

Ethernet has other problems associated with LAN drivers and the protocol stacks that are bound to the drivers. We'll discuss those problems in Chapter 17: What's This Driving Me Around?

chapter 16

Implementing FDDI

Characteristics

The Fiber Distributed Data Interface (FDDI) was the first access method designed specifically for large, high-speed internetworks. Like ARCNET, FDDI is an ANSI standard that is loosely based on IEEE 802.5 token-ring standards. FDDI operates at 100Mbps and uses a dual counter-rotating-ring topology to supply network traffic redundancy. FDDI automatically reconfigures itself if a single break in one of the ring's wires occurs. Like token-ring and ARCNET, FDDI is a token-passing access method. As a result, it offers the deterministic, predictable, and reliable features of ARCNET and token-ring, as well as many management functions similar to token-ring.

FDDI Terminology

To understand FDDI, a description of the terms the access method uses is necessary. They are as follows:

4B/5B—The method FDDI uses to encode data for transmission across the wire.

CCE—Configuration control elements. CCE is the protocol within the single-attached stations (SAS), dual-attached stations (DAS), and concentrators that controls the port and its configuration. When a failure occurs, the CCE determines the subsequent port configuration.

CDDI—Copper Distributed Data Interface. This access method is for FDDI over shielded and unshielded twisted-pair media.

Concentrator—A wiring device that allows stations to attach to one or both fiber rings. Concentrators are intelligent devices that allow attached node management.

Dual counter-rotating rings—In FDDI, two rings exist with data paths that travel in opposite directions. If the media of these rings do not run in parallel paths, FDDI responds to a break in a single ring by rerouting traffic to the second ring.

DAC—dual-attached concentrator. A concentrator that allows nodes to attach to both FDDI rings at the same time.

DAS—dual-attached station. A node that is attached to both rings.

Frame—The data and additional information required to transmit data to the proper node on the network. Also called a *packet.*

MAC—Media Access Control. Part of the FDDI access method that controls the signal to the physical media-dependent portion of the access method.

MIC—Media interface connector. The fiber-optic, keyed connector used to attach the adapter to the media.

NRZI—Non-return-to-zero invert on ones. NRZI is the FDDI signaling scheme.

Packet—The data and additional information required to transmit data to the proper node on the network. Also called a *frame.*

PMD—The portion of the ANSI standard for FDDI that handles the physical connection to the media. This portion includes the standards for Physical Layer Medium-dependent, single-mode fiber physical layer medium-dependent; and the new standards for the copper media access.

Ring—The path of the signal. In FDDI, the signal travels from node to node around the network until it returns to the original sending station.

SAC—Single-attached concentrator. A concentrator that allows nodes to attach to a single ring. SACs are used to create branches from the main ring.

SAS—Single-attached station. A station that attaches to a single ring.

SMT—Station Management Algorithm. The SMT provides the management functions within a station.

Station—In FDDI, a station includes both physical nodes and addressable logical network devices. Workstations, single-attached stations, dual-attached stations, and concentrators are referred to as FDDI stations.

Token—The frame that gives the adapter permission to transmit on the network.

Token-passing—A deterministic access method that requires a node to possess a token in order to transmit data. The token passes from adapter to adapter in turn.

How FDDI Works

As its name implies, FDDI is a fiber-optic–based access method used for high-speed applications and for transmitting data over long distances. Less-expensive nonfiber variants of FDDI have been developed for copper media and are called CDDI, the Copper Distributed Data Interface. Unshielded twisted-pair FDDI support is being developed, but is not yet available on a wide-scale basis.

The FDDI access method uses two rings that pass traffic in opposite directions called dual counter-rotating rings. If a break occurs along either of the rings, the network will use the configuration control elements (CCE) to reroute the network traffic to the remaining functional ring. (See Figures 16-1 and 16-2 on the next page.)

In FDDI, dual-attached stations connect to both rings. Single-attached stations attach to only one ring.

Tip

Single-attached stations do not have the same redundancy as dual-attached stations. If a break occurs in the media that extends from the station to the ring, the station's connection with the network is severed and that station is removed from the network.

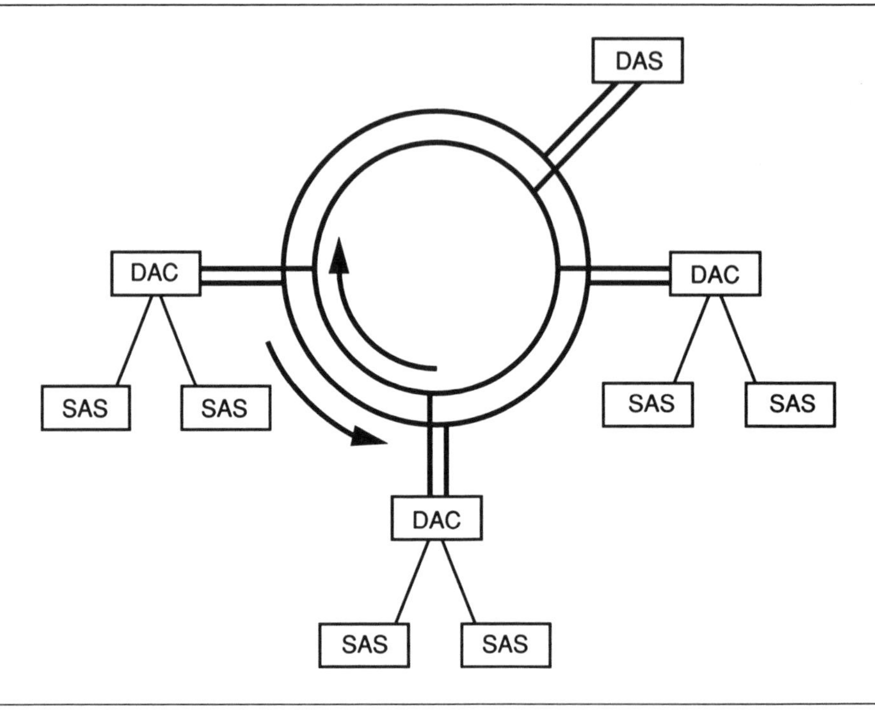

Figure 16-1. *The standard FDDI dual counter-rotating rings.*

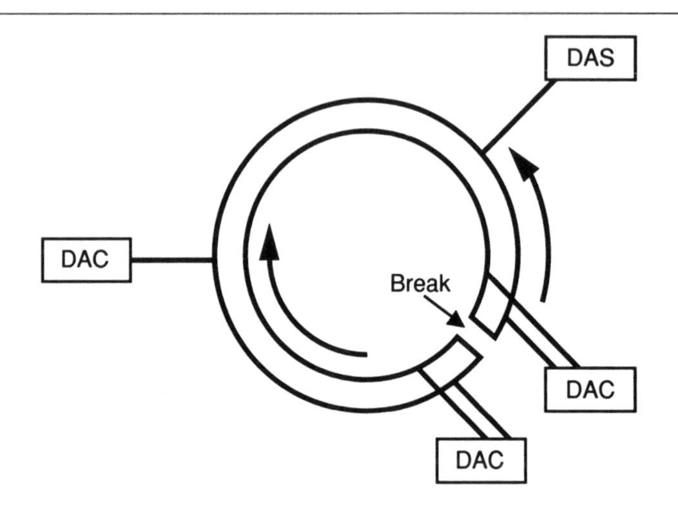

Figure 16-2. *After a break in an FDDI ring occurs, the CCE will reroute traffic to the other ring.*

Because they attach to both rings, dual-attached stations provide greater security and are more expensive than single-attached stations. Stations that use copper-based media cannot be dual-attached stations.

The maximum number of active stations on a FDDI network is 500, and the total network span is approximately 200 kilometers (120 miles). FDDI can use single-mode fiber-optic cable that passes one frequency of light, or multimode cable that passes several frequencies. The maximum span between multimode cabled stations is two kilometers and is 60 kilometers between single-mode stations. CDDI stations over either STP or UTP are limited to 100 meters from the adapter to the concentrator.

FDDI networks operate at 125MHz (approximately 100Mbps). To obtain these speeds, the access method uses an efficient signaling scheme called non-return-to-zero invert on ones and encoding called 4B/5B. This method is a two-step process that takes the initial signal and converts it to a five-bit NRZ (non-return-to-zero) signal stream. A signal of high polarity represents a binary 0, and a signal of low polarity represents a binary 1. The second step converts this signal to a NRZI signal. In this method, a signal transition represents a binary 1, and the absence of a signal transition represents a binary 0. This encoding method, also known as 4B/5B, guarantees that each transmitted signal contains at least one polarity transition every five bits. This transition is used to maintain the clock synchronization of the FDDI network. With a clocking rate of 125MHz, the effective transmission rate for FDDI with 4B/5B encoding is 100MHz.

The FDDI access method allows several types of frames to exist on the ring. The media access control (MAC) frames on an FDDI network operate in a similar fashion to token-ring MAC frames. They are responsible for ring initialization, timing, and error counters. Unlike other LAN access methods that transmit asynchronously, FDDI can transmit in both synchronous and asynchronous modes. In synchronous mode, the SMT preallocates the bandwidth necessary for the communication. In asynchronous transmission, the communication must contend with the other stations on the network for bandwidth.

The MAC layer is also responsible for maintaining timers for synchronous and asynchronous transmission. The token hold timer controls the length of time a station may transmit asynchronous frames. The token rotation timer schedules the transmissions on the ring.

Network management is defined by the SMT function and provides control to the station level for each station on the network. SMT provides current configuration information and connection and ring management information.

For FDDI communication, there are two types of frame formats: a token and a frame. Two types of tokens and eight types of frames exist. One of these tokens, called the *nonrestricted token,* is used by stations to transmit using the asynchronous bandwidth. Restricted tokens are used by a pair of stations to reserve all the bandwidth temporarily in a synchronous communication. These are the various FDDI frames:

void frame

station management frame

SMT next station addressing frame

MAC frame

MAC beacon frame

LLC frame

LLC information frame synchronous

LLC information frame synchronous

FDDI chips are currently manufactured by Advanced Micro Devices (AMD), Motorola, and National Semiconductor. Manufacturers currently producing FDDI adapters include Ascom Timeplex, Crescendo Communications, Digital Equipment Corp., Hewlett-Packard, IBM, Network Peripherals, and Madge Networks.

FDDI Cabling

FDDI uses two different cabling types: single-mode and multimode fiber. Each type uses two cables, one for transmitting data and one for receiving data. Special receptacles on the concentrators and adapters are used depending on the type of connection being made.

Single-mode fiber-optic cable is based on the X3.194 standard and is intended for campus-wide or metropolitan-area network (MAN) use. The light source for single-mode cable is based on lasers that allow a distance of up to 60 kilometers between stations. If you intend to install a single-mode fiber-optic network, it is best to consider using custom-made single-mode fiber and have it installed by a qualified technician.

Multimode fiber-optic cable is designed for standard FDDI installations. It allows distances of up to two kilometers between stations.

These are the allowable multimode cable specifications for FDDI networks:

62.5/125 microns
50/125 microns
85/125 microns
100/140 microns

Multimode fiber-cable uses LEDs as its light source. These LEDs have a wavelength between 1,270 and 1,380 nanometers. Multimode fiber, of the previously listed specifications, is readily available from many cable suppliers in pre-cut lengths. Although cable termination kits exist, installation of multimode fiber should also be left up to a qualified technician.

The ends of the fiber-optic cable must be terminated with a special keyed connector. A keyed connector has a structure that can be connected in one way and can only be put into a receptacle that accepts the key. This keyed connector is called a media interface connector (MIC). (See Figure 16-3 on the next page.) Keyed connectors are used for two reasons. First, FDDI connectors are keyed so you don't confuse the receive and transmit cables, and second, only specific keyed connectors can be used on certain concentrators or adapters. There are four types of keyed connectors as follows:

MIC A—The primary in/secondary out connector (dual-attached station to FDDI main ring)

MIC B—The secondary in/primary out (dual-attached station to FDDI main ring)

MIC M—A master connector that will fit into any connection receptacle

MIC S—A connector for single-attached-station (SAS).

Tip

Terminating the ends of fiber-optic cable and installing the connectors are not for the uninitiated user. Either attend a class on how to terminate a fiber-optic cable properly and purchase the proper termination materials, or leave it to professional cable installers. The money you will spend in trying to perfect the termination of the ends of fiber-optic cable is worth the price of a professional cable installer who will do it right the first time.

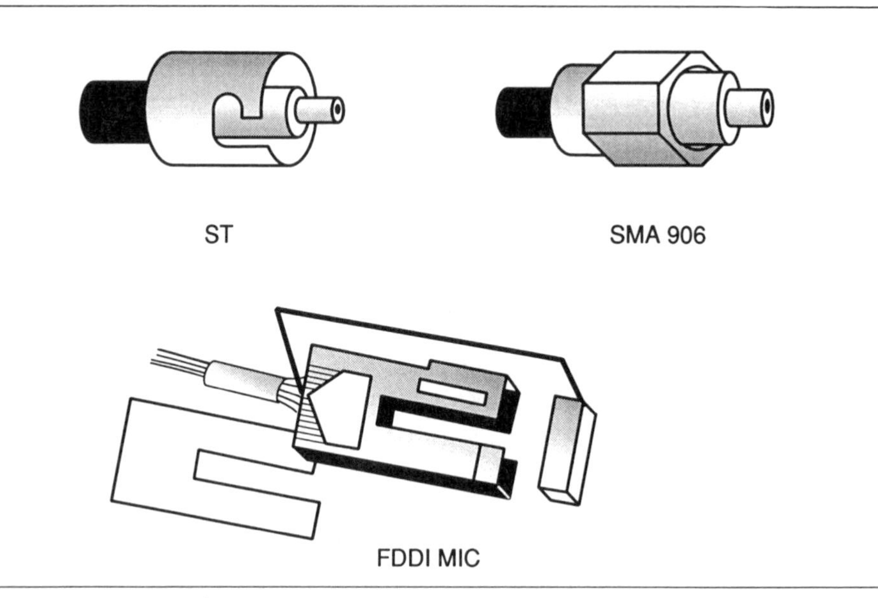

Figure 16-3. *Typical FDDI connectors.*

Troubleshooting FDDI

In most networks, the majority of problems involve media installation. FDDI is no exception. If you are installing FDDI or any fiber-based network, you'll want a device that can measure the power of the light source. This device is called a *time-domain reflectometer* (TDR). There are some TDRs on the market that balance price and functionality. The Link Confidence Tester from Fotec, Inc. is an example of a device designed specifically for FDDI cabling. Also, in fiber-optic connections, it is possible for dirty connectors to interfere with data transmission. You can clean fiber-optic connector ends simply by blowing out the ends with compressed air or by using special cleaning fluid. Remember, fiber-optic transmission consists of an optical signal and dirt can disrupt the signal easily. You should verify the quality of the cable and connection prior to installing the connector into adapters or concentrators.

Other FDDI troubleshooting checkpoints include the following:

1. Check that you have the properly keyed connectors on both ends of the cable.

2. Verify that all M connections are going to the correct ports. Remember that an M connector can use any connection.
3. Verify that all ports are operative.
4. In FDDI, rings will automatically segment if a problem exists. If an entire segment goes down, verify if the ring has been segmented and correct the problem.
5. If single-attached stations are no longer functioning, be sure that the ring to which they are attached is still active.
6. Using the SMT functions, verify whether a station or node is causing the ring to beacon. If so, the problem can be isolated to the station's upstream link. This process is similar to the fault domain isolation process in token-ring networks.

Card-Level Diagnostics

The majority of problems with FDDI adapters are related to a conflict with another adapter or a bus-timing issue. FDDI adapters use the following resources:

I/O port
DMA channel
interrupt request line (IRQ)

FDDI adapters that exhibit a conflict with another system resource normally fail to load the LAN driver. Look first for a conflict with the interrupt request line (IRQ). The default IRQ for an FDDI adapter is IRQ 2.

LAN Compass
Refer to the LAN Compass in the back of this book for a list of the common interrupts, DMA channels, and I/O ports devices use.

After interrupt conflicts, FDDI adapters have problems with shared RAM addresses. The settings for an FDDI adapter can range from C000h to DC000h. This address range can conflict with a variety of adapters and memory managers. Programs such as CheckIt LAN or Microsoft's MSD can be useful in verifying problems with shared RAM. Shared RAM problems most often occur with video adapters, SCSI controllers, or system shadowing.

Other problems with FDDI adapters are conflicts with adapters that use DMA channels, and especially with those adapters that use bus-mastering techniques to transfer data to system memory. The adapters that are most likely to cause DMA conflicts with FDDI adapters are

SCSI controllers
CD-ROM controllers
sound adapters
other network adapters

One of the hardest problems to diagnose in FDDI is when an FDDI adapter is installed with another bus-mastering device in an ISA machine. Both adapters may be set at different DMA addresses but still conflict with each other. Like token-ring, this problem is caused by bus-mastering priority, in which the DMA controller on the adapter controls the bus until it is finished with the data transfer or until the CPU must complete a memory refresh cycle. The problem occurs when two controllers want to control the bus at the same time. It is usually solved by the DMA channel number. The adapter with the lowest DMA channel number has bus priority. Priority is similar to interrupt priority in adapters that use IRQs for data transfer. However, to prevent one adapter from keeping the bus when other adapters need it, a concept known as fairness was developed. Some drivers implement fairness while others do not. If a driver does not implement fairness, the best idea is to configure the adapter at the highest DMA channel available to it. Doing this will usually solve the problem.

chapter 17

What's This Driving Me Around?

Where LAN Drivers Operate

The LAN driver is the interface at the Open Systems Interconnect (OSI) Physical and Data-Link layers between the adapter and at the Data-Link layer to the upper layers of the protocol stack. (See Figure 17-1 on the next page.) It is responsible for taking data from the OSI Network layer and handing it to the adapter as a packet of information the adapter can place on the wire.

The driver must be written to the needs of the adapter hardware, the computer system, the network operating system, and the operating system. It is responsible for taking data off the wire and sending it to the CPU memory, where it will hand the data off to the upper OSI layers. Depending on how it is written and the needs of the access method, the driver may be responsible for packet fragmentation; that is, receiving the packet as delivered from the upper-layer protocols, breaking it into pieces small enough to be fit into the Physical layer packet, and reassembling it at the other end. How the driver handles packets and manipulates the data in the transfer to the CPU determines much of the adapter's speed.

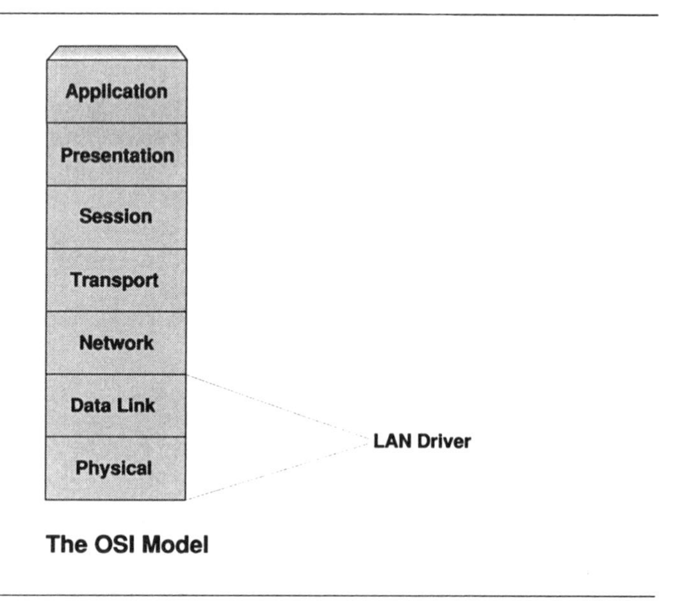

Figure 17-1. *The OSI model and LAN drivers.*

What a Data-Link Layer Packet Looks Like

Each access method has different data packets. Each packet consists of a series of octets (an eight-bit character field). The fields are broken down by access methods.

ARCNET Data Packet

The ARCNET data packet begins with a frame header that indicates the contents of the frame and a packet character. The source node ID and destination node ID follow. The next field (information length, or IL) indicates the number of octets in the data packet. It is followed by the data and, finally, by the error-checking cyclic redundancy checking (CRC) characters. (See Figure 17-2 on the next page.) The CRC detects errors in the packet. In a CRC, the number of 1s and 0s in the packet are counted before the packet is sent across the wire. The same count is also made when the packet is received. If the counts do not match, the

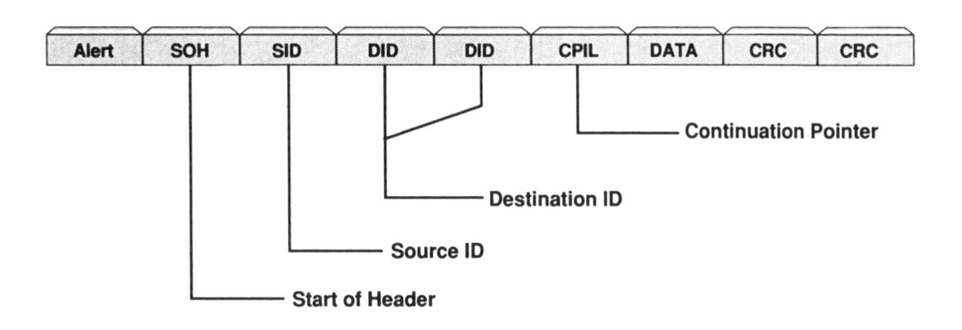

Figure 17-2. *The ARCNET packet structure.*

packet is rejected. ARCNETPlus uses a slightly different packet structure that remains compatible with standard ARCNET.

Token-ring Data Packet

The token-ring data packet is more complicated than the ARCNET packet because of the additional information token-ring requires to complete a transfer of data around the ring. The token-ring data packet appears as shown in Figure 17-3 on the next page.

The packet consists of:

A starting delimiter—One octet indicates the start of the frame.

The access control field—One octet contains the frame priority bit, the frame indicator bit, the monitor counts, and the priority reservation.

The frame control field—One octet contains information on the frame format, the address recognized bit, the frame copied bit, and the reserved bits.

The destination address—2 or 6 octets.

The source address—2 or 6 octets.

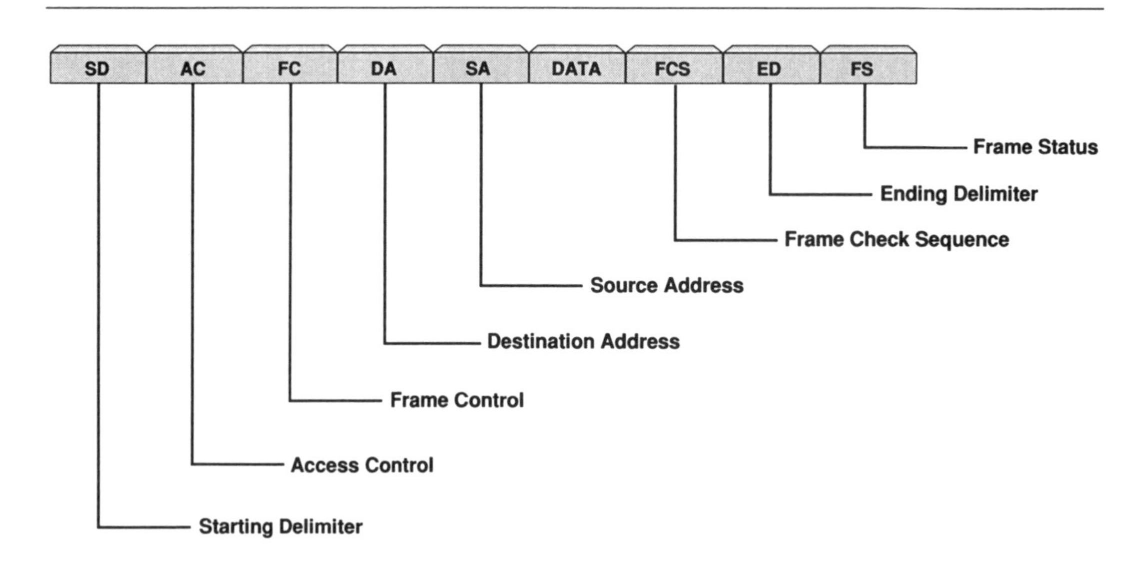

Figure 17-3. *The token-ring packet structure.*

Routing information—0 to 30 octets contain routing information for source routing.

Information fields—Of variable length.

Frame check sequence (FCS)—4 octets for error checking.

Ending delimiter—Contains the end-of-frame sequence and a bit indicating whether the packet is part of a multiframe transmission.

Ethernet Data Packet

The Ethernet frame is a standard frame size of 1,524 bytes. (See Figure 17-4 on the next page.) It consists of the fields listed below.

The preamble—8 octets alternating the 1010 pattern, ending in 10101011.

The destination address—6 octets indicating the burned-in Physical layer address of the destination Ethernet adapter.

The source address—6 octets indicating the Physical layer address of the source Ethernet adapter.

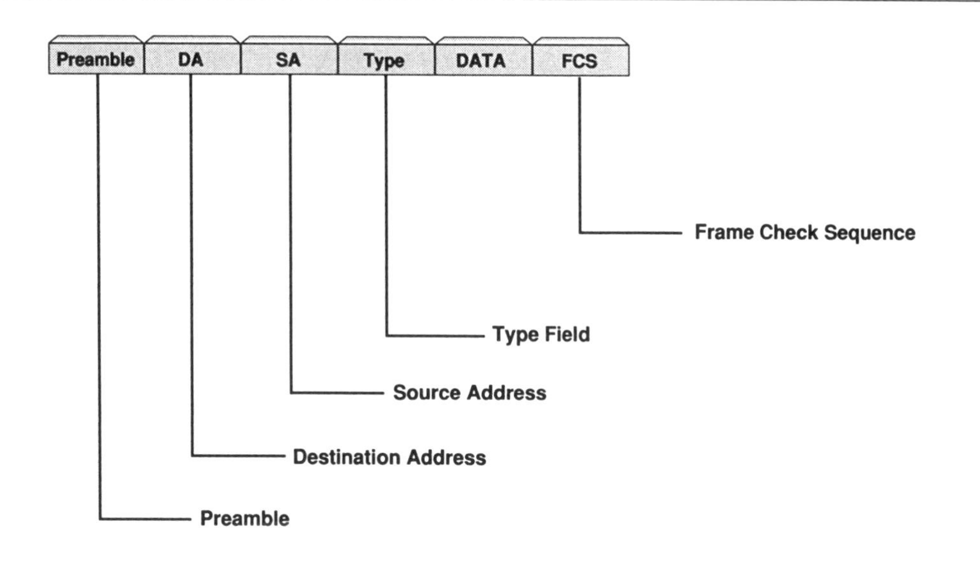

Figure 17-4. *Ethernet frame structure.*

The type field—2 octets indicating the higher-layer protocol, such as IP, XNS, or DECnet, used in the data field.

The data field—46 to 1,500 octets—The packet data including IEEE 802.3 Data-Link layer information, if needed.

The frame check sequence (FCS)—4 octets indicating the FCS for error checking.

In versions of NetWare that use drivers for systems previous to v3.12, a length field replaces the type field. The length field indicates the length of the data.

FDDI Data Packet

The FDDI packet is similar in structure to the token-ring packet. Figure 17-5 on the next page depicts its structure.

The frame consists of the following items:

Preamble—216 octets.

Starting delimiter—2 octets indicating the start of the frame.

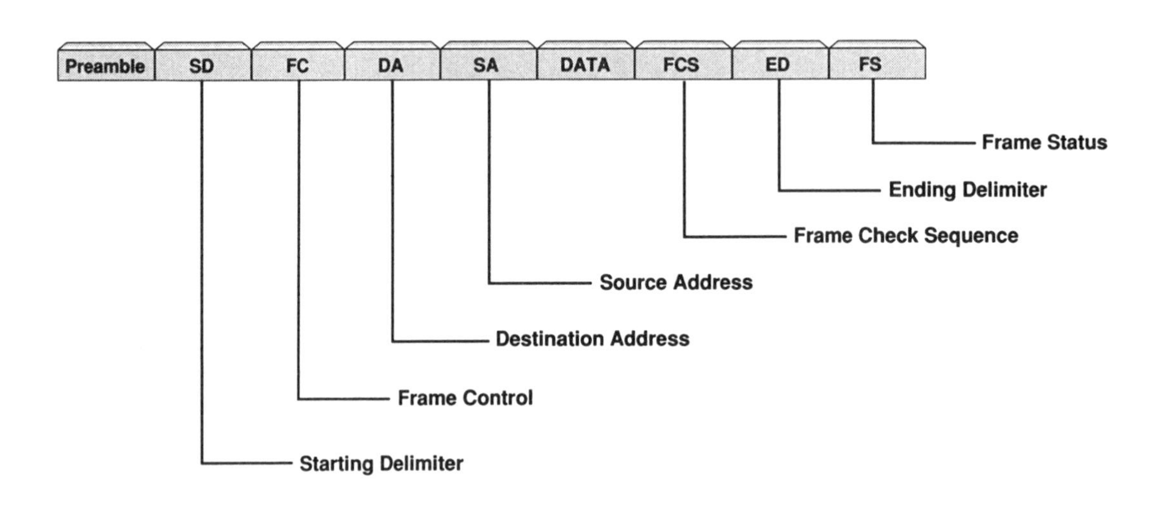

Figure 17-5. *FDDI packet structure.*

Frame control—2 octets indicating the FDDI class (asynchronous or synchronous), address length bit, and frame format bits indicating the type of frame.

Destination address—4 or 12 octets depending on address type.

Source address—4 or 12 octets depending on address type.

Information field—Of a variable length depending on packet type and size.

Frame check sequence—8 octets for error checking.

Ending delimiter—1 octet indicating the end of the frame.

Frame status—Variable depending upon the frame status.

Types of Adapters and Drivers

The network adapter manages the task of transferring data from one PC to another across the network. The requirements for this transfer are determined by various layers of the OSI model. The basic requirements are set by the access method—ARCNET, Ethernet, token-ring, or FDDI. These requirements include the Physical layer requirements of packet size, packet structure, acknowledgment, network access, and error recovery. The upper layers determine the other features of the network, including the network protocol and Logical Link Control (LLC) information.

The LAN driver acts as the link between the upper layer requirements and the lower Physical layer requirements of the access method, topology, and media. To perform, the driver is linked to one or more protocols, including:

IPX/SPX—NetWare's primary transport method.

TCP/IP—Transmission Control Protocol/Internet Protocol (TCP/IP). Developed by DARPA for large internetworks.

AppleTalk—A protocol designed for networking Apple computers.

The driver's primary responsibility is to transfer the data to and from the memory of the computer and hand it to the Physical layer for transport over the media. How this transfer takes place is in part determined by the access method and requirements of the network adapter. Much of the speed of the transfer is determined by how well the driver completes this task. The varying methods adapters use to transfer data to computer memory are shared-memory, DMA transfers, bus-mastering, pseudo-DMA, and I/O instructions only.

Shared Memory

Shared-memory is a data transfer method in which an area of memory is set aside as a buffer that the PC and the adapter share. Data is placed directly from the adapter buffer into the shared buffer in memory for use by the computer. The computer also places data in this shared-memory area to be transferred to the adapter for transmission on the network. Most adapters using shared-memory have buffer space on the adapter to store incoming and outgoing packets. Shared-memory data transfer requires the computer's CPU to monitor the shared-memory area for data and to control the transfer of the data.

In a typical shared-memory transfer, the adapter can use memory reserved in PC memory. The adapter's configuration determines the location of this memory. The LAN driver uses an event control block to move data from the adapter to the address space in the computer's CPU real memory.

Shared-memory is faster than I/O-based data transfer and often works in machines that don't support bus-mastering. Its disadvantages are that it is slower than DMA and bus-mastering, and the amount of RAM space on the adapter may be limited.

DMA Transfers

This data transfer method involves using the computer's DMA controller to take control of the data transfer from the adapter to a shared-memory location. This method does not require intervention of the computer's CPU for data transfer, freeing it for other processing and reducing its workload. DMA transfers are generally faster than shared RAM transfers. However, DMA adapters are more difficult to design and more expensive than shared-memory. Some clones and some memory managers do not support DMA adapters.

In a DMA transfer, the adapter signals the DMA controller that it wants to transfer data. The driver instructs the DMA controller where data is stored, the number of bytes to be transferred, and where they need to go. The DMA controller seizes control of the CPU's address and data lines to transfer data. When finished, the DMA controller relinquishes the lines to the CPU.

Bus-mastering Transfers

Bus-mastering is a form of DMA-based data transfer in which the transfer is controlled by a Bus-Mastering Interface Controller (BMIC) on the adapter. The adapter initiates the transfer by tripping one of the DMA channels and informing the DMA controller onboard the computer that it will control the transfer. With an ISA bus, the BMIC on the adapter takes control of the bus until the data transfer is complete or until the next video memory refresh cycle. In EISA and Micro Channel bus machines, the CPU and the bus-mastering adapter operate simultaneously.

Tip

Bus-mastering is possible on ISA-based machines. It is not as fast as EISA or Micro Channel machines and does not offer some of the advantages of EISA or Micro Channel bus-mastering, but it will increase throughput and reduce utilization, particularly on NetWare file servers.

Ethernet and token-ring commonly use bus-mastering data transfers. Bus-mastering eliminates shared-memory conflicts and, like DMA, is faster than shared-memory implementations. Bus-mastering adapters are also more expensive than non–bus-mastered adapters, and some clone PCs and memory managers don't support bus-mastering.

Bus Arbitration

An issue enters the bus-mastering arena when multiple bus-mastering adapters are used. Since the bus-mastering adapter controls the bus for the duration of the transfer, it is essential that a method for determining priority be established. Under ISA, there is no clear-cut method. The individual drivers for the various adapters must be responsible for allowing other devices on the bus (employing fairness). Under EISA, bus arbitration is controlled by the EISA standard and is implemented in hardware. Bus arbitration allows microprocessors to share the bus.

Burst Mode

The ISA, Micro Channel, and EISA standards also allow for a burst-mode data transfer capability. This method of data transfer can be up to three times faster than the transfer on standard ISA machines. In ISA burst-mode transfers, the adapter's DMA controller negotiates to transfer data on the bus. In EISA adapters, the logic on the system board handles the transfer, while in Micro Channel adapters, the arbitration is set up in software. Under Micro Channel, the standard calls for a series of arbitration levels from 1 to 8. The levels determine the priority of the individual devices for access.

NOVELL DRIVERS

Novell has developed specifications for Open Data-Link Interface (ODI) drivers for workstations and servers. These drivers conform to the specifications for a Multiple Link Interface Device (MLID). This specification allows multiple protocols to be assigned and linked to the driver for a single adapter and creates a series of logical attachments or boards for each protocol bound to the driver. Novell created the Link Support Layer (LSL) to control the various links between the protocols and the adapter's driver. The ODI specification began being used with NetWare v3.x and has been continued and updated in NetWare 4.x. See the appendices for details on the Open Data-Link Interface.

Workstation Drivers

The workstation driver is an MLID that interacts with the other parts of the ODI specification to link the protocols to the adapter and the upper layers of the network. Drivers written to this specification allow up to four logical connections or boards per physical LAN adapter. Multiple adapters may be placed in a single PC. Specific drivers are required for OS/2 and DOS. DOS drivers are installed manually by the user.

v3.x and 4.x

Under NetWare v3.12 and 4.x, DOS workstation drivers are installed through an installation utility provided in NetWare. This installation program creates a subdirectory and transfers all required files into it. It also creates a batch file called STARTNET.BAT that starts the network drivers and attaches the adapter to the network. All drivers certified by Novell are included in this utility. Updated drivers may be installed as well through this utility by selecting to use a driver supplied by the vendor. The utility will read the vendor-supplied disk and copy the driver.

The workstation driver settings are controlled by a configuration file called the NET.CFG file. This is a text-based file that contains the basic configuration information for all the network drivers on the workstation. It is found in the same directory as the other workstation files. The NET.CFG file can be edited by the user as needed with an ASCII text editor. The adapter driver portion of the NET.CFG file normally looks like this:

```
Link Driver TCNSW
        MEM D0000
        INT 2
        Frame Novell_RX-NET
```

To change the settings for the adapter, make the physical changes on the adapter as necessary and then edit the NET.CFG file. (For DOS 4.x and higher workstations, use the DOS EDIT command). The options available for the NET.CFG file for drivers are as follows:

DMA number—Used to configure the DMA channel the adapter uses.

INT number—Used to configure the interrupt the adapter uses.

MEM number (in hex)—Sets the starting memory address for the adapter.

Port number (in hex)—Sets the starting address for the I/O port the adapter uses.

Node address number (in hex)—Overrides the burned-in physical address on the adapter.

PS/2 slot number—Identifies the PS/2 slot the adapter is in. If only one adapter is used in the computer, you can omit the number, and the driver will scan for the adapter.

FRAME type—Used to specify the frame(s) the adapter uses. A different frame is required for each protocol bound to the adapter.

Look-ahead size number—Used to specify the number of bytes in the packet that the LAN driver sends to the LSL to determine how to route the packet.

Protocol name type—Specifies the new protocol to be attached to the adapter. "Name" is replaced with the hexadecimal protocol ID number, and "type" is replaced with the frame type to be associated with the protocol.

Send retries number—Specifies the number of times a packet will be resent after an error occurs.

Frame Types

Different access methods require different packet header information. The header information is specific to each protocol. The FRAME command in the NET.CFG file specifies the header information each protocol requires. A new frame must be identified with a particular protocol for each protocol bound to the driver. The following are the applicable frame formats for each access method:

Ethernet_802.3—Defines the default Ethernet frame type for NetWare v3.0, v3.1, and v3.11 networks. It should only be used with the IPX protocol.

Ethernet_II—Defines the unique packet header for Ethernet on Digital DECnet networks. Also used with TCP/IP networks.

Ethernet_802.2—Defines the default Ethernet frame type for IEEE and OSI frame types. Now also used on NetWare v3.12 and 4.x.

Ethernet_SNAP—Defines the default Ethernet packet header for TCP/IP networks.

Token-ring—Defines the default frame type for token-ring. This frame type assigns the standard packet header for the 802.2 networks IBM uses.

Token-ring_SNAP—Defines the 802.2 packet with SNAP header for use on networks that use the TCP/IP and AppleTalk protocols.

Novell_RX-NET—Defines a default packet header for ARCNET networks using IPX or TCP/IP. This frame is unique to Novell networks.

The frame type specified at the workstation must match the frame type specified at the server for each protocol bound. If not, the server will reject the packet, and communication will not be possible.

MLIDs versus Linkable Drivers

Versions of NetWare based on the 286 microprocessor model would allow only the IPX protocol to be bound to the adapter. The protocol (IPX) was actually linked into the driver along with the specific adapter settings, resulting in the IPX.COM file that was used to initialize the adapter. The adapter vendor supplied an object file (OBJ extension) that was linked into additional object files supplied by Novell. Linking was performed using one of two programs, either SHGEN or, more recently, WSGEN. The adapter settings were restricted to a specific set of combinations of settings contained in a table specified by Novell. During the linking process, you specified the adapter settings, and the WSGEN or SHGEN program created a final driver. The driver's settings could be viewed by adding the following switch to the driver statement:

IPX i (in which *i* stands for *information*)

Once the IPX.COM file was generated, settings could only be changed by running SHGEN or WSGEN again, or by using the DCONFIG utility. DCONFIG allowed you to choose from the other combinations of settings contained in the driver's settings table. More recently, Novell developed a utility called JUMPERS, which could be run against the generated IPX.COM file, and new values for the driver settings could be patched in. Drivers written to this specification were no longer restricted to the settings contained in a driver's settings table.

Additionally other settings could be patched in relative to other aspects of driver configuration, such as Early Token Release for token-ring networks.

The specifications for linkable drivers were supplanted by the MLID that allowed multiple protocols to be bound to the same adapter. ODI allowed IPX, TCP/IP, and other protocols to exist on the same adapter at the same time and also greatly extended the compatibility of NetWare to other network operating systems.

Server Drivers

The MLID for server drivers is similar to that for workstation drivers, but it corresponds to the unique demands of the NetWare file server. Server drivers carry a .LAN extension. This MLID also allows multiple protocols to be bound simultaneously to the same physical adapter. Under NetWare v3.x, LAN drivers must be manually loaded into server memory and bound to a specific protocol. Currently, the available protocols for use on the file server are

IPX
IP
APPLE

Additionally, Remote Initial Program Load (RPL) can be loaded and bound to a driver to allow it to remote-boot workstations attached to the network segment.

The server driver is loaded using the LOAD command at the console prompt (:):

```
LOAD TCTOK386.LAN
```

The server drivers can be stored in the SYS:SYSTEM subdirectory and loaded directly as just described, or they can be placed elsewhere on the server, on the DOS partition, or on the server's diskette drive. You must specify the path or drive specification after the LOAD command, as follows:

```
LOAD SYS:DRIVERS\TCTOK386.LAN
LOAD C:\TCTOK16M.LAN
LOAD A:\NW386\TCTOK16M.LAN
```

Driver settings and other specifications are placed after the driver name. The available driver settings and specifications include

DMA = *number*—Sets the DMA channel for the adapter.

INT = *number* (in hexadecimal)—Sets the interrupt channel for the adapter. This number is in hexadecimal, which is different from the workstation driver. This notation does not make any difference until you get to interrupts 10-A, 11-B, 12-C, or 15-F.

MEM = *number* (in hexadecimal)—Sets the starting memory address range for the adapter.

PORT = *number* (in hexadecimal)—Sets the starting base I/O address for the adapter.

Frame = *Type*—Sets the frame type for the communication protocol for each adapter.

Name = *string*—Allows you to assign a name to each adapter to help bind protocols and keep the individual adapters straight.

The adapter vendor may require additional variables in the LOAD statement.

Tip

A unique situation exists that can occur with ISA bus-mastering adapters and Novell file servers with more than 16 megabytes (MB) of RAM. An ISA bus-mastering adapter cannot use buffer space above 16MB. Therefore, enough buffer space must be reserved below 16MB for these adapters. The number of buffers is set in the server's STARTUP.NCF file using the SET command:

SET reserved buffers below 16 meg = xxx

where xxx is the number of buffers below 16MB. The maximum amount of buffers under NetWare v3.x is 200. You will also need to reserve a number of buffers for each ISA bus-mastering adapter you install in the machine and each protocol bound to the adapter. Consult your adapter manual for the exact number of buffers required and for the syntax for the LOAD statement for the driver.

The driver may be unloaded from memory using the UNLOAD command. The syntax for the command is as follows:

UNLOAD drivername

Replace "drivername" with the name of the driver you want to unload. When the adapter driver is unloaded from memory, all protocols are unbound as well. If you want to unbind only specific protocols, use the UNBIND command described ahead.

Protocols and Server Drivers

The server driver must be reloaded with an additional frame type for each communication protocol bound to the board. Each protocol requires that a unique frame type be attached to the LOAD statement. The frame type is specified as follows in the LOAD statement:

LOAD TCTOKH FRAME=TOKEN-RING_SNAP

The following frame types are available for server and workstation drivers:

Ethernet_802.3—Defines the default Ethernet frame type for NetWare v3.0, v3.1, and v3.11 networks. It should only be used with the IPX protocol.

Ethernet_II—Defines the unique packet header for Ethernet on Digital DECnet networks. Also used with TCP/IP networks.

Ethernet_802.2—Defines the default Ethernet frame for IEEE and OSI frame types. Also now used on NetWare v3.12 and 4.x.

Ethernet_SNAP—Defines the default Ethernet packet header for TCP/IP networks.

Token-ring—Defines the default frame type for token-ring. This assigns the standard packet header for the 802.2 networks IBM uses.

Token-ring_SNAP—Defines the 802.2 packet with SNAP header for use on networks that use TCP/IP and AppleTalk protocols.

Novell_RX-NET—Defines a default packet header for ARCNET networks using IPX or TCP/IP. This frame is unique to Novell networks.

The frame type specified at the server must match the frame type specified at the workstation for each protocol bound. If not, the server will reject the packet and communications will not be possible.

Binding Communication Protocols

Communication protocols must be bound to the individual boards using the BIND statement. This statement is performed from the console prompt (:) using the following syntax:

BIND protocol name TO board name

BIND IPX TO TCTOKH NET=21

If you are attempting to bind to a driver that is used with more than one adapter in the server, you must specify the settings of the adapter you are binding to in brackets. The bind statement in that event would appear as follows:

BIND IPX to TCTOK16M [int=3] net =21

Tip

This is where naming adapters comes in handy. When you must load and bind multiple frames to the same board, it can become confusing. By using Novell's naming convention, you can circumvent this problem. Name each adapter as the driver loads. Then use the adapter name instead of the driver name in the BIND statement. In this case, the LOAD and BIND statements would appear as follows:

```
LOAD TCTOK16M PORT=1A20 DMA=5 INT=2 NAME=TOKEN1
LOAD TCTOK16M PORT=2A20 DMA=6 INT=3 NAME=TOKEN2
BIND IPX TOKEN1 NET=333
BIND IPX TOKEN2 NET=666
```

These names will make configuration and recognition much easier when using multiple boards and multiple protocols.

Each protocol requires additional information after the BIND statement. This information includes

IPX—Requires that a unique network identifier number be added using the following syntax: NET=

IP—Requires, at a minimum, the IP address of the adapter using the statement ADDR=. The address is a series of four decimal numbers separated by periods such as ADDR=192.30.125.4.

AppleTalk—Requires that AppleTalk zones be set here or that they be set in a separate configuration file.

Individual protocols can be unbound from the driver using the UNBIND statement. The syntax for the statement is

UNBIND protocol drivername

The driver name can be replaced with the adapter name if a name was used in the original LOAD statement. This procedure simply unbinds the protocol from the driver. If you need to unload completely the driver from memory, use the UNLOAD command described previously.

The LOAD and BIND statements can also be placed in the AUTOEXEC.NCF file so that they will be loaded each time the server is restarted. To edit the AUTOEXEC.NCF file to include the statements for the drivers, either load INSTALL and select the System Options menu and then select EDIT AUTOEXEC.NCF, or use the EDIT utility to edit the file, by typing LOAD EDIT AUTOEXEC.NCF at the console prompt (:).

Novell Enhancements

With the advent of NetWare 4.0, Novell made two enhancements that affect driver performance greatly—they are the Packet Burst mode and the Large Internet Packet (LIP) Support.

Packet Burst

Under previous versions of NetWare, all packets sent required a response from the receiving node, and the NetWare Core Protocol required that only one packet be on the line at a time. With burst-mode, the workstation will make one request for a file. The server will respond with a stream of packets until the request is completed. At that point, the workstation will send a single response. Packet burst reduces network traffic and increases performance.

The packet burst in a given sequence is negotiated between the server and the workstation. The number is set at the workstation by setting the PB BUFFERS statement in the NET.CFG file. The number of buffers can be set between 0 and 10. If it is set to 0, packet burst is disabled; the higher the setting, the more memory required to provide buffer space. NetWare v3.x networks no longer support packet burst.

Large Internet Packet Support (LIPX)

Under previous versions of NetWare, packets crossing the internal router were immediately reduced to 576-byte packets. This represented the smallest packet size supported by Novell and occurred because a particular router might not have supported larger packet sizes. With LIPX, the workstation and server negotiate a packet size as if there were no intervening routers. NetWare ignores the router check during packet size negotiation. Remember, NetWare does not check for packet size on the router. If an intervening router cannot support the larger packet sizes, you must reduce the packet size or disable LIPX.

part

III

Toning Your Survival Instincts

Day-to-day life on the network can be a peaceful existence. You can prepare for problems with proper maintenance and monitoring techniques. When problems do occur, you'll be armed to take care of them with a minimum of panic and confusion.

This section provides some techniques you can use for LAN survival, the tools you can use to monitor your network, and the applications and methods you can use to address problems when they do occur. LAN life does not have to be the dubious prospect that it often is. A few common-sense tips and an arsenal of practical—even inexpensive—tools can keep problems at bay.

chapter 18

Monitoring Your Investment

What Is Network Monitoring?

Network monitoring is a catch-all phrase for everything from network mapping tools to LAN protocol analysis. Network monitoring should allow you to view the network performance, isolate and correct problems, discover potential problems, and avoid network down-time. With the addition of network management software, you also should be able to control network devices such as LAN adapters, hubs, and printers.

Novell Monitoring Features

NetWare supplies several menu-based or command-line utilities that let you monitor network operations. They are as follows:

MONITOR

VOLINFO

TRACK ON and TRACK OFF

CHKVOL

NMAGENT

MONITOR.NLM

The easiest-to-use and most valuable utility in NetWare monitoring is MONITOR.NLM, a NetWare Loadable Module (NLM) that ships with NetWare. (In NetWare v2.x, MONITOR operates as an .EXE file.) MONITOR allows the user to view the following network functions:

1. Overall activity and utilization
2. Cache memory status
3. Connection status
4. Disk drives and statistics
5. Mounted volumes
6. LAN drivers and their statistics
7. Loaded modules
8. File lock status
9. Memory usage

Typing LOAD MONITOR at the file server console's prompt (:) displays a screen that looks like that shown in Figure 18-1.

The main MONITOR screen offers the following statistics:

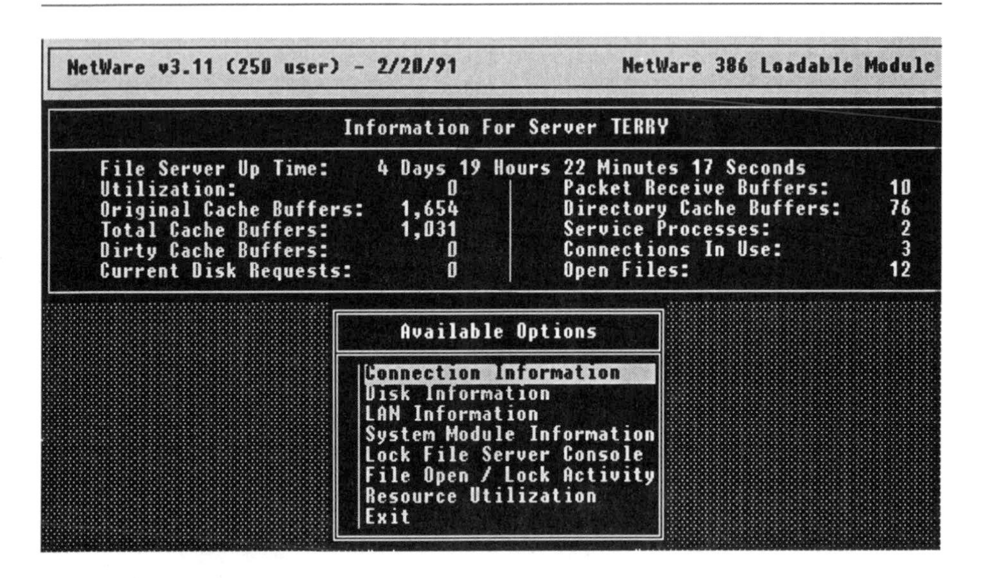

Figure 18-1. *MONITOR's main menu.*

File Server Up Time—Displays the amount of time the file server has been running.

Utilization—Displays the percentage (%) of time the processor is busy. This statistic shows 0 percent when you bring up MONITOR. To be accurate, bring up MONITOR when there is no network traffic.

Original Cache Buffers—Displays the number of cache buffers (in blocks) available to the server when it is booted.

Total Cache Buffers—Displays the number of buffer blocks currently available for file caching. You should monitor this number after loading all of your modules (NLMs and other programs) to verify that you have enough file server memory.

Dirty Cache Buffers—Displays the number of file blocks waiting to be written to disk.

Current Disk Requests—Displays the number of disk requests waiting for service.

Packet Receive Buffers—Displays the number of buffers available for requests from the workstation.

Directory Cache Buffers—Displays the number of buffers allocated to handle directory caching.

Service Processes—Represents the number of processes allocated for workstation requests. The server will allocate service processes as needed, but will not relinquish the memory for them unless the server is downed.

Connections In Use—Displays the number of stations currently attached to the file server.

Open Files—Displays the number of files the file server is currently accessing.

MONITOR's main menu gives you a good idea of the health of your network. You can also use this utility to make basic decisions about the network and your future needs. If your utilization is constantly above 75%, you should consider upgrading your file server. This number reflects how hard your server is working. A sustained high number means the file server is bottlenecking your network. If the number of dirty cache buffers becomes 50% of your total cache buffers for a sustained period of time, you should also consider increasing the amount of RAM in your file server. Both of these statistics could also indicate that you need to split your file server into two networks.

Other Information Screens

While the MONITOR utility is good to use, you will probably only need to view its Disk Information screen, the LAN Information screen, and the Resource Utilization screen on a consistent basis. These screens will give you an overall idea of your network's health.

The Disk Information Screen

MONITOR's Disk Information screen, shown in Figure 18-2 is selected from MONITOR's main menu. If you have multiple volumes on your file server, you will be presented with a second menu, Volume Segments on Drive. You must choose the volume you want to see. The disk information screen monitors this information:

Driver—The name of the disk driver (DSK) file loaded in the server's STARTUP.NCF file.

Disk Size—The size of the disk in megabytes.

Mirror Status—If the disk is mirrored, not mirrored, or remirroring.

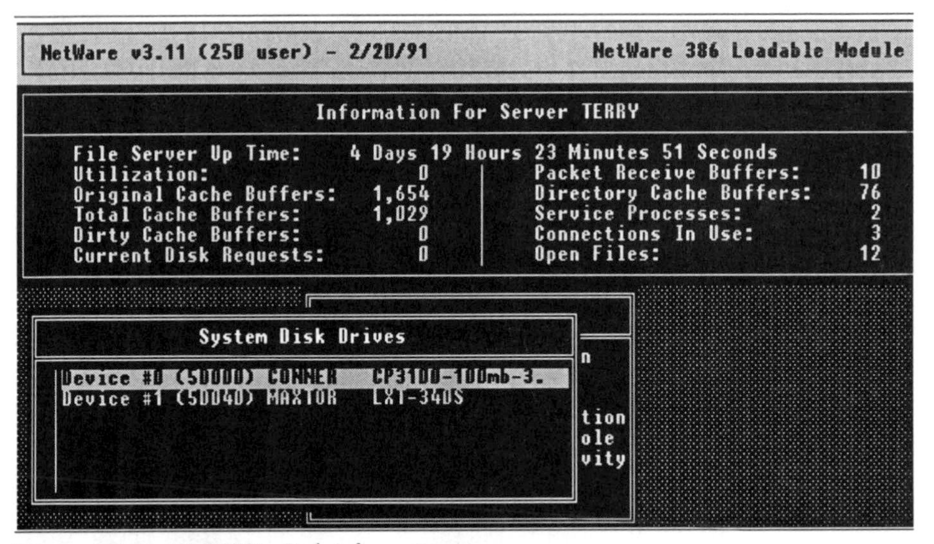

Figure 18-2. *MONITOR's Disk Information screen.*

Hot Fix Status—Whether Hot Fix status is normal or not (Hot Fix has failed).

Partition Blocks—The total amount of space on the volume shown in blocks.

Data Blocks—The amount of space available in blocks.

Redirection Blocks—The block size of the Hot Fix area.

Redirected Blocks—The number of blocks redirected to the Hot Fix redirection area.

Reserved Blocks—The blocks reserved for Hot Fix tables.
LAN Information Screen

The LAN Information screen gives you a great deal of information about the LAN driver and how well it is running. The LAN driver passes network information to the MONITOR screen. This information can be useful in determining exactly what is going on with your network. To view the LAN driver statistics, choose the LAN Information screen from MONITOR's main menu. If you have multiple adapters in the file server or multiple frame types bound to a single adapter, you will see a list of adapters to choose from. Remember, NetWare sees each bound protocol as a logical adapter.

Tip
Some drivers require that NetWare's Network Management Agent NLM (NMAGENT) is loaded prior to loading the LAN driver. Otherwise, these drivers will not pass network information to the MONITOR NLM. Most of these drivers will autoload the NLM if they do not find it.

The information in the LAN Information screen falls into two categories. The first category is information Novell requires. The second category is information that the vendor needs for the particular protocol or adapter to provide an accurate picture of the LAN driver. These information groups are called variables; the first category includes the standard variables for the access method; the second category contains the vendor's custom variable for the particular adapter. The standard LAN driver variables follow:

Driver Name—The long name of the driver the parameter is required to load.

Version—The version number of the loaded driver.

Node Address—The address in hexadecimal notation of the network adapter in the file server.

Protocols—The protocols bound to the adapter using the BIND statement.

Network Address—The network address assigned to the adapter when bound to the protocol using the BIND statement.

Total Packets Sent—The total number of packets sent from the file server through the adapter. Other packages can be used to obtain information about the network to compare the numbers.

Total Packets Received—The number of packets received by the file server through the adapter being viewed.

No ECB Available Count—The number of packets that could not be received because a buffer was not available. The server allocates more Packet Receive Buffers when this statistic increments, until the maximum available is reached. If you see this statistic increase after the maximum is reached, you can increase the maximum number of Packet Receive Buffers in the server's AUTOEXEC.NCF file or from the command line using the com-

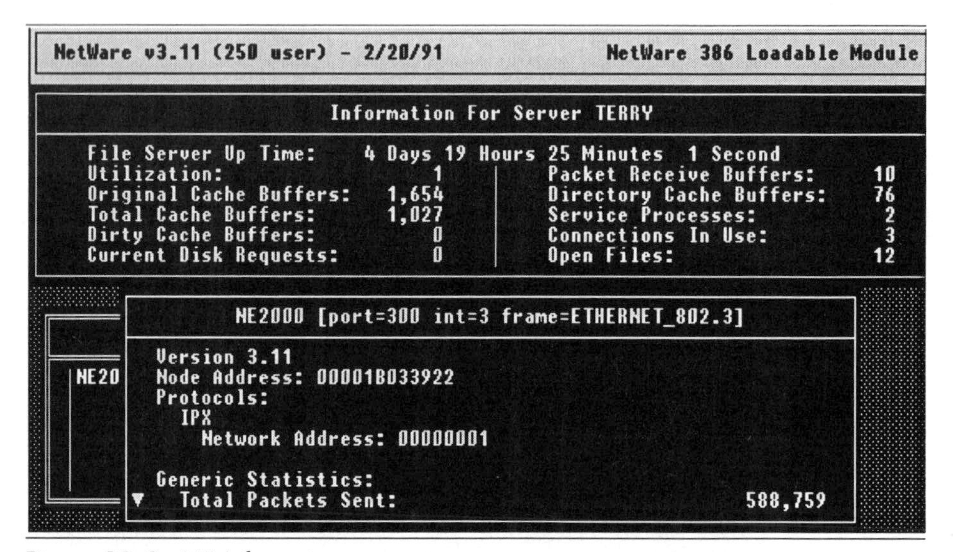

Figure 18-3. *LAN Information screen.*

mand SET MAXIMUM PACKET RECEIVE BUFFERS =XXX. The maximum number of Packet Receive Buffers in NetWare v3.x is 2,000, and in 4.x is 3,000.

Send Packet Too Big Count—The number of packets that could not be sent because they were too large. This statistic is an indication of a malformed packet.

Send Packet Too Small Count—The number of packets that could not be sent because they were too small. This statistic is an indication of a malformed packet.

Receive Packet Overflow Count—The number of packets received that were too big to store in a cache buffer. This statistic generally indicates poorly behaved software.

Receive Packet Too Big Count—The number of packets received that were too large. This is generally the result of an application error.

Receive Packet Too Small Count—The number of packets received that were too small. This is generally the result of an application error.

Send Packet Miscellaneous Errors—The number of errors that occurred when a packet was sent.

Receive Packet Miscellaneous Errors—The number of packets received with errors.

Send Packet Retry Count—Indicates the number of errors that occurred when the server tried to send a packet but could not because of a hardware error. If you see a large number of Send Packet Retry Counts, check for bad media.

Checksum Error—When a packet is sent, it includes a count of the number of 1s or 0s in the packet. If this count does not match the count the adapter at the other end of the communication reads, the packet is rejected.

Hardware Receive Mismatch Count—The number of errors when specified packet lengths have not been met.

Custom variables are provided by the adapter's vendor and include information specific to the access method and to the adapter. For Thomas-Conrad adapters, some of the custom statistics for token-ring include the following:

Auto-Removal Error—The number of times the adapter detected an internal hardware error, initiated the beacon process, and removed itself from the ring. The adapter will automatically reinsert itself when the error is corrected.

Burst Error—The adapter received a frame containing invalid data.

Lobe Media Fault—This indicates that the connection from the adapter to the multistation access unit has been lost. It indicates a cable problem.

Lost Synch with Adapter—The adapter's onboard processor lost communication with the driver. The driver will reinitialize itself.

Receive Congestion Error—The adapter could not accept a frame because its buffers were full. This is not uncommon on an extremely busy network.

Remove Received—The adapter received a "Remove Ring Station" media access control frame from a network manager.

Token Error—The active monitor detected a problem with the active token.

The Resource Utilization Screen

The Resource Utilization screen provides valuable information on the server's use of memory. To view this screen, select Resource Utilization from MONITOR's main menu. These statistics are represented as percentages indicating the amount of available memory. The In-Use column indicates how much available memory is being used in a particular memory pool. The displayed memory pools areas follows:

Permanent Memory Pool—This display provides statistics on both the Permanent and Semipermanent pools. Permanent and semipermanent memory is used for long-term needs such as directory cache buffers and packet receive buffers. This memory does not return to the regular memory until the server is rebooted.

Alloc Memory Pool—This display designates the Allocated Short-Term Memory pool. This memory is intended for short term use by NetWare Loadable Modules, drive mappings, and connection information.

Cache Buffers—Indicates the total amount of memory available in the cache buffer pool. Monitor this number closely. If it reaches 20 percent or more, you need to add more file server memory. For the short-term, you can increase the amount of this memory by unloading NLMs.

Cache Movable Memory—This pool lists the amount of memory buffers that are floating. NetWare can move these buffers at any time to help in memory management. This memory is returned when not in use to the Cache Buffer pool.

Cache Non-Movable Memory—Displays the amount of memory in this pool for buffer space temporarily allocated to another program.

Total Server Work Memory—Indicates the total amount of memory available for the server to use.

LANalyzer for Windows

Novell has developed a unique tool for network analysis. It is a low-level protocol analysis tool called LANalyzer for Windows. This product is currently only available for Ethernet and token-ring networks. It operates by utilizing the promiscuous mode of the Ethernet and token-ring chip sets. Promiscuous mode forces the adapter to copy all frames on the network to a buffer in memory. LANalyzer for Windows runs on a workstation that is attached to the network, but is not necessarily logged in. Therefore, it can work on both NetWare and non-NetWare networks. The LANalyzer is also available in a DOS-based version.

The first consideration for using LANalyzer for Windows is that you must have an ODI LAN driver that supports promiscuous mode. If you do not, you must obtain from your vendor a new driver that supports promiscuous mode, or obtain a new adapter.

Tip

IBM Token-Ring adapters do not currently support promiscuous mode.

LANalyzer for Windows provides these three real-time monitoring functions:

Packets per second—Indicates the number of packets on the network.

Utilization percentage—Indicates the percentage of bandwidth utilization at any given time period.

Errors per second—Indicates the number of errors generated on the network per second.

You may also set thresholds that will sound an alert when the limits are reached.

Below LANalyzer for Window's initial screen is a secondary screen that contains other basic network information. It lists each workstation on the network and the following information about each workstation:

Station—The individual node address of the workstation. Names can be substituted for these addresses by editing the node address list.

Kbytes out—The number of kilobytes transmitted by the workstation.

Kbytes/s out—The number of kilobytes transmitted per second by the workstation.

Kbytes in—The number of kilobytes received by the workstation.

Kbytes/s in—The number of kilobytes received per second by the workstation.

Pkts out—The number of packets transmitted by the workstation.

Pkts/s out—The number of packets transmitted per second by the workstation.

Pkts in—The number of packets received per second by the workstation.

Pkts/s in—The number of packets received per second by the workstation.

LANalyzer for Windows gathers information in real time. It also allows you to take this information and present it in graphical form to give a more visual representation of the network. With this information, you can determine the overall network traffic and which workstations generate the majority of the network traffic. You can also use this information to make decisions about the network layout and whether and how to segment your network or upgrade it. You can take the most heavily used nodes and place them on a different segment or on a faster access method. These functions, however, are only the most basic information LANalyzer for Windows provides.

The most important part of LANalyzer for Windows is the protocol analysis ability it gives you. This ability lets you capture actual network traffic and analyze it. You can determine whether you want to capture all packets, a small portion of the packets, or only the packets' header information.

Tip

LANalyzer for Windows will capture the entire packet but will only display the first four kilobytes of the packet. For normal network analysis and Ethernet networks, this size limitation is fine, but for token-ring networks that use a larger packet size than 4KB, this can cause problems. Also, any software-based protocol analyzer will miss or "drop" packets. Keep this in mind if you do not see what you expected.

LANalyzer captures the majority of the network packets and allows you to view them. This captured information can be extremely useful, provided you know what you are looking for. The analysis you can perform pays off with a relatively small amount of study. You will need to learn a small amount of how Ethernet and token-ring work and about the packet structure of each. In LANalyzer, packets are decoded and presented in a visual format based on the order in which they are received in the capture buffer.

NetWare Care

NetWare Care is Novell's pre-LANalyzer product for network analysis. It is not as complex or sophisticated as the LANalyzer, but it provides general information about the network. This information includes the following:

1. The number of transmitted packets
2. The number of received packets
3. The number of transmit collisions in Ethernet networks
4. The number of transmission errors
5. File server cache statistics
6. The file server routing table
7. Server performance in events per second
8. A network graph
9. Error statistics for workstations and the server

If you are planning to purchase LANalyzer, you will not need NetWare Care. However, with NetWare Care you can perform basic network troubleshooting such as identifying cable and network communication problems and overloaded or faulty network segments. Using NetWare Care's workstation error statistics, you can diagnose some application problems.

COMCHECK

While the NetWare utility COMCHECK is often used as an installation utility it can be used to check cable connections. (See Figure 18-4.) COMCHECK provides this information:

1. The adapter's network address
2. Unique user information for the workstation
3. The date and time
4. The status of the adapter to the rest of the network

To use COMCHECK, load LSL.COM, the workstation driver, and IPXODI.COM. Then type COMCHECK from the DOS prompt. You will be asked to provide a unique name for the adapter. COMCHECK will

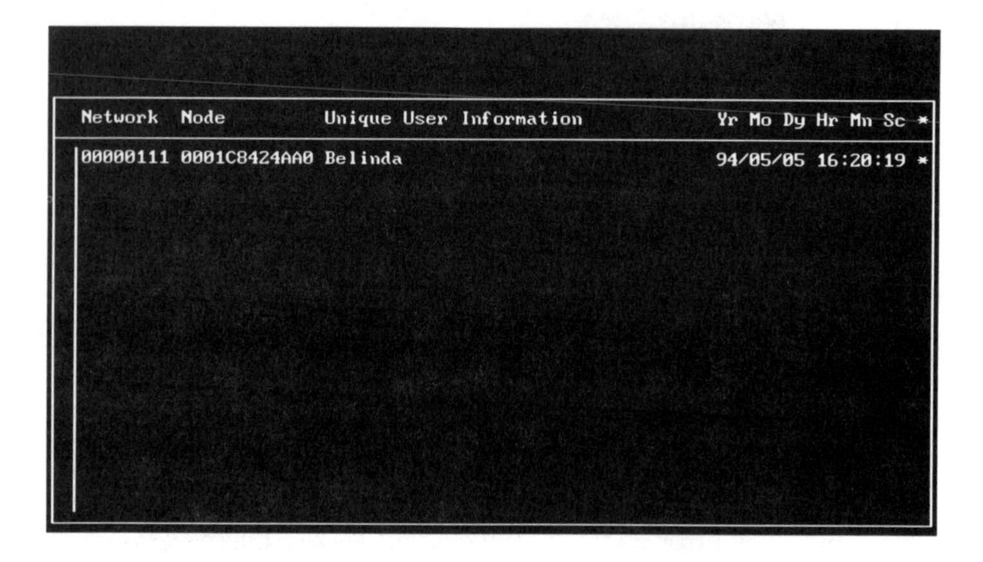

Figure 18-4. *COMCHECK's utility display.*

send traffic between all machines on the network in an attempt to identify cabling problems and determine whether a network adapter can send and receive information.

DISKED

DISKED is a NetWare utility that diagnoses problems with hard drives, disk co-processor boards (DCBs), or disk controllers. DISKED finds a specific hard disk sector and writes and reads disk data. DISKED provides this information:

1. The read status of the hard drive
2. The write status of the hard drive
3. The status of communications between the controller and the drive

CHKVOL and VOLINFO

CHKVOL and VOLINFO are NetWare command-line utilities that provide information about a specific volume on the file server. The utilities identify where the volume is located, its total space, the space used by files, the deleted file space, and the remaining disk space. To use CHKVOL and VOLINFO, enter the command name at the DOS prompt:

```
CHKVOL volume name
VOLINFO
```

TRACK ON

TRACK ON is a server-based utility that displays the network's router tracking screen. This screen displays all network packets the file server receives or sends. It displays the node ID, the network address, and related information for all packets destined for the server. You can use this information to decide if a station that is attempting to communicate with the server is actually sending information and if the server is sending a response. Or, TRACK ON can be used to check the routing of a packet through the network. To invoke TRACK ON, enter the command at the file server console. When you are finished using TRACK ON, you can turn it off by typing TRACK OFF.

Hardware-based Monitoring

NetWare provides assistance to vendors manufacturing hardware-based monitoring packages. In these packages, an additional device will often be attached to the network that can test every network event and cable integrity and provide protocol analysis. For simple analysis of network transmissions, many sophisticated cable-analysis devices are available that look for network transmission problems and malformed packets that result from faulty cables. Figure 18-5 depicts a cable tester.

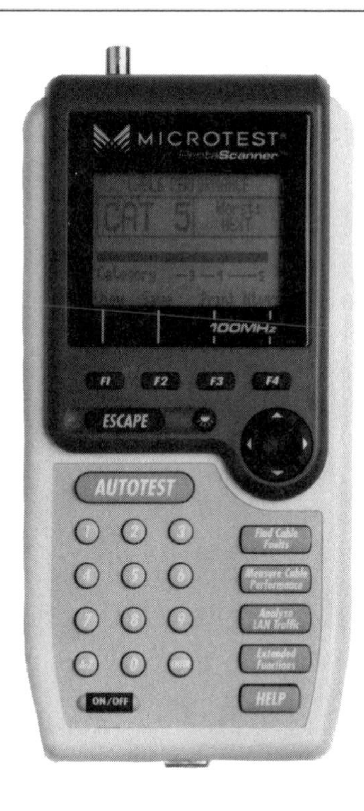

Figure 18-5. *A cable tester. (Reprinted permission of Microtest.)*

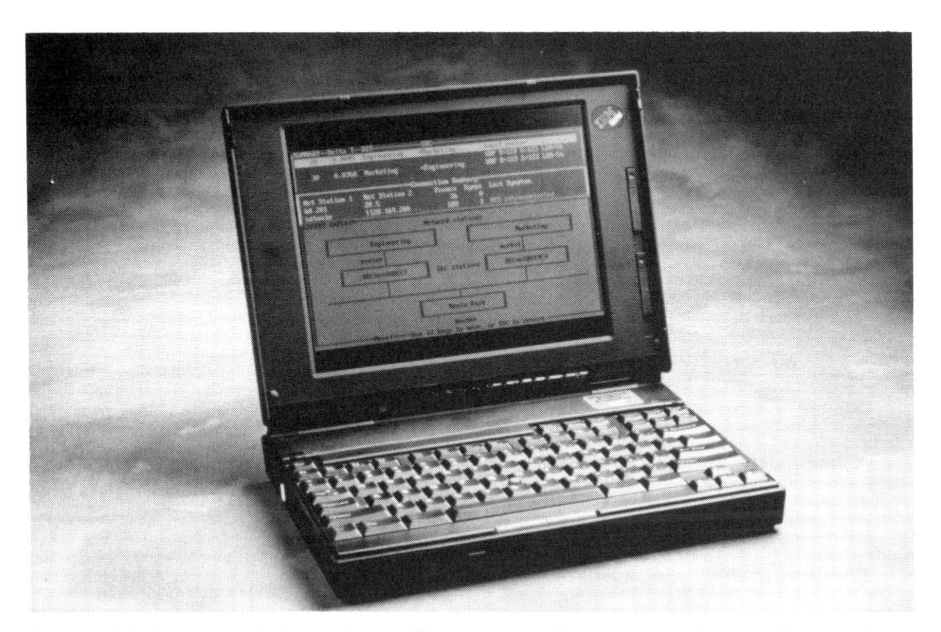

Figure 18-6. *Network General's Sniffer. (Reprinted permission of Network General).*

Network General also provides one of the most effective hardware-based protocol analysis tools on the market. Called the Sniffer, it provides analysis of the actual network packets. (See Figure 18-6.) The Sniffer attaches a specially designed Ethernet, ARCNET, or token ring adapter to the network to capture all network traffic. It then decodes packets as necessary. Unlike most software-based protocol analysis tools, the Sniffer captures all network traffic and provides more sophisticated analysis. Other hardware-based protocol analyzers are available from Network Communications Corp. and Hewlett-Packard.

Managed Hubs

The majority of Ethernet and token-ring hubs, concentrators, or multistation access units are not managed other than from LEDs on the front of the device. As networks became larger and more complex, the need increases to gather additional statistics on overall network traffic, monitor individual ports, and control those ports. A variety of companies have added software-based management into their hub products. The managed-hub business is led by companies such as Synoptics and Cabletron. These companies provide a central wiring device for most networks that can manage Ethernet, token-ring, and FDDI networks and automatically disable and reroute data from faulty nodes. While these devices do not extend or change the wiring rules of the access methods, they bring central control and remote monitoring to the user.

Called chassis-mounted managed hubs, these devices consist of a large box (chassis) that contains one or more power supplies and have the ability to accept a number of modules, each providing connections to network devices. Multiple power supplies provide redundancy in power supply failures. The back plane of the chassis provides interconnection between the modules when necessary for resegmentation of the network.

Additional management potential is realized in the managed hub with the introduction of management modules. These modules provide more sophisticated analysis of the network as well as the ability to control network actions. These modules gather information about each device attached to it and store the information in a database called a Management Information Base (MIB) for use by a management workstation. They also allow you to disable individual ports from the management station or reroute devices to a different segment.

The management station (a simple workstation) connects to the network or attaches to the hub via an RS-232 connection. This station runs management software to interpret the data sent from the management module.

The most common management protocol these devices use is the Simple Network Management Protocol (SNMP), which polls devices and gathers information for inclusion in the MIB database. This database and the information gathered correspond to criteria decided by the Internet groups responsible for the SNMP protocol. SNMP uses TCP/IP as its transport protocol to transmit control information to the hub.

In addition, these hubs often provide routing, bridging, and gateway modules to accomplish the actions necessary for internetworking.

Recently, Novell introduced the NetWare Distributed Management System (NDMS), which provides a framework for managed-hub operation within the NetWare environment. NDMS supports SNMP and allows NDMS-compliant network managers to control NDMS-compliant devices from a single management console. With NDMS, each hub vendor has a common set of instructions for information and managing their devices. NDMS has not been fully implemented yet.

Most of the functionality of managed hubs depends on the hub and accessories you purchase. You can scale the size and management functions to your individual needs.

Software Monitoring

Software monitoring can also run the gamut from simple packages to sophisticated protocol analysis with packages such as LANalyzer for Windows. Software-based network monitoring is often less expensive and less sophisticated than hardware-based monitoring or managed-hub products.

Tip
It is a good idea to store monitoring software on a local hard drive. If the network slows down or is not functioning, you can still collect statistics and analyze hardware problems.

Programs such as NetWare Care from Novell, ARCvision and Token Vision from Triticom, Monitrix from Cheyenne Software, and TXD from Thomas-Conrad Corp. are examples of inexpensive software-based network monitoring packages. To operate, these programs require that the devices' LAN drivers be loaded. They provide information related to the adapter's configuration, driver, and shell information. They can generate network traffic for analysis.

Programs such as LANalyzer for Windows, FTP's LANWatch, or Intel's NetSight Analyst provide extensive protocol analysis. For most small to medium-sized networks, these tools provide essential information at a reasonable cost.

Network Management Protocols

Network information gathering and management are based on sets of rules and guidelines provided by network management specifications. Two current specifications exist: SNMP and the Common Management Information Protocol (CMIP).

Each of these specifications establishes a method for gathering, using, and storing information for use by management consoles. SNMP is the oldest management protocol. SNMP defines the type of information that will be collected and how it will be stored. It provides a hierarchical control function that provides security.

CMIP is the Open Systems Interconnection model for network management. It also defines how CMIP-compliant devices interact on the network. The heart of CMIP is the Common Management Information System (CMIS), which defines the OSI standard for gathering and storing information on the network. CMIP functionality includes

Accounting management—Tracks the use of network resources

Configuration management—Allows the manager to reconfigure network devices

Fault management—Detects and corrects faults in network equipment

Performance management—Monitors network traffic

Security management—Allows system managers to control access to the information bases

CMIP is currently supported by IBM through its NetView management utility and by AT&T's Star Sentry management system. As OSI gains acceptance, CMIP and its related protocols will gain a wider acceptance in the marketplace.

Other Monitoring Applications

As the needs of the network managers grow, the list of applications will also grow to meet the needs.

Metering Software

Originally, software was written for use on standalone machines. As networks became prevalent, users discovered that they could share software with others by putting it on a network. Many programs were written for the network to allow multiple users and licensed on a per-user basis, meaning that each user who uses the software must have a license for it. Other programs, mostly those designed to run on the server as NetWare Loadable Modules (NLMs) or Value-Added Processes (VAPs) are licensed on a per-server basis.

Metering software monitors the application licenses in use and prevents use of applications in excess of the allowable licenses. Software metering saves money by performing license-compliance analysis and preventing you from purchasing more licenses than you need. Current metering software includes Integrity Software's Softrack, Frye Computer's Software Metering and Resource Tracking (SMART), and Saber Software's Saber Enterprise Application Meter (SEAM).

Inventory Software

As networks grow, the need to track the individual devices on the network increases as well. Inventory programs gather information on network devices and report that information to a central database of hardware and software configuration information. These packages may operate as an NLM and require terminate-and-stay resident (TSRs) programs on the workstations that allow the server NLM to gather device information. These programs help you maintain an accurate inventory of network hardware and software, providing the manager with better control of network assets.

chapter 19

Tracking Trouble

Tips and Tricks

Keep It Simple

Network troubleshooting follows many of the same principles that troubleshooting any problem or standalone computer does. You need to describe the symptoms of the problem, identify the potential problem areas, isolate the problem area, repair the problem, and document the changes or repairs you make. In this chapter, we give you some techniques to use, some questions to ask, and some tips that will help you solve the problems you will inevitably inherit along with the LAN.

What Really Goes Wrong on Networks

Network problems can be grouped into several categories, the majority of which are related to the media the network uses. Cabling problems account for almost 85 percent of all network problems. Of the remaining 15 percent, 90 percent are related to hardware or software configuration issues. These configuration problems can be grouped together as software anomalies, hardware configuration problems, hardware and software incompatibilities, or hardware failures. Very few happen because of poorly manufactured or designed software or hardware.

Tip

Yes, we know right now that you think we are just trying to protect network vendors because we've both worked for one. It's not true. Rarely does the hardware or software arrive damaged. Problems relate to improper configuration or incompatibilities between devices or software. If hardware or software incompatibilities exist (the equipment or software just won't do what it needs to), the sooner you call the vendor's technical support and get past them to talk to either test, hardware, or software engineers, the better off you will be and the faster you will solve the problem. Technical support staffs are excellent at resolving the majority of network issues you'll encounter and identifying the tough problems that need to be referred to engineering support.

The days of companies' technical support representatives pointing fingers at each other and leaving the user in the lurch are almost over. Most networking companies have formed support alliances to work on problems occurring between their products. If your vendor balks and tells you your problem is someone else's problem, find yourself a new vendor.

Isolate the Problem

When a problem appears, it manifests itself in some way. The operator may see a network error message. You may see an error at the file server console. The network may not work at all—users can't log in, or you can see that the file server has abended. Many network problems may be more discrete.

Network problems tend to follow Murphy's basic law: "What can go wrong, will go wrong." Isolating network problems can be a frustrating experience, but remember this: it is only equipment and it didn't really intend to ruin that vacation you had been planning for the last six months. In approaching a network problem, patience, logical thinking, and information are the cardinal virtues. Don't panic.

Gather as Much Information as Possible

When the problem occurs, find out exactly what is happening. The "shotgun approach" of trying everything unrelated at once that apparently solved the problem before can be time-consuming, counterproductive, and frustrating. Begin by assessing what went wrong. The first thing you need to do when problems occur is isolate the error. To do so, ask yourself some of these questions:

1. Who reported the error?
2. What is the reported error?
3. When did the error occur?
4. What was the user doing when the error occurred? What application was the user using? Was the user trying to log into the network and failed?
5. Is the user at fault? Is he or she doing everything right?
6. What has changed since the last time the workstation, server, or application worked?
7. What kind of machine are you having problems with?
8. What kind of LAN adapter does the machine use?

The list of questions depends on the circumstances, but the most basic question, "What has changed," is essential. Something caused the problem, and you need to find out what that was. At this point you need basic answers, not a laundry list of BIOS versions and IRQs.

Tip

In a small network you will probably know the answers to a lot of these questions already, but you should force yourself through the exercise of asking the questions and getting the answers each time a problem occurs. You will be surprised how helpful it is and how many solutions it turns up.

Experienced Experimentation

Problem isolation is a series of logical steps and controlled experiments based on the actual problem. Breaking the problem into a series of smaller problems that can be isolated by controlled experiments is essential. For example, you have a user that receives the message "File server not found." The first thing you need to do is break the problem into its basic components. When this message occurs, three fault zones exist. They are the following:

1. The file server
2. The cable and associated devices
3. The workstation and LAN adapter

The File Server

Verify that the file server is operating by checking to see if anyone else can log in. If others can log in, then your problem is almost certainly not in the server.

The Adapter

While cable is the obvious choice, you might choose to look at the workstation first. As part of checking the workstation, be sure that the cable is plugged into the adapter and is securely connected. Then, look to see if all the workstation's LAN drivers are loading. Rename the AUTOEXEC.BAT file to AUTOEXEC.SAV, reboot the workstation, and load the drivers manually in this order:

```
LSL
NE2000      ADAPTER DRIVER (MLID)
IPXODI
NETX
```

The driver you are most interested in is the adapter driver (the MLID). Not only must it load, it must load correctly. The driver should list the adapter's configuration when it loads. The network documentation in your LAN Survival Kit and your LAN Log should tell you the exact settings of the adapter. If the LAN driver loads but reports incorrect settings, or if the driver does not load, you probably have isolated the problem.

If not, rename both the CONFIG.SYS and AUTOEXEC.BAT files and reboot the workstation. Then load the drivers again. If they load normally and you find the server, you have isolated the problem. Then edit the CONFIG.SYS file and add back one statement at a time to see if any individual statement is causing the problem. If all statements load normally, you can then start testing the AUTOEXEC.BAT file.

One statement in the CONFIG.SYS file causes a lot of problems. It is the 386 memory manager statement that specifies proper memory exclusions. You must remember to exclude the range of memory that the adapter is using. This is usually a 16-kilobyte area such as D000-D3FF. The exclusion commands for memory managers are different; however, for DOS 5.x and higher memory managers, the EMM386.EXE statement should appear as follows:

```
EMM386.EXE X=D000-D3FF
```

Tip

Under MS-DOS and IBM PC-DOS 6.x, if you press the F8 key after seeing the statement "STARTING DOS" when you boot the machine, you will be able to step through the CONFIG.SYS and AUTOEXEC.BAT files one statement at a time. This tip can save a lot of time.

Tip

You can tell a lot when a driver improperly loads. Error messages may tell you where the problem lies. The error message "No interrupts from adapter" means that you have an interrupt conflict. An error stating that the "Adapter could not be reset or found" means a conflict exists with the port or shared-memory address the adapter is using. An incorrect node ID or a node ID of 0 can mean either a memory conflict or a timing conflict with the computer.

In any event, look to see what the error is, and look it up if possible in the documentation you have.

It is also a good idea to verify the NET.CFG and SHELL.CFG files for improper statements. One of the hardest things to remember is that when stating a memory address in the NET.CFG file, you must use the full hexadecimal address. For example:

Link Driver TCNSW
Mem D0000 (You must use four zeros, not just three)

Tip

Problems at workstations are often the result of configuration problems. Be sure to verify the FRAMETYPE the adapter is using. Verification is especially important in Ethernet workstations that use the latest Open Data-Link Interface (ODI) drivers on NetWare v3.11. The older driver specification called for Ethernet_802.3 as the default Ethernet FRAMETYPE. The current specification for drivers that are also compliant with NetWare 4.0 defaults to Ethernet_802.2. If the incorrect FRAMETYPE is specified, the adapter will not be able to find the file server. If this occurs, add the following line to the driver stat0ement:

```
Link Driver TCE16ATW
        frame Ethernet_802.3
```

If the drivers load properly but you cannot find the file server, circumstances become more interesting. A properly loaded driver does not mean that no workstation problem exists. Load NETX and then time the response until you see "A File Server Could Not Be Found" message. The NetWare shell (NETX) looks for approximately 30 seconds before returning the error. If the error returns almost immediately, you probably have a problem at the workstation. Go to the file server, and at the console prompt (:), type TRACK ON. TRACK ON brings up NetWare's router tracking screen. This screen shows all the basic router packets to and from the server. You are looking specifically for three statements. They are the following:

GET NEAREST SERVER—A packet sent by the workstation shell (NETX) to all file servers on the network

GIVE NEAREST SERVER—The server response to the GET NEAREST SERVER request from the workstation

ROUTE REQUEST—The response from the workstation requesting routing information

Each of these should appear as a single series of statements. Depending on other traffic on the network, they may be separated by other events. If a problem occurs, you should see one statement or the other missing. In some cases, you might see one of the statements repeat continuously. If the GET NEAREST SERVER statement is missing, either the cable is bad or there is still a problem at the workstation. If the statements are present, but you still can't find the server, investigate the bus timing on the card in the workstation or look for a bad cable.

The Cable and Associated Devices

If your network uses a bus topology access method, look to see if other devices on the same bus segment can log into the network. Doing this, and finding that workstations can log in, eliminates the bus cabling. From this point, look at the most obvious potential problems: the cable between the workstation and the bus, or the workstation itself.

Then, begin a careful analysis of the cabling system. If possible, attach a known good cable to the workstation. If you find the server at this point, you have isolated the problem to a cable or port on the hub, MAU, or concentrator. Use a cable scanner to test each cable segment. If all the cables check out, change to a different port on the wiring device.

The isolation process may seem long and tiresome. As you gain experience, you can cut back on some of the actions, but do not give in to a shotgun approach. Simply changing things in the hope of solving the problem will cause more problems in the long run and may leave you with an impossible mess.

Tip

No matter which approach you use, be sure to CHANGE ONLY ONE THING AT A TIME. Changing multiple things such as the cable and the port on the concentrator may solve the problem, but it will not give you an idea of the solution. This leaves you with a problem that is just waiting to happen again.

Repair and Replace

Once you isolate a problem, make the appropriate repair and try again. It is entirely possible that you have a combination of problems that will take several attempts to isolate. If you find a problem with an adapter, you may want to isolate the problem further by attempting to use the adapter again in a different machine that you know works. If the adapter still fails, contact the vendor for repair or replacement.

Tip

Verify the warranty with your vendor before you commit to repairs. If the adapter is out of warranty, it may in fact be less expensive to buy a new adapter instead of repairing the old one. However, many vendors offer lifetime warranties or the equivalent. That is one feature you receive by using a known vendor and not shopping on price alone.

If you used one of the adapters from your Survival Kit to replace a faulty adapter, be sure to replace the adapter with the repaired adapter or a new adapter. If the adapter has a problem that you can wait to repair, mark the problem spot and note it in your LAN Log.

Retrace Your Steps

In searching for the source of problems, review the recent past. Check your LAN Log for changes you may have made. Ask the user who reported the problem what changes he or she has made. Ask for, or consider the following:

1. If the user has made any changes to his or her workstation environment.
2. If the user moved a machine trying to reach a pencil, for example, that rolled under the system unit.
3. If the user made changes to the workstation's configuration, such as to the interrupts the workstation's network adapter uses.
4. If any equipment or software was changed, added to, or removed from the network.

Document Your LAN

Network documentation will help you with problem isolation and troubleshooting. Be sure to document everything that happens on the network. Write down events that occurred during installation, during configuration changes, when you added users to the LAN, when you removed devices from the LAN, along with any problems you've observed. Your LAN Log will help you reconstruct some of the factors that may be causing your current problems.

Network, Network, Network

One aspect of troubleshooting a person often forgets, sometimes until it is too late, is to establish communication with other network administrators or workgroup managers whose jobs are similar to yours. You should consider these users or administrators as excellent sources of information. You'll want to meet them at user groups, seminars, and training courses. In fixing network problems, avail yourself of these information sources. Also don't hesitate to call the vendor's technical support department for problems related to a specific piece of equipment.

Novell originally sponsored the Technical Support Alliance (TSA), a consortium of vendors that have been cross-trained on all TSA members' products. Realizing that a network problem cannot always be pinpointed to a single device, these vendors dispatch information in an attempt to provide support that is more accessible to users. Many TSA members have toll-free telephone numbers, and many staff their support lines 24 hours, 7 days a week. Avail yourself of these vendors' services when solving a problem. That is, contact them, after all else has failed, and you can accurately relate the symptoms of the problem.

Attend tradeshows, and read books. Do anything that will help you improve your skills. Listen closely as others troubleshoot your network, and learn from them how to do better the next time.

Ask for help. There are a variety of places to get help from, and all should be used from time to time including these:

Vendor technical support—If your problem is with a specific hardware or software product, you should contact the vendor for support. The staff should know the product better than you and should be able to give sound advice. They also have access to technical expertise that you do not. Many vendors also maintain forums on CompuServe or bulletin board services (BBSs) where users can get the latest drivers and software patches.

Novell Technical Support—If you have isolated the problem to a potential bug in NetWare or in a component Novell supports, contact Novell. Remember that Novell Technical Support is fee-based.

Technical Support Alliance—Most vendors of Novell-certified products are also members of the Technical Support Alliance. The members of the TSA are extremely useful in solving multivendor problems that otherwise would be difficult to solve via one vendor. TSA members will share information and equipment between themselves to help isolate and solve problems.

Check Your References

Make use of the on-line and electronic services available. Subscribe to NetWire, Novell's on-line service on CompuServe. Subscribe to CompuServe and read the PC network vendor forums, especially if you have their equipment. Prepare for a potential disaster by arming yourself with the information you can obtain from these services. Make use of the Novell information on the Internet. Consider buying NSEPRO, an on-line service for networking technical support, or the TECHs database, which will help you with a myriad of LAN problems. Use the LAN Compass in the back of the book to familiarize yourself with the information it provides.

NetWire is Novell's forum on CompuServe that presents an excellent opportunity to speak with others that may have encountered similar problems. It is also a great place to get upgraded software and patches. NetWire is extremely useful for generic problems or those intermittent problems that are hard to pinpoint. There are many NetWire SYSOPS (systems operators) that will answer your questions 24 hours, 7 days a week.

Assemble Your Tools

Once you've resigned yourself that the LAN isn't going to operate perfectly (or sometimes not at all), you'll want to assemble an arsenal of tools you can use when you need them. You should also remember that, like every survival kit, the ingredients need to be kept up-to-date. Older material needs to be replaced from time to time, and your software needs to be updated as necessary. Some of the equipment you might want in your LAN Survival Kit are the following:

1. Cable testers to test for breaks, frays, or distance violations on the type of cable you are using. Cable testers range from simple devices that examine only a single type of cable to expensive, sophisticated devices that will examine any type of cable and access method. We suggest you evaluate several manufacturers' products before making a final decision. MicroTest and Fluke are among the best manufacturers of cable-testing products. If you are on a budget, this is the one concession you may have to make to expense.
2. A basic tool kit that includes straight, Torx, and Phillips screwdrivers, nut drivers, needle-nose pliers, diagonal cutters, and a simple chip removal tool. From here you can expand into power tools or a soldering iron. The kit should also include a series of screws, bolts, computer slot covers, and drive-bay components. This is where pack-rat tendencies are useful—you will always have something that you can't use in another machine.
3. A basic cable kit that is designed around the cable that you use. For UTP cable, you will need a large number of RJ-45 connectors, cable, and a crimping tool. For RG-58 cable and RG-62 cable, you will need appropriate cable ends, a cable cutting tool, crimpers, T connectors, and terminators. For fiber-optic media, you will need

a much more extensive kit that can be purchased from your cable dealer. You should also keep on hand wall plates and plates for the wiring closet.

4. A Volt-Ohm Meter (VOM), which tests for electrical potential, resistance, and current. A good VOM is essential for verifying proper voltages on the wire, or current coming from a power supply to the appropriate pins on an adapter in the computer. The amount of resistance on a cable can be used to verify the cable's length or quality.
5. Protocol analyzers, which can capture network packets so you can examine them in trying to decide what is going wrong with the network.
6. Walkie-talkies or cellular telephones, which help you keep in touch either with other system managers that are helping you, or with users that may need help.
7. Diagnostic software that tests LAN adapters, cabling faults, and other hardware or software problems.
8. Extra LAN adapters for any type of network. At least one or two LAN adapters, a spare disk controller and video card, and any adapter you routinely use on the network, workstation, or server. The more mission-critical the device, the more you need a spare.
9. A Time-Domain Reflectometer (TDR), which verifies media integrity.
10. Manuals for every piece of equipment and software. A complete set of Novell NetWare manuals, specifically the System and Error Message manuals. Or, at a minimum, a copy of the Novell Support Encyclopedia on CD-ROM.
11. Diagnostic software like CheckIT LAN or Peter Norton's diagnostic software is essential. Also, a bootable DOS diskette with copies of the FDISK, FORMAT, and CHKDSK utilities. Many vendors now supply diagnostic software with their equipment.
12. Novell software that consists of a disk with VREPAIR and the associated NetWare Loadable Modules for the name spaces you use, DISKSET for setting up software for the disk co-processor board, and DISKED. A complete workstation boot diskette with the latest files on it. COMCHECK. For 286 NetWare workstations, the NetWare DCONFIG utility. And finally, a complete set of NetWare disks for your version of the operating system.

13. Protocol analysis software and hardware. LANalyzer for Windows or another protocol analysis tool. If you choose the more expensive hardware-based protocol analysis route, you should consider a device like Network General's Sniffer.
14. Vendor software. The latest drivers and setup software for all of the equipment on your LAN. For EISA and Micro Channel machines, be sure to have the latest setup software.
15. Network documentation for all equipment. User information. A network map and workstation documentation.

Tip
Maintaining spare LAN adapters is essential. This is also true for hubs, concentrators, hard drives and video adapters. Most vendors will cross-ship equipment, but that means that you will be down a minimum of 24 hours. If your network is critical to your business operation, the cost of a spare is small compared to the cost of 24 hours without the network.

Generic Network Problems

Although many of the problems you will find on a network are specific to a particular vendor's product, you will find that there are also many problems that are generic to networking. They are cabling, power problems, and problems with the file server or workstations.

Cabling

Cabling represents the majority of problems on a network by far. A good cable scanner is essential to isolating the problems you will encounter. However, there are a few simple rules to follow when troubleshooting cable:

Verify cable ends—The termination point of the cable is where the majority of stress on the cable occurs. Good quality, properly terminated ends are essential.

Cable terminators—The terminators for bus segments can fail over time and should be checked with a Volt-Ohm Meter to verify the cable's termination value. Also, remember that one of the ends of a 10BASE-2 or 10BASE-5 segment should be grounded.

Cable specifications—Be sure that you are using the proper type of cable for your network. UTP cable that worked well for 4Mbps token-ring may be out of specification for 16Mbps token-ring and cause immediate or intermittent problems.

Protocol specifications—Verify that you don't exceed the cabling specifications for your access method. Don't exceed the 10BASE-T specification of 100 meters. Follow rigorously the 5, 4, 3 rule. Exceeding these specifications can cause immense problems.

Power Problems

Although rare, power problems do crop up from time to time on a network. When you encounter them, they will be of two basic varieties: power supply problems and AC power and grounding problems.

Power Supply and Related Problems

A problem with a device's power supply can cause a variety of problems on your network. An errant power supply can allow unfiltered or over-voltage power on the network line. A noisy power supply can corrupt data. The first problem can create havoc on your network that is immediate and devastating. The latter can cause intermittent problems that are almost impossible to detect and cure.

Tip

One of the hardest problems we encountered with power was related to a voltage line on a computer bus that had gone bad. The adapter would not receive proper power on initial start-up, but if warm-booted, it would initialize and work normally. We traced this problem to a bad five-volt line on the bus.

A problem power supply many times will cause other problems on the computer that are unrelated to network problems. Replacing the power supply on a computer is a simple operation. Do not, however, attempt to replace the supply on a concentrator, multistation access unit, or hub. Send them back to the manufacturer for repair.

AC Power and Grounding Problems

Problems related to AC power and wiring are also generally rare occurrences on networks. You may run into them from time to time, and you should be prepared to respond to them. If you suspect a problem with the AC power, you can rent monitoring equipment, or in many cases the local power company will come in and verify the line for you. An AC power-line monitor is an expensive piece of equipment that you should consider renting if you feel you need one. AC power problems are often related to consistent low voltages or voltage fluctuations. Power conditioning equipment or battery backup systems can eliminate some of these problems. If brownouts or blackouts are a problem in your area, consider purchasing one of these systems.

Another potential problem related to AC power is proper grounding. In a properly grounded system, there should be little or no voltage on the ground line. Computer networks use the AC ground as part of the reference signal. If voltage is too high on the ground line or, worse yet, fluctuates between devices on the network, the result is a signal that is disrupted or corrupt. This causes data corruption and over time may damage your equipment. Have the local power company or a qualified electrician verify the grounding on the outside of the building and confirm that all AC outlets are properly grounded.

AC ground problems increase dramatically if you attempt to use copper cable between buildings or in areas of the same building that are on different AC grounds. There is no guarantee that the different buildings or areas have the same ground potential (the amount of voltage to ground). If you must run a cable between buildings or to different areas of a building on different AC grounds, use fiber-optic cable, which is immune to differing ground potentials, if at all possible. Fiber-optic will eliminate any ground potential problem. Because fiber-optic cable transmits the signal as a pulse of light, it does not require a ground plane for reference.

Tip

An improperly grounded system is an invitation to lightning-related power problems. Most systems that arrest or prevent problems from lightning are tied to the building AC ground. If the ground is faulty or nonexistent, surge protectors will not operate.

Nothing will stop problems related to a direct lightning strike on your building.

File Server Problems

The NetWare file server is the heart of the network. As a result, you should be especially wary of problems that arise there. NetWare will warn you of potential problems and give you a chance to correct them before disaster strikes. You can use the MONITOR utility to help isolate potential problems on the server before they happen. Some of the problems you might encounter include the following:

The server will not load—Look to see if an error message is displayed. This message will help you isolate the problem. A file server that will not load the SERVER.EXE program properly is often related to a mounting failure of the SYS or another volume.

VOL will not mount—At this point, run VREPAIR and see if you can repair the volume. It may be necessary to run VREPAIR more than once to be sure the volume is completely repaired.

Server abends (abnormal end)—A server will ABEND with a specific error message. Look up the error message and isolate it to the component that failed.

The server will no longer communicate—This failure may or may not be preceded by an error message. Unload the adapter driver and attempt to reload it. Verify the adapter for the appropriate LAN segment on the server. Check the settings in NetWare's MONITOR utility to verify proper configuration.

LAN driver will no longer load—Verify the adapter settings in the server. If the server is an EISA machine, verify the EISA configuration file. Replace the adapter if necessary. Verify the settings in the STARTUP.NCF and AUTOEXEC.NCF files that pertain to the adapter.

A new LAN adapter will not communicate—Verify that the LAN adapter driver is loaded and bound properly to the protocol stack (IPX). Verify that you have not duplicated a network address. Verify that you have set the following parameters according to the vendor's directions: MAXIMUM PHYSICAL RECEIVE PACK-

ET SIZE, MINIMUM AND MAXIMUM PACKET RECEIVE BUFFERS, and MINIMUM PACKET RECEIVE BUFFERS BELOW 16 MEGABYTES.

Hard drive dismounts—Verify the hard drive. If you are using mirrored drives, load the INSTALL utility and verify the mirroring status. The drives may have become unsynchronized. Check Hot Fix to see if the redirection area is becoming full. A nearly full redirection area indicates that a drive is about to fail.

You will also encounter file server problems when you attempt to add a new device to the server. With LAN adapters or controllers, the problem occurs because of a conflict with existing equipment. If you eliminate all conflicts and something is still wrong, look at timing issues between the machine and the new adapter.

Several problems can occur with ISA bus-mastering adapters. Some machines simply do not support ISA bus-mastering. If you see problems with bus-mastering adapters, disable bus-mastering on the device.

Another problem in a file server is related to bus-mastering priority, also called *fairness*. The problem revolves around bus access when multiple bus-mastering devices attempt to control the bus. Bus-mastering devices will hold the bus until they have completed the direct memory addressing (DMA) data transfer or until the CPU's next video refresh cycle. However, when multiple bus-mastering adapters are installed in the same machine, they must give up the bus more often. Because of this, bus-mastering adapters participate in prioritizing the DMA channel and fairness. For those adapters that do not invoke fairness, you will sometimes be able to manipulate the time on and off the bus. This can be performed when the driver loads under NetWare or with a physical switch on the device. Another alternative is to place the device that is not operating properly at a higher-priority DMA channel. To do this, place the device at a channel with a lower number than the device that will not invoke fairness. A final alternative for bus-mastering priority problems is to disable bus-mastering altogether. You will sacrifice performance but gain compatibility.

The arbitration level automatically sets bus priority between multiple bus-mastering adapters. EISA machines also have a unique priority system that eliminates the majority of issues with EISA bus-mastering adapters.

Memory Issues

File server memory is also an important issue when you are attempting to isolate server problems. NetWare uses separate memory pools and dynamically allocates memory between them. The majority of memory is assigned to cache buffers. If you do not have enough memory to accommodate the traffic on the network, performance will suffer and the server can become unstable. NetWare v3.11 will load with 2MB of memory, but if you attempt to run a production server with insufficient memory, you are asking for trouble. The amount of memory you need relates to the amount of disk and directory space you have, or to the number of LAN adapters and packet size the adapters use.

A good rule of thumb for calculating memory for disk size and directory space is that you should have at least 10MB of RAM for every 1GB of disk space. You need more memory if you add OS/2, Macintosh, or UNIX name spaces to the server. Each namespace requires about 2MB of RAM. A large number of additional files or directories may also require more memory.

The number of LAN adapters and the packet size they use will also affect the amount of memory the server needs. The more adapters you have in the server, the more RAM you will need. Also, the larger the packet size, the larger the amount of RAM you will need caching packets.

LAN Compass

Refer to the LAN Compass in the back of the book for configuring file server RAM.

Workstation Problems

On the workstation, problems are most often related to software configuration or hardware conflicts. LAN adapters will use one or more of the following settings:

Base I/O port

Interrupt

Shared RAM address

DMA channel

A conflict can occur with any of these settings. However, the most likely causes of conflict are the interrupt, a shared RAM address, or the DMA channel. Interrupt conflicts occur most frequently with modems and video cards. A program designed to poll the machine for devices and the ports they use is helpful in isolating the problem.

One of the most common workstation conflicts involves interrupt channels. Most adapters generate an interrupt before transferring data to system memory. ISA machines cannot share interrupts, so each interrupt a device uses must be unique. Many Micro Channel and EISA devices are designed to share interrupts at least with like devices. A list of the common interrupts devices use follows:

Interrupt 2/9—Video cards, LAN adapters, mouse

Interrupt 3—COM2

Interrupt 4—COM1

Interrupt 5—LPT2, mouse

Interrupt 6—Floppy controller

Interrupt 7—LPT1

Interrupt 10—Hard drive controller, PS/2 mouse

Interrupt 11—Hard drive controller

Interrupt 12—Hard drive controller

A shared RAM address can also conflict with the machine itself or other devices in the machine. Many machines shadow the BIOS and video into RAM. This shadowing can conflict with RAM address space of network adapters. Also, VGA controllers generally use the space from C000-C7FF for adapter RAM space.

Tip

A shared RAM address can occur between VGA controllers and sixteen-bit shared RAM LAN adapters. This conflict involves the way adapters send information along the bus. Data is sent in blocks of data. 16-bit adapters that occupy the same 128KB memory segment (from D000 to DFFF) must decode the information in the same way. The available sizes are 1KB and 128KB. If the sizes are different, only one of the adapters will work. The majority of video cards and shared RAM LAN adapters allow you to adjust this size to allow them to match.

Another source of problems with shared RAM LAN adapters is memory managers. You must exclude the area of memory the adapter uses. If the adapter is using range C800 to CBFF, you must exclude this area of memory. The exclusion statements for memory managers differ, but it must include a statement of exactly how much memory to exclude.

Tip

For Windows users, you may have to exclude the area of memory for shared RAM adapters in the SYSTEM.INI file. To do this, place the following statement in the [386enh] section of the SYSTEM.INI file:

EMMEXCLUDE=XXXX-YYYY

(where X is the beginning point of the shared RAM address, and Y is the ending address).

Tip

For ARCNET users, most vendors require a 16KB address space set aside for shared RAM. Of this space, only the first 8KB is critical. The last 8KB is reserved for boot ROMs, which allow a diskless workstation to boot to the network. If you are not going to use remote-boot, then you need only exclude the first 8KB. This action is especially helpful if the workstation is subject to RAM cram.

Conflicts will often occur between LAN adapters and other ISA devices using direct memory addressing. The other adapters that use DMA include SCSI device controllers. An additional problem can occur with bus-mastering devices. The problem revolves around sharing bus access with multiple bus-mastering devices. Bus-mastering devices hold the bus until they complete the DMA data transfer or until the CPU's next video refresh cycle. However, when multiple bus-mastering adapters are installed, they must give up the bus more often. The criterion for relinquishing the bus is based on the priority of the DMA channel and an algorithm called *fairness*. Most of the drivers for bus-mastering devices invoke fairness. Some do not. For those that do not invoke fairness, they will sometimes allow you to manipulate the time on and off of the bus. Another alternative is to place the device that is not operating properly at a higher-priority DMA channel. To do this, place the device at a channel with a lower number than the device that will not invoke fairness. Another problem related to DMA bus-mastering is ISA machines that don't support bus-mastering. If a machine you are using doesn't support bus-mastering, disable bus-mastering on the adapter. The majority of these problems do not appear with EISA machines or with EISA bus-mastering devices. With Micro Channel machines, you must set an arbitration level. The arbitration level automatically sets bus priority between multiple bus-mastering adapters.

NET.CFG Problems

The NET.CFG file contains the configuration statements for the NetWare components on the workstation. The values in this file are designed to override the workstation's default configuration set in the CONFIG.SYS file. The majority of the time the workstation's default configuration will work well. However, if you change the adapter from the default settings, you must place the changes in the NET.CFG file. The settings you place here must match the settings on the adapter. If the settings do not match, the driver will fail to load. The applicable NET.CFG statements are placed under the LINK DRIVER statement. The options include

DMA number—This option configures the DMA channel for the adapter.

INT number—This option configures the interrupt.

MEM number—This option specifies the beginning memory address range for shared RAM adapters.

PORT address—This option configures the starting port address for adapters using a port address.

FRAME type—This option overrides the default frametype. The driver will load if this option is incorrect; however, unless it matches the option set at the file server, you will not be able to find the file server.

There are more settings for network adapters, but they should not stop the driver from initializing the adapter. The various settings in the NET.CFG are discussed in detail in Chapter 6. What About Workstations?

Handling LAN Adapters

One of the most common problems that can occur is in the mishandling of LAN adapters. These are some rules you should follow:

1. Hold the adapter by its end bracket.
2. Don't touch the edge connector (gold fingers) that fit into the computer's expansion slot.
3. Discharge static equipment before touching the bracket or any part of the LAN adapter.
4. Don't touch any of the circuitry of the adapter.
5. If you are going to be carrying the adapter around, place it in an anti-static bag (the bag it came in) or wrap it in anti-static foam.
6. Don't force a LAN adapter into an expansion slot. Rock it gently.
7. Screw the LAN adapter into the CPU's chassis once you've determined that it works.
8. Keep the shipping contents and user documentation in case you have problems.
9. Don't install, reposition, or remove a LAN adapter when the machine is turned on.
10. Don't attempt your own repairs.
11. If a LAN adapter is dusty, blow it off with a can of compressed air.

AN OUNCE OF PREVENTION

Other techniques will help you prepare for anything that can go wrong on the network, or even forestall problems from happening. They are as follows:

1. Maintain some form of redundancy. In the file server, make sure that its drives are mirrored or duplexed. If you can afford it, duplex the file server with System Fault Tolerance (SFT) Level III. If you decide to do none of these, make sure that at least Novell's SFT I is enabled. SFT I provides transaction tracking, Hot Fix, duplicate FATs, Directory Entry Tables, and read-after-write verification.

2. Maintain a stock of spare equipment. Have plenty of terminators, T connectors, barrel connectors, and a supply of extra media. For adapters and hubs, concentrators, or multistation access units, consider a small quantity of spares that will be able to keep your

network operational while the original adapters or hubs are being repaired.

3. Perform periodic checkups of the workstations, tape backup units, printers, media, and the network file server.

4. Monitor your network's daily operations. Keep a close eye on the file server statistics via the MONITOR utility.

5. Preserve a clean environment. Periodically clean the file server, connectors, network adapters, tape drives, and printers.

6. Label each connection and cable, and document all changes in the LAN Log.

7. Install network components, devices, and media with care. Take the time to install the device the correct way.

8. Remember the distances allowed for each access method. Don't violate them just to squeeze a little bit more out of your network.

9. Remember that repairing network devices takes time. Have a plan for replacing these devices while they are out for repair. Document them in your LAN Log.

10. Many devices offer hot swappable modules such as power supplies that can be used in device failures. Consider them.

11. Consider sites that are similar to yours where operations can take place if the network is incapacitated.

12. Consider the human resources that you can count on to keep the network running in case something happens to you.

13. Evaluate power protection before you need it. Make sure to test the uninterruptible power supply regularly.

14. Have a troubleshooting and disaster-recovery plan.

15. Make sure that machines operate as standalone devices before installing them on the network.

16. Always power-down equipment when installing adapters or other components.

17. Test a device giving you trouble in a similar configuration.

By following these steps, most network problems can be avoided. Don't risk the safety of your network data or the work of network users by having an ill-planned or inefficiently operating network.

Make Some Hardware Checklists

Here are some things to look for if you are having network problems:

1. Duplicate node IDs
2. Loose connections
3. Distance violations
4. Media violations
5. Defective wiring, opens, shorts, crimps, kinks, or miswired connectors
6. Improper terminator or lack of termination
7. RECONs in ARCNET; collisions in Ethernet; and hard or soft errors in token-ring
8. Link integrity in Ethernet 10BASE-T networks
9. File server crashes; lack of file server disk space; improperly mounted drives; poor directory and file organization

Make a Software Checklist

Keep an eye on the software operations of your network with the MONITOR utility. Run the SECURITY utility to know where intruders may have tried to break into the LAN. Evaluate packages and utilities that provide virus protection, show file server statistics, or display rights and attribute problems.

On a regular basis, check the file server's cache statistics, check that all disks are mounted and operational, and evaluate the amount of disk space remaining on NetWare volumes. To protect the network's data, perform a trial backup and restore the data. Test the UPS regularly.

Most of these tips involve the type of common sense that will help you manage your LAN better. Consider each action before performing it, and learn from your mistakes. The LAN jungle is not as complicated as it appears as long as you keep your wits about you and follow these principles.

Vendor List

This appendix lists the leading vendors in each category you may be buying from. When you buy equipment or software, be sure you know what you are asking for and what you need, and make sure that you get the right answers from the companies on this list.

Backup Software and Hardware

Alloy Computer Products
(QIC, DAT, 8mm)
1 Brigham St.
Marlborough, MA 01752
(800) 800-2556
(508) 481-8500
Fax (508) 481-7711

Cheyenne Software (ARCServe)
55 Bryant Ave.
Roslyn Heights, NY 11576
(800) 243-9462
(516) 484-5110
Fax (516) 484-3446

CMS Enhancements (LANStack, QIC)
2722 Michelson Dr.
Irvine, CA 92715
(714) 222-6000
Fax (714) 222-6226

Colorado Memory Systems (QIC)
800 S. Taft Ave.
Loveland, CO 80537
(800) 432-5858
(303) 669-8000
Fax (303) 669-0401

Contemporary Cybernetics Group
(QIC, 8mm, autoloaders)
Rock Landing Corporate Center
11846 Rock Landing
Newport News, VA 23606
(804) 873-9000

Emerald Systems (QIC, DAT, 8mm,
XpressLibrarian, EmQ,
EmSave, autoloader)
12230 World Trade Dr.
San Diego, CA 92128
(800) 366-4349 or (619) 673-2161
Fax (619) 673-2288

Exabyte (8mm)
1685 38th St.
Boulder, CO 80301
(800) 392-2983 or (303) 442-4333
Fax (303) 442-4269

Gigatrend (DAT, LanDat SL,
SerVerDat SL, MasterSafe)
2234 Rutherford Rd.
Carlsbad, CA 92008
(619) 931-9122
Fax (619) 931-9959

Knozall Systems
(FileWizard for FileSafe)
375 E. Elliot Rd., Suite 10
Chandler, AZ 85225
(800) 333-8698 or (602) 545-0006
Fax (602) 545-0008

Legato Systems (Networker)
260 Sheridan Ave.
Palo Alto, CA 94306
(415) 329-8898
Fax (415) 329-8898

Maynard Electronics (QIC, DAT, 8mm,
LANStream, MaynStream, QICStream)
36 Skyline Dr.
Lake Mary, FL 32746
(800) 821-8782 or (407) 263-3500
Fax (407) 456-8887

Micronet Technology (QIC, DAT)
20 Mason
Irvine, CA 92718
(714) 837-6033
Fax (714) 837-1164

Mountain Network Solutions
(QIC, DAT, 8mm, FileSafe)
240 E. Hacienda Ave.
Campbell, CA 95008
(800) 458-0300 or (408) 379-7300
Fax (408) 379-4302

Palindrome (DAT, Network
Archivist, autoloaders)
600 E. Diehl Rd.
Naperville, IL 60563
(708) 505-3300
Fax (708) 505-7917

Performance Technology (Powersave)
7800 IH-10 West
San Antonio, TX 78320
(800) 327-8526 or (512) 349-2000
Fax (512) 366-0123

Storage Dimensions (LANStor, DAT, 8mm)
1656 McCarthy Blvd.
Milpitas, CA 95035
(408) 954-0710
Fax (408) 944-1200

Sytron (Sytos Plus)
134 Flanders Rd.
Westboro, MA 01581
(800) 877-0016 or (508) 898-0100
Fax (508) 898-2677

Tallgrass (FileSecure, FileSecure EnterPriz,
NetSecure)
11100 W. 82nd St.
Lenexa, KS 66214
(800) 825-4727 or (913) 492-6002
Fax (913) 492-2465

Tecmar (QIC, DAT, 8mm, ProServe)
6225 Cochran Rd.
Solon, OH 44139
(800) 422-2587 or (216) 349-0600
Fax (216) 349-0851

Communications Servers and Remote Access Software

Avalan Technology (Remotely Possible/LAN)
116 Hopping Brook Park
Holliston, MA 01746
(800) 441-2281 or (508) 429-6482
Fax (508) 429-3179

Brightwork Development (NETremote+)
766 Shrewsbury Ave., Jerral Ctr. W.
Tinton Falls, NJ 07724
(800) 552-9876 or (908) 530-0440
Fax (908) 530-0622

Cross Communications (Cross Star, LAN Modem, Cross Touch)
1881 Ninth St., Suite 302
Boulder, CO 80302
(303) 444-7799
Fax (303) 444-4687

Funk Software (Proxy)
222 Third St.
Cambridge, MA 02142
(617) 497-6339
Fax (617) 547-1031

Gateway Communications (Comsystem, G/Async 100 and 200, WNIM+)
2941 Alton Ave.
Irvine, CA 92714
(800) 367-6555 or (714) 553-1555
Fax (714) 553-1616

Intel (LANSight)
5200 N.E. Elam Young Pkwy., CO3-11
Hillsboro, OR 97124
(800) 738-3373 or (503) 629-7000
Fax (800) 525-3019

Microcom (Carbon Copy)
500 River Ridge Dr.
Norwood, MA 02062
(800) 882-8224 or (617) 551-1000

Microdyne (NetWare Async Communications Server)
207 South Peyton St.
Alexandria, VA 22314
(703) 739-0500
Fax (703) 739-1026

Multi-Tech Systems, Inc. (Multicom Async Gateway Series, Multi-Express)
2205 Woodale Dr.
Mounds View, MN 55112
(800) 328-9717 or (612) 785-3500
Fax (612) 785-9874

Norton-Lambert (Close-Up/LAN)
PO Box 4085
Santa Barbara, CA 93140
(805) 964-6767
Fax (805) 683-5679

Ocean Isle Software (Reach Out Network)
49 Royal Palm Blvd.
Vero Beach, FL 32960
(800) 677-4777 or (407) 770-4777
Fax (407) 770-4779

Shiva (NetModem/E)
One Cambridge Center
Cambridge, MA 02142
(800) 458-3550 or (617) 252-6300

Symantec (PCanywhere LAN)
10201 Torre Ave.
Cupertino, CA 05014
(408) 253-9600
Fax (408) 253-3968

Telebit (Telebit ACS, Modemizer)
315 Chesapeake Terrace
Sunnyvale, CA 94089
(800) 835-3248 or (408) 734-4333
Fax (408) 734-3333

Triton Technologies (CO/Session, CO/Session ACS)
200 Middlesex Tpke.
Iselin, NJ 08830
(800) 332-9440
(908) 855-9449
Fax (908) 855-9608

U.S. Robotics (Blast, Shared Access)
8100 N. McCormick Blvd.
Skokie, IL 60076
(800) 342-5877 or (708) 982-5001
Fax (708) 982-5235

Electronic Mail

Beyond (BeyondMail), a subsidiary of Banyan Systems
38 Sidney St.
Cambridge, MA 02139
(617) 621-0095
Fax (617) 621-0096

Da Vinci Systems (Da Vinci E-mail)
4200 Six Forks Rd.
Raleigh, NC 27609
(800) 328-4624 or (919) 881-4320
Fax (919) 787-3550

Enable Software (Higgins)
1150 Marina Village Pkwy., Suite 101
Alameda, CA 94501
(800) 888-0684 or (510) 865-9805
Fax (510) 521-9779

Futurus Corp. (Futurus Team)
211 Perimeter Center Pkwy., Suite 910
Atlanta, GA 30346
(800) 327-8296 or (404) 392-7979
Fax (404) 392-9313

Lotus Development (cc:Mail, Lotus Notes)
55 Cambridge Pkwy.
Cambridge, MA 02142
(800) 345-1043 or (617) 577-8500

Novell (NetWare MHS, FirstMail, NetWare Global MHS)
2180 Fortune Dr.
San Jose, CA 95131
(800) 638-9273 or (408) 947-0998
Fax (408) 435-1706

On Technology (Notework)
72 Kent St.
Brookline, MA 02146
(800) 767-6683 or (617) 734-4317
Fax (617) 734-4160

WordPerfect (WordPerfect Office), a Novell business unit
1555 N. Technology Way
Orem, UT 84057
(800) 451-5151 or (801) 228-5007
Fax (801) 228-5077

Xcellenet
5 Concourse Pkwy., Ste. 200
Atlanta, GA 30328
(800) 322-3366 or (404) 804-8100
Fax (404) 804-8102

Fax Servers

Alcom Inc. (LanFax Redirector)
1616 N. Shoreline Blvd.
Mountain View, CA 94555
(415) 694-7000
Fax (415) 694-7070

All the Fax Business Systems (Fax Pac Gateway)
58 West 44th St.
New York, NY 10036
(212) 840-5950
Fax (212) 840-7599

AMA Computers Inc. (SkyTek Fax)
1100 Burnhamthorpe Rd. West, Unit 27-31
Mississauga, Ont., Canada L5C 4G4
(416) 897-2153
Fax (416) 897-2151

Biscom Inc. (Faxcom for LAN)
321 Billerica Rd.
Chelmsford, MA 01824
(508) 250-1800
Fax (508) 250-4449

Calculus, Inc. (EZ-Fax)
1761 West Hillsboro Blvd.
Deerfield Beach, FL 33442-1530
(305) 481-2334
Fax (305) 481-1866

Castelle Inc. (FaxPress)
3255-3 Scott Blvd.
Santa Clara, CA 95054
(408) 496-1807
Fax (408) 496-0502

Cheyenne Software Inc. (FAXServe)
55 Bryant Ave.
Roslyn Heights, NY 11576
(516) 484-5110
Fax (516) 484-3446

Delrina Corp. (WinFax/Share)
6830 Via Del Oro, Suite 240
San Jose, CA 95119
(800) 268-6082
Fax (408) 363-2340

East Coast Software Inc. (Faxcess)
2221 Peachtree Rd. NE, Suite D429
Atlanta, GA 30309
(404) 455-8773
Fax (404) 448-3749

Excelltech Inc. (ExcellFAX)
300 W. 3rd St.
Yankton, SD 57078
(605) 665-5811
Fax (605) 665-8324

Extended Systems Inc. (axConnection)
5777 N. Meeker Ave.
Boise, ID 82704
(208) 322-7575
Fax (208) 377-1906

Fransen/King Ltd. (FormFax)
614 Regents Blvd.
Fircrest, WA 98466
(206) 564-4000
Fax (206) 565-9647

Futurus Corp. (Futurus TEAM FAX)
211 Perimeter Center Pkwy, Suite 910
Atlanta, GA 30346
(800) 327-8296 or (404) 392-7979
Fax (404) 392-9313

Gammalink (Gammanet)
133 Caspian Ct.
Sunnyvale, CA 94089
(408) 744-1430
Fax (408) 744-1549

Info Systems (Talki-Fax)
1110 Finch Avenue West, Ste. 614
Downsview, North York, Ont., Canada
M3J 2T2
(416) 665-7638
Fax (416) 665-4193

Intel (NetSatisFAXtion)
5200 N.E. Elam Young Pkwy., CO3-11
Hillsboro, OR 97124
(800) 738-3373 or (503) 629-7000
Fax (800) 525-3019

JetFax (JetFax)
978 Hamilton Ct.
Menlo Park, CA 94025
(800) 753-8329 or (415) 324-0600
Fax (415) 326-6003

Lane Telecommunications Inc. (Passport-3000 FAX Server)
5 Marineview Plaza, Suite 210
Hoboken, NJ 07030
(201) 798-0006
Fax (201) 798-0045

Lanier Worldwide (Lanier Link Plus)
2300 Parklake Dr. NE
Atlanta GA 30345
(800) 443-2948
Fax (513) 252-9541

Multi-Tech Systems Inc. (MultiExpress Fax Server)
2205 Woodale Dr.
Mounds View, MN 55112
(800) 328-9717 or (612) 785-3500
Fax (612) 785-9874

OAZ Communications (NetFax)
44920 Osgood Rd.
Fremont, CA 94539
(510) 226-0171
Fax (510) 226-7079

Optus Software Inc. (FACSys)
100 Davidson Avenue
Somerset, NJ 08873
(908) 271-9568
Fax (908) 271-9572

Pure Data (PureFAX)
180 West Beaver Creek Rd.
Richmond Hill, Ont., Canada L4B 1B4
(416) 735-6444
Fax (416) 731-7017

RightFax (RightFAX)
4400 E. Broadway, Suite 312
Tucson, AZ 85711
(602) 327-1357
Fax (602) 321-7469

SofNet Inc. (Fax/Works)
380 Interstate North Parkway, Suite 150
Atlanta, GA 30339
(404) 984-8088
Fax (404) 984-9956

File Servers

Advanced Logic Research (Powerpro)
9401 Jeronimo
Irvine, CA 92718
(310) 862-2926
Fax (310) 862-3395

AST Research (Premium SE)
16215 Alton Pkwy., PO Box 19658
Irvine, CA 97213
(800) 876-4278
(714) 727-4141
Fax (714) 727-9355

Compaq (SYSTEMPRO)
20555 SH 249
Houston, TX 77070
(800) 231-0900
(713) 370-0670

Core International (Core95)
7171 N. Federal Hwy.
Boca Raton, FL 33487
(407) 997-6055
Fax (407) 997-6009

NetFrame Systems (NF Series)
1545 Barber Ln.
Milpitas, CA 95035
(408) 944-0600
Fax (408) 434-4190

Samsung Electronics America (SystemMaster)
301 Mayhill St.
Saddle Brook, NJ 07662
(201) 587-9600
Fax (201) 587-9178

Tricord Systems (PowerFrame)
3750 Annapolis Ln.
Minneapolis, MN 55447
(800) 729-5055
(612) 557-9005
Fax (612) 557-8403

Unisys (U6000, PW2)
2700 N. First St.
San Jose, CA 95134
(408) 434-2146
Fax (408) 434-2122

Hubs and Network Interface Adapters

3COM (Ethernet, token-ring)
400 Bayfront Plaza
Santa Clara, CA 95052
(800) 638-3266 or (408) 764-5000
Fax (408) 764-5001

Accton Technology (Ethernet, token-ring)
46750 Fremont Blvd., #104
Fremont, CA 94538
(800) 926-9288 or (510) 226-9800
Fax (510) 226-9833

Accunetics (Ethernet)
190 Blydenburg Rd.
Islandia, NY 11722
(800) 446-7769
(516) 348-1566
Fax (516) 348-7246

Allied Telesis (Ethernet)
575 E. Middlefield Rd.
Mountain View, CA 94043
(800) 424-4284
(415) 964-2771
Fax (415) 964-1598

Andrew (Token Ring)
19021 20th Ave. N.E.
Bothell, WA 98011
(800) 776-6174 or (206) 485-8200
Fax (206) 487-5769

Artisoft/Eagle Technology (Ethernet, token-ring)
1160 Ridder Park Dr.
San Jose, CA 95124
(800) 733-2453 or (408) 441-7453
Fax (408) 436-0348

Asante Technologies (Ethernet)
404 Tasman Dr.
Sunnyvale, CA 94089
(800) 662-9686 or (408) 752-8388

Bytex (Ethernet, Token Ring)
Four Technology Dr.
Westborough, MA 01581-1760
(800) 227-1145 or (508) 366-8000
Fax (508) 366-0344

Cabletron Systems (Ethernet, token-ring, FDDI)
35 Industrial Way, PO Box 5005
Rochester, NH 03878-0505
(603) 332-9400
Fax (603) 332-4616

Chipcom (Ethernet, token-ring, FDDI)
Southborough Office Park
118 Turnpike Rd.
Southborough, MA 01772
(800) 228-9930 or (508) 460-8900
Fax (508) 460-8950

CNET Technology (Ethernet, token-ring, ARCNET)
2199 Zanker Rd.
San Jose, CA 95131
(800) 486-2638 or (408) 954-8000
Fax (408) 954-8866

Codenoll Technology (Ethernet, FDDI)
1086 N. Broadway
Yonkers, NY 10701
(914) 965-6300
Fax (914) 965-9811

Compex (Ethernet, ARCNET)
4055 E. La Palma, Unit C
Anaheim, CA 92807
(714) 630-7302
Fax (714) 630-6521

David Systems (Ethernet, token-ring, FDDI)
701 E. Evelyn Ave.
Sunnyvale, CA 94086
(800) 762-7848 or (408) 720-8000
Fax (408) 720-1337

Dayna Communications (Ethernet)
50 S. Main, 5th Floor
Salt Lake City, UT 84144
(801) 531-06600
Fax (801) 359-9135

D-Link Systems (Ethernet, token-ring, ARCNET)
5 Misick
Irvine, CA 92718
(714) 455-1688
Fax (714) 455-2521

Gateway Communications (Ethernet)
2941 Alton Ave.
Irvine, CA 92714
(800) 367-6555 or (714) 553-1555
Fax (714) 553-1616

IBM Corp. (token-ring)
Armonk, NY
(800) 426-2468

IMC Networks (Ethernet)
16931 Millikan Ave.
Irvine, CA 92714
(800) 624-1070 or (714) 724-1070
Fax (714) 724-1020

Intel (Ethernet, token-ring)
5200 N.E. Elam Young Pkwy., CO3-11
Hillsboro, OR 97124
(800) 738-3373 or (503) 629-7000
Fax (800) 525-3019

Intellicom (Ethernet)
20415 Nordhoff St.
Chatsworth, CA 91311
(818) 407-3900
Fax (818) 882-2404

Lantana Technologies (ARCNET)
4393 Viewridge Ave., Suite A
San Diego, CA 92123
(800) 666-4526 or (619) 565-6400
Fax (619) 565-0798

Madge Networks (token-ring)
42 Airport Pkwy.
San Jose, CA 95110
(800) 876-2343 or (408) 441-1300
Fax (408) 441-1335

Microdyne (Ethernet, FDDI)
207 S. Peyton St.
Alexandria, VA 22314
(703) 739-0500
Fax (703) 739-1026

Milan Technology (Ethernet)
894 Ross Dr.
Sunnyvale, CA 94089
(408) 752-2770
Fax (408) 752-2790

Motorola (Wireless)
20 Cabot Blvd.
Mansfield, MA 02048
(508) 261-4000 or (800) 446-6336

Network Interface (ARCNET)
15019 W. 95th St.
Lenexa, KS 66215
(800) 343-2853 or (913) 894-2277
Fax (913) 894-0226

Network Peripherals (FDDI)
1371 McCarthy Blvd.
Milpitas, CA 95035
(408) 321-7300
Fax (408) 321-9218

Networth (Ethernet)
8404 Esters Blvd.
Irving, TX 75063
(800) 544-5255 or (214) 929-1700
Fax (214) 929-1720

Olicom (Token Ring)
900 E. Park Blvd., Suite 180
Plano, TX 75074
(214) 423-7560
Fax (214) 423-7261

PC Office (100Mbps proprietary)
4901 Morena Blvd. Ste. 805
San Diego, CA 92117
(800) 726-8101 or (619) 273-1442
Fax (619) 273-2706

PlusNet (100Mbps proprietary)
21630 N. 19th Ave., B-16
Phoenix, AZ 85027
(800) 468-9032 or (602) 581-6771
Fax (602) 581-8545

Proteon (token-ring)
9 Technology Dr.
Westborough, MA 01581
(800) 545-7464 or (508) 898-2800
Fax (508) 366-8901

Proxim (Wireless)
295 N. Bernardo Ave.
Mountain View, CA 94043
(800) 229-1630 or (415) 960-1630
Fax (415) 964-5181

Pure Data (Ethernet, token-ring, ARCNET)
180 West Beaver Creek Rd.
Richmond, Hill, Ont., Canada L4B 1B4
(416) 731-6444
Fax (416) 731-7017

Racal-Datacom (Ethernet, token-ring)
155 Swanson Rd.
Boxborough, MA 01719
(800) 526-8255 or (508) 263-9929
Fax (508) 263-8655

Racore (token-ring)
170 Knowles Dr. #204
Los Gatos, CA 95030
(800) 635-1274 or (408) 374-8290
Fax (408) 374-6653

Standard Microsystems (Ethernet, token-ring, ARCNET)
80 Arkay Dr.
Hauppauge, NY 11788
(516) 435-6255
(800) 762-4968

Synoptics Communications (Ethernet)
4401 Great America Pkwy
Santa Clara, CA 95052
(800) 776-6895

SysKonnect (Ethernet, FDDI)
12930 Saratoga Ave., Suite D-1
Saratoga, CA 95070
(800) 752-3334 or (408) 725-4650
Fax (408) 725-4654

Thomas-Conrad Corp. (Ethernet, token-ring, ARCNET, 100Mbps proprietary)
1908-R Kramer Lm.
Austin, TX 78758
(800) 332-8683 or (512) 836-1935
Fax (512) 836-2840

Tiara Computer Systems (Ethernet, ARCNET)
1091 Shoreline Blvd.
Mountain View, CA 94043
(800) 638-4272 or (415) 965-1700
Fax (415) 969-0958

Xircom (Ethernet, token-ring)
26025 Mureau Rd.
Calabasas, CA 91302
(800) 874-7875 or (818) 878-7600
Fax (818) 878-7630

Network Management and LAN Utilities

Avanti Technology (Network analyzers)
13740 Research Blvd., Suite R-1
Austin, TX 78750
(800) 282-6844
(512) 335-1168
Fax (512) 335-7838

Blue Lance Software (Inventory, Security)
1700 W. Loop, Suite 1100
Houston, TX 77027
(713) 622-1381
Fax (713) 724-5269

Brightwork Development (Inventory, Security)
766 Shrewsbury Ave.
Jerral Ctr. W.
Tinton Falls, NJ 07724
(800) 552-9876
(908) 530-0440
Fax (908) 530-0622

Cabletron (Network management)
35 Industrial Way, PO Box 5005
Rochester, NH 03878-0505
(603) 332-9400
Fax (603) 332-4616

Central Point/Microcom (Inventory, Security, Server management)
500 River Ridge Dr.
Norwood, MA 02062
(800) 882-8224
(617) 551-1100
Fax (617) 551-1968

Cheyenne Software (Network management, Security)
55 Bryant Ave.
Roslyn, NY 11576
(800) 243-9462
(516) 484-5110
Fax (516) 484-3446

Chipcom (Network management)
Southborough Office Park
118 Turnpike Rd.
Southborough, MA 01772
(800) 228-9930
(508) 460-8900
Fax (508) 460-8950

David Systems (Network management)
701 E. Evelyn Ave.
Sunnyvale, CA 94086
(800) 762-7848
(408) 720-8000
Fax (408) 720-1337

Frye Computer Systems (Inventory, Server management)
19 Temple Pl.
Boston, MA 02111
(617) 451-5400
Fax (617) 451-6711

Horizons Technology (Inventory)
3990 Ruffin Rd.
San Diego, CA 92123
(619) 292-8331
Fax (619) 292-7152

Intel (Inventory, Protocol Analysis, Security, Server Management)
5200 N.E. Elam Young Pkwy., C03-11
Hillsboro, OR 97124
(800) 738-3373
(503) 629-7000
Fax (800) 525-3019

Knozall Systems (Server management)
375 E. Elliot Rd., Suite 10
Chandler, AZ 85225
(800) 333-8698
(602) 545-0006
Fax (602) 545-0008

LAN Support Group (Security, Server management)
2425 Fountainview, Suite 390
Houston, TX 77057
(800) 749-8439
(713) 789-0882
Fax (713) 977-9111

Magee Enterprises (Inventory)
2090 Langford Rd., Suite A600
Norcross, GA 30071
(800) 662-4330
(404) 446-6611
Fax (404) 368-0719

Microtest (Pair scanners)
3519 E. Shea Blvd.
Phoenix, AZ 85028
(602) 971-6963
Fax (602) 971-6963

Network Computing (Server management)
1950 Stemmons Frwy., Suite 3012
Dallas, TX 75207
(800) 736-3012
(214) 746-4949
Fax (214) 746-4955

Network General (Protocol analysis)
4200 Bohannon Dr.
Menlo Park, CA 94025
(800) 395-3151
(415) 688-2700
Fax (415) 321-0855

Ontrack Computer Systems (Security, Server management)
6321 Bury Dr.
Eden Prairie, MN 55346
(800) 752-1333
(612) 937-1107
Fax (612) 937-5815

Preferred Systems
2 Corporate Dr.
Trumbull, CT 06611
(800) 222-7638
(203) 459-1115
Fax (203) 459-1119

Protools (Network management)
14976 N.W. Greenbrier Pkwy.
Beaverton, OR 97006
(800) 743-4335
(503) 645-5400
Fax (503) 645-3577

Saber Software (Inventory, Menuing, Server management)
5944 Luther Ln., Suite 1007
Dallas, TX 75225
(800) 338-8754 or (214) 361-8086
Fax (214) 361-1882

Shany (Network management)
9724 Washington Blvd., Ste. 299
Culver City, CA 90232
(310) 204-0111
Fax (310) 204-0110

Thomas-Conrad Corp. (Network management)
1908-R Kramer Ln.
Austin, TX 78758
(800) 332-8683 or (512) 836-1935
Fax (512) 836-2840

Triticom (Network management, Inventory, Protocol analysis)
Box 444180
Eden Prairie, MN 55344
(612) 937-0772
Fax (612) 937-1998

Visisoft (Network management)
430 Tenth St., N.W., Suite 5008
Atlanta, GA 30318
(800) 847-4638 or (404) 874-0428
Fax (404) 874-6412

Xtree (Network management, Security, Server Management)
4330 Santa Fe Rd.
San Luis Obispo, CA 93401
(800) 634-5545 or (805) 541-0604
Fax (805) 541-8053

Printers

Hewlett-Packard (HP LaserJet)
PO Box 58059, MS511L-SJ
Santa Clara, CA 95051
(800) 752-0900
Fax (408) 323-2551

Lexmark International (IBM Laser Printer)
740 New Circle Rd.
Lexington, KY 40511
(800) 426-2468

Print Server Software and Hardware

ASP Computer Products (JetLAN)
160 San Gabriel Dr.
Sunnyvale, CA 94086
(800) 445-6190 or (408) 746-2965
Fax (408) 746-2803

Brightwork Development (PS-Print)
766 Shrewsbury Ave.
Jerral Ctr. W.
Tinton Falls, NJ 07724
(800) 552-9876 or (908) 530-0440
Fax (908) 530-0622

Castelle (LANpress)
3255-3 Scott Blvd.
Santa Clara, CA 95054
(800) 359-7654 or (408) 495-0474
Fax (408) 496-0502

Digital Products (LANprint)
411 Waverly Oaks Rd.
Waltham, MA 02154
(800) 243-2333 or (617) 647-1234
Fax (617) 647-4474

Emulex (Performance 2501)
3545 Harbor Blvd.
Costa Mesa, CA 92626
(800) 854-7112 or (714) 662-5600

Intel (LANSpool)
5200 N.E. Elam Young Pkwy., CO3-11
Hillsboro, OR 97124
(800) 738-3373 or (503) 629-7000
Fax (800) 525-3019

Milan Technologies (Fast Port)
894 Ross Dr.
Sunnyvale, CA 94089
(408) 752-2770
Fax (408) 752-2790

Northnet Research (JetStream!)
47 Arthur St. S.
Elmira, Ont., Canada N3B 2M6
(519) 669-1311
Fax (519) 669-4499

Rose Electronics (LANJet)
10850 Wilcrest
Houston, TX 77099
(800) 333-9343 or (713) 933-7673
Fax (713) 933-0044

Software Directions (PrintQ LAN)
1572 Sussex Tpke.
Randolph, NJ 07869
(800) 346-7638 or (201) 584-8466
Fax (201) 584-7771

Storage

Core International (LAN, SLAN-1000)
7171 N. Federal Hwy.
Boca Raton, FL 33487
(407) 997-6055
Fax (407) 997-6009

Iomega (Bernoulli)
1821 W. 4000 S.
Roy, UT 84067
(800) 456-5522

MicroNet Technology (AT, CPK, SB)
20 Mason
Irvine, CA 92718
(714) 837-6033
Fax (714) 837-1164

Micropolis (Raidion)
21211 Nordhoff St.
Chatsworth, CA 91311
(818) 709-3300
Fax (818) 709-3396

Sanyo/Icon (LANser)
18301 Von Karman, Suite 750
Irvine, CA 92715
(714) 263-3777
Fax (714) 474-1377

Storage Dimensions (LANStor)
1656 McCarthy Blvd.
Milpitas, CA 95035
(408) 954-0710
Fax (408) 944-1200

Uninterruptible Power Supplies

American Power Conversion (Back and Smart)
132 Fairgrounds Rd.
West Kingston, RI 02880
(800) 800-4272 or (401) 789-5735
Fax (401) 789-3710

Best Power Technology (Fortress)
38 Sidney St.
Cambridge, MA 02139
(800) 356-5794 or (617) 565-7200
Fax (617) 565-2221

Clary (Onguard PC)
320 W. Clary Ave.
San Gabriel, CA 91776
(818) 278-6111
Fax (818) 286-7216

Emerson Computing Power (AccuPower Gold)
9650 Jeronimo Rd.
Irvine, CA 92718
(800) 222-5877 or (714) 457-3600
Fax (714) 457-3788

Intellipower (Continuous Computer Powerline)
10-A Thomas St.
Irvine, CA 92718
(714) 587-0155
Fax (714) 587-0230

Minuteman Advanced Technology (Advanced Technology, Continuous Power)
1455 LeMay Dr.
Carrollton, TX 75007
(800) 258-7272 or (214) 446-9011
Fax (214) 446-7363

Oneac (ON)
27944 N. Bradley Rd.
Libertyville, IL 60048
(800) 327-8801

Panamax (Nonstop)
150 Mitchell Blvd.
San Rafael, CA 94903
(800) 472-5555 or (415) 499-3900
Fax (415) 472-5540

Tripp Lite (BC, Omni LAN, Unison)
500 N. Orleans
Chicago, IL 60610
(312) 329-1777
Fax (312) 644-4188

appendix B

NetWire, CompuServe, and the Internet

Making Use of On-Line Services

One of the most important ways to keep in touch with changes, additions, and deletions from NetWare is to subscribe to an on-line service. Here, you can bounce questions you might have about networking to other users, download patches and fixes that make NetWare better, and keep up-to-date with the latest NetWare information.

NetWare users commonly use three on-line services. They are: Novell's NetWire, which operates as a part of CompuServe; CompuServe, which has many NetWare-related areas; and the Internet, which has a large collection of NetWare information.

NetWire

Novell's NetWire requires only that you have a modem and some form of communications software that lets you log into CompuServe. Once in CompuServe, you'll type GO NETWIRE at the CompuServe prompt (!), which will take you to the on-line service. NetWire consists of forums where discussions of NetWare and its intricacies take place, libraries from which you can download information, and several LAN vendor forums, where product-specific information is supplied.

Once you have a subscription to CompuServe, you can join NetWire by typing GO NETWIRE.

CompuServe

CompuServe is an on-line bulletin board service that contains a number of vendors' product-specific forums. To access networking forums, type GO PCVEND at the CompuServe prompt (!). A number of vendors also have their own forums. To see these, choose the Computers options from CompuServe's main menu.

To get a CompuServe subscription, call 800-554-4079. You'll receive the first month free and a copy of CompuServe's DOS- or Windows-based CompuServe Information Manger (CIM).

The Internet

Users are increasingly turning to the Internet, an on-line service developed by the federal government to allow computers of different types to communicate with each other. NetWare information on the Internet is available by anonymous ftp, at ftp.novell.com or ftp.novell.de. When you use anonymous ftp, make sure that you use your user ID and entire Internet address as your password.

appendix C

NetWare Commands

In NetWare, the utilities are the tools you use to traverse and negotiate the networking jungle. Easy to use and extremely powerful, these utilities are divided into the following four types:

Command-line utilities—These utilities are executed from the DOS command line.

Console utilities—These utilities are restricted to use by the network supervisor only and run from the file server console.

Menu utilities—These utilities, which are executed from the DOS command line, operate via a series of menus from which the user can choose various tasks.

Windows utilities—These utilities, introduced with NetWare 4.x and operational on v3.12 networks, consist of a series of user and supervisor utilities that are run from within Microsoft Windows.

Command-Line Utilities

Command-line utilities are executed from the DOS command line on the workstation by either the user or the supervisor. Each version of

NetWare has different utilities it uses. We've marked the version number following the utility name. If you need help with the parameters a utility uses, many times you can put either a /? or a /H behind the utility name.

ACONSOLE (v3.12)—ACONSOLE allows you to access the file server remotely via a modem. No parameters are available.

ALLOW (v3.11, v3.12)—ALLOW lets you change or view a file's or directory's Inherited Rights Mask. You can also assign rights to files or directories with this command. The syntax is

ALLOW SYS:USERS\DENI\COMPASS.EXE R FS

ATOTAL (v3.12, 4.x)—In the NetWare accounting function, this utility lets you see the cumulative charges on a server including the connection time and the amount of disk storage used in a day. There are no parameters.

ATTACH (v3.12)—Allows you to connect to other servers after logging into a server. The syntax is

ATTACH servername

BINDFIX (v3.12)—You use this utility to repair the network's bindery if problems occur when you create, delete, or modify users, or change passwords, rights, or attributes. There are no parameters. When you run BINDFIX, all users need to be logged out of the server.

BINDREST (v3.12)—If the network still has bindery errors after you used BINDFIX, use BINDREST. This command restores the original bindery files.

CAPTURE (v3.12, 4.x)—CAPTURE redirects screen output to a printer or a file on a disk drive. A variety of parameters exist that are detailed in Chapter 9, Don't Forget the Applications, and in Chapter 7, Then There Are Printers.

CASTOFF (v3.12)—CASTOFF is used at a workstation when the user does not want to receive network SEND messages. If you don't want to receive BROADCAST messages from the file server, use CASTOFF ALL. Use CASTOFF when you are using communications or graphics packages, where CASTOFF will interrupt operations.

CASTON (v3.12)—Use CASTON after you have used CASTOFF. CASTON will allow the workstation to receive network broadcasts and to send messages.

CHKDIR (v3.11, v3.12)—CHKDIR allows you to view the amount of space on a volume or disk. To check the space on a volume or directory you aren't located in, use this syntax:

CHKDIR SYS:USERS\DENI

CHKVOL (v3.12)—CHKVOL lets you view volume information such as the total amount of space in the volume and the amount of space currently used or unused. Like CHKDIR, you can search either in the volume you are located in or in another volume. There are no other parameters.

COMCHECK—COMCHECK lets you test communications between network devices such as workstations, file servers, and printers. When you suspect that you may have cabling errors or duplicate node IDs, you should run COMCHECK.

CX (4.x)—CX is like the CD command in DOS. It allows you to change directories in NetWare 4.x.

DOSGEN (v3.12, 4.x)—This utility allows you to boot workstations from a file server, rather than from a local diskette drive or boot diskette. You use this utility for setting up diskless workstations. It has no parameters.

ENDCAP (v3.12)—Use ENDCAP to close a file after a CAPTURE takes place.

FLAG (v3.12, 4.x)—This utility allows a user or supervisor to view or modify ("flag") file attributes. FLAG has several parameters and allows you to set up to 16 attributes. It can be used in a directory you are located in or, by including the path statement, it can affect another directory. The syntax is

FLAG SYS:USERS\DENI\LIST +RO

FLAGDIR (v3.11, v3.12)—FLAGDIR lets you modify or view the directory rights and uses the same syntax as FLAG. Several parameters exist, and up to seven directory attributes can be set.

GRANT (v3.12)—This utility lets you grant rights to files or directories. Several parameters exist, among them ALL, which grants all rights to the specified file or directory. You can assign up to 10 rights with this command.

HOLDOFF (v2.2)—HOLDOFF is used when you are finished using a file and you want to allow other users to use it.

HOLDON (v2.2)—This utility prevents other users from using a file that you are using.

LISTDIR (v3.12)—This utility lets you see information such as the created date, last modified date, and the Inherited Rights Mask for a directory. It has several parameters. Among the five parameters are E to display effective rights and A to show all available directory information.

LOGIN (v3.12, 4.x)—LOGIN is the command a user or supervisor uses to access the network.

LOGOUT (v3.12, 4.x)—LOGOUT is the action you use to exit from a server or servers at the end of the day. If you are logged into several servers and only want to log out from one, enter the server name after the LOGOUT command for the server you want to exit.

MAP (v3.12, 4.x)—The MAP command lets you view, create, or modify the logical drives on the file server you are logged into in NetWare. Several parameters are possible. The syntax for mapping a drive is

MAP F: = SYS:\USERS\DENI

NCOPY (v3.12, 4.x)—NCOPY is NetWare's version of the DOS COPY command, which allows you to copy directories and files. NCOPY has several parameters, among them /S, which lets you copy all the subdirectories.

NDIR (v3.12, 4.x)—NDIR is the NetWare version of the DOS DIR command. It has numerous parameters, including the ability to sort files in a variety of different orders, the ability to show the rights and attributes assigned to the files, and the dates the file was created, modified, or last archived. To view the NDIR parameters, type NDIR /HELP from the DOS command line.

NETBIOS (v3.12)—This utility is necessary when you are communicating with devices or LANs that use IBM's NetBIOS. It has several options, one that lets you view information about the NetBIOS device, and another that lets you unload NetBIOS from memory.

NLIST (4.x)—This utility lets you view NetWare Directory Services objects.

NMENU (v3.12, 4.0)—This menuing utility, based on a menu from Saber Software, lets the user create menus from which users can choose applications.

NPRINT (v3.12, 4.x)—NPRINT allows you to redirect a disk file to a printer. In NetWare, use this command instead of the DOS PRINT command. NPRINT has several parameters.

NVER (v3.12, 4.x)—NVER displays the versions of the network operating system, the LAN drivers and the NetWare shell, that a workstation or file server is using. It has no parameters.

NWEXTRACT (4.x)—NWEXTRACT copies and expands the NetWare files from the CD-ROM for installation on the network.

PARTMGR (4.x)—PARTMGR lets you view the NetWare Directory and partition information.

PAUDIT (v3.12)—This utility lets you display information about NetWare's accounting system such as the times users logged in and logged out.

PSC (v3.11, v3.12, 4.x)—PSC is similar to the menu-based utility PCONSOLE. It has a number of parameters.

PSERVER (v2.1x, v2.2, v3.11, v3.12)—PSERVER.EXE allows you to create network print servers. It has no parameters. The NetWare Loadable Module of the same name loads the print server in NetWare v3.11 and v3.12.

PSTAT (v2.2)—PSTAT lets you see information about a network printer that includes whether the printer is on-line or off-line.

PURGE (v3.12, 4.x)—PURGE deletes permanently erased files that have been previously erased. PURGE allows wildcard use and has an option, /ALL, which allows you to delete all erased files.

QUEUE (v2.2)—This utility lets you create, modify, and view information about print queues. It has several parameters.

RCONSOLE (v3.12, 4.x)—RCONSOLE allows you to view and manipulate the file server console from a remote location on the network.

REMOVE (v3.12)—REMOVE lets you delete users and groups from the trustee lists for files and directories. It has two parameters.

RENDIR (v3.12, 4.x)—This utility allows you to rename subdirectories. It operates like the DOS RENAME command.

REVOKE (v3.12)—This utility allows you to remove trustee rights from files and directories. REVOKE has several parameters.

RIGHTS (v3.12, 4.x)—This utility displays the rights a user or group has in a particular subdirectory or to a specific file.

RPRINTER (v3.12)—Allows you to connect a workstation to a network as a remote printer server. It can also display the status of the printer and may be used to delete printer servers from the network.

SECURITY (v3.12)—SECURITY lists potential network problems. When you run SECURITY, it will pause as each page is displayed. To cancel pausing, use the /C parameter. SECURITY can be redirected to a printer by typing SECURITY >LPT1:

SEND (v3.12)—The SEND command allows users to send messages to other network users. It has several parameters.

SETPASS (v3.12)—This utility lets users change their passwords.

SLIST (v3.12)—This utility lets you view the file servers on the network and their status.

SMODE (v3.12)—This utility lets you create or modify the way programs search for files. It has several options.

SYSTIME (v3.12)—SYSTIME allows you to modify or view the time stamp on your workstation and coordinate it, if desired, with the time of the file server.

TLIST (v3.12)—This utility displays the trustees of a file or directory.

UIMPORT (4.x)—This utility, which replaces MAKEUSER, lets you create, modify, or delete users from an ASCII text file.

USERLIST (v3.12)—USERLIST lists the users and their network addresses that are currently logged into a file server. It has several parameters.

VERSION (v3.12)—This utility displays the version of NetWare the network is using.

WHOAMI (v3.12, 4.x)—This utility tells you your user name and workstation's network ID. It has several parameters, which are listed in the LAN Compass.

WSUPDATE (v3.12, 4.x)—This utility lets you update the NetWare shell on a workstation.

WSUPGRD (4.x)—This utility lets you update workstation files with newer versions.

Console Utilities

Console utilities must be run from the file server console. They control management and operations of the file server and are limited to use by a Supervisor or any user with access to the file server console. They are as follows:

ABORT REMIRROR (v3.12)—This utility stops remirroring.

ADD NAME SPACE (v3.12, 4.x)—ADD NAME SPACE allows you to store Macintosh, UNIX, or OS/2 files on the NetWare file server.

BIND (v3.11, v3.12, 4.x)—This utility is used at the file server console to bind LAN drivers with protocol stacks. It is also a workstation command used for the same purpose. BIND has several parameters.

BROADCAST (v3.12, 4.x)—This utility lets the administrator send messages to all users on the network.

CDROM (v3.12, 4.x)—CDROM lets you mount CD-ROM volumes on the file server.

CLEAR MESSAGE (v2.2)—This utility allows you to clear a message from the file server console when you are using the MONITOR utility.

CLEAR STATION (v3.12, 4.x)—CLEAR STATION lets you disconnect a workstation from the network (clear the connection).

CLIB (v3.11, v3.12, 4.x)—This utility allows a developer to use a set of standard functions in the development of NetWare Loadable Modules.

CLS (v3.11, v3.12, 4.x)—CLS, like the DOS CLS, allows you to clear the file server console.

COMPSURF (v2.1 and under)—In NetWare v2.1 and under, a disk needs to be prepared for NetWare installation. COMPSURF is the utility that performs a low-level format and surface analysis of the disk.

CONFIG (v3.12, 4.x)—This utility tells you the configuration of the file server including its adapter's node IDs, the adapter's hardware settings, and the file server's name.

CONSOLE (v2.2)—Used only in nondedicated systems, CONSOLE switches operations to the console screen.

DCONFIG (v2.2)—Used to change IPX.COM's configuration so that it will operate with a specific network adapter.

DISABLE LOGIN (v3.12, 4.x)—Allows you to prevent users from logging into the network during file server maintenance.

DISABLE TRANSACTIONS (v2.2)—See DISABLE TTS.

DISABLE TTS (v3.11, v3.12, 4.x)—Disables Novell's Transaction Tracking System (TTS).

DISK (v2.2)—Lets you look at the status of network disk drives.

DISKSET (v3.12, 4.x)—This utility loads information about disks connected to Novell's Disk Coprocessor Boards.

DISMOUNT (v3.12, 4.x)—Allows you to dismount a volume on a NetWare server.

DISPLAY NETWORKS (v3.12, 4.x)—This utility lets you display information about the number of networks, the number of hops between networks, and the network numbers.

DISPLAY SERVERS (v3.12, 4.x)—This utility displays the number of hops between servers and the names of all active servers.

DOMAIN (4.x)—DOMAIN allows you to load untested NLMs into protected space, until you are sure of their integrity.

DOS (v2.2)—This command allows you to change a nondedicated v2.2 file server to its DOS mode.

DOWN (v3.12, 4.x)—This utility lets you bring down the file server.

DSREPAIR (4.x)— Similar to VREPAIR, DSREPAIR repairs the NetWare Directory Services' database.

EDIT (v3.11, v3.12, 4.x)—EDIT is an ASCII text editor that operates on the file server console.

ENABLE LOGIN (v3.12, 4.x)—This utility allows you to reenable network logins.

ENABLE TRANSACTIONS (v2.2)—See ENABLE TTS.

ENABLE TTS (v3.11, v3.12, 4.x)—This command allows you to turn on Novell's Transaction Tracking System (TTS).

EXIT (v3.11, v3.12, 4.x)—This utility allows you to exit to DOS after DOWNing the file server.

HELP (v3.x, 4.x)—HELP is NetWare's on-line assistance and help function.

INSTALL (v3.11, v3.12, 4.x)—This utility is used to install NetWare on the server's hard disk. You also use INSTALL to mirror and unmirror drives, change the server's configuration, and create or modify volumes and partitions. INSTALL is loaded at the file server console by typing LOAD path INSTALL.

KEYB (v3.12, 4.x)—If you are using keyboards other than US keyboards, you will use KEYB to set the keyboard type.

LANGUAGE (4.x)—This utility lets you set the language NetWare will use. English is the default.

LIST DEVICES (v3.12, 4.x)—This utility tells you the devices that are attached to the file server.

LOAD (v3.11, v3.12, 4.x)—This command allows you to load NetWare Loadable Modules (NLMs).

MATHLIB (v3.11, v3.12, 4.x)—This utility needs to be used if you are using a math coprocessor. It runs from the LOAD command.

MATHLIBC (v3.11, v3.12, 4.x)—MATHLIBC is LOADed in machines that don't have math coprocessors.

MEDIA (v3.12, 4.x)—This utility allows you to load or remove different media on the file server.

MEMORY (v3.11, v3.12, 4.x)—This utility displays the amount of memory the file server can address.

MIRROR STATUS (v3.12, 4.x)—MIRROR STATUS shows the state of mirrored drives.

MODULES (v3.11, v3.12, 4.x)—This utility will show you the modules loaded in the file server.

MONITOR (v3.11, v3.12, 4.x)—One of the most important console utilities, MONITOR allows you to assess and monitor the condition of the file server console. See Chapter 18, Monitoring Your Investments.

MOUNT (v3.12, 4.x)—MOUNT allows you to load and mount volumes on the file server.

NAME (v3.12, 4.x)—Tells you the name of the file server.

NETBIOS (v3.11)—Used for workstations that use IBM's NetBIOS. Allows you to view NetBIOS information and unload it.

NLIST (4.x)—This utility lets you search for information about the various objects on the network.

NMAGENT (v3.11, v3.12, 4.x)—Stores information about LAN drivers that the system administrator can use to manage the network.

NUT (v3.12)—This utility must be loaded on NetWare v3.11 for the NLM user utilities to load.

NWSNUT (v3.12, 4.x)—See NUT.

OFF (v3.12, 4.x)—Like CLS in DOS, this command clears the file server console.

PROTOCOL (v3.12, 4.x)—PROTOCOL displays the protocols loaded on the file server or registers new protocols with the server.

PSERVER (v3.12, 4.x)—This command allows the system administrator to create a dedicated print server.

REGISTER MEMORY (v3.11, v3.12, 4.x)—This command is used in file servers that contain more than 16 megabytes of RAM.

REMIRROR (v2.2)—This utility allows you to remirror drives after you have added a new drive.

REMIRROR PARTITION (v3.12, 4.x)—If for some reason a partition stops being mirrored, you'll use this command to remirror it.

REMOTE (v3.11, v3.12, 4.x)—This command lets you load the RCONSOLE utility and is used for remote file server monitoring.

REMOVE DOS (v3.11, v3.12, 4.x)—This command allows you to remove DOS from the file server's memory.

RESET ROUTER (v3.12, 4.x)—When RESET ROUTER runs, it updates corrupted router tables.

ROUTE (v3.12, 4.x)—In token-ring networks, you use this command to create and control the routing process.

RS232 (v3.11, v3.12, 4.x)—RS232 lets you access the file server console from a remote asynchronous connection.

RSPX (v3.12, 4.x)—This command is used with REMOTE.NLM to let you communicate with the file server console via RCONSOLE.

RTDM (4.x)—Although this command sometimes is used as an acronym for "Read the Darn Manual," in NetWare 4.x, it is used to migrate data to a device like a CD-ROM.

SBACKUP (v3.12, 4.x)—SBACKUP allows you to back up and restore data on a NetWare file server.

SCAN FOR NEW DEVICES (v3.12, 4.x)—This utility will display the new devices that have been added to the file server since it was brought up.

SCHDELAY (4.x)—This utility lets you prioritize file server CPU processes.

SEARCH (v3.11, v3.12, 4.x)—This command is used on the file server console to set search drives for NLMs and other files such as the AUTOEXEC.NCF and STARTUP.NCF files.

SECURE CONSOLE (v3.11, v3.12, 4.x)—This command lets the system administrator lock the file server console.

SEND (v3.11, v3.12, 4.x)—SEND lets you send messages to specified groups of workstations.

SERVER (v3.11, v3.12, 4.x)—SERVER is used to load NetWare on the file server and enable it.

SERVMAN (4.x)—A management utility, SERVMAN lets you manage the processes, NLMs, volumes, users, and name spaces on the file server.

SET (v3.11, v3.12, 4.x)—SET allows you to change network operating system parameters and configurations.

SET TIME (v3.12, 4.x)—This command lets you change the file server time and date.

SPEED (v3.11, v3.12, 4.x)—SPEED displays the speed of the NetWare file server.

SPOOL (v2.2, v3.12)—This command allows you to create, maintain, and modify spooler mappings in network print queues.

SPXCONFG (v3.11, v3.12, 4.x)—SPXCONFG lets you configure NetWare's SPX.

TIME (v3.12, 4.x)—Shows the time and date of the file server console.

TIMESYNC (4.x)—This utility is used to synchronize the time on all the network's file servers.

TOKENRPL (v3.11)—Used to boot diskless token-ring workstations.

TRACK OFF (v3.12, 4.x)—Disables TRACK ON.

TRACK ON (v3.12, 4.x)—Displays all server requests and packets the server sends.

UNBIND (v3.11, v3.12, 4.x)—Allows you to "unbind" a protocol from a LAN adapter.

UNLOAD (v3.11, v3.12, 4.x)—This utility lets you unload NLMs.

UNMIRROR (v2.2)—UNMIRROR allows you to unmirror drives.

UPS (v2.2)—This utility lets you display the status of an uninterruptible power supply.

UPS (v3.11, v3.12, 4.x)—This utility lets you load software to monitor an uninterruptible power supply.

UPS STATUS (v3.11, v3.12, 4.x)—This utility operates the same as the UPS utility in v2.2.

UPS TIME (v3.11, v3.12, 4.x)—UPS TIME lets you change the discharge and recharge times on the UPS attached to the file server.

VAP (v2.2)—Shows the VAPs loaded on the file server.

VER (v2.2)—Shows the version of NetWare operating on the file server.

VERSION (v3.11, v3.12, 4.x)—Shows the version of NetWare loaded on the file server.

VOLUMES (v3.12, 4.x)—Shows the volumes available on the file server.

VREPAIR (v3.11, v3.12, 4.x)—Use this utility to repair disk drive problems.

WATCHDOG (v2.2)—In v2.2, this utility lets you monitor the connections to the file server.

XCOPY (4.x)—XCOPY installs NetWare's Electrotext documentation and copies NetWare files from the server to a workstation.

Menu Utilities

NetWare ships with a variety of menu utilities, which allow users and supervisors to choose actions from the file server console. For more information on using these utilities, refer to the Novell documentation.

ATOTAL (4.x)—ATOTAL is part of the network's accounting system and lists information such as the number of server requests, the number of blocks written, and the number of blocks read. ATOTAL information can be redirected to a disk file.

AUDITCON (4.x)—This utility allows a network auditor to view the security of the network.

COLORPAL (v3.12)—COLORPAL allows the user or network administrator to change the color scheme the menu utilities use.

DSPACE (v3.12)—DSPACE displays the amount of space available to network users and allows system administrators to change the amount of disk space or limit it initially.

FCONSOLE (v3.12)—FCONSOLE displays information about the network to supervisors, supervisor-equivalents, or FCONSOLE operators. From FCONSOLE, you can broadcast messages, change to another file server, view connection information, down the file server or lock it, view LAN driver information, purge files, view network statistics and the status of the network, and view version information.

FILER (v3.12, 4.x)—FILER allows a user to manage directories. Within FILER, a user can view current directory information, directory contents, and volume information, and also set filer options. In addition, users can view the Inherited Rights or Maximum Rights Mask, directory attributes, directory create dates, and directory rights.

MAKEUSER (v3.12)—MAKEUSER lets you create, edit, and modify information about users.

MIGRATE (v3.12)—MIGRATE replaces v3.11's UPGRADE.EXE.

NETADMIN (4.x)—This utility lets you look at, create, view, or modify the NetWare Directory Services objects.

NETUSER (4.x)—This utility lets users manage print jobs, send messages, and map drives.

PARTMGR (4.x)—The partition manager, PARTMGR is used in NetWare 4.x to manage partitions.

PCONSOLE (v3.12, 4.x)—This utility lets you create print queues and print servers.

PRINTCON (4.x)—PRINTCON displays and creates print configurations.

PRINTDEF (v3.12, 4.x)—Allows you to create or modify forms and create network printer definitions.

SALVAGE (v3.12)— SALVAGE allows you to recover files that have not been purged.

SESSION (v3.12)—The SESSION utility lets users map drives, change drives, and send messages to other network users.

SYSCON (v3.12)—Perhaps the most important utility the supervisor uses, SYSCON allows you to create and edit login scripts, grant file and directory rights and attributes, enable the NetWare accounting system, change user passwords, view information about the network, create and display work-group managers, or display groups users belong to. Users can also use SYSCON to display information about their accounts or to change their passwords.

USERDEF (v3.12)—With USERDEF, you can create commands that allow you to add users to the network, change their attributes and account balances, and edit or create login scripts.

VOLINFO (v3.12)—VOLINFO displays information about the NetWare volumes such as the amount of space used and available.

Windows Utilities

In NetWare v3.x and 4.x, Novell created several Windows utilities that take the place of traditional DOS menu or command-line utilities. These Windows-based utilities are the NetWare Administrator, NWTOOLS, and NWUSER. The NetWare Administrator is for use by the system manager and allows the system manager to create, delete, or modify objects, create user templates, modify trustee rights, view the Inherited Rights Filters, search for objects, and create, modify, or delete replicas. In addition, the NetWare Administrator lets you add or delete trustees from files or directories, and create print servers, queues, and printer objects.

NWTOOLS (4.x) lets users map drives, create and send messages, and configure print jobs.

NWUSER (4.x) lets users manage print jobs, capture printer ports, send messages, map drives, and attach to other servers.

appendix D

The Open Data-Link Interface

In 1989, Novell and Apple Computer introduced the Open Data-Link Interface (ODI) to make life easier for network adapter and protocol stack vendors and, most importantly, the network user. ODI specifies a standard method of allowing a LAN adapter and its driver to communicate with a protocol stack such as NetWare's, Apple's AppleTalk Filing Protocol, or TCP/IP's Internet Protocol.

What Once Was, Is No More

Formerly, when the administrator installed a LAN adapter, he or she needed to link the LAN adapter's driver to the IPX protocol stack or any other protocol stack the driver needed to communicate with. If the user wanted the workstation to be able to communicate concurrently with more than one stack, it meant that the user needed to buy and install multiple adapters, each with drivers capable of addressing the preferred stack. Vendors introducing LAN adapters needed to write a number of drivers depending on the protocol an adapter needed to communicate with and the version of NetWare it was working with. Each time Novell changed the NetWare shell (the redirector or requester) or made changes to IPX, a new LAN driver needed to be written and the user needed to relink the driver with the new shell or

IPX version. Drivers were called linkable or dedicated IPX drivers and were the common form of drivers used until ODI was introduced.

In addition, if a vendor did not have an adapter with a driver of the appropriate type, the user sometimes had to purchase adapters elsewhere and install two or more LAN adapters in a workstation or file server that met their needs to address multiple protocol stacks. The end result was cumbersome: LAN adapter vendors had to keep writing new drivers, and users had to keep relinking the LAN drivers with NetWare's IPX.

Enter ODI

ODI solves this cumbersome process by providing a specification that allows LAN adapter vendors to write a single driver that will communicate with any number of protocol stacks. And, in turn, it allows users to buy a single adapter with a driver that can communicate with numerous protocols—that is, as long as the vendor writes drivers that are ODI-compliant.

The ODI specification consists of three layers: the Multiple Link Interface Driver (MLID) the Link Support Layer (LSL), and the protocol stack itself. The LSL is further divided into two sublayers, the Media Support Module (MSM) and the Hardware-Specific Module (HSM).

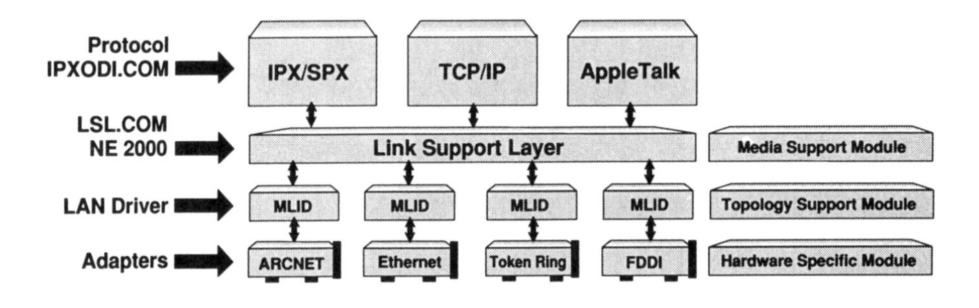

Figure D-1. *Novell's Open Data-Link Interface.*

The MLID represents the LAN driver. The LSL is an interface between the LAN driver and protocol stack that keeps a database, which tells it which adapters belong to which drivers and which drivers are linked to each protocol stack. In reverse, the LSL informs the protocol stack of which drivers it can address. The protocol stack is what it implies—IPX, AppleTalk, Sun's Network File System, UNIX, or NetBIOS. (See Figure D-1.)

Installing ODI Drivers

More detailed information on ODI drivers is included in Chapter 6, What About Workstations, and Chapter 19, What's This Driving Me Around. To load an ODI driver, the user must place statements in the workstation's AUTOEXEC.BAT file, or else enter these commands from the DOS command line:

```
LSL
IPXODI
NETX
NE2000
```

LSL represents the Link Support Layer. IPXODI is the NetWare protocol stack IPX. NETX is the NetWare shell (redirector or requester). NE2000 is the name of the MLID. In an Ethernet network, the NE2000 is a common driver type.

appendix

E

GLOSSARY

This appendix contains some of the words and acronyms you'll see everyday in your assault on networking jungle.

10BASE-T A star-wired Ethernet implementation that runs on unshielded twisted-pair (UTP) cabling.

10BASE-2 A bus-based Ethernet implementation that runs on RG-58U coaxial cabling.

10BASE-5 A bus-based Ethernet implementation that runs on RG-8, thick Ethernet cabling.

802.2 The Logical Link Control Layer of the Open Systems Interconnect Model, the upper part of the Data-Link Layer, provides a method for the upper layers to communicate with the Media Access Control (MAC) layer of the Data-Link Layer.

802.3 The Institute of Electronic and Electrical Engineers (IEEE) specification for the Ethernet access method.

802.5 The Institute of Electronic and Electrical Engineers (IEEE) specification for the token-ring access method.

A

ABEND Stands for "abnormal end." When an application causes the server to go down.

access control rights These NetWare file and directory rights let users change the Inherited Rights Mask and trustee rights for files or directories.

ACS (asynchronous communications server) A specialized server that allows dial-in and dial-out communications, or a software package that allows communication with multiple asynchronous modems.

active hub In the ARCNET and token-ring access methods, hubs can be either active or passive. Active hubs regenerate the signals to their original strength after attenuation occurs.

adapter Commonly, adapter refers to the network interface card that allows communication between the PC and the network.

address In NetWare, several addresses exist for each device. Each workstation has an address that identifies it to the network and an address that tells which network it belongs to. Each file server has an external network address and an internal network address. The external network address identifies the segment the server is on. The internal network number represents the logical network the server belongs to.

ADMIN The 4.0 equivalent of the SUPERVISOR in v2.x and v3.x. This user has all rights on the network.

archive To prepare a data file for long- or short-term storage.

ARCNET A 2.5Mbps token-passing access method.

attach After logging into a file server, network users can attach to additional file servers.

attributes In a file or directory, attributes determine what can be done to a file.

AUTOEXEC.BAT The file that provides the environment for the PC.

AUTOEXEC.NCF Similar to the AUTOEXEC.BAT file, this file controls the booting and environment of the file server.

B

backbone A backbone consists of several file servers or devices joined together along a bus to speed network traffic and improve network efficiency. FDDI is commonly used as a backbone.

backup system The means provided for saving the data, files, and directories on the network so that they are not harmed or destroyed if network errors occur.

bandwidth The effective throughput of a network access method.

base I/O address The starting address of an I/O port, which the microprocessor uses for communication with the device. Commonly used by LAN adapters.

base memory address A buffer the adapter uses for processing data in memory.

BBS (Bulletin Board System) An electronic service accessed via a modem that facilitates communications between users.

BIND When a communications protocol is assigned to a LAN adapter, a process called binding is used.

bindery A database that keeps information about users, devices, and servers on the network.

BIOS (Basic Input/Output System) Programs inherent in the CPU's firmware that allow the CPU to address other attached devices.

block The network reads and writes data as blocks. The default block size in NetWare is 4 kilobytes (KB).

boot files The files the client workstation and file server use to boot the network.

buffer An area a device uses to store data until it can be used.

burst mode In burst mode, the adapter's DMA controller, software, or system board logic negotiates use of the bus to transfer data. Burst mode allows faster data transfer than shared-memory adapters.

bus The system architecture that peripheral devices such as LAN adapters and video adapters attach to, which serves as the method for transporting data between the device and the machine's CPU.

bus-mastering Commonly implemented in LAN adapters, bus-mastering allows the adapter to take control of the bus, leaving the CPU free for other processing.

bus topology A LAN topology in which workstations and network devices extend off a central media.

C

cache To hold data in RAM so that it can be accessed faster than reading it from disk.

CAPTURE A command used to redirect data to a file so that it may be used or printed later.

CD-ROM An increasing common media used for near-line data storage.

client In NetWare, this term is synonymous with any device that receives services from a server. A client may be a DOS, OS/2, UNIX, or Macintosh workstation, or a printer that receives print jobs from a print server.

coaxial cable A solid- or stranded-core copper cable surrounded by a protective, insulating sheath that is commonly used in ARCNET, Ethernet, token-ring, and FDDI access methods.

collisions In Ethernet, when two workstations attempt to transmit data at the same time, a collision occurs, destroying both data packets. Ethernet is also called Collision Sensing with Multiple Access and Collision Detection (CSMA/CD).

CONFIG.SYS The file that sets the environment for the DOS workstation.

connection The term used to describe a device's physical and logical attachment to the network.

console The console in the network refers to the device on a server that allows a person to monitor the operations of that device. Commonly used to refer to the file server console or the print console.

controller This device allows a device to attach so it can communicate with the system or another device.

CNE (Certified NetWare Engineer) A person who successfully passes tests that certify that he or she is knowledgeable about the network. Unfortunately, CNE certification can be obtained solely by reading manuals and passing tests. Often, holders of this certification have no practical network experience.

CSMA/CD (Collision Sensing with Multiple Access/Collision Detection) See **Collisions.**

D

Data-Link The second layer of the OSI model responsible for defining the cable access method.

data striping In this method of writing to disk, data is written to a collection of drives, thus speeding access and writing of the data.

DCB (disk coprocessor board) In NetWare, an adapter that provides the interface between the CPU and the system's hard disks.

dedicated A machine that performs one function only. Commonly used on the NetWare file server.

device A printer, file server, workstation, or other piece of equipment on the network.

directory entry An entry in a table that contains information such as the location, name, and owner of a file or directory.

DMA (direct memory access) A technique some LAN adapters use, in which a DMA controller moves data to RAM. DMA transfer is faster than shared memory, but more difficult and expensive to design.

DR DOS Now called Novell DOS, this version of DOS was developed by Digital Research and is currently developed and marketed by Novell.

driver The software that provides instructions to the network device that allows it to communicate on the network.

duplexing A SFT Level II mechanism that ensures data integrity by duplicating data on disks with their own redundant controllers.

dynamic The ability in NetWare v3.x and higher to allocate memory on the fly and return it to the system when no longer needed.

E

ECNE An Enterprise Certified NetWare Engineer. This person is one level higher than a CNE, and normally it means that a person has practical experience on the network.

effective rights In NetWare security, these are the rights a user has in a file or directory.

elevator-seeking In NetWare, reading and writing from and to the server's disk drive is done by elevator-seeking, which operates much like an elevator picking up and dropping off requests in a logical travel pattern.

EISA (Extended Industry Standard Architecture) The EISA bus was developed by a consortium of vendors in response to IBM's Micro Channel Architecture bus. The EISA bus is a 32-bit bus.

e-mail (electronic mail) The service that allows users to communicate electronically with each other across the network or multiple networks from their PCs.

Ethernet A contention-based access method that operates at 10MBps. Also called CSMA/CD, because devices on an Ethernet network may communicate simultaneously, resulting in collisions.

F

fault tolerance Fault tolerance implies the ability of the system to provide redundancy for failed or failing components. In NetWare, three types of fault tolerance exist. SFT Level I includes duplicate directory entry tables and file allocation tables, transaction tracking, and read-after-write verification. SFT Level II includes server mirroring and duplexing, and SFT Level III includes full-server mirroring.

FAT (File Allocation Table) A table that records the locations of all pieces of a file in memory.

FDDI (Fiber Distributed Data Interface) This access method allows communication at 100Mbps. It is a token-passing access method used for applications that need high speeds such as graphics, database operations, and imaging.

fiber-optic Fiber-optic media consists of a solid glass core surrounded by a protective, insulating, reflective sheath. Fiber-optic media is used for long distances, in areas with high electromagnetic and radio-frequency interference, and where high speed is needed.

file server In NetWare, this is the device (PC) that services file requests from clients.

FTP (File Transfer Protocol) The Transport layer protocol used in the Department of Defense TCP/IP model.

frame Sometimes called a packet. Strictly, a frame is the portion of the packet that represents the protocol variation of the packet such as Ethernet_II or Ethernet_SNAP.

G

gateway A device or software package that allows a LAN to access a heterogeneous device such as a mainframe that use different protocols. It may also allow two LANs that use different protocols to communicate with each other.

group In NetWare, a defined collection of users that have common rights and needs.

GUEST When NetWare is installed, two accounts are created. They are SUPERVISOR and GUEST. The GUEST is just what it implies, a visitor to the network with limited access to the network's files and directories.

H

hub A device that centralizes the communications access of clients on the network.

I

IDE (Integrated Drive Electronics) An architecture hard disk drives use.

IEEE (Institute of Electrical and Electronic Engineers) This group is responsible for the development and formalization of LAN standards.

Inherited Rights Mask A group of rights for files and directories that controls the rights a user inherits.

INT (Interrupt) See interrupt.

Internet An electronic forum created to allow communications between a variety of different machines.

internetwork A collection of more than one network.

interrupt An interrupt signal that indicates an intent to perform a certain task. Interrupts can be hardware or software.

IPX (Internetwork Packet Exchange) The Network layer protocol NetWare uses for network communications.

IPXODI The IPX protocol stack in Open Data-Link Interface implementations.

IRQ (Interrupt Request Line) See **interrupt**.

ISA (Industry Standard Architecture) A 16-bit bus architecture.

L

LAN (local-area network) A locally limited collection of PCs that can communicate with each other via media.

LAN Workplace A software package developed and marketed by Novell that allows a PC workstation to communicate with an IP-based network or machine.

LANalyzer A protocol analyzer developed by Novell and now marketed and further developed by Network Communications Corp.

LLC (Local Link Control) The interface between the upper layers of the OSI Model and the Media Access Control (MAC) layer.

log in The action a user performs to access the network. In NetWare, this process consists of entering a user name, and optionally, a password.

login script Three login scripts exist that control the NetWare environment. They are the system login script, the profile login script, and the user login script.

LSL (Link Support Layer) The interface between the protocol stack and the Multiple Link Interface Driver that manages communication between the two.

M

MAN (metropolitan-area network) A local-area network or internetwork dispersed across a geographic metropolitan distance.

MAU (multistation access unit) A hub used in token-ring to attach workstations to the network.

MCA (Micro Channel Architecture) A 32-bit bus architecture developed by IBM.

media The cabling used to connect workstations and other devices on the network, permitting communications among them.

media access control The Media Access Control Layer of the OSI Model provides access to the media and defines the format of frames, node addresses, and integrity of the frame.

MHS (Message Handling Service) Novell's e-mail standard.

mirroring A form of SFT Level II in which data on a drive is duplicated to another disk on the same disk channel.

MLID (Multiple Link Interface Driver) The name of the LAN driver in an Open Data-Link Interface environment.

N

Name space Clients on the network require name spaces, which handle the file-naming conventions for their native operating system

NetBIOS A network layer protocol used by IBM machines, mainframes, and minicomputers.

NetWire A BBS operated by Novell to communicate with its NetWare users.

NETX.COM Commonly called the NetWare shell, this software program differentiates between and handles DOS and network client requests.

NETX.EXE Commonly called the NetWare shell, this software program performs a similar function to the NETX.COM file.

NFS (Network File System) The network operating system used by Sun Microsystem's workstations.

NIC (Network Interface Card) See **adapter**.

NLM (NetWare Loadable Module) A program that runs as an integrated part of the network operating system.

NOS (Network Operating System) Like the client's operating system, the network operating system provides the framework for communications between workstations.

node A device on the network that may be a printer, client workstation, or file server.

O

ODI (Open Data-Link Interface) A specification that allows LAN adapter vendors to write one LAN driver that can communicate with a number of protocols such as IP, IPX, and the AppleTalk Filing Protocol. In reverse, ODI allows protocol vendors to write to a common specification that can communicate with multiple LAN adapters.

OS (operating system) The framework and intelligence of the client workstation and file server that allows it to operate as an intelligent PC.

OSI (Open Systems Interconnect) A model designed by the International Standards Organization that specifies the rules and methods for communication between devices.

P

packet Also called a frame. This is the data unit transported between devices on the network.

partition In NetWare, the file server's disk drive is divided into sections. These sections, called partitions, contain either NetWare or the native operating system.

password When users log into the network, they may be asked to enter a combination of letters and numbers that are unique and identifies them to the network.

print queue In NetWare, print jobs are sent to queues where they are stored until the printer can print them.

R

RAM (random access memory) The dynamic storage in a computer used for caching data.

read-after-write verification Part of NetWare's SFT Level I, read-after-write verification ensures that the data is read after being written to disk, thereby verifying its integrity.

remote-boot In remote boot, a boot ROM fits on the LAN adapter, allowing the client to boot to the network without a hard drive or diskette drive.

rights The rights are the permissions a user has to a file or directory.

ROM (read-only memory) This form of memory is permanent.

S

SAP (Service Advertising Protocol) File servers on the network advertise their services on a periodic basis. SAP is the protocol servers use to let other devices know that they are ready to service requests.

security equivalence In NetWare security, security equivalence gives a group or user the rights of another group or user.

SFT (System Fault Tolerance) See **fault tolerance**.

SCSI (Small Computer System Interface) An interface that allows up to eight devices to be attached.

shared memory A type of memory transfer an adapter uses. In shared memory, the LAN driver moves data from a shared RAM location on the adapter to an area in real memory. Shared memory is faster than I/O and simpler to implement than DMA and bus-mastering.

SMS (Storage Management Services) Novell's standard for data backup and protection.

SPX (Sequenced Packet Exchange) The Transport Layer protocol NetWare uses to guarantee communications between device.

supervisor The administrator of the network who has access to all network services, files, and directories.

SYS:LOGIN This directory, created by NetWare, contains several files that allow a user to log into the LAN.

SYS:MAIL The MAIL directory, created by NetWare, contains the user login scripts, the printer definition files, and the user mail subdirectories.

SYS:PUBLIC One of the directories created by NetWare that contains files and utilities used commonly by users.

SYS:SYSTEM One of the directories created by NetWare that contains system files and Supervisor utilities.

T

TCP/IP (Transmission Control Protocol/Internet Protocol) The suite of protocols developed by the Department of Defense to allow communication between a variety of computer equipment.

topology The physical and logical layout of the LAN.

TP (twisted-pair) Collectively applied to unshielded and shielded twisted-pair media.

trustee rights A series of permissions that designate a user's or group's access to directories and files.

TSA (Target Service Agent) In NetWare backup, the TSA is a program that allows the device it runs on to be backed up.

TSR (terminate-and-stay resident) A program that is loaded into memory on the workstation to control tasks or network operations.

TTS (Transaction Tracking System) The transaction tracking system, a form of SFT Level I, protects transactional data if a network error occurs.

U

UPS (uninterruptible power supply) A device that provides power in the event that the power to a device is interrupted.

user The person who sits at a workstation and maintains an account on the network.

UTP (unshielded twisted-pair) A media that consists of a stranded copper core surrounded by a protective sheath used in ARCNET, Ethernet, and token-ring networks.

V

VAP (Value-Added Process) A program that operates on the file server in NetWare v2.x workstations.

Volume A unit of disk storage. In NetWare, the first volume's name is always SYS.

W

WAN (wide-area network) An internetwork that is geographically distributed and connected by media other than cabling.

WORM (write-once, read-many) A device commonly used for near-line storage.

INDEX

W